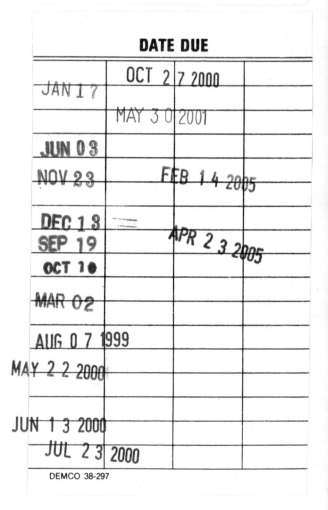

DATE DUE

JAN 17	OCT 2 7 2000	
	MAY 3 0 2001	
JUN 03		
NOV 23	FEB 1 4 2005	
DEC 1 3		
SEP 19	APR 2 3 2005	
OCT 1		
MAR 02		
AUG 0 7 1999		
MAY 2 2 2000		
JUN 1 3 2000		
JUL 2 3 2000		

DEMCO 38-297

THE
NAZI HUNTERS

ALSO BY CHARLES ASHMAN

The People vs. Angela Davis
Martha Mitchell: The Mouth That Roared
Kissinger: The Adventures of Super Kraut
The Finest Judges Money Can Buy
Connally: The Adventures of Big Bad John
The Disappearance of Jimmy Hoffa
The CIA-Mafia Link
The Gospel According to Billy (Graham)
Diplomatic Crime

ALSO BY ROBERT J. WAGMAN

Hubert Humphrey: The Man and His Dream
Taxpayer's Guide to Effective Tax Revolt
Tax Revolt 1980: A How-to Guide
Hostage! The Story of the Iranian Hostage Crisis
Lord's Justice: The Story of the Dalkon Shield
Instant Millionaires: America's Lotteries and Their Winners

THE
NAZI HUNTERS

Charles Ashman

Robert J. Wagman

PHAROS BOOKS
A SCRIPPS HOWARD COMPANY
NEW YORK

Cover design: Nancy Eato
Interior design: Elyse Strongin

Copyright© 1988 by Ashman-Wagman Writing Partnership

First published in 1988.

Library of Congress Cataloging-in-Publication Data
Ashman, Charles
  The Nazi hunters.

  Includes index.
  1. War criminals—Germany.   2. Criminal investigation.
3. World War, 1939-1945—Atrocities.   I. Wagman,
Robert J. II. Title.
D803.A84   1988   364.1'38'0922   88-60373
ISBN 0-88687-357-6

Printed in the United States of America

Pharos Books
A Scripps Howard Company
200 Park Avenue
New York, NY 10166

10 9 8 7 6 5 4 3 2 1

Contents

This book is dedicated to the victims . . . and to those who are committed to continuing the hunt for their killers so as to finally bring them to justice.

The Authors

Authors' Preface and Acknowledgments

This book had its germination in 1982, but we didn't realize it at the time. We were in Yugoslavia witnessing the production of the first cooperative film effort between the government-regulated Yugoslav motion picture industry and an American studio. The film focused on resistance to the Nazis when they invaded Yugoslavia. Many in Yugoslavia felt that freedom fighters in other countries had been glamorized while Yugoslavia had never received proper credit or world recognition for the resistance by its partisans to the vastly larger German army. It was a point of pride for those who wanted Tito memorialized more as an anti-Nazi than as a communist leader.

It was in the town of Novisad, reminiscent of Omaha, and in the "midwest" of Yugoslavia, that we met former resistance and partisan leaders who were on hand to keep the film authentic. And it was there that we heard for the first time the name of Kurt Waldheim (now president of Austria) in a context other than that of immediate past secretary-general of the United Nations. We registered the facts and moved on to other projects.

Our three years of research and investigation for the book *Diplomatic Crime* had led to the discovery of several former Nazis serving in key diplomatic posts throughout the world, including the highest ranks of the United Nations. That, too, became part of this story.

Thousands of documents at the Berlin Document Center, the United Nations and elsewhere verify the worst fears of historians with respect to the killing and jailing of Jews under the Nazi regime, and the humiliation forced upon them for no reason other than their faith. Reading these documents helps to explain a little about the spirit of the remaining Nazi hunters and the passion of survivors of the Holocaust.

It was not simply a case of a sudden barbaric act of violence. Some experts in criminal justice believe that more often than not one who kills commits his crime out of emotion felt at the moment. It may happen when something goes out of control during the commission of a lesser crime. In fact, many homicides are triggered by outbursts of emotion.

Not so in the case of the killers being hunted for war crimes. In almost every instance, premeditation is clearly established by the policies and actions taken against the Jews in Germany starting eight years before the United States entered the war. Constant humiliation, coupled with the deprivation of all basic human rights, was a pervasive policy even before Jews were carted off to die horrible deaths. Is it any wonder that survivors of the Holocaust and the relatives of those who died are not willing to end the hunt, despite those who argue that the criminals are old now and should be spared?

★ ★ ★

There is just no way in this one book, or in five such books, to document fully each and every case of interest, past or pending, involving accused war criminals. We have elected to focus on the hunters—that amazing band of public and private individuals in Washington, D.C., Toronto, Tel Aviv, Vienna, Melbourne, Paris, London, and elsewhere—many of whom were not yet born when Hitler was trying to turn the world to his way. We were fascinated by these men and women who, with limited resources, have doggedly pursued the Nazis, most of whom are buried deeply in the fabric of American society and that of half a dozen other nations. We became intrigued with their methods and with the many roadblocks they have had to overcome.

Seldom has any issue of international concern seen such amazing private sector involvement. An official of the United States government, or any government concerned with the hunt for Nazis, would readily admit the indispensable role of Simon Wiesenthal, the World Jewish Congress, the Los Angeles-based Simon Wiesenthal Center and others. From Vienna, Wiesenthal has almost single-handedly kept the spirit of the hunt alive. Meanwhile, the World Jewish Congress has spearheaded the drive to expose Waldheim.

It's interesting that the Nazi hunt weaves in and out of both liberal and conservative concerns. On the one hand, investigations by the U.S. Department of Justice under Attorney General Edwin Meese, during the conservative administration of Ronald Reagan, placed Kurt Waldheim on the Watch List. That same agency, dependent upon a conservative U.S. administration for funding and support, has successfully prosecuted individuals who were deported to the Soviet Union and to West Germany for lying on their applications for American citizenship about their wartime pasts. Nevertheless, the conservative political arm in the United States, with such powerful spokespersons as Patrick Buchanan, repeatedly attacks the Office of Special Investigations for its dependence upon evidence secured from the Soviet Union. Unquestionably, Buchanan and other conservatives believe that the Soviets were merely using our so-called Nazi trials for their own ends, and that any evidence received from them must be tainted. We learned how the FBI is called upon to reexamine and reevaluate very thoroughly all of the evidence that comes from the Soviet Union before it is used by the Justice Department in any of the cases it prosecutes in the United States.

It should be noted that our own differences as individuals have been helpful to us in balancing the material for this book. One of us is a traditional Catholic with a midwestern background and many years of experience as an investigative journalist for newspapers. The other is Jewish with a New York-Los Angeles background, now acting as foreign correspondent for various newspapers, most of them British, interested in American political events.

When we made the emotional, financial, and time commitment to devote the several years necessary to making this book a reality, we had no idea what we were getting into. First, there was the frustrating fact that each time we opened up a closet, we found both evidence and more closet doors to open. After forty years there were still unanswered questions about the Nuremberg trials and, more recently, about Adolf Eichmann and his trial. In light of Glasnost, our understanding of historical and political machinations among the allies took on new meaning and had to be reinvestigated. There was new relevance to what we had learned about Kurt Waldheim and tucked away in our memory banks four-and-a-half years before anyone pointed a finger at him and shouted "Nazi!" Unquestionably, the exposé of Waldheim's Nazi past by the World Jewish Congress and others became a primary factor in giving direction to this book as it progressed.

One of the most difficult tasks in journalism—and almost impossible in writing a book—is keeping ahead of a breaking story. As this book was being prepared, we found it necessary to share discoveries through newspaper articles as we went along. In Arizona, we found a critical witness who had been a hostage in Yugoslavia during World War II. Miograd Cedic told us, and lie detectors verified his truthfulness, that his family had bribed Kurt Waldheim to spare his life. That story appeared in *Wiener* Magazine on December 15, 1987, and we were notified the next day that the Austrian state police, at Waldheim's order, had confiscated all copies of the issue so the story would not get out. Now we can write that story fully, including the bizarre developments since Cedic first reached us to say that he had been trying to get someone to listen to his claims that Waldheim was a Nazi for more than forty years.

It was gratifying to be seated with the ambassador from Israel on network television when the United Nations' Nazi archive was opened, and to be credited with having contributed substantially to the atmosphere that forced open those critical files. We had not expected to be signing affidavits for use in various trials, or to be asked to meet with members of an official commission investigating Waldheim at the request of the Austrian government. Our dealings with General James Collins, the American member of that commission, and the investigation by him and his colleagues, are an essential part of this book.

As we were tracing former German officers who had served with Waldheim in an effort to corroborate documents that we had located, we stumbled upon an incredible development. We learned that the East German government, which since 1953 had refused even to consider paying reparations to world Jewry, had changed its mind. West Germany has paid $47 billion in goods and services to Israel and to individual Jewish survivors whose property was confiscated by the Hitler regime. Now we discovered and reported that East Germany has accepted, in principle, its responsibility and will do the same. Secret negotiations were well under way, with the international claims conference set up by the World Jewish Congress and others some years ago.

Most of the Nazis whom we talk about in this book have burrowed deeply, in an effort to hide forever. There is one glaring exception. You will meet and learn a great deal about Alois Brunner, the man described by Adolf Eichmann as his "best right hand man," and by witnesses against Eichmann and at Nuremberg as "the most brutal killer of them all." Brunner specialized in the killing of women and children when he was a prison camp commandant and a top aide to Eichmann for the elimination of millions of Jews and others.

Brunner has been interviewed periodically by British and German journalists in recent years. When we reached him in 1987, we heard nothing new, but a brazen reconfirmation of shocking statements given the German magazine *Bunte* a few years ago which astounded the world. Brunner feels no remorse and no regrets. He claims that the killing of Jews and others was justified.

We hope that through this book you will understand that the United States government does not have the authority to prosecute any foreign Nazi war criminal for any crime whatsoever, because those crimes did not occur in the United States. The Office of Special Investigations is limited to conducting civil procedures, whereby one can be deported or extradited as punishment for lying on an application to come into this country. Unfortunately, in not one of those cases resulting in deportation to West Germany has that person faced criminal prosecution when he got there.

West Germany has bound itself with extraordinarily imposing criteria for trying criminals for crimes committed long ago, making it next to impossible for it to prosecute all but a handful of the most heinous of the remaining Nazi war criminals. In fact, there is in West Germany a frustrated public prosecutor whose job description implies that he would be constantly prosecuting hundreds, perhaps even thousands, of former war criminals. He knows who they are. Some have been shipped to him by the United States after deportation proceedings. Others have been discovered by his own investigators, or international organizations. Yet he cannot prosecute them. In most cases, including bloody, provable, torturous murders involving children, he is helpless.

The opening of the United Nations Nazi war crimes archive was the solution to a mystery that many never knew existed. For them and for those who knew but have forgotten the mood of America at the end of World War II it would be a revelation. Few are shocked anymore to hear the gory details about the Nazi past of several "American" scientists who helped launch our space program. Nevertheless, it is still disturbing to find more and more former Nazis in positions of major responsibility throughout the world.

Access to this archive means renewed attention in the media to the horrors of World War II. It means more inquiries by students and academicians and more discussion by intellectuals on the impact of Nazi history. It could be argued, quite sincerely, that with all of the problems in the world today, we should not get bogged down in committing the dollars, efforts or emotions required to reexamine what happened more than forty years ago. But there are Nazis in the United States and elsewhere who would like to see it happen all over again. Hate is their weapon. Spotlighting their current activities while finding out all about those whom they seem to idolize is freedom's weapon. They require us to be accurate and to segregate fact from theory, whether in the case of Waldheim, or that of the next individual deported by the United States.

Shortly after the decision to open the U.N. war crimes archive was made, we were asked to comment for various newspapers and the broadcast media on the significance of that decision. We believe it is essential for all concerned to realize that unlocking the secrets of wartime atrocities raises critical legal, moral, political, and journalistic questions.

After the U.N. archive was opened, it became common for local and national television stations and newspapers to feature individual cases with sensational publicity: "Tonight on Channel Two, we disclose a Nazi living among us!" This points up the danger that the irresponsible will lump the worst villains, who are described in detail in the U.N. archive, with others who may have been foot soldiers at the wrong place, at the wrong time, and stand accused without proper evidence. It is essential in revealing the identity of known Nazis to distinguish between a nineteen-year-old who was assigned as a guard to a concentration camp and lied about it on his application to come into the United States and the man who gave the orders at that camp for thousands to be killed. Decency, fairness, and humanity command that those distinctions be made.

We have tried extraordinarily hard to be fair. We have been adamant in distinguishing between fact and theory, whether in the case of Waldheim, Alois Brunner, or that nineteen-year-old guard. We have tried to avoid the pitfall of assuming that an individual with a particular name is identical to one so named in the U.N. Nazi war crimes archive. Unfortunately, there are just too many seemingly "familiar" names involved, since many German or Slavic surnames are as common as "Smith" or "Jones" in English-speaking countries. A researcher must be very careful; an unforgivable error is quite possible.

As a result of access to the U.N. archive, our research uncovered the Nazi background of various U.N. officials and members of the diplomatic corps around the world. One such person is Gunther van Well, for many years one of West Germany's most distinguished diplomats. He served as foreign minister for that country and was then appointed ambassador to the United Nations, where he worked very closely with Waldheim, who was then secretary-general.

Van Well subsequently went to Washington as West Germany's ambassador to the United States. He met regularly with the president of the United States and the secretary of state and was an instrumental participant in complex negotiations between West Germany and our other allies. Van Well was a Nazi, and he now admits it. Although there is no evidence he committed any war crime, he does not wish to talk about what he did during Nazi service. He has since retired from diplomatic life and refused to talk further.

Just as there is a danger of jumping to erroneous conclusions when there are unsubstantiated accusations in the U.N. files, there is a risk of assuming that the files contain everything about everyone. Is it possible that there are important former Nazis, many of whom may be guilty of war crimes, who are not listed? Authorities in the United States, the United Kingdom, and West Germany all agree that it is more than possible and is, in fact, quite likely.

In 1987 the Simon Wiesenthal Center delivered lists of known Nazi criminals to the heads of government in the United Kingdom, Australia, Canada, and several Latin American countries. We tracked those lists and the lack of activity that followed in most cases. But while writing this book, we were able to help focus attention on one Nazi war criminal living in Scotland. Our colleagues in the British media, who had received innumerable warnings from their lawyers not to do so, final revealed who he was and what he had done. He is still living in Scotland, but there may be light at the end of this tunnel.

The Canadian story is double-edged. On the surface, there appears to have been some action toward the prosecution of Nazis discovered by private investigations in recent years. However, scratch that surface and you will find procedures so unrealistic as to make it unlikely that much will happen.

At this writing, there is scattered talk in the United Nations of trying to resurrect the Nuremberg concept of a world tribunal for those cases that cannot be tried in any other acceptable forum. In the United Kingdom, for example, which has no extradition treaty with the Soviet Union, there is no realistic way to take action against individuals whose crimes were committed in the Eastern theater of operations. Britain is now discussing changes in its laws.

We hope that by documenting the role of the Nazi hunters, disclosing their quarry, and analyzing their methods, we can remind the world that we are not talking about mere numbers. So often, we hear and read about six million Jews who died in the Holocaust, or twelve million Jews, Slovaks, Russians, Gypsies, and others the Nazis killed. It would be better to remember in terms of hearts and souls, broken bodies, and lost opportunities rather than just statistics.

Writers hope to persuade readers to share their points of view on historical heroes and villains, who are usually painted in black and white because too many grays would be confusing. As you begin to relive the horrors of Nazi brutality and follow the hunt for the worst of the perpetrators, be aware that while we began as objective chroniclers of Nazi hunting, at some point we, admittedly, crossed a line and became, to a degree, hunters ourselves. But we have not allowed that to impose upon our efforts to remain fair.

A word about usage. As we will discuss at length in chapter 3, it was decided early on that mere membership in the National Socialist German Workers' Party (Nazi Party) did not in itself constitute a war crime. But over the years, "Nazi" has come to stand not only for actual members of the Nazi Party, but for the whole range of collaborators, auxiliary police force members, and other ancillaries of the Third Reich.

As a result of this book there has been a counterattack of threats, economic pressure, insults, and slander designed by those who still want to protect individuals who believed in the Final Solution. As we became involved in the research, we found ourselves exchanging information with the World Jewish Congress, other private groups, and in some cases official organizations, as to the whereabouts of war criminals. As a result, when our investigation turned for several months primarily to the Waldheim situation, some of the Austrian president's supporters fought back. Newspaper publishers, the publisher of this book, and associates of ours received anonymous phone calls and letters attacking us. We received threats in the mail—the cowardly kind that remind you they know your whereabouts without revealing the writer's identity. Slander was employed to compromise our efforts to make this book totally accurate, timely, and thorough.

Despite these crude attempts at intimidation, we proceeded and were literally blessed with the highest level of cooperation either of us has known in the preparation of a book or story. Many dedicated individuals, after satisfying themselves as to the legitimacy of our goals, opened their files and their hearts. Some were Holocaust victims, many were public officials. They represented the leadership and membership of half a dozen organizations throughout the United States and a like number in the United Kingdom and internationally.

We make repeated reference herein to Neal Sher, Director of the Justice Department's Office of Special Investigations, and his staff. Sher has brought a remarkable blend of professionalism and humanity to the job. He has assembled a band of archivists, investigators, historians, and lawyers who have the spirit that has kept the hunt for Nazis alive despite every imaginable internal and external obstacle.

There is no more knowledgeable or effective organization in the field than the World Jewish Congress. It is said that the world is crowded with Jewish organizations, and that their causes may often overlap. If this is true, it reflects even more favorably upon the World Jewish Congress, which has become such an effective clearinghouse for Jewish communities around the world. Without the talent of its leaders and the commitment of its entire staff, this book would not exist, Kurt Waldheim might never have been exposed, and the world would know dangerously less about Nazis than it does.

President Edgar Bronfman provides strong leadership and financial underwriting for the World Jewish Congress. Israel Singer, its secretary-general, is the organization's heart and soul, and Elan Steinberg, its indefatigable executive director, provides the organization with the means and strategies for both offense and defense. The three form a brilliant and effective team.

This book is also the story of well-known figures like Simon Wiesenthal, who survived concentration camps to devote his life to hunting down those who engineered and executed the Holocaust. It is the story of those who carry on in his tradition and in his name: Rabbis Marvin Hier and Abraham Cooper of the Simon Wiesenthal Center for Holocaust Studies in Los Angeles, their able colleague in Toronto, Sol Littman, and Elliot Welles, director of the Nazi Crimes Task Force of the Anti-Defamation League of B'nai B'rith. But it is also the story of the unknown, including a woman in her eighties who works in an office on New York's Madison Avenue locating former victims around the world to testify at those few trials of Nazis that still take place.

A handful of major newspapers not only provided invaluable information, making it possible to crosscheck our own research, but served as outlets for key stories during the past year, including the Waldheim case, the opening of the Nazi war crimes archive by the United Nations, and related matters. In Great Britain, *The Sunday Express* and *The Star* were most effective in detailing every aspect of the Waldheim story and of the efforts to motivate the British government to initiate prosecution of known Nazis living in that country.

After we provided the *Express* with the names that appeared on the list of seventeen Nazis delivered to the home secretary by representatives of the Wiesenthal Center, a few of the accused sought injunctive relief from British courts to prevent publication of their names and pictures. The matter is still pending before those courts, but this does not prevent us from identifying those involved in a book published in the United States.

In Canada, *The Toronto Sun* has repeatedly published our articles and taken a leading role in focusing attention in that country with respect to the hunt for Nazis. In the United States, *The Las Vegas Sun*, and *The Arizona Republic* must be commended for their determination to keep the story of war crimes alive.

★   ★   ★

You don't devote the amount of time that we have committed to this book without imposing heavily upon those around you. Our families must be thanked for their tolerance and understanding.

Research is indispensable in preparing investigative books and articles. Ours was performed thoroughly by Angela and Barrett Ford, Shireen Liane-Smith, Richard Brodsky, and Beth Fox in the United States, and Michael May and Kelvin O'Shea in London. In the U.S., long-time friends at CBS, ABC, and CNN were indispensable. We enjoyed ready access to the Yad Vashem Center in Israel, the National Archives in Washington, and the collections and libraries of UCLA and the University of California at Berkeley. We owe a special thanks to our friend Joe Sills, senior information officer at the United Nations. To borrow slightly from Shakespeare, we have been "at a great feast of material and stolen some of the scraps."

Our editor, Hana Lane, has more than a sharp pencil. She has been a demanding guide as we tried to cull down from potential volumes into a single book the most relevant and provable facts concerning the hunt for Nazis.

To those with whom we work on a daily basis and who gave us understanding as we preoccupied ourselves with the completion of this task—thank you.

★ ★ ★

Finally, we must turn our attention to a question that has been put to us from Melbourne to Munich and from New York to London, and at almost every stop between: "Why don't you just let the old men die? It's ancient history." We have come to call this the "isn't it time to forgive and forget" argument. Its proponents are, by and large, well-meaning persons who believe it is simply better to let the past lie after all these years. Among them are those who hold that the phrase "Nazi hunters" should be put away for all time. Some are motivated by humane concerns about old men who today could harm no one being dragged through court proceedings that would destroy what is left of their limited lives. Others fear, with some justification, that there is a direct relationship between the increase of anti-Semitism in the United States and around the world and efforts to hunt down Nazis. Proponents of closing the books on the war crimes of Nazi Germany argue that except in the rare case of a major Nazi figure who has still not been brought to justice, it would be better to simply forgive and forget.

There are signs in many hospitals that say time heals all. We do not accept that. Time can never heal the Holocaust. To more than six million Jews, it is too late. World Jewry will never be the same again. The synagogues will not be restored to their former grandeur. Hitler's memorial is, in a sense, the partial destruction of the Jewish people and the critical wounding of all civilization.

But rather than attempt to answer those who would close the books on the Nazi horrors of the past, we'll let others speak. Elan Steinberg believes that to ignore war criminals who remain free "would amount to an amnesty for the Holocaust, and that is morally reprehensible."

Robert E. Conot, whose *Judgment at Nuremberg* stands as the definitive work on the war trials, writes, "While many of the principles of Nuremberg have been incorporated into international law, practices have changed little. The impacts of Nuremberg have faded. Nuremberg has become an abstract rather than a dire precept."

Another answer comes from America's chief Nazi hunter, Neal Sher, who says simply that he has no time for such debate. "It's an argument I will not be drawn into," states Sher. "If a person has persecuted others because of race, religion, or political beliefs, I will pursue them whether it can be shown that the persecution was committed against thousands or a single individual. I believe justice demands an accounting no matter the passage of time, and it is not the kind of thing that can or should be quantified."

The argument is also lost on the victims of Nazi persecution, to whom forty years is but a day. Among the most eloquent is Nobel laureate Elie Wiesel, who wrote in his 1960 personal account of the death camps:

Never shall I forget that night, the first night in the camp, which has turned my life into one long night, seven times cursed and seven times sealed. Never shall I forget the little faces of the children, whose bodies I saw turned into wreaths of smoke beneath a silent blue sky.

Never shall I forget those flames which consumed my faith forever.

Never shall I forget that nocturnal silence which deprived me for all eternity of the desire to live. Never shall I forget those moments which murdered my God and my soul and turned my dreams to dust. Never shall I forget these things, even if I am condemned to live as long as God himself.

Never.

Perhaps the last word on this subject should go to Simon Wiesenthal, who was a lone voice of conscience for so many years. "This matter must remain open as a warning," Wiesenthal says, "because the murderers of tomorrow might be alive today."

Most Wanted

It will never be possible to assess accurately the number of Nazis and others responsible for crimes against humanity, but the governments of many nations and some private Nazi-hunting organizations have periodically fixed figures as a guideline in the ongoing hunt for war criminals. But the wide-ranging, still imprecise definition of "war crime," and the varied interpretations of crimes committed by those accused, makes both Nazi-hunting and the gathering of statistics an inexact science.

Nevertheless, officials of the primary organizations still hunting Nazis, and the governments of West Germany and the United States, believe that between 150,000 and 200,000 Germans and others were responsible for committing atrocities before and during the war years. Fewer than 2,000 were convicted by the Americans at Dachau and the secondary trials at Nuremberg. Another 1,085 were convicted by the British, 2,107 by the French, 75 by the Belgians, 10 by Denmark, 197 by the Netherlands, 92 by Norway, and 5,452 by Poland. Yugoslavia, the Soviet Union, and East Germany combined convicted approximately 25,000 others. In short, just over 35,000—some 20 percent of those believed responsible for major war crimes—have been hunted down, captured, and convicted.

One area of general agreement among Nazi-hunting organizations and individuals is that some very notorious war criminals are still at large. Whether you subscribe to the concept of a "ten most wanted" list or any other numerical combination, there are a handful of major Nazi war criminals who must be brought to justice—and "brought to justice" is the correct phrase, because some of the most notorious are living quite openly.

At the top of everyone's list is Alois Brunner, chief deputy to Adolf Eichmann. Brunner, who now lives in Damascus, Syria, was responsible for the deaths of more than 100,000 Jews and some 60,000 others. The man described by Eichmann during his trial as "my most consistently effective aide" has lived under the name of Dr. Georg Fischer in Syria for more than twenty-five years. He deserves detailed examination, and his is one of the few cases where such an examination can be both thorough and current, since he has boasted widely of his identity and "achievements."

Space does not permit detailing the exploits of each and every Nazi on the "most wanted list," but, for reasons no one has ever explained to our satisfaction, Brunner's is a blank page in the books that describe Nazi atrocities. We assembled what we could from Elliot Welles of the Anti-Defamation League, from the Berlin Document Center, French authorities, and the United Nations Nazi war crime archive to piece together the life of this monster who, as you read this, sleeps peacefully in the security of Syrian government protection.

In 1961, as the world's attention was focused on the Eichmann trial, a small but bulky letter was delivered to a forty-nine-year-old man in Damascus. The nameplate on his door said Georg Fischer, but the man inside was Alois Brunner, former aide to Eichmann and a key organizer of the murder of millions of Jews and others.

We know now that the bulky parcel exploded as Brunner, alias Fischer, opened it. When he was released from the hospital, he had lost two fingers on his left hand. The parcel had originated in Israel, but had been taken by a Mossad agent to Paris and remailed to give it a French postmark, thereby avoiding suspicion. A senior Israeli intelligence officer told us that "There are many freelancers out there who have gone after major Nazi war criminals, but in the case of Brunner, I think you will find that we would not hesitate to take 'official credit' for originating the efforts to kill him."

A second letter bomb to Brunner took out one eye, but he has been quoted by three separate journalists who interviewed him in Syria as saying, "Israel will never get me," adding, "I won't be another Eichmann."

For some reason, despite his horrendous career, Brunner did not receive the notoriety that others have in the post-war years. Yet a small band of people was dedicated to tracking him down and bringing him to justice. None was more dedicated than Elliot Welles, director of Task Force on Nazi War Criminals of the Anti-Defamation League of the B'nai B'rith.

It's difficult for Welles to be objective, since he was there when Brunner sent his mother to her death; he knows a great deal about this particular killer. Welles told us that his years of hunting for Brunner and "trying to get him" resulted in evidence from a half-dozen countries, from former victims, former Nazis, and outraged bystanders who could not accept the fact that Brunner went unpunished. Welles told us that for "nearly thirty years the government of Syria has provided sanctuary and protection to Brunner." We corroborated that independently through French, Austrian, and English sources.

Third Reich records reveal that Alois Brunner belonged to a cadre of deportation experts who attempted to fulfill *der Führer's* dream of "the Final Solution of the Jewish Question*—ultimately, the extinction of the Jewish race. As a director of the Nazi plan to deport all non-Aryans to death camps, Brunner made his mark as one of the cruelest, most cold-blooded, most ruthlessly efficient officers in Eichmann's command. Files and eyewitness testimony reveal that the SS *Hauptsturmfuhrer* cut a wide swath through Europe and the Mediterranean, enforcing mercilessly the German plan to rid the world of "unpure" blood in the pursuit of a German Master Race.

Experts who have analyzed the motives of the most brutal of the Nazis point out that Brunner, like Hitler, Himmler, Goering, and Eichmann, did not conform physically to the Aryan ideal of a blond, blue-eyed *Ubermensch* (member of the master race) . None of them would have been a good model for Mengele's breeding goals. Records show that Brunner was 5 feet, 8½ inches tall and never weighed more than 130 pounds. Former Nazi officers who worked with him described him at Nuremberg as "poorly built, puny, with wicked little eyes, and a very monotonous voice." At the Eichmann trial, another description enumerated the traits "small, dark, nervous, with a long and pointed nose, slightly bowlegged and slightly hunchbacked." Dieter Wislenceny, one of Brunner's close friends among the Nazi hierarchy, who was executed for war crimes in 1948, described him as "a man with bad posture, black kinky hair, dark eyes, thick lips and a hook nose. He must have had some Gypsy or Jewish blood."

Brunner was born in Rohrbrunn, Austria, in 1912. He attended school in Furstenfeld, Austria, after which he became an apprentice merchant, took trade school courses, and later worked in a department store. The Nazi Party beckoned, and Alois Brunner heeded the call on May 21, 1931, becoming, at the age of nineteen, a member of the Furstenfeld branch. He joined the party after he was turned down on his application to become a policeman. Shortly thereafter, he also became a member of the Nazi SA.

He worked at a savings and loan firm for a few months, and when it closed in the midst of Germany's deep economic depression, he leased and opened a cafe. That, too, closed after four months, wiping out his finances.

The Austrian Legion, a paramilitary Nazi organization that was outlawed by the government, enrolled Brunner as a member in September 1933, and he re-

---

* According to testimony at the Nuremberg war crimes trials, the term "final solution" was probably first contained in a memo from Heinrich Himmler, the head of the SS, to Adolf Eichmann, head of the Gestapo's Jewish Section. According to Dieter Wislenceny, Eichmann's deputy, Eichmann explained the term to him. "He said the planned biological annihilation of the Jewish race in the Eastern Territories was disguised by the concept and the wording 'final solution.' In later discussions of the subject the same words would appear over and over."

mained one until March 1938, the time of the *Anschluss*. However, Brunner's Nazi Party membership had been voided on April 1, 1933, apparently because the young man failed to pay his party dues. (Later Brunner claimed he had paid them, and blamed the Furstenfeld organization for failing to send them to Hartberg, where he had moved.) He appealed to his group leader, who praised him as an exemplary Nazi, "a tireless and enthusiastic fighter . . . [who] sacrificed his free time to the movement." Nonetheless Brunner's membership remained void until May 17, 1939. Meanwhile, he joined the SS in November 1938, one week after *Kristallnacht*. On his SS application, Brunner lied about his employment history: he claimed he had lost his job as a department store clerk because of his membership in the SA. In fact, Brunner had resigned the position, but he realized at that early stage that the SS respected such sacrifice, and he used the mantle of nobility to further his cause within the hierarchy.

Brunner's self-serving attitude paid off; he worked as a manager of SA Intelligence and Communications in both Eisenstadt and Oberpullendorf. In 1938 he became an employee of the Central Office for Jewish Emigration in Vienna, as Adolf Eichmann's personal secretary. As one of the office's earliest employees, Brunner saw his star rise quickly, and he became an officer in the SS Security Service, known as the SD.

By 1942 the young officer had become director of the Central Office for Jewish Emigration in Vienna, where he was responsible for Eichmann's brainchild, the deportation of Vienna's Jews to "resettlements" in Poland. In that year, Brunner also forwarded his application to the SS for permission to marry. He had chosen Anni Roder, a former typist for the Hitler Youth Propaganda Office and, since 1939, a stenographer in his own office. After a strenuous investigation of the couple's political, genealogical, and physical histories, the SS deemed them fit to bear children who met Aryan standards.

Brunner's office served as the model for the German plan of mass deportation. His supervision of the Viennese deportations gained him respect in the eyes of his Nazi superiors in Berlin. He was promoted to captain in the SS Security Service and as representative of the Reich Security Main Office (RHSA), was the absolute authority behind the Central Office in Vienna. His method of dealing with the Viennese Jewish population proved so successful that by 1941 no Jews were allowed to emigrate to any area except Poland. Jewish resistance to the deportation policy and escape attempts were ruthlessly put down.

By organizing the Viennese Jewish community into a single entity, Brunner was able to make the *Kultusgemeinde*, as the community organization was known, the unwitting participant in its own destruction. The group was ordered to provide the Central Office with detailed lists of resident Jews and family members, which, in turn, would be used to determine deportation transport roles. Brunner used the organization against itself: by balancing threats with favors, he could ensure cooperation on the part of the Jews. An offer would be made to free Jews from the German concentration camps of Dachau and Buchenwald in exchange for the ex-prisoners' voluntary deportation to Poland. *Kultusgemeinde* employees were promised exemptions from deportation if they managed to fill the Nazis' transport quotas.

The Nazis also developed categorizations by which certain persons were exempt from deportation. These exempted Jews included wounded or decorated veterans, *Kultusgemeinde* administrators, invalids, and those with Aryan spouses, or spouses who were prisoners of war. Such supposed "relaxations" of deportation policies gave the Jewish population a false sense of security: if they might be exempted through their cooperation, then Jews would aid the Nazi cause. Routinely, those scheduled for deportation would be ordered to relinquish all their assets; payment was promised in the form of scrip certificates "to be issued in zlotys" upon their arrival at a resettlement. To many, this was the first indication that their true destination was Poland.

Finally, exemptions disappeared altogether. It became clear that, under Eichmann's orders, all Viennese Jews were to be deported. By the end of summer, 1942, fewer than 10,000 Viennese Jews remained in the city. Brunner's transports were responsible for the deportation of 47,000 Jews, many of whom were interned in the Nazi camp at Theresienstadt, outside of Prague, or sent to the Polish ghettos of Riga, Minsk, and Lublin. By the fall of 1942, a new phase of Eichmann's Final Solution had begun, and future transports would discharge most of their human cargo directly to mobile killing vans or mass execution sites in the Rumbula Forest near Riga.

In early 1943, Eichmann sent Brunner to Salonica, Greece's third largest city. There Sephardic Jewish culture had flourished since the fifteenth century, when the Jews fled Spain to escape the Inquisition. Brunner was joined in Salonica by SS *Hauptsturmführer* Dieter Wislenceny, who announced that the SS would take over from other commands in Greece the "actions against the Jews."

Next Brunner was posted to Paris, opening a new phase of depravity and sadism. Assigned to command the German transit camp at Drancy, just outside the French capital, he assumed his new command with relish. On his first day, Brunner began personal interrogations of every one of the 3,000 inmates of Drancy. Three days later, he had his deportation lists. On June 21, 1943, the first transport ordered by Brunner left Drancy, ending a period of three months without transports to the Nazi death camp at Auschwitz.

Brunner was cold-blooded in his command of Drancy. Inmates reported that "Every Jew arrested or brought to the camp submitted to a brutal interrogation by Captain Brunner or his acolytes." The camp was called by its prisoners "*Drancy la Creve*" (Drancy the Killer). Witnesses testified that Brunner's office walls were marked with bloodstains and bullet holes, vivid proof that he ruled with sadistic abandon. Others recalled that during walks through the camp, he would occasionally draw his pistol and fire at random into crowds of prisoners. Evidently enjoying such cruelty, he would also visit the camp for regular hour-long beatings of prisoners with a horsewhip.

Brunner was as efficient as he was sadistic. He organized the camp to suit his needs, categorizing its inmates into several groups. The most dreaded, "Category B," meant that one was subject to immediate deportation to Auschwitz.

He also exerted strong central authority, dismissing the French guards who had manned the camp and replacing them with a band of twenty-five hand-picked SS soldiers, described by Drancy inmates as "thieves and pilferers from Vienna." They were "sworn body and soul to Brunner" and were able to oversee the several thousand prisoners, whom Brunner had placed under the charge of Jewish administrators, chosen from the camp itself. By assigning the day-to-day running of the camp to the Jews themselves, Brunner was able to ensure the inmates' cooperation in their own demise. He also established the Order Service, a group of Jewish inmates who supervised the handling of prisoners and delivered them to the death-camp transports. The slightest infraction by anyone in the Order Service would result in placement on the next transport.

Closing the camp to French authorities, Commandant Brunner assigned the task of provisioning it to the *Union Generale des Israelites des France*, or UGIF, a Nazi-initiated Jewish council. Brunner's first requisition to the UGIF indicated clearly his intent: 40,000 index cards and 500 arm bands imprinted *Jewish Order Service*. Soon the UGIF was forced to play a part in the deportation process: the transports themselves were provisioned at extraordinary expense by the Jewish council, although testimony from transport survivors reveals that no food was made available to them "and only once during the journey did we obtain drink." On supply orders, Brunner usually added a note to the effect that "these precious food supplies not be used for the camp inmates."

The UGIF served other needs for the brutal commandant as well. Its officials were held accountable for the actions of inmates involved in escape attempts. When two prisoners escaped during the summer of 1943, Brunner ordered the UGIF's Paris leaders held hostage. When that action failed to turn up the escaped prisoners, the leaders were deported to Auschwitz. That September, an escape tunnel was discovered in the camp at Drancy; Brunner's response was swift and brutal: the chief of Jewish camp administration and sixty-five assistants were tortured and deported.

Deportees were issued the standard scrip, now bearing the legend "the equivalent amount will be reimbursed in zlotys by the Council of Elders of the Jewish Community in Poland." It suggested that goods would be available for deportees to buy once they reached their destination—a deception perpetuated by the Nazis at Drancy. The RSHA proposed that the name of Auschwitz not be used, but rather vague references to Polish resettlements, about which the security office disseminated glowing reports. In Drancy, the Nazis showed inmates pictures of a quiet village.

Brunner's reputation grew as he managed to speed up the deportation transports to Poland. Despite the fact that the French Vichy government had agreed with the Reich that no Jews of French nationality were to be deported, Brunner's operations stretched throughout northern France, identifying Jews for arrest and deportation. The UGIF was forced to submit detailed lists of Jewish organizations, and was informed that any organization not listed would be considered illegal and its members subject to immediate deportation to Auschwitz. Thus compelled to be thorough, the UGIF helped to further the Nazi cause.

At first, Brunner managed to circumvent the agreement not to deport French Jews by identifying those who had become French through naturalization. Arguing that they were not technically French, Brunner justified their deportation. Later, in August 1944, he cosigned a secret order with Helmut Knochen, supreme police chief of France and Gestapo *Obersturmführer*, which stated, in effect, that all Jews in France, without regard to nationality, were subject to immediate arrest and deportation. The order made no provision for exemptions, targeting penal institutions and prisons directly.

Also targeted directly were the Jewish children of France. As early as 1942, Brunner had pressed the UGIF for information on Jewish orphanages and children's centers, stressing that any attempt to hide the children or aid in their rescue from Nazi internment would result in the arrest of UGIF leaders. As the UGIF realized that even children from recognized "legal centers" were being sent to the Eastern camps, secret children's homes were instituted, but even these were not completely safe. Several were raided and the children sent off to die in extermination camps.

In one three-night period during in June 1944, Brunner rounded up and shipped to death camps 500 children from centers whose records had been supplied by the UGIF. When a UGIF official appealed to Brunner about the arrests, the commandant of Drancy responded with his own brand of Nazi zealotry: the children were "future terrorists," he asserted, and deserved the same fate as every other enemy of the Reich.

Brunner's deportation of Jews from southern France did not run as smoothly as his operations in the north. The Italians, Germany's fascist allies, had controlled large portions of Southern France since 1942, when Germany first overran the area. French Jews found the Italian authorities quite amenable, allowing them freedom from prosecution and implementation of the Final Solution. With the actions of a sympathetic French prefect protecting Jews around Nice, the region, especially the Cote D'Azur, became a haven for Jews. This recalcitrance on behalf of French and Italian authorities galled Brunner, who strove to evacuate every Jew in France.

However, the relative safety of southern France was short-lived because the Allied armistice with Italy in September 1943 brought Italian withdrawal, opening the area to Brunner's henchmen. At first the Nazis were frustrated in their search for Jews: secret Resistance presses had been printing forged identification papers in southern France at a rate of about 20,000 per month, allowing Jews to adopt non-Jewish identities. Unable to get his hands on a list of Jews in the area, Brunner resorted to more desperate methods.

Reducing the participation of French authorities to a minimum, Brunner instituted block-by-block sweeps. As eyewitnesses recalled, "the Nazis barricaded a street, burst into the hotels and gathered up all those who by identity card or physiognomy appeared to be Jews." When the Germans doubted the authenticity of a man's papers, a "medical examination" was made: "Prisoners have to take down their pants. They were classified Jews or Aryans by whether or not they are circumcised," according to testimony at the Eichmann trial.

Brunner's special team of twelve to fourteen torturers rounded up large numbers of Jews—men, women, and children. One of Brunner's Jewish aides, brought from Drancy to assist in Nazi operations, stated that "Among the arrested there were the ill and feeble, the elderly, nursing babies, pregnant women; all underwent the violence and torture of these brutes."

French cooperation with, and participation in, these Nazi operations suffered, as word spread of the true scope and methods of the Final Solution. Brunner flew into apoplexy when the BBC broadcast a report on Nazi activities in Drancy. Upon discovering two inmates attempting to smuggle letters to the outside world, he had the men whip each other almost to death. But Brunner's command at Drancy was drawing to a close, as Allied forces approached Paris late in the summer of 1944. As the distance from the front grew shorter, Brunner still endeavored to fill one last transport, rounding up 1,300 Jews from any source, including children's homes, and shipping them off to Auschwitz.

On the day the Germans abandoned Paris, August 17, 1944, the commandant sent one last carload of fifty-one Jews to Birkenau, attached to the last German military train. The next day Brunner abandoned Drancy, stating, "To hell with the camp." Upon his departure, the Red Cross assumed jurisdiction. Brunner's last act before escaping France was to order the deportation lists from Drancy destroyed—lists containing 67,000 names. However, the camp files were saved, fulfilling Brunner's greatest fear. The names of 23,500 victims sent to the camps at Brunner's command testify to the cold-blooded commandant's complicity in the murders of more than 99 percent of his deportees. From Paris, Alois Brunner was sent to Slovakia, a German satellite. Transports of Jews had been sent to the Eastern camps from Slovakia until 1942, when word had leaked to the Slovakian government about the actual fate of Jewish deportees sent to the supposed resettlement camps. Deportations ceased for nearly two years after 55,000 Slovakian Jews had been deported and the country's remaining 25,000 Jews were placed in forced labor camps.

At the end of August 1944, an insurrection broke out in Slovakia, involving 15,000 anti-Nazis from Slovakia, Hungary, and neighboring areas. Brunner's posting to Slovakia was the Nazi response, aimed at breaking the back of the insurrection. Within two weeks Brunner had reinstated the transports of deportees that had worked so well in Vienna, Salonica, and France. On one night in September, his forces rounded up 1,800 Slovakian Jews in Bratislava.

The Slovakian Jews had prevented deportations from August 1942 through August 1944 by entering into a ransom plan with the Reich, whereby they offered up to $2,000,000 for the guaranteed safety of the entire Jewish population. A Slovakian Jewish leader had contacted Brunner's SS crony Dieter Wislenceny and offered the Germans the funds made available by a Jewish charitable organization, the Joint Distribution Committee (JDC). Although the offer had resulted in a two-year moratorium, the German government had cooled on the scheme, and Brunner's response to the ransom negotiations upon his arrival was to place the negotiators and their families on the next available transport.

In October 1944, after a direct appeal by a Slovak Jewish leader to Brunner for renewed negotiations, the Nazi captain had her arrested and placed in Slovakia's Sered transit camp. There he interrogated her for hours, offering to help her in exchange for information about her contacts with Jewish organizations abroad, and on Jews hiding in Bratislava. She refused to assist Brunner, and he had her deported to Auschwitz, where he made arrangements to have her killed upon arrival.

In March of 1945, the Soviets were approaching the Sered camp. Brunner stepped up his transports and sent Jewish prisoners to other camps, including Theresienstadt, when the route to Auschwitz was cut. Finally, the Soviets were close enough to bombard the camp, and Brunner realized that he must flee. As at Drancy, he managed to put the Sered camp's remaining Jews on a transport to Theresienstadt, remaining ruthlessly consistent in his efforts to exterminate every Jew in his command.

By the spring of 1945, the Nazis had lost the war. Eichmann's deportation policy had been implemented with cold precision, and Brunner's command in

Slovakia was directly responsible, from September 1944 until April 1945, for the deportation of 14,000 Jews from the Sered camp to Auschwitz and to the concentration camps of Theresienstadt and Sachsenhausen.

With the collapse of the Eastern Front and the Soviet liberation of Sered, Brunner fled to Austria, where he was last seen by his fellow Nazi officer Wislenceny in Vienna on April 2, 1945. Brunner was among the Nazi officers arrested and interned in Germany immediately after the war and held under joint British-American supervision. He used the alias Alois Schmaldienest and had military papers to back up that name with a lower rank. Near the end of the war, it was common for top Nazis to hold forged papers in the event they were captured. He did not have the telltale SS blood-type tattoo. (His friend Wislenceny said in 1948 that "Brunner did not have a tattoo because the needle would have killed him.")

Brunner was released by the British-American forces and spent seven months as a civilian truck driver in Munich— working for the U.S. occupation forces. Records show that after that he lived undetected in a small town outside of Germany for nearly a decade. Throughout those years, the name Brunner was very high on the list of those wanted for the worst crimes against humanity in Austria, Greece, Czechoslovakia, and Germany. The U.N. War Crimes Commission assembled a file on Brunner, and many hunters considered him their number one target, but during the 1950s they could not locate him.

Finally, France, based on numerous eyewitness accounts from victims and other officers, condemned him to death in absentia in 1954. Although it is not known exactly when, Nazi hunters believe that sometime between 1955 and 1957, Brunner fled Europe, fearing that hunters armed with the French death warrant would find him. He went first to Cairo, then moved on to Damascus, Syria.

Under the name Dr. Georg Fischer, Brunner was an assistant manager in a trading company that represented West German firms. A handful of those in the network designed to hide Nazis knew where Brunner was at that time, but protected him.

In 1960 Brunner was arrested by Syrian authorities and accused of using the trading company to smuggle drugs. Police records show that he asked to see the captain in charge at the time of his arrest and risked identifying himself by true name and former Nazi rank, and, perhaps more importantly, true deeds. "Welcome to Syria. The enemies of our enemies are our friends," the police captain reportedly told him.

According to Elliot Welles, Brunner then met with Syrian officials and assembled a scheme to free Adolf Eichmann from captivity in Jerusalem. Welles says that a team of Syrian agents under Brunner's command tried to penetrate

Israeli security, but found it too tight and abandoned the plan. Then the group plotted to kill the leaders of the World Jewish Congress in Vienna in 1961. Brunner arranged Austrian contacts who could be trusted to handle the logistics of getting the Syrian bomb in and out. The bomb was found when Viennese police were tipped off. But Brunner had shown his loyalty to the Syrian government and had an extremely effective credential in the fact that he was perhaps the most hated man alive to the Israelis. More than once, the theme "the enemies of our enemies are our friends" was repeated.

Brunner became a "security advisor" to the Syrian government, and the Mossad believes that he was responsible for at least a dozen anti-Israeli incidents throughout the world. He helped train Syria's security police in "effective interrogation methods" and became a personal advisor to the brother of Syrian president Hafez Assad.

When the Austrian government uncovered the 1961 plot to kill the leaders of the World Jewish Congress, it also learned of Brunner's involvement and tried to have him extradited, using the death warrant issued when he was tried in absentia in France. The Syrians admitted to the French that Brunner was in their country, but said that "because of certain and special circumstances" he was not a common criminal and therefore could not be extradited through normal diplomatic channels.

The Israelis talked several times of an Eichmann-type raid into Syria to bring Brunner out to face trial, but a top aide to former Israeli prime minister Ben Gurion told us that "There were just so many far more important and delicate political matters going on between the nations in that part of the world that it was impractical to risk the negative public reaction of another Eichmann situation." However, the Mossad kept an active file, Elliot Welles kept tracking him, and many of the free-lance Nazi hunters exchanged information on the day-to-day movements of the man at the top of their wanted lists.

In 1974 some journalists found Brunner and confirmed that he was working for the Syrian government as an advisor on "Jewish affairs." That convinced the government of Austria, France, and anyone else who was interested in getting Brunner out through diplomatic channels that it would never happen. But ten years later, an aggressive prosecutor in Cologne obtained new evidence of Brunner's murder of Germans, in addition to the documented cases of his participation in the murder of more than 100,000 Jews and tens of thousands of others from different countries. Based on "fresh material and documents," the West German government officially requested extradition of Brunner by the government of Syria.

At first, Syria flatly denied that Brunner was in the country. But they added, as a bizarre footnote, that even if he was in Syria, they would not honor the request, because they had no formal extradition treaty with West Germany. After this incredible exchange, a team of West German journalists from *Bunte* magazine tracked down Brunner, alias Georg Fischer, to his home at 7 Rue Haddad in Damascus.

The reporters took photos of Brunner walking through the streets of Damascus, which showed him to be a gaunt, balding man with only one eye and a deformed hand. (The missing eye and the hand injury, as mentioned earlier, were the results of letter bombs.) *Bunte* reported that Brunner was accompanied by two or three armed, uniformed bodyguards provided by the Syrian government.

Its reporters interviewed government officials, neighbors, and finally, Brunner himself. He told *Bunte* that he had "no bad conscience" for getting rid "of that Jewish garbage"; he actually bragged about sending Jews to their deaths. The Brunner world view, as expressed in 1985, was that "the Communist East is bad, the capitalist West is much worse. Jews, with their Christian and Islamic sects, are the crowning achievement of the devil."

There was outrage throughout West Germany when the *Bunte* interview appeared, and the West German government renewed its demand for Brunner's extradition for trial. France followed suit. Alfred Streim, chief prosecutor of West Germany's Central Office for the Investigation of Nazi Crimes, says, "Brunner is the most incriminated Nazi still alive." Newspapers in the United States, Great Britain, Canada, and Australia began editorializing about Syria's abuse of international law by harboring the murderer Brunner. *The Boston Globe* said, "the very survival of a man like Brunner is a shame that taints several nations. His escape from justice is one of many signs that the evil he personifies still flourishes."

After the sensational Brunner interview, Elliot Welles, working from his small, cluttered office in New York, continued his efforts to get the former Nazi. Simultaneously, American relatives of victims of Brunner's atrocities held meetings with private adventurers to determine whether or not it was realistic to send a group into Syria to bring Brunner out and turn him over to either the French or the Israelis for trial. In 1987 meetings were held in London and Manchester, England, Atlanta, Georgia, and New York City about just such a campaign.

This was one of the few occasions that we became part of the posse in the course of reporting on Nazi hunters. We were asked by two wealthy American businessmen, who were willing to issue a blank check to any group that could get Brunner out to stand trial, to approach the Israeli government and find out how they would treat him if he suddenly appeared outside Syria's border. The sensitivities of ten years before had increased, we were told by a leading member of the Israeli mission to the United Nations. The delicate problems that Israel faced in staying militarily strong and trying to gain understanding from the U.N. member nations made it impossible to launch an Israeli raid on an official basis. "But if Brunner showed up outside the borders of Syria, there would be a free-for-all as to which country would get him to try him first. We're very fast in a foot race of that kind."

In late 1987, we were able to confirm firsthand what the *Bunte* reporters and later a team of British journalists had also discovered. First there was the address, 7 Rue Haddad, and the fact that Brunner was still living there. Then there were those who thought the *Bunte* article had exaggerated, or even misstated, Brunner's boasts. *Bunte* was accurate; Brunner repeated his assertions about the Jews in a telephone interview with us, saying, "they deserved to die, and I would do it all over again because they were human garbage."

The Canadians, among America's Western allies, have the best access to Syria, and the Canadian Jewish community is a vital one. Several things came together to make our interview with Brunner possible. Since you cannot telephone Syria from the United States unless Syria wants you to, it was necessary to have assistance inside the country.

Through two free-lance journalists, we were finally able to arrange the call, during which the interpreter spoke German, English, and French, while Brunner spoke German.

It was a brief call. Expecting that Brunner would disconnect the minute he realized that he was speaking for American publication, we used the premise that the interview was for the London *Sunday Express*. We started by asking about the interview in *Bunte*, and he repeated what he had told the German reporters two years earlier, almost as if it were a script. And, more recently, in yet another interview with a British journalist, Brunner again repeated these outrages. But one thing that *was* clear in this interview was the tone of his voice. He spoke clearly and without hesitation, but without inflection.

After Brunner confirmed what he had told *Bunte*, we tried to get him to expand on his present feelings about Israel, the United States, the Soviet Union, and even Kurt Waldheim. He would have none of it and hung up.

Within three hours of that conversation, a free-lance television crew arrived outside of 7 Rue Haddad. They had been sent by the international desk of ABC News in London. The guards chased them away, making sure the Syrian among them knew how dire the consequences would be if he came back. Next morning, a photographer took pictures of the house and verified with neighbors that Brunner was there and then he, too, was chased.

Our ABC news contact told us that London had received a disturbing message from their Syrian cameraman. Quite simply, it pointed out that he would be in serious physical danger if he went back on that assignment, and it just wasn't worth it.

After the worldwide publicity caused by our brief telephone interview, the television news visit, and the photographer's attempt to see Brunner, the former Nazi was moved by Syrian authorities to the outskirts of Damascus, where he is living at this writing. The house at 7 Rue Haddad is boarded up. There will be no more phone calls to Mr. Brunner from reporters.

In late 1987, a former British Special Forces Officer, now retired and working as an international "consultant" to businesses with offices in sensitive areas, visited Damascus with a Canadian who was there on behalf of several trading companies. They toured the city, managing to drive past 7 Rue Haddad a dozen times, and used their skills and contacts to find out where Brunner was, how well guarded he was, and whether it would be possible to get him out. Brunner had been moved some three miles away to a heavily guarded private home; there were now four guards instead of two. The visitors arranged for a British photographer to seek out Brunner's new location, if he could, and to photograph the house. His camera was confiscated by the Syrian police guarding Brunner, and the photographer was told that he would be arrested if he returned to that street. The plan to kidnap Brunner was abandoned.

In November 1987, West Germany renewed its request for Brunner's extradition. And ironically, in the middle of the Waldheim crisis in Austria, members of the political party most supportive of the Austrian president processed another request of the same kind. (Austria had been relatively quiet on the issue since Waldheim took office.)

It has been suggested that even if Syria wanted to release Brunner for trial in France, West Germany, or Israel, it could not do so, because Brunner knows too much about Syrian intrigues and terrorism around the world.

★ ★ ★

There is some disagreement about the next most important war criminal still at large, but that dubious honor probably belongs to Heinrich Müller. Most Nazi hunters believe that the former head of the German Gestapo and administrator of the Nazis' program of extermination is still alive. He would be eighty-five years old now.

It's believed that Müller fled to Albania and has been hiding in Eastern European countries since World War II. Many rumors have placed him in Russia, Albania, or East Germany, but none of the sightings has ever been confirmed. His family insists that he died and was buried in Germany. In 1964 West German officials examined his exhumed remains, but according to experts on the scene, the results were inconclusive. Aaron Breitbart of the Simon Wiesenthal Center said at the time, "We're not sure, but we believe he is still alive and may have gone to work for the Russians after the war."

Then there's Josef Schwammberger, seventy-five, known as the "mass murderer of Poland" for the atrocities he committed as a Nazi SS captain in charge of two Jewish ghettos and a work camp in Occupied Poland. He has been sought for extradition by the West German government since 1973 for his role in the deaths of as many as 15,000 Jews in Poland, many of them at Auschwitz.

Schwammberger has lived in Argentina since 1949. According to information uncovered by several Nazi hunters connected with Simon Wiesenthal, Schwammberger was arrested in Austria in 1945, but managed to talk his way out of captivity. He eventually made his way to Argentina using an Italian passport in his real name. Apparently, he spent most of his almost forty years in Argentina in the La Plata region, thirty miles southeast of Buenos Aires, in the predominantly German community of Villa General Belgrano, near Cordoba. Local records show that he became an Argentine citizen in 1965, worked for Petroquimica Sudamericana, an Argentine company in La Plata, and voted regularly in elections since 1973. Reportedly, his wife, who arrived with him in 1949, went back to West Germany in 1964.

It has been known since 1962 that Schwammberger is in Argentina. He was spotted that year at Bariloche, a mountain vacation resort, and twice more during the next several years in Buenos Aires. What kind of man is Josef Schwammberger? An educated Austrian, he joined the SS in 1939 and rose quickly to become commandant at Poland's Rozwatdeva Ghetto and Przemysl work camp. Those who were not deported to Auschwitz died from forced labor under his command.

Witnesses say that on a single day, September 3, 1943, he murdered fifty Jews. According to an Austrian police report compiled after the war, Schwammberger stood the victims up against a wall and shot them in the neck from less than a foot away. "As long as the victim showed any signs of life, Schwammberger shot again and again into the temple."

In the files of the VVN *Bund der Antifaschisten* (Anti-Fascist League) in Frankfurt is an eyewitness account by Siegfried Kellermann, who saw Schwammberger leading a roundup of some 1,000 Jews in Przemysl in 1943. "There was a huge wood pile, which was set on fire, and all people had to strip naked and give up any gold, money and jewelry," Kellermann told Austrian police in his 1946 statement. "Schwammberger and two or three other men killed the people, and their bodies were immediately thrown into the fire." Kellermann said that children's heads "were beaten against a wall, and then they were thrown into the fire." By his account, 900 people died that day, and he saw the whole thing happen from a hiding place. Two other eyewitnesses to Schwammberger's brutality joined California Democratic Congressman Henry Waxman at a Wiesenthal Center press conference in 1987 to demand Schwammberger's extradition from Argentina.

Bernard Goldberg, who was a prisoner of Schwammberger's, stated that

"One day seventeen boys were talking among each other about how the conditions were better in one labor camp than another. Schwammberger got very angry and killed the seventeen boys. He had a cart that was drawn by two gray horses. One day, the horses brushed up to an electric fence and were killed. Schwammberger went crazy. He walked into the office of the chief doctor, a Jewish woman from Kracow, killed her, and then killed the Jewish man in charge of the inmates. In the middle of that night, Schwammberger walked into my barracks, took out a gun, and killed five other boys."

Cesia Zimmerman Miller added that, "It was very late one night in the late spring of 1943, and a German soldier was on his way out of an apartment when he was startled by a Jewish man. The Jewish man was faster and grabbed a knife the soldier was carrying and stabbed him. The soldier who was stabbed survived." Schwammberger threatened to wipe out the entire ghetto if the man who had stabbed the soldier did not step forward. He took fifteen Jews as hostages. The Jewish man came forward on the promise that Schwammberger would punish only him and would release the hostages. Schwammberger then hanged him and two boys who had been caught in the forest. Present at the hanging were the Nazi commandant and every Jew in the area, who was forced to watch.

Last year the West German government offered a reward of nearly a half-million dollars for Schwammberger's arrest. He was also put at the top of a "10 Most Wanted" list widely circulated by the Wiesenthal Center. Within days, Schwammberger reportedly moved to Huerta Grande, a small village in the hills of Cordoba Province, 500 miles northwest of Buenos Aires and some 600 miles from his long-time home in La Plata. But the flight was unsuccessful. On November 17, 1987, Argentine federal police arrested him without incident.

According to Rabbi Marvin Hier, dean of the Wiesenthal Center, "His picture had appeared in all of the newspapers, and people who were anxious to collect the reward led Argentine police to his hide-out. The whole sequence in the Schwammberger case shows, once again, that the only thing standing between mass murderers and the bar of justice is worldwide apathy."

As this is written, it appears that Argentina is going to turn its back on forty years of its recent history and return Schwammberger to West Germany. Before and during World War II, Argentina had close ties with Germany. Most of the South American country's officer corps were trained at German military academies and many German immigrants settled in Argentina in the 1930s. Under the Perón government and a succession of military regimes, former Nazis—including accused war criminals—were welcomed openly in Buenos Aires and the German cities of Argentina. But now Argentine president Raul Alfonsin says he wants to break with the past and that Schwammberger will be returned to West Germany. Argentine secretary of justice Enrique Paixao, on Alfonsin's orders, told government prosecutors to seek revocation of

Schwammberger's citizenship. He stated that the charges pending are "so severe that the government considers it unworthy for him to possess [Argentine citizenship]." He told reporters that Argentine authorities would not have granted Schwammberger citizenship in 1965 had they known of the West German charges against him.

Schwammberger has gone into court in Argentina to fight both his denaturalization and the extradition request. But even if he is extradited, there is some question that he will ever stand trial. He is seventy-five years old and has a heart condition. He was hospitalized briefly for heart problems in mid-November 1987, in the La Plata prison medical wing, after his initial two-hour closed appearance before Federal Judge Vicente Bretal, during which he admitted his identity.

Walter Kutschman, a former senior Gestapo officer, was another Nazi war criminal also tied to Argentina. Kutschman, who would be seventy-four, was found living in the coastal town of Miramar under the name of Pedro Ricardo Olmo. He was a top aide to the commandant of Drohobycz death camp in Poland, and had personal responsibility for the deaths of 2,000 Polish Jews. He was also involved in the killing of countless others. In 1983 Kutschman was interrogated by an Argentine judge because of pressure brought by Simon Wiesenthal. After that interrogation, he was released. He died September 1, 1986.

Others high on any most-wanted list of Nazi war criminals, based on the accusations against them and the documentation of their crimes, include Eric Gruen, chief doctor at the Majdanek death camp from 1940 to 1944. During those four years, an astounding 1,380,000 persons were murdered there. Among those hunting for Gruen are relatives of the few who survived. He will be sought until there is confirmation of his death.

Another doctor accused of personal responsibility for the deaths of thousands is Heinz Wilhelm Konig, who worked at Auschwitz with Mengele on his bizarre experiments. Konig, who would be seventy-five years old now, was reportedly seen early in 1988 in Scandinavia. As this book goes to press, Nazi hunters are looking for him all over Finland and Norway and are optimistic about his capture again.

Two important Eichmann aides were Antone Burger, deputy commandant of Theresienstadt, and Friedrich Warzok, commandant of the Janowska camp in Poland. Both were intimately involved in the application of the Final Solution. Warzok is accused of personally supervising the killing of 40,000 people. Burger's "specialty" was selecting pregnant women for deportation and execution. He was also a slave-labor organizer. Their names were often referred to in the Eichmann trial, and the record of their misdeeds can be found not only in American war archive, but in the Berlin Document Center.

Burger was caught and imprisoned after the war, but he escaped from Allied soldiers in 1948 and his present whereabouts is unknown. Today he would be seventy-six years old. Periodic reports that he has been seen in South America have not been confirmed.

Leon DeGrelle, a former Nazi general, was the head of the Belgian SS during the war. DeGrelle, now eighty-two, was sentenced to death in absentia in 1945 by a Belgian court as a traitor. He found asylum in Spain in 1954 under General Francisco Franco and became a Spanish citizen through adoption by an elderly woman. He lives openly in the town of Torreblanca, on Spain's Costa del Sol.

Belgium tried unsuccessfully on six occasions to have DeGrelle extradited during the Franco regime. Now the statute of limitations has run out in his case. Belgium can no longer pursue him; instead, it has banned him from ever returning. DeGrelle, like Brunner, is an unrepentant Nazi. He actually gives lectures and participates in seminars on Nazi history, and contributes articles to publishers around the world who want "his view" of the "so-called Holocaust." But this activity has recently gotten him into trouble. Violeta Friedman, an Auschwitz survivor, has sued DeGrelle on grounds that he insulted her honor by doubting the existence of Nazi concentration camps in a 1985 interview published in *Tiempo* magazine in July 1985. It quoted DeGrelle as saying: "I doubt very much that the gas chambers ever existed, because two years ago someone in the United States was offering a prize of $50 million to anyone who could bring proof, but no one has showed up to collect the money."*

Mrs. Friedman's case is now in an appeals court. A lower court dismissed it in 1986, ruling that DeGrelle never referred to her by name. She remains determined and says that if she loses again, she will appeal either to the Spanish Supreme Court, the European Human Rights court in Strasbourg, France, or both.

Horst Schumann, another Auschwitz doctor on Mengele's staff, is also on the wanted list and believed to be alive. So too is another Eichmann deputy.

---

* DeGrelle was wrong. In fact someone did show up and has collected. In 1980 the Institute for Historical Review, an organization preaching the view that the Holocaust is a myth of Jewish propagandists, offered a $50,000 reward to anyone who could "prove" that the Nazis gassed Jews in concentration camps. Mel Mermelstein, a Holocaust survivor, took them up on their offer. Assembling eyewitness accounts by Auschwitz survivors, he submitted the data and claimed the reward. When the institute refused to pay, he sued.

In July of 1987, a superior court judge in Los Angeles ruled that the Holocaust was an established fact, that Mermelstein had furnished more than adequate proof, and that the institute was required by law to pay him the $50,000.

Ultimately, the institute agreed to pay, but it continues to publicize its position that the Holocaust never happened and to promote the revisionist historians who seek to eliminate a minimum of 6 million deaths with a verbal eraser.

Ralph Gunther is the subject of conflicting reports as to whether or not he has survived. He organized huge deportations as a member of the team implementing the Final Solution. None of the Nazi hunting organizations has been able to confirm whether or not he is alive, and until there is evidence of his death, they will not quit.

★   ★   ★

Since we received the list of seventeen accused Nazis living in the United Kingdom that was given to the British government in 1987, we have traced them as best we could. It has been a tedious task to compare the information we had with partial evidence in London, the United States, and the Soviet Union in order to be sure that we were locating the right people rather than someone who had a similar name or background. *The Sunday Express,* with whom we have worked closely, assigned two of their best investigative reporters, Michael Dove and Chris Logan, to trace down these mysterious persons independently.

The moment the questions started, several of the former Nazis got very nervous. We learned that a few of them were dead, and, in at least two cases, we simply could not confirm that they were still alive, or still in the United Kingdom. But there are Nazis living in Britain, and there is no reason why we cannot name them. A court injunction has been issued against Thames Television, which affects all of the media in the United Kingdom. As a result of that injunction, the names of three of the Nazis located have not appeared in the *Sunday Express* or any other newspaper, and their names and images have not been seen on British television.*

You do not publish a person's name and location and accuse him of war

---

* On February 12, 1988 a letter was delivered to the legal department of the Express Newspapers at 121 Fleet Street in London. It came from Shacklocks, Ltd., a firm of solicitors in Nottingham. The letter pointed out that the firm had already secured an injunction from the British Court of Appeals (Britain's trial-level court) prohibiting Thames TV from broadcasting the identities of these three alleged Nazi war criminals. The letter went on to threaten contempt proceedings against the newspaper if they published "any material identifying our clients whether by name, photograph, photograph of their residence, place of work, family or any other means whatsoever."

Contrary to the practice in the United States where "prior restraint" is not allowed, British law permits courts to enjoin publication until a matter is fully resolved in the courts, or until a higher court strikes down the injunction. The lawyers for the newspaper, knowing full well that the British system rigidly enforces such injunctions, complied—at least for the time being.

Isn't it odd, though, that three accused Nazis living in totally different parts of England suddenly come together to be represented by the same attorney acting to prevent publication of the very different allegations against them?

crimes without being sure. We are. It is true that the evidence on many of these men originated in the Soviet Union, but all information has been corroborated by other sources. Witnesses, documents, and clear records in each case ensure the status of those who are named.

The first of the accused British war criminals who is trying to hide behind the British injunction is Augus Vilis Abakukas. He was a deputy to the chief of administration in the Abrene District in Latvia. As such, he is accused of collaborating with the Nazis and being personally involved in the persecution of civilians. Abakukas came to England and served as chairman of the Latvian National Council. He is currently living in the Coventry area, and his neighbors and friends have no idea that he worked with the Nazis. Since his name has not appeared in the British press, publication of this book will create a shockwave. Anticipating this reaction, we took into our confidence a local police official who investigated Abakukas to determine whether or not he had any criminal record in England. "It's as if this man does not exist," the official told us. "I can't remember any case where there is less information about anyone. He is a mystery."

The second accused war criminal to seek injunctive relief against media disclosure of his identity is Leopolds Fricis Rumba. He is living in Surrey and has been identified as a former senior officer in the Fifteenth Latvian SS Division, which documents show was responsible for the massacre of many Jewish civilians and others over a two-year period during World War II.

The third is Janis Friszalds, born June 10, 1923, in Code, Bauska, Latvia. He was a stormtrooper with the Latvian SS Legion and holds personal responsibility for the persecution and killing of Jews by order of Nazi command headquarters, which insisted that Latvian legions enforce the Final Solution.

Among the other accused war criminals living in Britain is Janis Andrups. Nazi hunters accuse him of being a Gestapo informer, Nazi propagandist, and SS war correspondent who served as editor of a monthly Latvian publication that was viciously anti-Semitic and dedicated to justifying the Final Solution. Now eighty-three years old, Andrups is living in West London. He is a journalist editing a Latvian magazine. When confronted with the charges he said, "These allegations are ridiculous and hurtful." He added that if there is any evidence to suggest that he was pro-Nazi, or an informer or collaborator, it is forged. He says that the KGB is trying to discredit him and others who were in the Baltic states during World War II because "we are so strongly anti-communist."

Another accused Nazi collaborator and war criminal is Arvidas Derzinkas, who is seventy-one years of age and lives on a British pension in a Nottingham council house. Captured wartime records show that he participated in the murder of Jews in Lithuania. Derzinkas is angry at being accused and denies that he had anything to do with the killing of Jews. He says he was horrified when he watched the Nazis herd 20 Jewish families into a village synagogue and then take them to a Jewish cemetery for execution: "It was the most terrible thing I had ever seen."

Witnesses against Derzinkas agree that the incident he remembers took place, but disagree that he was an innocent bystander. He is accused of collaboration with the Nazis on more than one occasion. Derzinkas retired five years ago after working for twenty-four years as a machine operator in an iron foundry in Nottingham. We talked with people from the factory, and neighbors who were shocked to learn of the allegations against someone they knew as a quiet retiree. One neighbor told us that "He seemed like such a very nice man. It's hard to imagine that he would be responsible for hurting anyone. But on the other hand, I guess if he is hiding from his Nazi past, we could not expect him to act differently without raising suspicion."

Fricis Kurseitis is accused of having served as an officer in a Latvian division that was responsible for mass killings of Jews and others. He is now seventy-six and admits that he was a Latvian soldier. He lives in Corby, Northhamptonshire, with his Latvian-born wife, Elenoara. Kurseitis is well known in the community, having worked there for twenty-five years as an industrial chemist. He, too, claims that Soviet agents duped Jews into believing that he had collaborated with the Nazis because he had campaigned for Latvian independence against the communists. But there is evidence to the contrary, both in the Soviet Union and, now, in the United Kingdom.

Pauls Reinhards is said by Nazi hunters to have been "in charge of the recruitment of Latvians from various villages to serve in police battalions and a Latvian SS legion responsible for the killing of thousands of Jews during World War II." Reinhards, now eighty-four, is living in Gravesend, Kent. He admits that he has lived in England for forty-one years, and he works at the Latvian offices in London. He is angry about the allegations, admiting that he was involved in military activities but claiming that "I never recruited for the police or the SS. It is a monstrous thing to accuse me of."

Juilja Valvars is accused of having been a collaborator who not only worked with the Nazis as they slaughtered innocent people, but also wrote anti-Semitic articles to stir up Latvian hatred for Jews and to justify the violence against them. Valvars now lives in Leeds, in the Yorkshire area, where he has been for nearly forty years. He refused to talk with us, but his wife insisted that "My husband is an innocent man and never did anything to hurt anyone." There are documents reflecting Valvars' involvement with the Nazi cause and witnesses ready to testify against him.

In Scotland, the seventy-two-year-old retired engineer is known as Antanas Gecas. He lives in an elegant Georgian terraced villa in the wealthiest suburb of Edinburgh. But during the war years, and before he Anglicized his name, he was Antanas Gecevicius—the most notorious Nazi war criminal living in the United Kingdom.

According to a massive dossier assembled by the Wiesenthal Center, as commander of a unit of the Lithuanian Auxiliary Police *(Schutzmannschaft)*, Gecas was personally involved in the mass murder of Jews in the cities of Kovno, Minsk, Slutsk, and Kletsk. Right after the war, he fled to Britain, where he changed his identity and became a mining engineer with the Coal Board.

Captured Nazi documents and evidence from the Soviet Union (evaluated by Lithuanian-speaking examiners) show clearly that Gecas was one of a handful of key officials in Lithuania responsible for carrying out the Final Solution. He was so adept at his duties that Hitler awarded him the Iron Cross.

When confronted with the accusation, Gecas denied everything. His lawyer, Nigel Ducan, admitted that Gecas is from the Lithuanian area but said that his client "denies all allegations." Gecas fell back on a familiar refrain: the whole thing was a "KGB plot" to discredit him because he was a staunch anti-communist. But Scottish television newsmen put the lie to Gecas's denials. After spending seven weeks investigating the case in the U.S.S.R., they produced an hour-long special that carefully documented the fact that Gecas had ordered the liquidation of 10,000 Jews. Witness Juozas Aleksynas related that "The condemned Jews were driven into the pits, ordered to lie down, and then shot where they lay." Other witnesses said that groups of condemned people then lay down on top of the corpses and were shot. Gecas was seen issuing commands to his soldiers to line up the victims by the pits and massacre them.

At least two witnesses said that if anyone survived the mass shootings, Gecas went down to the pit to finish him off. On each occasion, thousands were killed. Another eyewitness, Moteyus Migonis, testified that "people doomed to death were stripped naked, driven to the pit, and on Gecas's command, shot. I saw everything clearly."

In addition to the original list given to the British government by officials of the Simon Wiesenthal Center, and discovered by us through Nazi-hunting connections in the United States, thirty-four other alleged war criminals living in the United Kingdom have been identified by various Nazi hunters and Nazi-hunting groups. These cases are in the early stages of investigation, and documents are being gathered to determine whether or not there is sufficient evidence to point the finger of accusation at them.

A ranking member of Parliament dedicated to the ongoing hunt for Nazis told us that "It would appear that of the thirty-four about half may well be dead or no longer living in the United Kingdom, but of the remaining seventeen at least four or five are locatable. They may, however, prove to be 'small fish' and not in a league with Gecas and others."

New lists of known Nazis have been given to the governments of Australia, Canada, Venezuela, and Sweden* by both Simon Wiesenthal and the Wiesenthal Center. Information also comes from the United States Department of Justice, which has been checking out thousands of tips from former victims and relatives of those who were victimized. As evidence develops, the information is given to the nation concerned.

On October 1, 1986, officials of the Simon Wiesenthal Center turned over evidence on forty suspected Nazi war criminals living in Australia—the result of many years of research about war crimes committed in Latvia, Lithuania, and Byelorussia. When the information was given to the Australians, Rabbi Marvin Hier, dean of the center, said, "The suspects on this list are accused of having participated in some of the most atrocious crimes of World War II in the wanton slaughter of men, women, and children forced from the towns and cities of Latvia and Lithuania."

When the Germans invaded the Soviet Union on June 22, 1941, it marked a turning point for the Jews. Within hours of that invasion, Jews in Poland, Latvia, Lithuania, Estonia, and the Ukraine were killed by Nazi squads and collaborators. Local policeman and Nazi sympathizers who wanted to ingratiate themselves with their conquerors often launched vicious pogroms against the Jews with whom they had lived for many years as neighbors. (Rosters of these killer police auxiliary forces uncovered many war criminals living in the United States; denaturalization and deportation proceedings are being started, as detailed below.)

All along the Eastern front, there was looting, burning, and killing. Tens of thousands of Jews were massacred every month by Nazi collaborators. One statistic shows, in the most horrifying way, the effectiveness of their work. When World War II began, there were some 225,000 Jews living in Lithuania; by 1945, 2,500 survived. Latvia had some 95,000 Jews at the beginning of the war; at war's end there were fewer than 500.

Various organizations have presented the Canadian government with lists of dozens of suspected war criminals living in the country. Last year a government commission reviewed the matter and declared that, in fact, 20 accused war criminals were in Canada and that an additional 218 suspects should should be investigated.

Recently, the Canadian government brought formal charges against the first name on its list of twenty war criminals. Imre Finta, seventy-six, was arrested

---

* Sweden claims it is powerless to do anything about war criminals living there. The country has a strict twenty-five-year statute of limitations on all crimes, including war crimes. As Sweden interprets its statute of limitations, it cannot even extradite a criminal to a second country for a crime that was committed more than twenty-five years ago. Given this interpretation, Sweden could become a major haven for war criminals.

by the Royal Canadian Mounted Police as he boarded a bus in Hamilton, Ontario, bound for Buffalo, New York. A former captain in the Hungarian Gendarmerie, he is charged with deporting 8,615 Jews from Szeged, Hungary, in April, May, and June 1944, to their deaths at Auschwitz. The charges were brought under the new Canadian law that allows for the prosecution of war criminals for the crimes they actually committed: Finta is charged with illegal confinement, kidnapping, and manslaughter. According to the indictment, the manslaughter charge is included because Finta is alleged to have "unlawfully caused the death of those Jews who died within three train transports used for their deportation, prior to them reaching their destination." The trains left the Rokus railway station in Szeged.

Evidence against Finta was gathered by Sol Littman, the Canadian representative of the Wiesenthal Center, and Sabina Citron, an Auschwitz survivor, of the Holocaust Remembrance Association. Finta is probably the best known of an estimated 500 members of the Hungarian Gendarmerie who emigrated to Canada in the postwar years. He once ran a popular Toronto restaurant, the Moulin Rouge, which was frequented by movie stars and government officials, and during the 1950s and '60s, his name was often in the newspapers. This fact outraged members of the Toronto Jewish community, who knew him for very different reasons. But Finta was quick to sue any publication that linked him with war crimes for libel. Shortly after his arrest, he was released on $100,000 bond, which was posted by an unnamed Hungarian family in Toronto. His trial—a test case of the new Canadian law—began in 1988 and is expected to escalate into a legal battle that will last for years.

★ ★ ★

The subject of suspected war criminals living in the United States presents us with a difficulty. Neal Sher, head of the Office of Special Investigations, admits openly that he is working on more than 500 files, many of which will result in the instigation of denaturalization or deportation proceedings. We have been able to identify in the following pages some of the war criminals living in the United States, but we will not identify all whom we have located. In some cases, former war criminals living in the U.S. have already received their subpoenas, and the government is proceeding in its efforts to force them out of the country, but in others, publication of their names could result either in their disappearance or in evasive legal action. Accordingly, out of respect for Sher's proceedings, and because we have been asked to do so by U.S. prosecutors, we have limited identification in selected cases to the crimes involved and the war criminal's current whereabouts.

As Nazi hunters have come to learn, in the wave of emigration to the United States under the postwar Displaced Persons Act, members of the same units often settled in the same parts of the country. The prime example is that of the 2nd Lithuanian Police Battalion, mentioned earlier in connection with Antanas Gecas, now living in England. Under direct SS supervision, this group was responsible for killing thousands of civilians in both Lithuania and Byelorussia during the period 1941-43.

The overall commander of the Lithuanian *Schutzmannschaft* was Major Franz Lechthäler, of the German 11th Police Reserve Battalion. After the war he was tried and convicted of war crimes by a German court. The Second Battalion was commanded by Antanas Impulevicius, who in 1962 was tried in absentia as a war criminal and sentenced to death by the Soviet Union. It was established later that Impulevicius had become Antanas Impulionis, an American citizen living comfortably in Philadelphia. Twice the Soviet Union demanded his extradition, but it was during the coldest part of the Cold War period, and the United States refused to hand him over. Impulevicius died peacefully at the age of sixty-three in 1970. But many in his command are still living in the United States, some of them also in the Philadelphia area. They have become a major target of the Office of Special Investigations.

Both Matthew Katin (formerly Motiejus Katinauskas), seventy-three, and Vytautas Gudauskas, seventy, were living the quiet life of retirement a few miles from each other in Massachusetts, near Worcester, when their seclusion was rudely interrupted: The OSI began denaturalization proceedings against them in 1985. Katin came to the United States in 1949 and became a citizen in 1966; Gudauskas arrived two years later and became a citizen in 1975. The government alleges the two men volunteered for the battalion as privates in 1941 and served until 1943. According to the government's suit, while serving in the SS, the two "arrested, detained and murdered" civilians. Both men deny the charges completely. Katin claims to have worked on his father's farm during the period, and Gudauskas says he was a shoemaker. Their lawyers have tied up proceedings for years and the cases against them are still pending.

Katin and Gudauskas are not the only Massachusetts residents the U.S. government has accused of committing war crimes as members of the *Schuzmannschaft*. In 1956, in one of the earliest attempts to deport an alleged war criminal, the INS began an action against Felix Krasnauskas, also of Worcester. An INS judge ordered him deported, but the Board of Immigration Appeals overturned the verdict, saying that the government had failed to provide eyewitnesses tying Krasnauskas to a specific crime. It is believed that he still lives in the Worcester area.

Juozas (Joseph) Kisielaitis, a former Boston resident who entered the United States in 1963 and was never naturalized, was accused in 1984 of the murder and persecution of Jews while a member of the Lithuanian 2nd Battalion. He fled to Canada in 1985 before his deportation trial could begin. It is believed that he continues to live there. He has been added to the Watch List, so he may not re-enter the United States. Canada has shown no interest in pursuing him.

The Krasnauskas case is not the only one against a *Schutzmannschaft* member that the government lost in the early days of deportation efforts (see chapter 7). In 1952 the INS attempted to deport Antanas Spokevicius, who had entered the United States only the year before. Spokevicius, a resident of Chicago, admitted that he had lied on his visa application, but said he had done so out of fear that he would be repatriated to the Soviet Union. The trial judge ruled against him, but the Board of Immigration Appeals reversed the ruling in 1953, saying that fear of political persecution if repatriated overrode even a willful misrepresentation of fact on the application. It is believed that he still lives in the Chicago area.

Bronius Kaminskas, a resident of Hartford, Connecticut, was another member of the Lithuanian 2nd Battalion whom the federal government tried to deport. Proceedings against him were started in 1976, on grounds that he took part in the murder of several hundred Jews, including sixty children, in August and September 1941. His deportation hearing never took place. A court-appointed doctor found him incompetent to stand trial, and he continues to live in the Connecticut capital. Another Lithuanian 2nd Battalion member residing in Hartford is Antanas Bernotas. He never became a citizen, although he arrived in 1949. OSI began deportation proceedings against him in 1983, and the action is still pending.

Living in Clifton, New Jersey, is Juozas Kungys, another member of the Lithuanian 2nd Battalion. The OSI started denaturalization proceedings against the retired seventy-one-year-old dental technician in 1981. Kungys entered the United States in 1948 and became a citizen in 1954; he has been accused of taking part in the 1941 massacre of more than 2,000 Jews in the ghetto in Kedainiai. In September 1983, U.S. District Judge H. Curtis Meanor ruled in favor of Kungys, saying that the government had failed to provide enough evidence for denaturalization, specifically that Kungys had personally taken part in the atrocities. The decision was overturned by the Third Circuit Court of Appeals in June 1986. In May 1988, the U.S. Supreme Court ruled that the Third Circuit must again review the case to redetermine whether the lies Kungys made on his citizenship application were sufficiently serious to deny him citizenship.

Also appealing a denaturalization order is another *Schutzmannschaft* member, Jonas Klimavicius of Kennebunkport, Maine, who entered the United States in 1949 and was naturalized in 1954. He is accused of the murder of Jews as a member of both the Lithuanian 2nd Battalion and the Gestapo-led Iron Wolf terrorist squads. He was ordered stripped of his citizenship in September 1987, for his repeated refusal to appear for a deposition despite court orders to do so. That order is now on appeal.

Mecis Paskevicius (aka Mike Pasker) is a resident of St. Petersburg, Florida, who entered the United States in 1950, lived for years in Los Angeles, and was naturalized in 1962. Another member of the Lithuanian 2nd Battalion, he is accused of the murder and beating of Jews, and denaturalization proceedings against him were started in 1977. In 1979 he voluntarily consented to revocation of his citizenship, and deportation proceedings began, but on December 16, 1980, he was found mentally unfit to stand trial. Periodic reexaminations since that date have resulted in the same conclusion.

Because of the advanced age of accused war criminals, Nazi hunters say that they are in a race against the clock. This is borne out by the fact that several of the accused Lithuanian *Schutzmannschaft* members died before proceedings against them could be completed. Both Chicago resident Henrikas Benkunskas, accused in the killing of Jews in Kaunas in 1941 and later in the Minsk-Slutsk area, and Jurgis Juodis, a 2nd Battalion officer, of St. Petersburg, Florida, died in 1986 while denaturalization cases were pending against them.

For many survivors of the Holocaust, the Nazi unit that personifies the horrors they can't forget is the SS Death's Head Division (SS-Totenkopf Sturmbann), whose battalions staffed most of the major death camps and carried out the mass murders of the Final Solution. The division is also accused of machine-gunning hundreds of surrendering British troops during the German invasion of France. A number of this division's former members are now living in the United States and are a major target of the OSI.

Jakob Habich of Norwood Park, a suburb of Chicago, known to his neighbors and customers of his former butcher shop as "Jake," is accused of being a Death's Head guard at three concentration camps. Habich, now in his mid-seventies, came to the United States in 1955 and acquired citizenship in 1962. Now retired, he has lived for more than a decade in Norwood Park. He and his wife, Katharina, are well liked; as his next door neighbor puts it, "He seems like a perfect gentleman."

According to the accusations against him, Habich enlisted in the SS in 1943. He served first as a guard at the Majdanek death camp in Poland, where at least 200,000 prisoners died. Then he was transferred to the smaller Flossenbürg concentration camp, where more than 20,000 prisoners died, and finished out his career at the infamous Auschwitz. The OSI began denaturalization proceedings against Habich in November 1987. When asked to comment about the charges, he said simply, "I did nothing wrong. I just want to be left alone." Also late in 1987, the OSI ended an investigation of many years by starting deportation proceedings against another Death's Head guard, Josef Eckert of La Puente, California. Although Eckert entered the United States in

1956, he has never been naturalized. He, too, is accused of being a guard at Auschwitz, and at the death camps at Katowitz and Gleiwitz, all of which were in Poland.

Another Californian, Bruno Karl Blach of La Habra, near San Diego, lived a quiet life as a grocery clerk for many years after arriving in the United States. That ended when the OSI accused him of being a member of the SS Death's Head who worked as a guard and dog handler at the German death camps of Dachau and Wiener Neudorf. At a sensational 1986 trial, eyewitnesses pointed him out as the man who had beaten up and "stomped" two Yugoslav prisoners before they were shot to death in 1945 and machine-gunned an elderly Jew. His defense, based on mistaken identity, maintained that even if he were the guard in question, he was only following the orders of superiors, and should not be deported for the "sins of the Third Reich." At the end of an emotionally charged two-week trial, the judge found the evidence against him convincing, and on April 27, 1987, ordered him deported to his native Czechoslovakia to face trial. He continues to live in southern California while he appeals that order.

Albert Ensin of Stoughton, Massachussetts; Liusdas Kairys of Chicago; Stefan Reger of Yardville, New Jersey; Peter Quintus of Detroit; and Leonid Petkiewytsch of Cincinnati have all been identified as former concentration camp guards—Ensin at Auschwitz, Kairys at several death camps, including Treblinka and Lublin in Poland, Reger at the Auschwitz subcamp known as Birkenau, Quintus at several camps in Poland, and Petkiewytsch at Kiel-Hassee.

Kairys was stripped of his citizenship by U.S. District Judge James Moran in December of 1986, after the case had dragged on for more than six years. On July 27,1987, he was ordered deported to the Soviet Union to stand trial. Deportation proceedings were suspended pending a decision on an appeal of the denaturalization order by the Seventh U.S. Court of Appeals. Petkiewytsch admits that he was a death camp guard, but claims that he submitted documents to that effect with his visa application; a postwar British tribunal had found him innocent of any war crime. His case is still pending and those of Ensin, Quintus, and Reger have yet to be heard.

Still another SS Death's Head member was more than a guard. Conrad Schellong of Chicago is accused of being an officer at several death camps, including Sachsenburg and Dachau where he was in charge of training new SS guard recruits. He was stripped of his citizenship on August 24, 1983. That verdict was upheld on appeal by the Seventh Circuit in October 1986, and the Supreme Court refused to review the case in April 1987. Nevertheless, Schellong is still free in Chicago pending deportation proceedings. Additional appeals could take years.

One Death's Head guard who slipped away was Stefan Leili, seventy-seven, of Clifton, New Jersey. Leili has admitted in a deposition taken by OSI investigators that he was a guard at the Mauthausen concentration camp in Austria. He also admitted shooting a French Jewish prisoner, seventeen-year-old Leon Axelroud, in December 1943, as the youth tried to run from two other SS guards who were beating him. Leili claimed that the other two guards deliberately "chased prisoners away so they would be shot at." He denied that his was the fatal bullet, as another guard had shot the prisoner in the face after he went down. But he admitted that the shootings were unnecessary, because the victim had no chance whatsoever of escaping.

Question: "Could he have escaped?"

Leili: "No. He couldn't have gone through that ditch and over the barbed wire fence."

Question: "You shot him because it was your duty as a guard, even though there was no real possibility that he could escape?"

Leili: "Yes."

After the 1986 deposition, but before a court could act, Leili, according to his family, slipped out of the United States and is now living in West Germany. Nevertheless, OSI went to court, and, using the deposition as evidence, U.S. District Judge Harold Ackerman of Newark ordered Leili's citizenship revoked and directed that a copy of the evidence be forwarded to West Germany for possible criminal action there.* Leili's name was also placed on the Watch List, so he may not reenter the United States.

Another Death's Head guard who slipped away was former Chicagoan Mar-

---

* As in the case of others who have been deported, or who have voluntarily returned to West Germany, prosecutors there say there is not enough evidence to start prosecution under German law. In fact there is a small "club" of former Death's Head guards who have gone back to West Germany and are living quietly with no fear that they will ever face justice for their actions. Two are former Chicagoans: Reinhold Kulle and Hans Lipschis. Another lived for many years in the San Francisco area—Josepf Wieland of Burlingame, California—and Joseph Leprich lived in Clinton Township, Michigan.

Kulle was accused of serving as an SS guard and group leader of prisoners at the Gross-Rosen death camp in his native Silesia and participating in the murder and persecution of prisoners. During Kulle's service at Gross-Rosen more than 50,000 prisoners were either starved or executed. He was stripped of his U.S. citizenship and ordered deported to West Germany after final appeal to the U.S. Supreme Court was denied.

The stories of Leprich and Wieland are identical. Accused of persecution of Jews while guards at the Mauthausen concentration camp in Austria, both departed immediately for Germany after being stripped of their citizenship in different actions. Similarly, Lipschis, after being accused of serving as a guard at Auschwitz, agreed to depart for West Germany rather than face the charges. (See chapter 12 for details of the West German situation.)

tin Bartesch, a native of Grossau, Romania. He said on his 1966 citizenship application that he had served in the German army from July 1943 to May 1945, but he was actually a guard at Mauthausen from October 1943 to July 1944. Bartesch was accused of killing a young French Jew, Max Ochshorn. Camp records (Daily Log entry #302) showed that Bartesch took credit for the killing so that he could apply for extra leave time. As part of a settlement agreement to avoid trial, he departed for Austria on May 27, 1987. He was stripped of his citizenship two days later and has been added to the Watch List.

Still another former Death's Head guard has found a safe haven in Paraguay, the point from which he entered the United States in the 1950s. Chester Wojciechowski of Chicago agreed to depart voluntarily in 1987 rather than face charges about his guard service at the Majdanek concentration camp in Poland in 1944. Reportedly he is now living quietly in Paraguay.

Another unit that seems to have sent a number of former members to live in the United States is a Latvian Security Auxiliary Police unit known as *Arajs Kommandos.*

According to a Justice Department complaint seeking the denaturalization of one of its former members, the unit was used by the Nazis "primarily to aid in the persecution and murder of those persons considered to be racially undesirable or enemies of Nazi Germany." The unit was named for its founder, Victros Arajs, who died in 1988 in a West German prison where he was serving a life sentence for mass murder.

So far the OSI has brought complaints seeking the denaturalization of three alleged members of the unit.

— Konrads Kalejs emigrated to Chicago from Australia, whose citizen he became after the war. He is accused of taking part in the 1942 destruction of the Latvian village of Sanniki, and the killing of most of its inhabitants, as a member of the unit. Kalejs fled Chicago after the complaint was filed and was found in Miami. Arrested, he was released on bond. If ordered deported, he will return to Australia.

— Valdis Didrichsos of Mercer Island, Washington, is a retired civil engineer who moved to the Seattle suburb from Chicago in 1979. He is accused of killing civilians while serving in the unit from 1941 to 1942. His case is yet to be heard.

—Mikelis Kirsteins of Utica, New York, is accused of killing and persecuting Jews and other civilians while a member of the unit for a six-month period in 1941. He suffered a heart attack shortly after the case was filed.

Other accused war criminals who are still living in the United States as they await denaturalization hearings or appeals pending after revocation of citizenship include:

— Alexander Lehmann, resident of Cleveland. A West German citizen who entered the United States in 1957 and was never naturalized, he is accused of ordering and assisting in the murder and persecution of numerous Jews and other civilians while serving as deputy police chief of Zaporozhe, in the Ukraine. In February 1984, he was ordered deported to West Germany, but the order was stayed pending an appeal and then stayed again for health reasons. Appeals are still pending.

— Kazys Palciauskas of St. Petersburg, Florida. He was the mayor of Kaunas, the capital of Lithuania, from June 1941 until May 1942. In that capacity he allegedly ordered the internment of the city's 20,000 Jews, signed deportation orders sending many to death camps, confiscated Jewish property, and generally collaborated with the Nazis. He was ordered denaturalized in March 1983, and the verdict was affirmed on appeal on June 18, 1984. Deportation proceedings then began and are continuing.

— Vladimir Sokolov, a New Haven, Connecticut resident. Sokolov was a Russian language and history instructor at Yale University from 1959-76. His case represented a departure for OSI in that he is accused of being a Nazi propagandist who helped create the atmosphere in which the Holocaust could take place by his writings in a Russian-language newspaper under Nazi control. His past caught up with him in 1976, when some of those articles and speeches surfaced, and he was forced to resign from the Yale faculty. A denaturalization effort did not begin until 1982, and he was stripped of his citizenship in 1986. A first appeal was denied in March 1987, and the U.S. Supreme Court refused to hear his case in May 1988. The OSI has started new deportation proceedings.

— George Theodorovich of Albany, New York. He is accused of murder and persecution of Jews while a member of the police force in Lvov in the Ukraine. He was denaturalized on January 31, 1984, and after several appeals failed he was ordered deported in October 1987. Further appeals of that order are still pending.

— Antanas Virkutis of Chicago. Virkutis is accused of the murder and torture of Jews, other civilians, and Allied prisoners while warden of the Nazi prison at Siauliai, Lithuania, from 1941 to 1944. Although the case was filed in 1983, he is still awaiting trial.

— Juris Kauls of Sun City, Arizona, who entered the U.S. from Canada in 1951, is accused of being the deputy chief in charge of guards at fourteen concentration and slave labor camps in and around Riga, Latvia. His case also has not yet been heard.

Many more actions will be undertaken by the Justice Department in the near future. We know of war criminals living in the Chicago and Boston areas; the New York City boroughs of Manhattan, Brooklyn, and Queens; Passaic and Jersey City, New Jersey; the Phoenix area; and a suburb of Wisconsin.

One of those likely to be among the first charged with having lied about his background on his application for citizenship served as a Nazi police official in the town of Braetz in Poland, at a facility known as *Erweitertes Polizeigefängnis.* This known Nazi is a retired supervisor who was employed by a factory near Chicago. Now in his late seventies, he is living a quiet life with his wife and their children and grandchildren who live nearby. The Justice Department has received information about him through Nazi-hunting sources in this country, and backup information has come from Europe.

In New Jersey, there are former residents of Nikolayev, located north of Odessa in Lithuania, including two men who were responsible for wartime activities as members of Lithuanian police units. Both are under active investigation and should soon be standing in court to explain why they should not be expelled from the United States.

In Arizona, there is a former Nazi concentration camp guard who served Hitler in Lublin, Poland. Victims of that concentration camp have provided testimony to help identify him and he, too, is under active investigation with respect to his false entry into the United States.

In Boston, a man who resided in Skaudiville and served as a Lithuanian police officer in 1943 and 1944, is enjoying his retirement from his working life as a machinist in various New England communities. Records received from the Soviet Union identify him as a police officer who commanded other Lithuanian officers to beat Jewish victims without cause.

In addition to those specified, there are at least three former officials of the Lithuanian security police who served in Vilna, the site of some of the war's most brutal persecutions of Jews. Documents on one former Vilna official show that on several occasions "he ordered other police officers to kill civilians and then shot some himself when they had hesitated to fire."

In northern Florida, just outside Jacksonville, is a man in his late seventies who served with Latvian collaborators in carrying out SS orders against Jews in 1943. He retired to the adult community in Florida when he gave up managing a nursery near Atlanta, Georgia. He, too, is among those who will be arrested imminently for war crimes and there are eyewitnesses available to testify against him.

Milwaukee, Wisconsin, is the home of a vibrant German community. Tens of thousands of German-American families there are among the most patriotic Americans in the United States. Infiltrated into that community, however, are former Nazis. Officials at the Office of Special Investigations know they are there but have had difficulty isolating them because of similarities among names and reluctance to bring charges against or investigate someone who might be guilty of nothing more than kinship with a war criminal. Nevertheless, the search has narrowed and arrests will be made in the near future.

Behind Closed Doors

Behind locked doors on the eleventh floor of a nondescript office building sixteen blocks south of the United Nations in New York City are the secrets of the greatest crimes in the history of man. The building is owned by the United Nations, which has been for forty years the custodian of the accusations and, in many cases, the proof of the atrocities committed by thousands of Germans and others under the banner of Hitler's "Final Solution."

For years the staff, consisting of sixty-year-old Alf Erlandsson, chief archivist of the United Nations, and twenty-four clerical assistants, has gone about its business quite routinely. The documents in their charge, 8,500 files reporting World War II Nazi war crime allegations against 36,000 people, are stored plain gray cardboard boxes, each labeled as to its contents. Many are so brittle with age that they disintegrate when touched. Exposure to light over the years has yellowed many to the extent that they are all but unreadable.

Erlandsson, a Swede trained as a historian, has transferred most of the files to microfilm since 1980, and, to make it much more usable, has assembled a detailed fifty-six-page inventory of the files' contents. "This is a very important source on the darkest chapter of the Second World War," Erlandsson says. "It is very depressing reading. It is an extremely sad thing."

The files are the final product of the United Nations War Crimes Commission, which was established in London in 1943. It compiled thousands of dossiers about Nazi war criminals before it closed shop in 1948, when it was decided to bury the names of accused Nazi war criminals who were not to be tried immediately; most of the evidence was kept by the accusing nation.

First, it was felt that 25,000 Nazi criminal trials would require a commitment of manpower, money, and time that the Western Allies were unwilling to make. They had to get on with the Cold War and the monumental task of readjusting to a peacetime economy and social milieu*.

---

* Of the 36,000 files, 11,000 deal with suspects and key witnesses; 25,000 were direct accusations of war crimes against known individuals.

Second, there was the decision by Roosevelt, later endorsed by Truman and by the British government, to overlook the criminal acts of those who could be important to building a solid scientific and research team to combat competition from the Soviet Union. That attitude of "forgiveness" extended beyond the arena of science, according to many officers of the OSS, who made the selections as to which former Nazi officers would be treated leniently.

Once the documents were placed in crates marked *Secret*, the new United Nations was the logical repository. They were turned over with the mandate that they not be opened without express direction from the original seventeen members of the commission. When the commission sealed those files, it gave particular distinction to 25,000 accused war criminals, each of whom was designated *A*, indicating sufficient evidence existed to justify bringing charges of war crimes against them. (The famous Nuremberg war trials were limited to prosecuting a handful of major Nazi figures, and relied not upon information from the War Crimes Commission, but on the tribunal's own investigation.)

For forty years the files were made available only on a very limited basis to representatives of the seventeen original nations, when and if they were involved in prosecution of a particular case. No American, Briton, or other national could go in on a "fishing expedition," but only to examine specific files for specific material. It is almost unbelievable that in all that time, only three of those files have ever actually been used for an investigation. The red tape involved in securing access made it next to impossible, even for an aggressive prosecutor like the Justice Department's Neal Sher to use the documents as he sought evidence against those who had lied to gain entry to the United States.

As early as 1979, representatives of the Office of Special Investigations held preliminary meetings with the archivists and staff members of U.N. Secretary-General Kurt Waldheim about broader U.S. access to those files. An agreement was worked out, subject only to the United Nations' concern that the files' contents not be disclosed to the press, because that would violate the mandate of secrecy. Even so, on several occasions, despite the agreement-between U.S. Attorney General Benjamin Civiletti and Waldheim, American investigators were turned away from the file rooms.

Before March 1986, when Nazi hunters discovered the scope of material in the archive—and the fact that one file was about Waldheim—none of the hundreds of journalists covering the U.N. paid much attention. But the discovery of a file on the secretary-general caused a furor. Now, reflecting upon the pressures felt by Waldheim as he completed his service at the U.N., it is evident why he was not anxious to have those files opened to the world.

While some of the files consist of general accusations without much evidence to support them, in most cases, the evidence is damning. And those who have examined even a handful of files know that the U.N. archive is probably the greatest source of information about war crimes ever compiled.*

Indifference to genocide is unconscionable. Would it be unfair, then, to compare the indifference that would have kept these files closed to that which allowed the Holocaust to occur? The U.N. was, in fact, founded on the ashes of Nazi horrors and had as its mandate a pledge to prevent the repetition of such horrors. When the seventeen nations finally approved opening its files, it took a giant step—albeit a very late one—toward fulfilling the original U.N. goals.

As we interviewed U.N. delegates, prosecutors from many nations, frustrated historians, and officials of concerned organizations about the opening of the files, the mystery deepened as to why they had been locked up in the first place. Clearly, the last several years of the war were not the time to stage a series of trials and to punish individual war criminals, but it was absolutely ridiculous that evidence that could have saved lives before the war ended, and helped locate war criminals, was not used, much less buried.

★ ★ ★

In order to understand the story behind the years of secrecy, it's necessary to go back to the fall of 1942, when reports were trickling into London from escaping refugees, neutrals, and prisoners of war supporting the suspicion that Hitler was carrying out the most horrendous massive deportation and execution of a people in the annals of war. An impatient Adolf Eichmann was overcoming the resistance of a few officers around him, and, on a near-daily basis,

---

* We have now had an opportunity to study many of these files. We know the original secrecy decision has kept sealed incredible details about the horrors of the Holocaust. The files have kept from the world lists of Gestapo personnel and details of their activities. They even contain outlines of property confiscated and reports on entire Jewish communities that were wiped out as part of the Final Solution.

Most agonizing is the realization that after this documentation was so meticulously gathered by the Allies, it was concealed. It is believed by many historians that perhaps millions could have been saved had there been wide and immediate dissemination of the material as it began to accumulate in 1943. The more that historians, researchers, journalists, and politicians review the history of the original U.N. War Crimes Commission, the more convinced they become that many known and perhaps some still unknown pressures were brought to bear in the decision to seal the files.

Unquestionably, the Allies are embarrassed by the disclosure that they supported Waldheim as secretary-general despite their prior knowledge of his Nazi past (see chapter 4). And undoubtedly, what has become known as the "Paperclip Conspiracy"—the decision to overlook war crimes so as to secure the services of essential scientists and researchers for the West—still causes political embarrassment and moral questions. Many of those scientists are named in the U.N. war crimes files.

tens of thousands, mostly Jews but others as well, were being transported to their deaths in gas chambers at camps in Poland. However, London and Washington, perhaps preoccupied with the fact that the tides of war were gradually turning in their favor, were still skeptical about the appalling reality of the Final Solution. Not even when Berlin Radio boasted of the deportations of thousands of Jews from the Drancy transit camp outside Paris, did Britain and the United States realize the extent of what was happening.

If there was one person who seemed to understand the horrors that were taking place, and who committed himself to doing something about them, it was Lord Chancellor John A. Simon—chief legal advisor to Churchill and counsel to Foreign Minister Anthony Eden. On August 5, 1942, John Winant, the American ambassador in Great Britain, forwarded a detailed proposal from Lord Simon to the State Department for setting up a United Nations Commission on War Crimes.*

By September 1942, Anthony Eden was pressing the Roosevelt administration for a reply to Lord Simon's proposal and for FDR's views on demanding the immediate surrender of war criminals in the event of an armistice, rather than waiting to deal with the issue in some future peace treaty.

On September 28, 1942, the State Department sent Eden a vague memorandum that agreed in principle with the British demand for prompt action, but left most questions unanswered. The British were dissatisfied: pressure was mounting in England as more and more evidence of atrocities came to the attention of politicians. The Foreign Office urged the U.S. ambassador to get a clarification from his government. (In the great tradition of American bureaucracy, it was finally admitted after the war that many of the communiqués from Britain on this subject had been mislaid at the State Department.) The British set October 7th as the date for announcing the creation of the U.N. Commission, and American approval arrived by courier one day before.

The new entity was to be called the United Nations War Crimes Commission (UNWCC). But, when he agreed to its creation, Roosevelt made a small but vital change in the announcement text. Lord Simon's draft had stated that the commission's purpose would be "the punishment of individuals who are proved to be themselves responsible, whether as ringleaders or actual perpetrators, for war crimes." The Roosevelt version reduced the potential for prosecu-

---

* There has been considerable confusion over the use of the term "United Nations" by the Western Allies even before World War II ended in 1945. Although the international organization known as the United Nations was not formed until after the war, Roosevelt and Churchill had used the term to describe those nations fighting and working in concert since 1942. Thus "United Nations" in the name of the War Crimes Commission does not refer to the international organization that was formed after the war, and which would eventually become the repository of the files of the commission..

tion from a multitude of tens of thousands to the punishment of a very few by defining the commission's purpose in the words: "punishment shall be meted out to the *ringleaders* responsible for the organized murder of thousands."

Nevertheless, plans for the commission proceeded and arrangements were made for thorough investigation of war crimes allegedly committed against the Allied nationals. (There was no mention of crimes against nationals from Axis countries, or stateless victims.) The commission would gather testimony as to such crimes from each of the member nations and would give periodic reports to their governments on its evaluation of the evidence and any successful identification of those responsible. Obviously, the primary concern was with the most serious atrocities.

Lord Simon was a practical man. Although he knew that a detailed gathering of evidence was essential, he stated in the House of Lords, "We can discuss all of these points about the evidence until the crack of doom. But we must also find the wanted men." The commission staff members were not policemen or detectives. They were bureaucrats who, in most cases, had been appointed because they could be spared by their governments from the more pressing duties of wartime planning.

In order for the commission to function effectively, close cooperation with the Soviet Union would be required. Much of the evidence against accused war criminals would have to come from the Soviet Union, because so many of the crimes had taken place in territories under that nation's control. Despite the bickering between the Allies and the Soviets and the fear that the next war, a cold one this time, was already beginning between the West and the Stalin government, there would have to be a joint effort to make the commission effective.

Since the British had set a deadline for announcing the formation of the U.N. Commission, the other Allies had to be notified of that deadline. On Saturday, October 3, 1942, the British Foreign Office, at the direction of Anthony Eden, sent by courier messages to the London representatives of all the Allies inviting them to participate in discussions on the formal creation of the commission. For some reason, the letter that was delivered to the Soviet embassy was treated as a routine delivery and brought to no one's attention until the following Tuesday, one day before Lord Simon was to address in the House of Lords on the the Allied plans.

The Russians were angry at what they perceived as a snub and, at the same time, questioned the decision itself. *Pravda* condemned American and British plans to set up the commission. The Russians were particularly suspicious and critical of Britain, pointing out that Churchill had given refuge to Rudolph Hess, Hitler's deputy, who had flown to Britain on May 10, 1941, in one of the most bizarre missions in military history.*

Stalin knew that Hess had been a major architect of the subsequent invasion of Russia, and insisted that the British bring Hess to trial immediately, or turn him over to Moscow. But doctors had told the Foreign Office that Hess was mentally unstable, and anything they tried to do with him publicly would make that fact obvious to the world. Churchill called it "a medical matter, not a political one." It was agreed that for practical purposes, the disposition of the Hess case would have to wait until after the war; consequently, the British continued to refuse Stalin's demand. The Hess affair became a key factor in the deteriorating relations between the Western Allies and the Soviets, and the efforts of those who were trying to launch an aggressive hunt for Nazis before the end of World War II.

But if the Soviet Union was not to participate in the commission and was, in fact, undercutting it, the effort would be dead in the water. Churchill sent special instructions to Sir Archibald Clark Kerr, the British ambassador in Moscow, and asked him to deal directly with Stalin on the issue of the War Crimes Commission, and, if necessary, to brief the Soviet leader on the Hess case.

Although Stalin was reportedly dubious at first, he finally softened his position somewhat, but insisted on knowing whether or not Hess would be tried. The record of those conversations between Stalin and Kerr includes such questions from Stalin as "is it not the custom after a war to repatriate prisoners? Will Hess be repatriated? If Goebbels or Hitler himself were to land in Great Britain tomorrow, would he, too, become a prisoner and then be repatriated to Germany after the war?"

Stalin demanded immediate action as a gesture for those in his country who had suffered at the hands of the war criminals. Ambassador Kerr could assure the Soviet leader only that Hess would not be sent back to Germany after the war; the actual trials and punishments would have to wait, as his government saw it. Kerr thought he had convinced the Russians to participate in the War Crimes Commission and ignored their objections, at least temporarily. He was wrong. Stalin was adamant that Russian participation depended upon Allied agreement that a war criminal would be tried and executed, or otherwise punished, as soon as he was found. The British refused, and on November 24, 1942, Soviet Foreign Minister Vyacheslav Molotov told Ambassador Kerr that

---

* On a Saturday night, just weeks before the Nazi invasion of the Soviet Union, Rudolf Hess, Deputy Fuhrer of the Third Reich, took off from an airfield near Munich. Hours later he was having tea in the cottage of a farmer in Renfrewshire, Scotland. The man who was closest to Hitler was a prisoner of the Home Guard.

Volumes have been addressed to answering the questions surrounding Hess's flight. Why would a man of such high rank in the Nazi organization undertake such a bizarre journey? Was Hitler aware of his key deputy's plans? But regardless of the disagreements of historians as to the truth behind the Hess trip, there are certain facts in evidence that play a vital part in understanding the subsequent hunt for Nazis.

his nation would not participate in the commission unless the demands they had made were met.

As the year ended, the British themselves seemed to be dragging their feet in getting the commission into action. Lord Simon wrote to the foreign minister on January 12, 1943, stating, "I am concerned that there will be a challenge to our government as to why we have not gone further." There were pressures from others in London as well, including members of Parliament, who were demanding reports. The Foreign Office was stalling.

When members of the House of Commons found out that the British had received confirmation in November 1942 from a diplomat in Switzerland that the "Final Solution" was an actuality, they were outraged. It seemed there were still some in the Foreign Office who were skeptical about the story, but the European governments in exile, world Jewish leaders, and some Americans pressed hard for action.

In late November, Rabbi Wise, head of the World Jewish Congress, gave President Roosevelt a file entitled "Blueprint for Extermination." It contained the same material as that which had been assembled by Sidney Silverman in the British Parliament, which he, in turn, had handed over to the British minister of state, Richard Law. Both files were explicit in their accounts of the killing of Jews at Belsen, Treblinka, Chelmno, and Auschwitz. Refugees from Poland had helped piece together evidence of massive killings in the Warsaw ghetto, details of which were also in the files.

Some of those critical of the British government's foot dragging during late 1942 and early 1943 explain it as being linked to the country's strained situation in the Middle East. If Britain were to accept fully and openly the charges of mass killing of Jews, it would be unable to resist demands that Jews who escaped from the Balkans or other lands be allowed to settle in Palestine. Massive settlements of that kind were inconsistent with British foreign policy.

Records of the World Jewish Congress detail the circumstances surrounding pressures brought by Rabbi Wise and others on the U.S. State Department to take a firm and public position with respect to Hitler's acts. A senior U.S. official, Robert Reams, made a notation that when reviewing correspondence with the World Jewish Congress and with the British "we must be careful not to make it appear that we are officially confirming Rabbi Wise's contention." Both the British and the State Department finally drafted an official position, but some subtle changes were made by Secretary of State Cordell Hull. The British version had arrived for his review stating that the evidence gathered:

> . . .leaves no room for doubt that the German authorities, not content with denying to persons of Jewish race, in all the territories over which their barbarous rule has been extended, the most elementary human rights, are now carrying into effect Hitler's oft repeated intention to exterminate the Jewish people in

Europe. From all the occupied countries, Jews are being transported, in condi-
tions of appalling horror and brutality, to Eastern Europe. In Poland, which
has long been the principal Nazi slaughterhouse, the ghettos established by the
German invaders are being systematically emptied of all Jews except a few
highly skilled workers required for war industries. None of those taken away
are ever heard of again. The able-bodied are slowly worked to death in labor
camps. The infirm are left to die of exposure and starvation, or are deliberately
massacred in mass executions. The number of victims of these bloody cruelties
are reckoned of entirely innocent men, women and children. We condemn in
the strongest possible terms this bestial policy of cold-blooded extermination.

Despite the testimony of refugees, prisoners of war, and objective observers
who had no reason to fabricate stories, Cordell Hull—while not disputing
much of what was being said about Nazi barbarism—disagreed with the certainty expressed in the statement "no room for doubt," Accordingly, Hull,
with Roosevelt's approval, softened the declaration to read: "We have numerous reports."

Yet, this declaration was to give the sufficient impetus to the War Crimes
Commission and initiate the hunt for Nazis. It was published in Moscow and
broadcast from Washington, D.C., by President Roosevelt on his regular
"Fireside Chat" program. It was delivered in the House of Commons by Anthony Eden, and it had a dramatic impact throughout the world.

Finally, in March 1943, it appeared that the United Nations War Crimes
Commission would become a reality. It was still not clear whether or not the
Soviet Union would participate despite their demands that Hess be tried. The
Soviets had also insisted on bringing along representatives of Lithuania, Latvia, and Estonia, to which the British objected because all three countries had
been seized by Stalin and and would, presumably, be extra puppet voters for
the Soviets.

In bureaucratic Washington, the policy seemed to be that the Roosevelt-
Churchill creation of a War Crimes Commission should be recognized, but it
should not impede the many things still to be done to win the war. No one of
real substance could be spared from the war effort. Herbert Pell, a middle-lev-
el political crony of Roosevelt and a former congressman and Democratic Party loyalist, was appointed to represent the United States at the new commission. No one thought he would make much of a fuss, but they were mistaken.

When Pell agreed to serve on the commission, the State Department was
bogged down in bureaucratic infighting and didn't get around to briefing him
for months. Meanwhile, Britain, with American support, was, trying to get the
still Soviets to commit themselves to participation.

The first meeting was scheduled for September 1943, but there were many loose ends: the British Foreign Office cautioned the State Department that the hunt for Nazis might be delayed. Meanwhile, Pell was still forgotten by his state department superiors. The would-be delegate besieged the White House with repeated letters and phone calls urging pressure on the State Department, but to no avail. Aides to Roosevelt reported that the president was more than a little annoyed when, on October 29, 1943, in response to several official inquiries, the State Department finally told him that "Pell's group met without Pell." The War Crimes Commission on which Pell was to represent the United States had held its first official meeting in London on October 19. Pell was not the only one absent; the Russians did not show up either.

In one sense, Pell did not miss much. Rather than launching an international hunt for war criminals, the first meeting of the War Crimes Commission had been a rather routine and boring discussion of procedural details. Allied fortunes of war were improving, and Pell and a handful of others who wanted the commission to move forward forcefully realized that the time was right to get the hunt going. The Germans were retreating on the Eastern front, and Allied forces were building up. Anthony Eden, the British foreign minister, was not getting along with Prime Minister Winston Churchill, his boss. Churchill was pushing for action by the commission he had initiated, while Eden was treading water and sending memos suggesting that he had never intended the commission to move aggressively before the war ended. But despite Eden's behind-the-scenes attempt to sabotage Churchill's enthusiasm and a comparable hesitancy on the part of some of Hull's advisors, Roosevelt and Churchill personally insisted on moving ahead.

On December 23, 1943, Moscow Radio reported that three German soldiers and a Russian collaborator had been convicted in a three-day trial in Kharkov. They were hanged publicly and the world soon knew about it. In London and Washington, there was concern that the Soviet action was being misinterpreted as encouraging immediate trials and execution of criminals—this was not the policy of the commission. Hull's personal files reveal that in the middle of the war, he sent a secret communiqué to Switzerland, which acted as an intermediary for the Germans. Hull promised that notwithstanding the formation of the War Crimes Commission, in accordance with the Geneva Convention, ordinary German soldiers would not be tried if they had not been involved in atrocities. He issued a press release to this effect, thus dissociating the United States from the Soviet decision to hang the three German soldiers.

The impact was predictable, and the Soviets became still more estranged from the Americans and the British. Hull's announcement was the death blow to Soviet participation in the War Crimes Commission, which continued to suffer from governmental preoccupation with the war effort and political infighting. As an "outsider" trying to integrate itself into existing political machinery, the commission was at a disadvantage. Classified information was withheld by the British, because disclosure would have meant sharing it with the Allies. The United States, too, was reluctant to share information through Pell, who finally arrived in London when the hearings were well under way. On December 7, 1943, Pell had his first meeting with his British counterparts and realized that there was no evidence on which the commission could proceed. One suggestion was that the BBC broadcast a worldwide appeal for the collection of evidence, but the idea was rejected because it might provoke reprisals from the faltering but still powerful Nazi organization.

Pell's assistant, Lawrence Preuss, had been designated an aide who would be the liaison with the State Department. He was, in effect, Hull's man, sent to make sure Pell stayed in line and that Hull knew everything that was going on. When Pell insisted that Preuss push the State Department for information, the aide wrote a lengthy memorandum to the department's legal advisor, Judge Green Hackworth. Now a public document, the memo shows that the State Department was being asked to appoint someone to collect evidence for the commission. The response was incredible: "If the cases are to be prepared by the government, then it would seem that the commission would have very little to do." In fact, Hull and the State Department, despite Roosevelt's enthusiasm for the commission, treated it as a British project and, having appointed a mediocre delegate in Pell, felt it should now all but ignore the new commission.

Hull's attitude was inherited by his successor, acting Secretary of State Edward R. Stettinius, Jr., who felt that the War Department might cooperate with the commission. But the War Department was not interested; War Secretary Henry Stimson considered the War Crimes Commission strictly a State Department creation. It was passing the buck. On March 13, 1943, Stimson stated in a memorandum that the War Department certainly accepted responsibility for war crimes policy, but "in view of the shortage of personnel," it would be too much work for his department to pass along any information to the commission. Stimson was concerned with winning the war, not with becoming a communicator for the State Department. When the War Crimes Commission specifically requested the names of top Nazi officers later that year, the War Department declined to comply for "security reasons." Two months later, the U.S. Joint Chiefs of Staff sent a memorandum to the secretary of state saying that they rejected the concept of referring any cases to the commission, because it would limit the jurisdiction of American military courts and cause delays. In other words, as far as the U.S. government was concerned, the commission had been created for cosmetic reasons, and the Nazi hunt, at least for the time being, was all talk.

Pell got angry. Frustrated by the State Department, but hesitant to criticize it publicly, he took on the British Foreign Office and Anthony Eden in particular. He told those in diplomatic circles that Eden's lack of interest and his department's restrictions on cooperating were emasculating the commission. He also filed a report with the U.S. State Department saying that "the punishment of war criminals from this war will degenerate into another farce, as it did after the last war." All he got in response were generalities and evasions.

Finally, by December 1944, however, as a result of public pressure, the State Department decided it was better to appear concerned about the commission's lack of activity than to be blamed for it. A State Department representative told the British ambassador in Washington that the United States was very worried and blamed the British for the commission's failure to act. He asked what would happen if the war were to end suddenly and the Allies were not in a position to deal with the war criminals. Everyone agreed that the Allies would appear ridiculous and inept.

Pell was the commission member who pushed for a broad base from which to gather evidence. He had arrived in London committed to the principle that the commission should try to document every single atrocity committed at any time, in any place, including those inflicted by Germans on Germans in the late 1930s. As an international Jewish-inspired press campaign waxed stronger, and Pell became more and more outspoken, the State Department's Preuss grew very nervous. Pell was telling everyone that he had President Roosevelt's personal endorsement for widening and accelerating the commission's mandate to launch the hunt for Nazis. On February 16, 1944, he wrote to Roosevelt insisting upon his promised support, pointing out that "if the question of the Jews in Germany is not taken up by the War Crimes Commission, there will be no organization in the world that can touch those who have persecuted these unfortunate people on account of their religion and their race."

Meanwhile, on another political front, the War Refugees Board was disturbed by the British government's denial of entry visas for Jewish refugees coming to Palestine. It had lobbied Roosevelt on behalf of Jewish organizations to ensure that the policy of extermination of the Jews was kept in the forefront of any declaration on war crimes. The White House had wanted the board's director, John Pehle, consulted on Pell's problems, but State Department staff members saw Pehle as a threat to their position and went around him.

While the War Crimes Commission was bogged down in procedural red tape and hampered by lack of support from either the British or American governments, Adolf Eichmann was deporting hundreds of thousands of Jews from Hungary to Auschwitz (Oswiecim), Poland. On April 15, 1944, massacres had begun in Hungary, and half a million Jews had been forced into cattle trucks and sent to Auschwitz at the rate of 15,000 per day. Captured Nazi records show that each truck to Auschwitz had two buckets—one for water and one for excretion. Many died from suffocation on the road even before they reached the death camp. The trip took four to six days.

It was no longer possible for the British, the Americans, or anyone else to pretend that the Holocaust was not happening. The fate of the Hungarian Jews was too well known and too easily proven. It seemed impossible that anything could prevent the War Crimes Commission from identifying war criminals for trial when the conflict ended. Technically, under the guidelines established for the commission, the Hungarian Jews, as citizens of an Axis ally, were in the same position as the German Jews: outside the commission's mandate.

On May 25, Joel Brand, a Hungarian Jew set free by Adolf Eichmann, arrived in Istanbul with a message to British and American authorities. Eichmann had the audacity to invite the Allies to barter for the lives of Hungary's remaining Jews. If the British and Americans would supply tons of coffee, tea, cocoa, soap, and 10,000 trucks, the Jews would be set free to leave for Palestine. Brand received no attention in Turkey and went on to Cairo, where he was arrested by British officials as a suspected Gestapo agent and accused of trying to divide the Allies.

On August 26, 1944, Charles De Gaulle marched proudly through the streets of Paris as the city was liberated by the Allies. As a result of that liberation, first-hand reports of German brutality during the French occupation reached the world, encouraging action against war criminals. The United States could not allow the policy of war crimes investigation to remain solely a British matter.

Four days later, a press conference was held in London, chaired by Sir Cecil Hurst, the British delegate and chairman of the War Crimes Commission. The first question was whether or not Adolf Hitler was on the Commission's list of war criminals. The answer was no. Then someone asked how long the list of war criminals was. Hurst hemmed and hawed before admitting that the list was "not a very long one," but he refused to give the actual number of names.

The next day, newspapers around the world labeled the commission a failure and, worse, a bumbling failure. It turned out that, as the date of that press conference, there were 184 names on the list.

Lord Simon's January 12, 1943, letter predicting embarrassment had turned out to be prophetic. In Washington, the monies necessary to keep Pell on the commission were canceled, and his resignation was announced by the State Department. Pell agreed to continue without pay, but his offer was refused. He went public and told the media that there were State Department officials who did "not want to punish Nazi war criminals despite going through the motions." Pell became a martyr and received a great deal of attention from Jewish leaders, the War Refugee Board, and other international organizations.

Then Hurst, the chairman of the commission, resigned. Eden stated that

Hurst had resigned because of serious illness, and that he was not expected to recover. Hurst disappointed him by living for another seventeen years. He had, in fact, resigned in anger over Eden's refusal to take the commission seriously and to cooperate with it. Subsequently, a British government, preoccupied with the threat of Soviet communist expansion in Eastern Europe, slowed the War Crimes Commission to a crawl before the war ended. U.S. red tape and America's growing concern about Soviet expansion didn't help.

It was suggested by the British Foreign Office that the commission be shut down, but anxiety about how the media would treat such a step prevented it. Others said perhaps the commission "would fade away" out of boredom. But it didn't fade away, it continued, and eventually it received the attention and cooperation of all the Allied nations.

One by one, the nations of Europe came forward, some with remarkably detailed documentation of war crimes committed on their territory and the identities of those who had committed them. In many cases, photographs and affidavits substantiated first-hand accounts. Time and effort had been expended to render their presentation to the War Crimes Commission effective. Some, unfortunately, did not have more than brief descriptions of individuals, improperly spelled names, and spurious evidence.

The War Crimes Commission now included seventeen member nations: Australia, Belgium, Canada, China, Czechoslovakia, Denmark, France, Greece, India, Luxembourg, the Netherlands, New Zealand, Norway, Poland, Great Britain, the United States, and Yugoslavia. (South Africa was originally a member, but soon dropped out.) It had survived internal bickering and high-level efforts to sabotage its work, and devoted the last twenty months of its existence to culling through the mass of material and compiling the huge files of horror now finally being shared with the world.

★   ★   ★

By early 1987, great pressure was being brought to bear on U.N. Secretary General Javier Perez de Cuellar. Historian David Wyman—considered a distinguished expert on the Holocaust—wrote to say that "Opening of these archives is indispensable for any full understanding of the Holocaust." Finally, Perez de Cuellar decided to reconvene the seventeen member countries of the original War Crimes Commission to get their permission to open the files to historians, researchers, and journalists.

When the seventeen first reconvened to decide about access to the archive, only Israel publicly pressed for opening it. But Israel was not an official member of the commission, because the State of Israel did not exist in 1943. The Israelis were allowed to sit in on the first phase of the deliberations as an observer with an obvious interest. The Israelis believed that a systematic examination of the U.N. material would not only help identify war criminals who might still be in hiding, but would also help strengthen cases against individuals already under suspicion.

The Israelis argued that it was more than a matter of new evidence of war crimes that was at stake. Repeatedly, spokespersons for Israel said that regardless of what future prosecutions might take place based on the new evidence, history must include the full record of Nazi crimes. Perhaps the person most responsible for articulating the arguments in favor of disclosure and setting the strategy that achieved that goal was Israel's then permanent representative to the United Nations, Ambassador Benjamin Netanyahu. The ambassador told everyone that opening the archive meant more than filling in the gaps in history books: it was "indispensable to justice." Netanyahu believed that when the evidence was released, public scrutiny would force reluctant governments finally to prosecute known Nazis in their countries. He was concerned that the "hourglass is emptying."

In the weeks before the final decision was made, Netanyahu told us that "in a few years, there just won't be any more criminals to try, and no witnesses to testify. If that happens, we shall have neither truth nor justice." Netanyahu pressed hard at the U.N., but his first request, in June 1986, was rejected. He was told by the secretary-general that the files "might disclose unproved rumors against innocent people." Netanyahu countered that the identities of the accused were already known. (Historians searching in a dusty warehouse of the National Archives in Maryland in 1986 had discovered a complete list of the 25,000 accused by the War Crimes Commission. That list had previously been made public and widely distributed among journalists.)

For a year, Ambassador Netanyahu and his colleagues lobbied other nations at the U.N. Some nations argued vehemently that opening the archive to general inspection would be grossly unfair—since the evidence gathered by the commission forty years ago had not been used, it would be stale. Baseless accusations could be made, embarrassing and even endangering certain individuals. First, it was Poland that objected most strongly, but without giving any specific reason. Finally, the Poles capitulated, and the big stumbling block came down to one nation—France. Because France was a founding member of the U.N. (along with the United States, Great Britain, the U.S.S.R., and China) it had the political muscle to block the opening by its single vote.

French representatives lobbied the other members on the dangers of releasing massive lists of people all over the world, many of whom might be alive and against whom there was no compelling evidence. It has been suggested that French reluctance to reopen the war's history books is based largely on unwillingness to refocus attention on the cooperation between fascists in the French government and the Nazis. Critics have repeatedly expressed disgust over the quick surrender of France to Hitler's war machine. The government had then cooperated too closely with the invaders, and reopening the diaries of those days would only remind the world of France's role.

Perhaps even more to the point, the names of seventeen French citizens appeared in the files—not Germans who invaded France and committed atrocities—but Frenchmen whose collaboration was such that the Allies wanted them brought to trial for the most serious of war crimes.

Those who favored opening the files insisted that they would do it in such a way as to distinguish clearly between bland accusations and credible documentation. The United States, passive at first, finally began to champion Israel's cause. The political mood in the United States after the exposé of Kurt Waldheim as a former Nazi, and the ban against his ever returning to America, motivated the U.S. representative to insist on opening the files.

Finally, French opposition crumbled under the political weight of the other members of the commission, strong public support for Israel's insistence on opening the files, and leverage from the international media. On December 2, 1987, the first persons permitted into the archive under the new policy walked into the room and came away appalled at what they had read. It took less than three hours to examine a handful of files so filled with documentation of the most horrible atrocities that even seasoned journalists and tough-skinned historians and prosecutors were shaken.

But Ambassador Netanyahu* and Elan Steinberg and Israel Singer at the World Jewish Congress, and people like Robert Rhodes-James, a British historian and leading back-bench Member of Parliament, celebrated with good cause. They had led the fight to open the files, and they had won. They had insisted that continued secrecy at the U.N. did not protect the innocent, but the guilty. They had argued that keeping the files closed was giving credibility to those who would deny history and who said, by their silence, that we would learn nothing from the horrors of World War II.

---

* Ambassador Netanyahu has resigned to return to his country. He protested Secretary of State George Shultz's meeting with P.L.O representatives claiming accurately that it violated long-standing agreements between Israel and the United States.

Netanyahu's departure left a major void at the world body. In addition to his leadership in the fight to unlock the sealed secrets of war criminals, he had been a consistent champion of human rights, an outspoken ally of the United States and Israel's most informed and persuasive voice of reason.

It is expected that he will enjoy rapid political success in Israel. He is described as a potential future Israeli prime minister.

Who Is A War Criminal?— What Is A War Crime?

If the battle over whether a War Crimes Commission should be established was long and convoluted, an even longer battle was fought among the Allies over the more basic question of how the guilty should be punished and what they should be punished for. Long before D-Day, long before the specific horrors of Auschwitz, Buchenwald, Dachau, and the other death camps were known, long before there was any certainty that the Allies would defeat Nazi Germany, there was spirited debate at the highest levels of government over how, or even whether, those guilty of committing atrocities in the name of Adolf Hitler should be brought to justice.

As we have seen, for President Franklin Roosevelt there was no question. On October 7, 1942, he told a news conference, "It is our intention that just and sure punishment shall be meted out to the ringleaders responsible for the organized murder of thousands of innocent persons in the commission of atrocities which have violated every tenet of the Christian faith." But London wavered. As early as June 22, 1942, a plan to prosecute major Nazi war criminals for a wide range of atrocities had been placed before the legal officers of the Crown. Lord Chancellor Simon, although he favored establishment of a War Crimes Commission, recommended against the plan, which he said might set troubling precedents for the future. His reasoning was labored, to say the least. Simon felt what was being proposed would be a break from the traditional rules by which victors had punished the vanquished after a war ended. He believed the proposals would establish ex post facto laws and open the way for victorious states, after future conflicts, to prosecute anyone they found it convenient to brand a war criminal. Some factions within the British Foreign Office wanted to limit prosecutions to those guilty of violating clearly established and long-standing rules of war.

Simon put forth a counterproposal. Why not simply put top Nazis up against a wall and shoot them as they were captured, especially if hostilities were continuing? The plan was formalized in a position paper entitled "The Punishment of War Criminals" and approved by Churchill before it was submitted to the

Americans. The proposal was designed to take care of "the Hitler and Mussolini gangs, the Japanese warlords and the rest." Simon proposed that 100 persons, to be declared world outlaws, be listed by agreement of the Allies. When any one of them was arrested by any Allied soldier, he could be shot to death within six hours of identification by an officer holding the rank of major general or above, with no need for a trial or approval by civilian authority.

The British cabinet was split over the Simon idea. While many of them liked the idea of shooting German leaders on sight, it did little for international law to discard the concept of an international tribunal, upon which even the Soviets were insisting.Tom Bower, the British author and historian who has focused effectively on the political motivations of Britain's leaders at the war's end, says that there was a "deadlock" and a "bankruptcy of ideas" in London at that time.

Either as a compromise or a stalling tactic, the cabinet asked the Foreign Office to prepare a list of war criminals who would be so repugnant to the conscience of mankind that the "decision on their fate would not only be accepted but expected." Sixty days later there was still no list.

Angered, Churchill demanded action and the Foreign Office finally produced a list. Instead of the 100 names that Churchill had requested, it had thirty-two Germans and five Italians. Among those selected for immediate execution should they be found, in addition to Hitler, were Max Amann, a Nazi publisher; Bernard Rust, the Nazi minister of education; and several others who were totally unknown to the British and perhaps even to many Germans.

After weeks of argument, a much shorter list, prepared by Lord Simon, emerged. It contained only five well-known names (Hitler, Himmler, Goering, Goebbels, and Ribbentrop). The hunt was on, and the hunted had been designated.

The British position was unacceptable to Roosevelt and to the U.S. government. Publicly, they said they could not understand the legal stance assumed by the British. Privately, they speculated that London's position was quasi-political, developed, perhaps, out of fear that history would end up recording as "war crimes" some questionable activities undertaken by the British in the early years of the war.

Both the United States and Great Britain were deeply disturbed by the abstention of the Soviets as the War Crimes Commission was being formed, but it was agreed that the commission would hold its initial meeting in London without Soviet participation in the hope of pressuring them into joining. The tactic resulted in a wider agreement on the punishment of war criminals, as mentioned in chapter 1.

On November 1, 1943, Cordell Hull, the U.S. secretary of state, met with his British and Soviet counterparts in Moscow, where the United States, Great

Britain, and the Soviet Union signed "The Declaration of German Atrocities," commonly referred to as the Moscow Declaration. That declaration stated in part that:

> *Those German officers and men and members of the Nazi party who have been responsible for, or who have taken part in . . . atrocities, massacres and executions, will be sent back to the countries in which their abominable deeds were done in order that they may be judged and punished according to the laws of these liberated countries and the free governments that will be created therein.*
>
> *Germans who take part in wholesale shooting of Italian officers, or in the execution of French, Dutch, Belgian or Norwegian hostages, or of Greek peasants, or who have shared in the slaughters inflicted on the people of Poland or in the territories of the Soviet Union which are now being swept clear of the enemy, will know that they will be brought back to the scene of their crimes and judged on the spot by the people they have outraged. Most assuredly, the allies will pursue them to the uttermost ends of the earth and will deliver them to the accusers in order that justice may be done. This declaration is without prejudice to the case of the major criminals whose offenses have no particular geographical location and who will be punished by a joint decision of the government of the allies."*

Roosevelt trumpeted the news of the pact and warned that "None who participated in these acts of savagery shall go unpunished. All who share in the guilt shall share the punishment."

Four weeks later, at Teheran, the first three-power conference in which Stalin participated took place. According to Elliott Roosevelt, who accompanied his father to Teheran, Stalin rose at the concluding banquet and offered the following toast: "I propose a salute to the swiftest possible justice for all Germany's war criminals—justice before a firing squad. I drink to our unity in dispatching them as fast as we capture them, all of them, and there must be at least 50,000 of them."

According to Elliott Roosevelt, this brought Churchill instantly to his feet in protest: he was not about to abide wholesale slaughter. "Any such attitude is wholly contrary to our British sense of justice. The British people will never stand for such mass murder." Roosevelt says that his father tried to defuse the situation with humor, joking that he was sure Stalin was wrong—that there were not more than 49,500 such war criminals.

If nothing else, this exchange shows the confusion that prevailed on the subject among Allied leaders. Summary execution for a handful of top Nazis was the remedy suggested by Lord Simon, but rejected out of hand by Roosevelt as barbaric. Stalin embraced the idea not from any concern about the future course of international law, but out of a clear passion for revenge. The State Department was torn between these extremes. Some key Roosevelt advisors leaned toward endorsing the idea of executions, swayed either by Simon's fears about precedent, or Stalin's desire for revenge. Others supported an international tribunal.

Despite White House prodding for resolution of the war crimes issue, the War Department moved with caution during the summer of 1944. Two separate plans for an occupied Germany were drawn up: "Handbook of Military Government for Germany" and the "Interim Directive on Occupation Procedures" (later known as Joint Chiefs of Staff Order 1067). The plans focused almost entirely on the initial occupation and purposely avoided attention to the long term. The handbook contained a long and detailed list of some 250,000 Nazi Party, government, police and military officials—by position, not by name—who were to be automatically detained. The list avoided most members of the regular German Army, who were to be considered prisoners of war and treated under the provisions of the Geneva Convention. It did contain members of the Gestapo, the German State Security Service (SD), and the officer corps—but not the enlisted personnel—of the SS.

The Interim Directive also called for the detention of those suspected of committing war crimes. It stated that "Adolf Hitler, his chief Nazi and Fascist associates, and collaborators (and individuals) suspected of having committed war crimes, including those whose names shall appear on lists drawn up by the United Nations, shall be arrested and held for future investigation and subsequent disposition."

This was the only mention in either document of war criminals as opposed to high-ranking government or Nazi officials. It was inserted in the Interim Directive with some hesitancy and against the backdrop of a heated philosophical battle between London and Washington. Great Britain was still a very reluctant participant in the evolving definition of war crimes, particularly as applied to a nation's persecution of its own nationals. British legal experts admitted that such persecution violated national and international law, but argued that it did not come within the traditional definitions of war crime.

Interestingly, this view now found adherents in Washington. Judge Hackworth, the State Department's legal advisor, agreed strongly with the British position that a country's persecution of its own nationals should not be considered a war crime. He also strongly supported the proposition that actions carried out before the actual onset of hostilities could not be considered war crimes. In the case of Nazi Germany, this applied to the invasion of Poland, which began on September 1, 1939. Hackworth found an ally in President Roosevelt, who, in fact, instructed Pell, the U.S. representative to the War Crimes Commission, to put forward as the official U.S. position that no act before the start of hostilities should be deemed a war crime. Later, at Nuremberg and after, this would become the subject of heated international debate.*

Roosevelt remained torn by the bitter debate that continued to rage behind the scenes in Washington. It was a three-way battle. Members of the State Department, including Secretary Hull, were still troubled by the long-term legal ramifications of trials under an expanded definition of war crimes. They conceded, very reluctantly, that executions were the way to proceed, but only after military courts-martial of some kind. At the other end were those, like Treasury Secretary Henry Morgenthau, Jr., who were so repulsed by the scope of Nazi atrocities that they supported Lord Simon's idea of summary executions. In the middle were those who wanted specific war crimes trials.

Now another factor entered into the equation.

After D-Day, June 6, 1944, General Dwight D. Eisenhower became incensed over reports of wholesale executions of Allied prisoners by the Germans. He insisted upon a formal investigation of the matter in preparation for punishing the guilty when they were eventually captured. Put in charge of the investigation was Lieutenant Colonel Murray Bernays, who would soon emerge as the pivotal figure in the war crimes movement.

Bernays was a noted legal scholar who had emigrated from Poland to the United States with his family in 1901, at the age of six. After graduating from

---

* The Nazi plan, based on blatant anti-Semitism, that led to the extermination of millions of Jews began well before the invasion of Poland. When we visited the Berlin Document Center, perhaps the most fascinating revelation was the large number of persons who would become key wartime Nazi officials who were involved in oppression of Jews as early as 1933.

Civil oppression of the Jews began on April 1, 1933, with the first official boycott of Jewish shops, lawyers, and doctors, and the public demand for the removal of Jewish pupils from schools and universities. Hitler's close friend Rudolf Hess was among those who scripted key documents that outlined the Nazi plan. By 1935, the infamous Nuremberg Laws, designed to protect the German bloodline, were enacted. Intermarriage with a Jew was made a serious crime.

In the summer of 1936, Adolf Hitler moderated the party's anti-Semitic campaign. The Olympics were scheduled, and with the athletes came the world press—and a magnifying glass focused on German life. We talked with a seventy-five-year-old retired newspaper publisher who remembers, in great detail, what it was like when the Olympics came to Berlin.

In 1937 it became possible for any Jewish business owner to be stripped of his company without any legal justification.

On March 13, 1938, Austria died. The forced *Anschluss* (union) of that country with Nazi Germany meant that all anti-Jewish rules and regulations already in force in Germany would be applied immediately. Jews were required to come forward and register and to reveal their wealth.

On June 9, 1938, the main synagogue in Munich was destroyed in view of a cheering crowd. On August 10, the same devastation struck the main synagogue in Nuremberg.

Harvard University and Columbia Law School, he had joined the Army during World War I. After the war, he returned to New York, where he established a law practice and became a close friend of Judge Samuel Rosenman, who by 1940 had emerged as one of Roosevelt's closest advisors. When World War II began, Bernays was called back into service.

Rosenman favored the idea of trials and saw an ally in Bernays. He persuaded U.S. Army Colonel Mickey Marcus, who had been charged with formulating policy for postwar Germany, to appoint Bernays to make the plans for bringing Nazi leaders to trial. Marcus was privately worried that the British-held view that Nazis leaders should be summarily executed would prevail. That concept and its potential ramifications frightened him, as it did Bernays, when he learned that such a course was being considered seriously.

Bernays's immediate problem was to come up with some kind of legal theory that would extend the existing concept of war crime to cover the acts of atrocity that would have to be punished. He wrestled long and hard with the question and admitted he was having difficulty formulating anything that would win the day in the ongoing debate. Then he was introduced to a book by Rafael Lemkin that was about to be published. Lemkin was a world-renowned legal scholar who had escaped from Poland as the German invasion began. Eventual-

---

As of October 5 of that year, Jews could no longer hold passports unless a red letter *J* appeared on them; later that month, 17,000 former Polish Jews were expelled from Germany.

On November 9 and 10, 1938, the Nazis showed their true colors to the world, in the "Crystal Night" pogrom, so called for the enormous number of windows broken by Nazi thugs. All over Germany, synagogues, shops, homes, and flats belonging to Jews were destroyed. In those two days, 20,000 Jews were imprisoned without specific charges and 100 were killed outright. On November 12, the Nazis assessed the cost of all this destruction and demanded that German Jews repay their fellow Jews. Three days later, all Jewish students were expelled from German schools.

The year 1939 began with Nazi confiscation of all Jewish valuables. Goering's name is clearly visible on the Berlin Center document that sets forth the details of that confiscation. Within months the Nazis had imposed a curfew: Jews could no longer be out of doors after 8 P.M. in the winter and 9 P.M. in the summer, and they were not allowed to have wireless sets. The actual deportations of the Jews from Germany, mainly from the province of Pomerania, began on February 12, 1940.

On March 7, 1941, German Jews were designated compulsory laborers, and by July 31 Goering had ordered the evacuation of all European Jews in all German-occupied territories. By the end of that year, incredible restrictions were placed on those Jews who were not already in concentration camps—restrictions on when they could go out of their homes, where they could walk, and what time they had to return.

January 20, 1942 was the date of the Wannsee Conference which detailed the Final Solution of the Jewish problem. From this time forward, many of those whose names appear high on the list of the wanted were involved in carrying out the most massive persecution of a people in contemporary times.

ly he ended up in the United States, where he went to work for the OSS (Office of Strategic Services) and began researching a book on German activities during the early years of occupation of Eastern Europe. As Bernays was pondering his inability to formulate a comprehensive legal theory on war crimes, he was given an advance copy of Lemkin's *Axis Rule in Occupied Europe.*

Lemkin postulated the premise that organizations like the Nazi SS and Gestapo were nothing more than criminal organizations. Seizing on this premise, Bernays began to evolve a theory that the extermination of the Jewish population of Eastern Europe, the mass execution of Allied prisoners of war, and the atrocities committed against the native populations of many captured nations were all related to a collective criminal conspiracy and could be dealt with legally as such after the war. As Bernays stated it:

> *The crimes and atrocities were not single and unconnected, but were the inevitable outcome of the basic criminal conspiracy of the Nazi Party. . . . A conspiracy is criminal either because it aims at accomplishment of lawful ends by unlawful means, or unlawful ends by legal means. Therefore, such technicalities as whether the extermination of fellow Germans by Nazi Germans was unlawful, or whether this could be a 'war crime' if it were committed before there was a state of war, would be unimportant if you recognize as the basic crime the Nazi conspiracy. . . . Therefore, the thing to do is to try the organization along with the Nazi leaders on the conspiracy charge and having convicted the organization, the convictions would serve as* prima facie *proof of the guilt of any of its members.*

Bernays proposed to accomplish this through an international tribunal. Thus was born the idea that would become the Nuremberg trials.

In short order, both Secretary of State Hull and Secretary of War Henry Stimson embraced Bernays's conspiracy theory of prosecution; now they had to convince President Roosevelt. In September 1944, the president had traveled to Quebec with Treasury Secretary Morgenthau to meet with Churchill on plans for the postwar economic recovery of Europe. With Churchill at the meeting was Lord Simon. After the economic talks, the subject turned to war trials, and both Morgenthau and Simon argued passionately for summary executions. In the end, they won over both Churchill and Roosevelt. The two leaders signed a one-sentence communiqué that read: "The President and the Prime Minister have agreed to put to Marshal Stalin Lord Simon's proposals for dealing with the major criminals and to concert with him a list of names."

Morgenthau returned to Washington flushed with victory. By now, Hull had become uneasy, and Stimson was thrown into a panic at the thought of summary executions. Using Bernays's theory as a theme, they drafted joint a memorandum entitled "The Trial and Punishment of European War Criminals," which they submitted to Roosevelt in late November. They argued vehemently that the United States could not go along with any plan advocating executions without trials. This, they argued, would violate the basic principles on which the nation was founded. They maintained that by adopting Bernays's theory the problem of establishing a dangerous precedent could be avoided.

On December 18 of that year, a military report to Allied headquarters that landed on General Eisenhower's desk made all of the political bickering academic. It was that moment of truth when death replaced diplomacy as the topic of the day for those concerned with the War Crimes Commission. The signal had come from the U.S. First Army in the Ardennes Forest, on the German border with Belgium. It said that "SS troops had captured U.S. soldiers, approximately 200, who after being searched were lined up and shot with machine guns." One wounded soldier escaped to report what had occurred. The mass murders became known as the Malmedy Massacre and were attributed to Hitler's desperation in the war's last German offensive—the Battle of the Bulge. But the massacre so affected people on both sides of the political discussion surrounding the prosecution of war criminals that debate came to a halt. In the United States, Secretary Stettinius, Secretary Stimson, and Attorney General Francis Biddle agreed to back the Hull-Stimson memorandum as the basis for a war crimes policy. They agreed on U.S. backing for international trials, including the prosecution of Germans for crimes as far back as 1933. Most importantly, they agreed that the trials did not have to have their legal basis in allegations that defendants had violated either established norms of war or established international law: they could be justified simply on the fact that defendants had committed crimes against humanity. The group took the plan to Roosevelt and he quickly agreed.

The plan was unveiled on February 1, 1945, at a press conference at the State Department. Joseph Grew, undersecretary of state, announced the plan as the official U.S. policy. It included the assurance that stateless Jews were indeed victims and that crimes against Axis nationals would also be prosecuted. In other words, Nazis would be punished for their crimes "wherever committed." Those who would become the Nuremberg prosecution staff were assembled to begin amassing evidence for a postwar trial or series of trials.

Roosevelt intended to get approval from Churchill and Stalin at Yalta in February 1945, but the British continued to balk at the concept of war crimes trials under any theory that expanded their scope beyond violations of established rules of war. So the item was withdrawn from the agenda for the Yalta Conference. In April Roosevelt sent a delegation headed by Rosenman to London to negotiate some solution with the British. They were unsuccessful. In a letter from London, Rosenman confided to a friend that the British still maintained that "executions without trial is the preferable course."

On April 12, 1945, Roosevelt died, and Rosenman returned from London for the funeral. In a meeting with President Harry S. Truman, the legislator explained the problem and added that with the impending fall of the Nazis, it must become a top priority, and somehow the British must be won over. Truman agreed and huddled with his advisors to form a plan. Chief Justice Robert Jackson (Roosevelt's long-time attorney general) would be drafted to head the prosecution teams for the trials even before the British agreed to them. Truman's advisors believed that Jackson's preeminence as a legistator would send an unequivocal message to Churchill and Simon that the United States was dead serious about going forward with the plan for war crimes trials. Rosenman was dispatched to the Supreme Court to get Jackson's assent. The chief justice not only said yes, he supported the concept enthusiastically and threw himself into the effort.

At this point, the scene of the war crimes debate had shifted to San Francisco, where the Allies were meeting to draft the charter of the United Nations. Jackson had agreed on May 1 to head the U.S. prosecution team. The next day, as the announcement was being made public, a straightforward message was delivered to Foreign Secretary Anthony Eden in San Francisco: the United States was prepared to go forward with war crimes trials, with or without British participation. Eden was told that President Truman was dispatching a delegation headed by Rosenman to San Francisco to receive Britain's answer, and a meeting was demanded for the next afternoon, May 3.

Eden cabled London frantically for instructions. At 6:00 P.M. London time, four hours before Eden was due to meet with the delegation, an emergency cabinet session convened to consider the matter.

Lord Simon, as he had for the past three years, argued against trials and in favor of summary executions. But many cabinet members now saw that position as untenable. Finally, Minister of State Richard Law came up with what he believed would be a workable compromise. Britain would go along with the trials plan if it were guaranteed that the legal theory employed would not expand upon traditional definitions of crimes. If the trials were held under Bernays's theory of criminal conspiracy—which, interestingly, had all but gotten lost in Washington's planning—Britain could agree without compromising what it had long described as its basic reservations.

That advice was cabled to Eden, who was told to proceed slowly, agreeing to trials in principle but holding back on final approval until a complete plan was drafted. The meeting was convened, and it included Marshal Molotov and a Soviet delegation. Eden put forward Whitehall's new instructions, and hours of what Rosenman later described as "spirited debate" followed. Finally, an agreement was reached. Britain would drop its plan for summary executions and would participate in war crimes trials subject to final approval of technical arrangements and a philosophical underpinning, plus an agreement by the Soviets that they, too, would participate. Each delegation appointed technical advisors to begin working out details.

The first meeting of the technical experts was on May 5, 1945. Among the U.S. participants were Rosenman, Judge Hackworth of the State Department, and Bernays. A major problem became apparent immediately. Neither the British nor the Soviet participants had received instructions on how to proceed. Consequently, much time was spent on insignificant details. The U.S. delegation wanted to move forward with more deliberate speed, so, at a second meeting three days later, they presented a draft proposal and pushed for its adoption. The British delegation was willing to move ahead under the assumption that London would be all but forced to approve whatever final draft came out of the group. But the Russians and the French, who were not a part of the prior discussions (but who had to be included in the decision as founding members of the still unchartered United Nations), had not heard from Moscow and Paris, respectively, and little progress was made. In fact, much time was spent debating what was fast becoming the central focus of the sessions: the definition of "crime" that would be adopted. All parties pushed for their own positions, which were still far apart.

Two days later, on May 10, the Soviet and French delegations were still awaiting word from home, and Rosenman announced that he was going back to Washington until they had received instructions. At this point, the central argument had come down to whether the group could simply declare a given act illegal, or whether legal precedents had to be cited as the basis for declaring such an act a crime. This point was crucial to the Americans, who admitted that they were having difficulty coming up with precedents for any number of activities that they wanted to include in the list of indictable crimes.

Neither the French nor the Soviets ever received their instructions, and the San Francisco meeting never resumed. Rather, it was decided that the United States would come up with a final proposal and send it to the other parties, after which another meeting would convene to hammer out details.

That turned out to be easier said than done, because there were still pockets of sharp disagreement within the U.S. government. Effectively, what the U.S. delegation had presented in San Francisco became a starting point, called in retrospect Draft 1. When the delegation returned to Washington, suggestions from the other representatives were incorporated into the initial draft, and Draft 2 was produced. But with that second draft came a long commentary that was in itself almost as detailed as the second draft, and which a number of persons involved dubbed Draft 2A. This commentary became important, because it included a much-expanded concept of war crimes for which the Nazis could be prosecuted. It did so by advancing what commentator Bradley Smith characterizes as an "extremely elastic definition of international law," stating that "International law shall be taken to include the principles of the law of nations as they result from the usages established among civilized people, from the law of humanity, and [from] the dictates of public conscience."

Draft 2 quickly became Drafts 3 and 4. But the expanded concept of international law contained in the commentary on the second draft stuck. In a way, it became the basis for the eventual definition of war crimes.

While Draft 2 had been formulated as a revision of the document produced by those who had been to San Francisco, the next revision became the work of Justice Jackson and his staff during the four-day period May 15-19. What emerged in Draft 3 was the much-expanded definition of war crime. Some in Washington had problems with Draft 3, especially a provision that would have allowed for prosecution of anyone accused of waging what was called "aggressive war," which was basically defined as a war that violated existing treaties. Some members of the War Department said that this was going too far, so revisions were made, many by Jackson himself. Among them was a redefinition of aggressive war to delete the reference to treaties and to speak only of invasions "in violation of law." But during the international debate that would follow before the final adoption of a definition of war crime, the definition of aggressive war drifted back to what it had been in Draft 3.

By late May, Draft 4 was complete and all concerned believed the document was ready to present to the other Allies. On May 28 Jackson took the proposal to London, where he presented it to Eden and the Lord Chancellor. The British were more than a little taken aback, unaware that the proposal had undergone such substantial change from the one they had discussed in San Francisco. They started to balk again, but Jackson put it bluntly. Most of the Nazi hierarchy was already under U.S. control, and the United States was perfectly prepared to go it alone and start the trials based on the legal theories embodied in the new draft. Get on board, he told the British in effect, because the train is about to leave the station without you.

The British capitulated, and Churchill appointed Attorney General Maxwell Fyfe as Britain's chief prosecutor. Jackson returned to Washington in triumph. After meeting with Truman, Jackson decided to move his headquarters to London and agreed with Fyfe that the chief prosecutors for the four Allied countries—the United States, Britain, France, and the U.S.S.R.—would meet there to work out details and sign the protocol.

The meeting, which has become known as the London Conference, began on June 25, 1945. Jackson believed it would take only a few days to hammer out a final agreement, but he was too optimistic. Preparations for the coming trials went forward even as the Allies inched toward agreement on the key document on which the prosecutions would be based. June became July, and July, August. At one point the argument became so heated that Jackson suggested it might be better for each nation to try those it held captive itself, using whatever theories of international or domestic law it thought best.

Both the French and the Soviets had grave problems with aspects of the American proposal. One of the most heated debates surged around the definition of a war criminal as one who persecutes on the basis of political belief. Several participants argued that wars are fought primarily over such differences. There was a fear that inclusion of this phrase would effectively limit the definition of just war, especially as waged by an aggressor state, and open the door for a future victor to brand all members of a defeated nation as war criminals (this, of course, was the British fear first expressed by Lord Chancellor Simon almost four years earlier).

Then, too, there was bitter debate about the American demand that "wanton" destruction of civilian property be included as a war crime. The problem was partly one of language. How would the concept of wanton translate into the many languages in which the eventual definition would have to stand? It was argued that wanton had imprecise nuances peculiar to English, and was not readily translatable. Also, the Soviets feared that inclusion of this phrase would open them to charges of war crimes for their scorched-earth policy in the counterinvasion of Germany. In the end, the word was allowed to remain in the English version, but the caveat "not justified by military necessity" was added. That seemed to satisfy the Soviets, who could argue that what they had done was justified by military necessity.

Finally, on August 1, the respective heads of state intervened. Truman, Stalin, and Britain's new prime minister, Clement Attlee, meeting in Potsdam, issued a directive that their representatives in London reach an agreement quickly and that the war trials begin. Six days later, the agreement was completed. Several changes had been made in the draft that Jackson had brought to England, but none of major significance. The United States had its agreement that Nazis would be tried under a very broad definition of acts that could and would be considered war crimes. On September 5, the London Agreement was signed by the United States, Britain, the Soviet Union, and France. It was also acceded to by the nineteen other countries that now comprised the United Nations War Crimes Commission. This agreement established a definition of war criminal that remains the basis for prosecuting those accused of committing atrocities during the Second World War.

Using the broad basis favored by Jackson, a war criminal, under the London Agreement, was considered someone guilty of "crimes against peace," "war crimes," and "crimes against humanity." Borrowing from the theory originally advanced by Bernays, conspiracy to commit one of these acts also constituted a separate crime:

Article 6. *The Tribunal established by the Agreement . . . for the trial and punishment of the major war criminals of the European Axis countries shall have the power to try and punish persons who, acting in the interests of the European Axis countries, whether as individuals or as members of an organization, committed any of the following crimes:*

The following acts, or any of them, are crimes coming within the jurisdiction of the Tribunal for which there shall be individual responsibility:

(a) CRIMES AGAINST PEACE: Namely, planning, preparation, initiation, or waging of a war of aggression or a war in violation of international treaties, agreements, or assurances, or participation in a common plan or conspiracy for the accomplishment of any of the foregoing.

(b) WAR CRIMES: Namely, violations of the laws or customs of war. Such violations shall include, but not be limited to, murder, ill-treatment or deportation to slave labor or for any other purpose of civilian population of or in occupied territory, murder or ill-treatment of prisoners of war or persons on the seas, killing of hostages, plunder of public or private property, wanton destruction of cities, towns, or villages, or devastation not justified by military necessity.

(c) CRIMES AGAINST HUMANITY: Namely, murder, extermination, enslavement, deportation, and other inhumane acts committed against any civilian population before or during the war or persecutions on political, racial, or religious grounds in execution of or in connection with any crime within the jurisdiction of the Tribunal, whether or not in violation of the domestic law of the country where perpetrated.

Leaders, organizers, instigators and accomplices participating in the formulation or execution of a common plan or conspiracy to commit any of the foregoing crimes are responsible for all acts committed by any persons in execution of such plan.

The Nuremberg Tribunal carefully spelled out its view that its Charter, and especially the crucial Article 6, did not really constitute new law, but simply a further codification of existing international law, particularly the 1907 Hague Convention on the laws and customs of war and the 1929 Geneva Convention on the treatment of prisoners of war. The Tribunal wrote: "The Charter is not an arbitrary exercise of power of the victorious nations but in the view of the Tribunal it is the expression of international law existing at the time of its creation; and to that extent is itself a contribution to international law."

It is important to note the clear distinction made in Article 6 between "war crimes" and "crimes against humanity." As we saw, over the course of the three years and more of debate leading to the London Agreement, Lord Chancellor Simon and his allies on both sides of the Atlantic had argued that the term war criminal should be limited to one who had broken the established rules governing civilized conflict. But the American view prevailed in delineating clearly that a war criminal is also one who has committed atrocities against a civilian population—even if the victims might be of the same nationality as the perpetrator—or persecuted others on political, racial, or religious grounds.

Since the adoption of Article 6 at London in 1945, the world has repeatedly reaffirmed this new standard for defining a war criminal, especially the distinction between war crime and crime against humanity, and the clear inclusion of the latter in defining the term.

The third resolution passed by the new United Nations General Assembly in 1946, "Extradition and Punishment of War Criminals," adopted "the definition of war crimes and crimes against peace and humanity contained in the Charter of the International Military Tribunal." The United Nations War Crimes Commission specifically adopted the definition of war criminal in Article 6 as defining the acts that came within its jurisdiction. Article 38 of the Statute of the International Court of Justice, adopts the definition verbatim.

Six times since 1946, the U.N. General Assembly has adopted various resolutions that specifically embrace the Article 6 definition of war criminal, including crimes against humanity. In 1968, for example, a resolution was passed asking member nations to adjust their statute of limitations so that war criminals would not go unpunished. The resolution's preamble stated that "war crimes and crimes against humanity are among the gravest crimes in international law." Today no one will argue that the Nuremberg definition of war criminal is not the accepted standard.

Another distinction must be noted and discussed, for it has tended to become blurred in the years since Nuremberg. The terms "Nazi" and "war criminal" are not, nor have they ever seriously been considered, synonymous. A "Nazi" was a member of the *National Sozialistiche Deutsche Arbeiter Partei* (NSDAP), which translates as the National Socialist German Workers Party. Even when Bernays and others were drafting a war criminal statute based on organizational guilt and a conspiracy theory, they never advanced the idea that mere Party membership should brand someone as a war criminal. The organizations that they defined as criminal were those like the Gestapo. (By the same token, the point should also be made that relatively few members of the Germany military, especially in the enlisted ranks, were party members and, in fact, regulations prohibited party membership, except in certain assignments.)

There is ample reason why the distinction drawn at the time of Nuremberg between mere Party membership and criminal conduct has all but gotten lost. Clearly, every high-ranking member of the Reich, and for that matter of the German military's officer corps, was a Party member, as was virtually every member of the Gestapo. But they have been charged as war criminals for their violations of specific provisions of Article 6, not simply for party membership. In the United States, as prosecutions have sought to denaturalize those who lied on entrance visa applications, the distinction between Party membership and war crimes has become increasingly blurred. By statute, Nazi Party membership is sufficient for denying an entry visa and lying about party membership is a sufficient cause for denaturalization. But here, too, Party membership alone does not brand the accused as a war criminal. This applies only if the accused committed specific acts against humanity or war crimes as defined in the London Agreement. But media treatment of many of these cases has failed to make this distinction.

In 1945 the Nuremberg Tribunal's work began. To support its efforts, a small city had to be established within the Palace of Justice in Nuremberg, including a cafeteria, a barber shop, a dentist's office, a tailor, and a post office. Five thousand people had to be housed, including the prosecution team and court officials, security guards, cooks, waiters, journalists, and VIP visitors from many nations. The United States alone had a team of more than 600 prosecutors. The British sent 160 people and the French and the Soviets had scores of lawyers and assistants rotating in and out of Nuremberg.

Prosecutors assembled a list of more than 5,000 potential defendants. By mutual agreement, 24 of them were chosen to stand in the dock at the first trial:*

Of these defendants, Ley committed suicide, Krupp was considered too infirm to stand trial, and Bormann escaped and was tried in absentia. Thus twenty-one defendants stood trial jointly.

The trial started on November 20, 1945, and continued through August 31, 1946. Four-hundred and three open sessions were held. By the time it ended, it was the longest trial in history. Over 3 million documents were produced, and 80,000 feet of film had been introduced into evidence along with 88,000 affi-

---

* *Hermann Goering,* Commander of the German Air Force and Hitler's designated heir; *Rudolf Hess,* Hitler's deputy and second in line to succeed him; *Joachim von Ribbentrop,* Minister of Foreign Affairs; *Robert Ley,* Labor Minister; *Wilhelm Keitel,* head of the High Command; *Ernst Kaltenbrunner,* head of the Security Police; *Alfred Rosenberg,* Minister for the Occupied Territories; *Hans Frank,* Governor of Poland; *Wilhelm Frick,* Interior Minister; *Julius Streicher,* newspaper editor and propagandist; *Walter Funk,* head of the Reichsbank; *Hjalmar Schacht,* Finance Minister; *Gustav Krupp,* munitions industrialist; *Karl Doenitz,* Naval admiral and Hitler's actual successor; *Erich Raeder,* Navy Commander-in-Chief; *Baldur von Schirach,* Youth Minister; *Fritz Sauckel,* Assistant Labor Minister; *Alfred Jodl,* head of planning for the High Command; *Martin Bormann,* head of the Party Chancery; *Franz von Papen,* Vice Chancellor; *Arthur Seyss-Inquart,* Governor of the Netherlands; *Albert Speer,* Munitions Minister; *Constantin von Neuarth,* Governor of Czechoslovakia; *Hans Fritzsche,* propagandist and Radio Minister.

davits signed by a total of 150,000 people. Another 150,000 persons had submitted documents on behalf of various organizations around the world. Thirty-three witnesses had been questioned exhaustively for the prosecution and sixty-one for the defense.

The world was listening on October 1, 1946, to a special radio hookup originating at Nuremberg when the tribunal's president, Britain's Lord Justice Geoffrey Lawrence, read the various sentences. In the end, eighteen men were convicted. For varying technical reasons, Schacht, Papen, and Fritzsche were acquitted. Of the eighteen men convicted, eleven—Goering, Ribbentrop, Keitel, Kaltenbrunner, Streicher, Seyss-Inquart, Rosenberg, Jodl, Frank, Frick and Sauckel—were sentenced and eventually hanged.

At 6:15 A.M. on the 16th day of October 1946, the Allied control council in Berlin announced to the world, "The sentences of death passed by the international military tribunal at Nuremberg on October 1, 1946, on the undermentioned war criminals were carried out this day. . . ." Then in a footnote it added: "Hermann Wilhelm Goering took his own life on October 15, 1946." The ashes of Goering and all the others were disposed of secretly after the cremation that had been ordered by the court.

Three of the other defendants received life sentences and four were given sentences ranging from ten to twenty years. By 1970 all of these seven had either died or been released from custody except for Rudolf Hess, who remained the sole inmate of Spandau Prison until his death in 1987.

Of Hess, the Lord Justice said, "Hess had been in prison with Hitler in 1924 and became his closest confidant, a relationship which lasted until his flight to the British Isles. As Deputy to the Fuhrer, he was the top man in the Nazi Party, with responsibility for handling all party matters. Throughout the pre-war years, he supported Hitler's policy of vigorous armament. Between 1933 and 1937, Hess occasionally made speeches advocating international cooperation. But nothing he said or did can alter the fact that Hess knew better than any other individual how determined Hitler was to realize his ambitions and how fanatical and violent a man he was."

Five organizations were declared criminal conspiracies under the terms of Article 6: the Gestapo; the SS; the SD, a state security service; the SA, a paramilitary organization; and the leadership corps of the Nazi Party. But the judges held that no member of these organizations could be could be considered a war criminal per se by reason of party membership. If members of these groups were tried later, they would have to be convicted of committing specific acts in violation of Article 6.

As the trial drew to a close, debate raged as to the next step. American Telford Taylor had been designated Justice Jackson's successor as chief war crimes prosecutor. He was prepared to move forward with the trials of up to 400 more accused at a half-dozen separate sites throughout the Occupied Zone. Washington was opposed to the idea because of the cost that would be involved. The Soviets disliked it because of the time involved. Even Jackson opposed the plan as too grandiose and simply not worth the trouble.

In the end, an additional 185 defendants stood trial over the next two-and-a-half years. But the prosecutions became progressively more difficult, and the results more mixed. In case after case, a separate tribunal established to review sentences lowered or commuted them altogether. Finally, Cold War considerations prevailed: Americans now saw the Soviet Union as "the enemy," and the heart went out of Nazi prosecutions. In 1949 the Nuremberg prosecutors closed up shop.

At the same time that the International Tribunal at Nuremberg was doing its work, "lesser offenders," as they were termed, were being tried by other Allied tribunals, German state courts—which the London Agreement had given jurisdiction in perpetuity over war crime cases—and so-called Denazification courts. American military tribunals eventually heard another 184 cases, which resulted in 130 convictions. Twelve convicted defendants were executed, twenty received life sentences, and the others were sentenced to shorter terms. By 1958 all those imprisoned had been set free. Those accused and tried before other Allied military tribunals did not fare as well: 462 were eventually executed, most by the Soviets.

Under the designation of criminal organizations established by the International Tribunal, and other standards, almost 3.5 million persons were potential defendants before the Denazification courts. Fewer than one million were ever brought to trial, mostly in very large groups, of whom only 9,600 were sentenced to prison. By 1949 all but 300 of them had been released.

The record of the German state courts is even more mixed. Since 1945 only 6,481 individuals have been convicted of war crimes. Of those convicted, only 12 were sentenced to death and executed; another 158 were given life sentences. Few, if any, are still in prison today. (See chapter 12.)

Even before the International Tribunal had completed its work, a fierce debate had broken out on both sides of the Atlantic. The London Agreement had clearly specified that the International Tribunal was being set up to try "major" Nazi figures. Almost everyone could agree that an Eichmann or a Mengele was a war criminal. But what about the men who carried out Eichmann's orders for a Final Solution? Again, there might be little doubt that the man who operated the gas ovens at Auschwitz was a war criminal, but what about those who designed or built the ovens? What about the guards at the camp, or on the trains that brought millions of Jews to the camps? What about those who operated and scheduled the trains? And what about the propagandists who created the climate that allowed the whole terrible business to take place?

Clearly, under the conspiracy theory advanced by Article 6, all of them could be considered war criminals. But the further down the line one went from those giving the orders, or actually committing the atrocities, the greater the debate over whether defendants were actually culpable.

Then, too, there was considerable debate over whether Article 6 even applied to accused who were not major figures. Could, for example, a guard at Auschwitz be accused of a "crime against humanity" because he personally persecuted on the basis of race, religion, or political belief? Or, even more difficult, because he was part—albeit a very small part—of what would be termed today a "criminal enterprise" that persecuted on these bases? To an extent, this debate has been more theoretical and academic than real, for once the Allied military tribunals and the Denazification courts ended their work in 1950, almost every war crimes prosecution has been for specific acts committed by specific individuals against specific victims, as opposed to generalized prosecutions based on the commission of crimes against humanity within the framework of Article 6.

There has never been serious debate in the United States about trying accused war criminals in U.S. courts for the crimes of which they are accused. It has always been assumed that U.S. courts lack jurisdiction over such crimes, committed in distant lands, and such prosecution would be unconstitutional.

Justice Department prosecutions are for violations of the immigration laws, leading to denaturalization and deportation. In these proceedings the defendant is often accused of specific acts, but only to show the materiality of concealing facts on the original visa or citizenship application, or the absence of the "good moral character" required for naturalization and U.S. citizenship. Those few postwar prosecutions around the world that have been based on generalized "crimes against humanity" have been against defendants like Eichmann, who would have been tried at Nuremberg had they not successfully fled or hidden. However, at this writing a debate over the application of Article 6 to rank-and-file defendants is emerging in Canada, Australia, and Great Britain. (see chapters 10 and 11). For years, these three countries all but ignored the question of whether war criminals were living in their midst. But as the result of a 1987 reexamination of the problem, the Canadian Parliament has decided not to follow the U.S. model of trying simply to denaturalize and expel war criminals. Rather, it will seek jurisdiction and try the accused for their crimes, wherever committed, and those prosecutions will be based on the definition of war criminal contained in the London Agreement. Australia, too, has passed such a law and Britain is starting what will probably be a long debate in Parliament on whether to take this approach. It will be years before the high courts in these countries finally decide whether such prosecution is possible.

Waldheim: What Is The Truth?

No one accuses former United Nations Secretary-General Kurt Waldheim, now president of Austria, of being a Nazi war criminal on the scale of a Mengele, an Eichmann, or any of those hanged at Nuremberg. But in the last few years, a firestorm of debate has arisen over what role Waldheim played in World War II and whether he was connected with war crimes or perhaps even committed them himself.

As the world has been caught up in the Waldheim debate, there has been renewed interest in the whole subject of hidden war criminals. In great measure, the search for the truth about Waldheim became a symbol for today's on-going hunt for war criminals.

The Waldheim case study is uniquely important for anyone trying to understand the philosophy behind the ongoing hunt for Nazi war criminals.

Certainly, in and of itself, this is a mystery with every possible appeal. A powerful statesman in charge of an international organization has a secret past that is discovered just as he is seeking a national presidency. He wins the election despite the revelations, and this accelerates the investigation of his own career and that of other Nazis. But, in addition to the personal aspect of the Waldheim situation, and the hurt and anger it evokes in many who worked with him at the United Nations, his life is very much a symbol of what the Nazi hunt is all about.

In January 1980, Kurt Waldheim was comfortably situated in his glass-enclosed office with a magnificent view of Manhattan from atop the United Nations building on the East River. He was serving his second term as leader of the most prestigious international organization the world has ever known. At twelve o'clock noon daily, his press aide would meet with members of the United Nations press corps. Most of them were regulars who spent considerable time tracing stories of particular interest to the countries where their newspapers, radio stations, or TV outlets were based. As a rule, nothing very significant happens in a press briefing, except before the arrival of a head of state, or just after a significant vote.

After the regular questions on a dozen routine matters were concluded on January 16, a hand went up in the back of the room. Hillel Seidman stood up and asked in a clear, but accented voice: "How is the secretary-general going to answer the serious charges that he was a member of a Nazi youth group and a member of the Nazi Party?"

Seidman sat down. The press spokesman for Waldheim dismissed the question by saying, "That is ridiculous."

To the shame of all the journalists present, no one reported the story. No wire copy reached the newspapers of the world, and radio and television audiences heard nothing about the fact that a man named Hillel Seidman had asked the secretary-general of the United Nations such a shocking question. Who was this man?

Seidman was born in Poland in 1915. He was the only member of his family to survive the mass killings by the Nazis in the Warsaw ghetto. During the war years, he worked as a secretary to the Jewish members of the Polish Parliament and led a variety of Jewish community activities. He planned to escape by getting credentials from a friend to travel to Paraguay, but that hope did not materialize. He was jailed for being Jewish, spent several months in prison, and was then interned in a ghetto for a year and a half. After the war, he finally realized his dream of emigration and came to the United States in 1946.

Seidman spent many years working as a journalist, and his fascination with international events often focused his attention upon the United Nations. When Waldheim was a candidate for his second term as secretary-general, Seidman became curious about his background. Seidman went about his research methodically, and began by getting all the handout biographies and *Who's Who* material he could find. But he was disturbed see that there seemed to be a gap in every biographical work: it simply was not clear where Kurt Waldheim had been from 1943 to 1945.

As in all police work and journalistic investigation, a tip can help a great deal, and a member of Waldheim's U.N. staff guided Seidman's research by telling him exactly where to look and what he would find.

It seemed too impossible to take seriously. After all, Kurt Waldheim was one of the most respected and powerful diplomats in the world. Based on the documentation he reviewed, Seidman became convinced that the secretary-general of the United Nations had indeed been a member of the Nazi youth movement and later a member of the Nazi Party.

Even the World Jewish Congress was skeptical at first, but Seidman's sincerity, and the nature of the congress itself, made it inevitable that the group would be instrumental in getting his story told. The World Jewish Congress suggested that the journalist write to Congressman Stephen Solarz, a liberal Jewish Democrat who represented Seidman's section of Brooklyn. Solarz says he was shocked by the suggestion that the secretary-general of the U.N. had been a member of the Nazi Party. But shortly thereafter he ran across a brief reference in an issue of *The New Republic* to the effect that Waldheim had been a member of the Nazi student union. This persuaded Solarz to pursue the matter. (That *New Republic* item by journalist-author Shirley Hazzard was the initial published revelation alerting the world to the existence of the Waldheim-Nazi connection. It is grossly unfair that her outstanding work has not received the credit it deserves in subsequent detailing of the story.)

After discussing the charges with friends in New York and staff members of the House Foreign Affairs Committee, of which he was a key member, Solarz wrote to Waldheim and asked for clarification of his background. At the same time, he made an official request to the Central Intelligence Agency for any information in their files that would bear on Waldheim's background and the secretary-general's activities during World War II.

Waldheim responded almost immediately. It is now clear that he lied when he responded to Congressman Solarz: "First of all, I wish to say that I was never associated in any way with the Nazi youth movement.... I certainly had no contact with or connection with any extermination units. I myself was wounded on the eastern front, and being incapacitated from further service at the front resumed my law studies at the University of Vienna where I was graduated in 1944."

At the same time, the Central Intelligence Agency responded in a way that seemed to back Waldheim's position. The agency said it had no information in its files whatsoever about Waldheim's background. Further, it had made "inquiries" which led to the conclusion that Waldheim had no meaningful World War II service in the German Army. "We believe Waldheim was not a member of the Nazi youth movement, nor was he involved in anti-Jewish activities," the CIA said. This, coming on the heels of Waldheim's flat-out denial, was enough to satisfy the curious Congressman and anyone else who would seriously entertain Seidman's claims or Hazzard's charges.

Years later, we were able to confirm that at the time the CIA denied having any files on Waldheim it did have a copy of a background report on him prepared prior to the end of the war by its predecessor, the Office of Strategic Services. The CIA apparently considered the report so embarrassing that in 1988 it still refuses to release it, citing national security considerations. We also have confirmed that the new CIA "inquiry" that the agency referred to in its response to Solarz's request had been limited to asking the Austrian Foreign Office for details.

Years passed and nothing more was heard about charges of Waldheim's Nazi service. In 1982 Waldheim retired as secretary-general and returned to Austria. Four years later something seemingly insignificant happened to change all that. In January 1986, a move was underway in Austria to establish a memorial at the Vienna Air Force Academy honoring General Alexander Loehr, a founder of the modern Austrian Air Force. But, during the war, he had also been the commanding officer of infamous German Army E Group in the Balkans, and had later been executed by the Yugoslavian government as a war criminal. There was overwhelming evidence that Loehr had been personally responsible for the killing of tens of thousands of innocent civilians.

In a January issue of the Austrian magazine *Profil,* there was a favorable discussion of the proposal to build the memorial to Loehr. The article included a comment made by Manfried Rauchensteiner, a prominent Austrian, stating that Loehr was "a man to be admired" and pointing out that outstanding men like Kurt Waldheim had "served in his command." Today, as Waldheim remains in the Austrian presidency, disgraced by the findings of his country's hand-picked commission of historians and the subject of editorials worldwide demanding his resignation, that magazine article seems particularly ironic. Its support for paying tribute to a senior Nazi officer responsible for mass murder is justified by associating him with a distinguished political leader whose Nazi background was not yet known to the world.

Rauchensteiner's off-hand comment received little notice, but it struck a jarring note with Elan Steinberg at the World Jewish Congress offices in New York. He had never forgotten the charges that had been leveled against Waldheim by Hillel Seidman seven years earlier. This was the first time he had seen anything that even began to corroborate what Seidman had said.

Immediately, the World Jewish Congress dispatched an investigator to Austria to find out more about the relationship between Waldheim and Loehr. He returned to New York armed with a now famous photograph taken on May 22, 1943, on a German airstrip in Podgorica, Yugoslavia, which shows Waldheim in his Nazi uniform with an Italian officer and two-high level Nazi officers, including General Arthur Phleps, commander of the 7th SS Division. The investigation also bore documents detailing Waldheim's military service and showing clearly that both the letter written by Waldheim to Congressman Solarz and the CIA report on Waldheim were false and misleading.

★ ★ ★

It was 3:00 P.M. in Vienna on February 10, 1986, and Kurt Waldheim, candidate for the Austrian presidency, was attending a meeting of his senior advisors who were briefing him on European economic matters. At the same hour, a meeting was convening in an office building in New York, which was to have an indelible impact on Kurt Waldheim's life and would rewrite recent history.

Edgar M. Bronfman, president of the World Jewish Congress and a multimillionaire business executive, was being briefed by Elan Steinberg, executive

director, and Israel Singer, the WJC's secretary-general. They showed Bronfman the photograph and documents their investigator had found in Austria
and requested permission to move ahead with a full-scale, worldwide investigation of Kurt Waldheim.

The political ramifications were enormous for the World Jewish Congress
and for world Jewry. It should be noted that Waldheim and his defenders have
often charged that the flood of derogatory information about his wartime career was generated by political opponents in Austria during his presidential
campaign. The three men meeting in that New York office were not even
aware of, nor had they any interest in, internal Austrian politics except as it affects the Jewish community.

The World Jewish Congress had no significant history as a Nazi-hunting organization. It had been designed to coordinate positive efforts of Jewish communities throughout the world. Nevertheless, despite the risk and sensitivity
of the issue, Bronfman initialed and approved a memorandum outlining what
was necessary for a full-scale investigation of Waldheim. He wrote "Do it."

And they did.

While WJC investigators dug into archives in several European capitals, they
located the former head of the CIA's Questioned Documents Division, Robert
Crown. They hired him as a consultant to verify the authenticity of the photograph of Waldheim with SS General Phleps, and a second photo discovered by
WJC investigators, this one showing a group of Nazi officers, including Waldheim and the infamous General Loehr, gathered around a map table on December 3, 1944. This photo was especially incriminating, because it showed
that Waldheim was still on Loehr's staff at the end of 1944. Steinberg was determined that nothing should be made public about Waldheim unless it was irrefutable, or the whole effort would fail.

By the last week in February 1986, Steinberg believed he had enough solid
evidence to make the story public. He turned his documents over to *The New
York Times* and said the newspaper could authenticate them in any way it
chose. The *Times* put reporters to work in Vienna, Bonn, and New York, and
within a week was ready to go into print.

On March 4, 1986, the *Times* published its first story on Kurt Waldheim's
hidden past; it created a media and political shockwave around the world.

"Files Show Kurt Waldheim Served Under War Criminal," read the front-
page headline. The story, datelined Vienna, began:

> *Kurt Waldheim, former secretary-general of the United Nations, was at-
> tached to a German Army command in World War II that fought brutal cam-
> paigns against Yugoslav partisans and engaged in mass deportations of Greek
> Jews, according to documents made available here.*

The documents also show that, as a young man, he was enrolled in two Nazi Party organizations. . . . Documents about his military service were made available to the Times *by the World Jewish Congress and were corroborated independently by the* Times.

The story went on to detail how Waldheim had denied all previous charges of membership in any Nazi organization, and it pointed out that all of Waldheim's authorized biographies described him as having been discharged from the army after his wounds on the Russian front.

In an interview granted the *Times*, Waldheim for the first time acknowledged his membership in the two Nazi youth organizations. But he claimed they were "totally harmless, completely uninteresting" groups established by a few students "for social gatherings, coffee parties and things like that." He also acknowledged his service under General Loehr, but insisted that he had been only a very low-level staff interpreter. He acknowledged the authenticity of the photograph of himself with Loehr, but claimed this was the only occasion during his service career that he had been with the general. Another document that had been uncovered showed that Waldheim had been decorated with a special Croatian service medal—the King Zvonimir Silver Medal for "heroic bravery in battle against the insurgents"—in the latter half of 1942. Waldheim dismissed the fact, stating that "they were handed out like confetti," as a kind of good-conduct medal. Later research shows that although some 20,000 German officers were eligible for the medal, only three, Waldheim and two others, were awarded the honor. As for forgetting two-and-a-half years of military service in his official biography, Waldheim stated boldly, "I never said my book made any claim to completeness."

On March 7, 1986, three days after the first *New York Times* article appeared, the telephone rang at World Jewish Congress headquarters in New York: Kurt Waldheim was asking for Edgar Bronfman. Because Bronfman was traveling, Waldheim talked to Elan Steinberg, claiming that he was innocent of everything he had been accused of in *The New York Times* and by the wire services and world newspapers that were picking up the *Times* story. Steinberg cleverly asked him to put his thoughts into writing so that he could review them point by point with Bronfman.

Waldheim then made perhaps the most serious tactical mistake of his post-United Nations career. He did put it in writing. Former Nazis would do better to restrict their confessions and their lies to the telephone.

Waldheim telegraphed Bronfman claiming that *The New York Times* article and all of the press reports based upon it were fabricated to "damage my international standing and my position as a candidate in the Austrian presidential election. The timing, two months before election, and the fact that during thirty years of service for my own country and ten years as Secretary-General of the United Nations, such accusations had never materialized or have been substantiated are self-explanatory."

Waldheim claimed that his political reliability had been checked by the Austrian authorities and the intelligence services of various nations without any confirmation of "my membership in Nazi organizations or in military activities that could be considered war crimes." He went on to state specifically, that "I was not a member of the SA or any other organization of the Nazi regime," and to deny having served in any army unit linked with war crimes against partisans operating in the Balkans and with the deportation of Greek Jews. He said, "I wish to state categorically that I had nothing whatever to do with such atrocities." He concluded that everything said about him was "completely unfounded and unsubstantiated." It is ironic that after Austria's International Commission of Historians filed their report, Waldheim admitted most of the things he had denied in this early telegram.

Elan Steinberg has a journalist's nose for news, a trial lawyer's ability to dig out facts, and a good detective's willingness to spend the time necessary to find the truth. Apparently, material about Kurt Waldheim and his activities during World War II was abundant in Europe. Now Steinberg began to wonder, if European archives contained so much material on Waldheim's army service, what U.S. archives might contain. Robert Herzstein of the University of South Carolina is a respected historian on World War II. Steinberg recruited him and dispatched him to Washington to determine what might be in official U.S. archives about General Loehr's command. In fact, given the CIA response to Congressman Solarz's request years before, neither Steinberg nor Herzstein was very hopeful. But almost as soon as Herzstein started poring through microfilm in a National Archives annex in suburban Maryland, he began finding records of Waldheim's wartime Nazi service.

The most damaging evidence by far was a 1948 list of known war criminals compiled by the U.S. Army on the basis of War Crimes Commission records. Scanning the long list, entitled "Combined Registry of War Criminals and Security Suspects (CROWCASS) Final Consolidated Wanted List," Herzstein flipped through to *W*. There it was, entry 313622—Lieutenant Kurt Waldheim, listed as a criminal at large. An adjacent column cited "Reason Wanted." Waldheim's listing had a one-word entry: "murder."

The newly found U.S. documents were given to *The New York Times* and, on March 25, the paper printed the full story. It took only a few days for reaction stories to appear around the world. Now the floodgates were open, and public opinion was turning rapidly against Waldheim: neither he nor the hunt for Nazis would ever be the same.

Philosophers or jurists might argue as to who is responsible for a killing. Is it only the person who pulls the trigger, or does it include the one who made the gun and delivered it to the killer knowing how it would be used? At what point do you break the chain of guilt? Answers to these questions can be found and their relevance to the ongoing search for Nazis understood only by examining carefully the life of Kurt Waldheim.

First, there is the life that he was believed to have lived, as documented in the most comprehensive defense to date—an official Austrian government publication known as the "White Book." This 297-page book, entitled *Kurt Waldheim's Wartime Years—A Documentation,* was written by Karl Gruber, the former Austrian Foreign Minister who first brought Waldheim into government service after the war, and Ralph Scheide, a Foreign Ministry officer. Scheide says the book is a compilation of documents and an assessment refuting all accusations that have been made against Waldheim. Actually, the White Book is essentially an accumulation of press releases rehashing Waldheim's denials.

Second, there is the life documented in the United Nations archive, the Berlin Document Center, files in Zagreb, Yugoslavia, and a dozen other nations.

We went to each of the primary sources that document Waldheim's life and have included nothing in this bizarre story that has not been corroborated by at least two independent sources with evidence to support their positions. There has been little in common between the accounts of Waldheim and his supporters and those who have painted the picture of Waldheim the Nazi war criminal. The Waldheim position was founded on the outright lie that he was not serving in the German army at the time of the atrocities to which he has been linked. After it became obvious that photographs, affidavits, and witnesses could place him amid those atrocities, the Waldheim story changed and changed again. (As one commentator put it succinctly: "First he said he wasn't there. Then he admitted he was there, but didn't know what was happening. Finally, he said he knew, but that he had no control or authority.")

The world was then told that indeed Kurt Waldheim had served in the German army in 1943, 1944, and 1945, but was at no time in any area where atrocities took place. After still more evidence was introduced, yet another variation of the story said that apparently Waldheim *was* in those areas where atrocities were committed, but was not aware of them. The current variation is that Waldheim was admittedly in areas where atrocities occurred and had some knowledge of them, but certainly never participated in them. Wrong again!

In 1918, Kurt Josef Waldheim was born in Sankt Andra-Wordern in lower Austria, where his father served as a school administrator. We now know that when Waldheim was eighteen, he volunteered for military service in the Dragoon regiment at Stockerau and told friends he wanted to become a diplomat. At the same time, he began studies in Vienna, later joining the Nazi student union and later the Brown Shirts. Then he was drafted by the Wehrmacht—

the German Army—shortly after the war began and assigned to the 45th infantry division.

Waldheim was sent to the Russo-Polish border, where brutal battles were fought in 1941. The death toll was huge, and tens of thousands were injured. Waldheim was wounded in the leg, and, in December 1941, was sent to a convalescent center. After he had recovered, he was assigned to Army Group E becoming an intelligence officer and sent to Yugoslavia. What happened in the months that followed is the basis for the most serious charges of personal involvement in war crimes on Waldheim's part.

The young officer served under the previously mentioned General Loehr. His unit had the mission of eliminating pockets of partisan resistance. All sense of humanity was forgotten as partisans were taken hostage and executed and their property confiscated at the whim of any German officer. And Kurt Waldheim was guilty of "murder" and "hostage executions," according to a Yugoslav criminal file compiled in 1947.* (Why the Yugoslavs kept quiet will become clear later in this chapter.)

By examining the Yugoslavian documents and comparing them with U.S. Army records and statements from those who were on both sides of the battlefield, we end up with a dossier that confirms the fact that Waldheim helped plan reprisal measures by the German armies that resulted in the execution of thousands of civilians. The formal indictment by Yugoslavia was based on eyewitness testimony, documentary evidence, and lists and photographs referring to twenty-one villages burned to the ground. The file on Waldheim concludes that "based on everything herein exhibited, the State Commission declares Kurt Waldheim a war criminal, responsible for the war crimes qualified and described above." It describes him as "presently a fugitive" and adds that "apprehension of this criminal. . . and his extradition for trial to the Yugoslav authorities is compulsory."

While the Yugoslavs were describing Waldheim as a fugitive, the United States and its allies were apparently overlooking it for the time being, because Waldheim was permitted to join the postwar Austrian Foreign Office, which had a stated policy against accepting Nazis.

---

* Case File No. 25572, Yugoslav State Commission for Establishing of War Crimes, 1947, Belgrade. This document was submitted to the United Nations War Crimes Commission and became a part of the permanent file at the United Nations. Prior to the decision by the United Nations to open its Nazi archive, the case file was obtained by the authors from a cooperative member nation of the War Crimes Commission. A few of the documents contained in it have been discovered as exaggerated or fabricated. But the basic facts have been documented from other sources.

Among the statements against Waldheim in the Yugoslavian file are those of seven German officers and soldiers who worked with him. The file also contains captured Nazi documents stating that it is "correct to take hostages" and that "reprisal measures shall consist of executions by firing squad or by hanging and destruction of the populated areas." The Yugoslav authorities who investigated Waldheim concluded that "He was responsible for the implementation of the above-mentioned criminal order and other similar orders and for the development, creation and issuance of criminal orders."

In 1948, in London, the United Nations War Crimes Commission was asked by Yugoslavia to endorse its indictment of Kurt Waldheim. After reviewing the seven-page document of findings against Waldheim, it assigned the dossier an *A* classification, signifying that the evidence clearly justified his prosecution as a war criminal. The footnote added by the commission to the Yugoslavian documents states that "from April 1944-May 1945, Waldheim was a German intelligence officer responsible for the retaliation actions carried out by the Wehrmacht units in Yugoslavia. In this connection he is charged with murder and putting hostages to death."

One of the major sources of information for the International Commission of Historians and for the U.S. Justice Department, prior to its determination to bar Waldheim from America, were captured Nazi personnel rosters. They reflect that by December 1, 1943, Waldheim was serving as a key intelligence staff officer at the high command of Army Group E, with headquarters in Arsakli, Greece. Waldheim's commanding officer was Lieutenant Colonel Warnstorff. After steadfastly defending Waldheim's position, Warnstorff talked with the historical commission investigating Waldheim, and his testimony is a startling part of its final report.

Waldheim has claimed repeatedly that he knew nothing of Jewish deportations in Greece, but Professor Hagen Fleischler of the University of Crete, an expert on the German occupation of Greece, says that Waldheim's specific role, according to the documents he has examined, made him "one of the best informed men in the German forces, with knowledge of virtually all aspects of the occupation of the Balkans."

We were able to obtain a sample duty roster for the period when Waldheim was serving as an intelligence officer with that unit, which specified his responsibilities. They included: (1) Preparation and signing of morning and evening intelligence reports based on information from the field that included German casualties and action taken against hostages. (2) Recording such sensitive matters. 3) Responsibility for German staff briefings including discussion of the most effective use of hostages and civilian slave labor. 4) Involvement in special tasks, or *Sonderaufgaben,* a catchall description for those jobs relating to mass terror, torture, or execution, according to experts who testified at the Nuremberg Trials. Waldheim's personnel records state clearly that his duties included just such "special tasks."

It is now known that Kurt Waldheim kept under lock and key many of the most sensitive Nazi documents outlining Hitler's plan for the Balkans during the last years of World War II. Evidence found in the U.S. National Archives confirms that these documents, labeled *Geheim* (Secret), had been issued by the high command of Army Group E and dealt not only with the retaliation program against civilian hostages, but also with the strategic plan for control of the Balkans by the Nazis.

Gerald Fleming, the respected British historian, author of *Hitler and the Final Solution* and a member of the International Commission of Historians, stresses that responsibility for holding these top secret documents was delegated by the high command to "the most trusted officer within intelligence." He adds that this responsibility "indicated that the high command had complete trust in [Waldheim] and he would have knowledge of all that was happening."

Controversy arose over the revelation that Waldheim and his deputy, Helmut Poliza, were the only high-command officers of Army Group E on the personnel roster of December 1, 1943, with responsibilities for "prisoner interrogation." We have seen nineteen documents confirming Waldheim's authorship of interrogation reports of Allied prisoners. Professor Herzstein observes that "interrogation under the Germans often involved torture and almost always ended in execution."

Hitler had issued the so-called Commando Order, which required that all enemy troops captured behind German lines be "shot immediately after interrogation," or at once if not needed for interrogation. On April 5, 1944, seven British commandos and three Greek partisans were captured by the Germans and sent to Rhodes for interrogation by the high command's expert questioners. On April 24, at Group E headquarters in Arsakli, Waldheim received a report on those interrogations, accepted and signed them, and sent them on to the Gestapo. The outrage in the United Kingdom and in Greece today is based upon the belief that with a stroke of the pen, Waldheim had indicated that the interrogation was over and Hitler's mandate of death could be carried out.

Perhaps the most damaging document is the memorandum from Waldheim's intelligence unit to the commander-in-chief of the Southeast forces saying that further interrogation of prisoners in the area would be "fruitless." The Historical Commission, the U.S. Justice Department, and those who have evaluated the documents independently, have concluded that this sequence of events meant that Allied prisoners were to be turned over to the SS for the "special treatment" the Führer had ordered.

In March 1942, Waldheim completed three months of rest and home leave and returned to active military service. West German records and U.S. archives show that he arrived at Army High Command (AOK) 12 on March 14 and soon thereafter was assigned to the German liaison command of the Bader Combat Group *(Kampfgruppe Bader),* headquartered in Pljevlja, Yugoslavia. Its mission was to clear the Sarajevo-Dubrovnik-Pljevlja area of partisans and their suspected supporters. A joint German-Italian operation, it required a liaison staff between the two armies, and Waldheim was fluent in Italian. Command of the group consisted of 12th Army officers and staff officers.

The Bader Combat Group was notorious for its harsh treatment of partisans and civilians. On March 19, 1942, shortly after Waldheim's arrival, the Wehrmacht commander of the Southeast Army issued his directive on the treatment of partisan resistance fighters in Serbia and Croatia:

> *Localities in the vicinity of which attacks, destruction, explosions, or other acts of sabotage have taken place and which are suspected of having been used by the insurgents as refuges, are to be destroyed. Removal of the population to concentration camps can also be useful.*
>
> *If it is not possible to apprehend or seize the insurgents themselves, reprisal measures of a general nature may be in order, for example, the shooting of male inhabitants of nearby localities, according to a specific ratio, for example, 100 Serbs for one German killed, 50 Serbs for one German wounded.*

By the end of May, the Bader Combat Group had completed its mission successfully. In the words of the Wehrmacht report of May 23, 1942: the "resistance movement in the German area of East Bosnia has been destroyed by the Trio and Foca campaigns of the General Bader Combat Group."

Evidence of Waldheim's direct involvement in what has come to be known as the Kozara massacres begins with his assignment to the West Bosnian Combat Group *(Kampfgruppe Westbosnien)* in June 1942, after it absorbed certain members of the recently disbanded Bader Combat Group. Captured Nazi documents obtained from Croatian archives show that Waldheim was a member of the Command Staff *(Führungsstab)* of the West Bosnian Combat Group, which carried out the Kozara operation. During the summer of 1942, in the Kozara mountain region, this group directed a vicious anti-partisan campaign in West Bosnia (now Yugoslavia) under command of the notorious General Friedrich Von Stahl. Five thousand resistance fighters and unarmed civilians were killed. Twelve thousand—many of them noncombatants—were taken prisoner. In the "cleansing operation" (destruction of whole villages) that followed, thousands of peasants were shot, and more than 68,000 inhabitants, primarily women and children, were deported to concentration camps in forced marches on which most of them died. Indeed, a German chronicler of the 714th Division candidly refers to the operation as "the final liquidation" of "subhumans" *(untermenschen),* carried out "without pity or mercy," because only "a cold heart can command what needs to be commanded."

On March 16, 1986, Kurt Waldheim assured the Yugoslavian newspaper *Vecernje Novosti* that he had taken no part in any operations in the Balkans. On March 26, after the paper published excerpts from Yugoslav War Crimes Commission files, he admitted: "At the time of 'Operation Kozara,' I was in that territory, but was not directly involved in the fighting." When a reporter asked him how he could have denied taking part in military operations, he replied: "Who can remember everything from the war period?"

On April 6, 1986, Waldheim issued a 13-page memorandum defending himself in which he claimed that although he had been appointed to "Combat Group West Bosnia" as an "interpreter" in April 1942, "this was followed by immediate assignment as a liaison officer" to an Italian unit 125 miles away. A second version of the memo on April 12 told the same story.

However, as mentioned earlier, documentary evidence discloses that for his performance at Kozara, the Croatian government awarded Waldheim the Zvonimir medal, with oak clusters, on July 22, 1942—at the recommendation of General Von Stahl. And in the commemorative roll appended to the German military account, only 34 men (of the 20,000 who participated in the campaign) were mentioned. Twenty-fifth on the list was Kurt Waldheim.

German war documents also reveal that Waldheim was a member of the small German detachment responsible for the deportations from Kozara to Nazi concentration camps. Until October 1986, Waldheim had denied being at the site of the deportations, but in a dramatic admission to *The Washington Post,* he conceded that his long-standing account was incorrect and that he was indeed serving in Kozara at the time of massacres and deportations. While insisting he had nothing to do with such crimes, Waldheim told the *Post* that he "was assigned as a special missions staff officer to the staff of the Quartermaster" and "had the duties of supply officer." However, a series of captured German documents reveals that Waldheim's Quartermaster unit was assigned direct responsibility for the concentration camp deportations that led to the deaths of tens of thousands of innocent civilians. They contain the special orders for deportation, including a June 4, 1942, order from General Von Stahl assigning Waldheim's unit the task of establishing "prisoner collecting points." A secret order dated the previous day instructed Waldheim's Quartermaster unit to advise headquarters in advance of all prisoner deportations to Belgrade, specifying "anticipated arrival date and numbers." The unit was "to reach agreement with the Croatian government" concerning deportation to "Croatian camps." However, on June 5, revised orders came through to the effect that "deportation of prisoners to Croatian concentration camps is to be handled by the German unit itself."

In late July 1942, Waldheim arrived at headquarters of the German 12th

Army in Salonika, Greece. On July 13, shortly before his arrival, 9,000 Jewish men and young boys were summoned to Liberty Square at dawn and made to stand in the blazing Greek sun from 8 A.M. until late afternoon. If anyone moved or shaded his eyes, he was beaten senseless by the German soldiers who ringed the square. The brutality continued for several weeks.

In his memorandums of April 6 and 12, 1986, Waldheim said that he worked as an "interpreter" in Arsakli (a hilltop site, on the outskirts of Salonika, known locally as "Panorama" because of its clear view of the city below) until he went on "study leave"—in mid-November 1942—to write his doctoral thesis on the 19th-century Pan-German Nationalist Konstantin Frantz.*

During Waldheim's absence from the Balkans, the war intensified and the Wehrmacht High Command received the following orders from Hitler and relayed them to forces in the field:

> *If this struggle against the guerrillas is not conducted both in the East and in the Balkans with the most brutal means at hand, in the foreseeable future there will no longer be enough forces available to overcome this pestilence.*
>
> *The Armed Forces are therefore entitled and obligated to utilize every means in this struggle without restriction, even against women and children, as long as it brings success.*
>
> *This struggle has nothing to do with soldier chivalry or with the obligations of the Geneva Convention.*

In January 1943, AOK 12 was absorbed by the newly created Army Group E, headquartered in Arsakli and commanded by Loehr. The deportation of the Jewish community of Salonika began in mid-March 1943. Over the next two months, Wehrmacht personnel serving under Loehr worked alongside the SS in directing the deportation of Salonika's Jews to the death camp at Auschwitz (Oswiecim), Poland, where they were killed in gas chambers.

Waldheim has repeatedly admitted returning to headquarters in Arsakli by March/April 1943. Thus he was there during the period when more than 40,000 Jews—about one-fifth of Salonika's population—were deported. Almost daily, 2,500 Jewish men, women, and children were packed into Wehr-

---

* The thesis was made public during hearings of the House Subcommittee on Human Rights on April 22, 1986, and it reveals something of Waldheim's own "mindset." Applying Frantz's 19th-century ideology to his own time, Waldheim wrote:

> [I]n consequence of the current great conflict of the Reich with the non-European world, in magnificent collaboration of all the peoples of Europe under the leadership of the Reich, the way is being prepared against the . . . danger from the east [Russia]. The realization of the [Reich concept] is the rational calling of Germany . . . through the concept of the Reich these words . . . will be realized: Europe has fallen through Germany, but it is through Germany that it must be resurrected.

macht freight trains and hauled off to Auschwitz. Waldheim admits that he ventured into the city occasionally, but insists not only that he had nothing to do with this atrocity, but that he did not even notice that the Jews were disappearing. (On March 9, 1987, Colonel Roman Loos, former head of the German Secret Field Police in the area, was quoted by the Associated Press as stating, "He didn't know about that? That was known to everybody.")

When the World Jewish Congress discovered the photograph of General Phleps, Commander of the Prinz Eugen Division, with Kurt Waldheim, it did not know just how much that photograph suggested. Phleps had been responsible for launching "Operation Black" against the partisans in Yugoslavia, who were fighting mainly in Montenegro. From May 15 to June 15, 1943, the most extreme reprisal measures were taken, because the German and Italian armies had been unable to crush partisan resistance in Yugoslavia.

The order for Operation Black stipulated that "The troops must move against the hostile populace without consideration and with brutal severity, and must deny the enemy any possibility of existence by destroying abandoned villages and securing existing supplies." A May 22 meeting Waldheim attended at Podgorica was a key strategy session for the ongoing execution of this operation. The following day the Prinz Eugen Division attacked just east of Podgorica to "clean up" the area. Waldheim's superior, Colonel Macholz, directed coordination of the German units and the 14th Italian Army Corps under General Roncaglia.

Ultimately, Operation Black resulted in the murder of more than 16,000 of the "enemy," including 12,000 persons described in German reports only as communists. According to Professor Jozo Tomasevich of San Francisco State University, "the shooting of partisan prisoners, a practice consistently followed by the Germans, probably reached its peak during Operation Black." Thus, a captured Wehrmacht document notes that of the 498 prisoners taken by one German unit during this operation, all were shot. A May 30, 1943, order from one of the combat groups involved commands, "Now that encirclement is complete . . . let no able-bodied man leave the circle alive."

Yugoslav survivors have described the horrors perpetrated by German forces against civilians during Operation Black. The testimony of one such survivor, Mrs. Marcia Blagojevic, on the fate of inhabitants of the village of Bukovac, is quoted in a 1947 report by the Yugoslav War Crimes Commission. The Germans had rounded up the villagers and taken them to a nearby hillside. Mrs. Blagojevic described what followed (There is a dispute among historians as to the accuracy of Mrs. Blagojevic's description.):

The Germans immediately opened fire from machine-guns and tommy-guns on the people herded on the slope. One could hear the horrible cries of women and children and the shouting of men. A couple of Germans tore from my hands my six-year-old child and slaughtered him in front of me. Then they cut him to pieces and forced me to take the pieces into my hands. I also saw a group of people being shot in front of a house after they had been bestially thrown into the house, and the whole thing set on fire. . . . Another lot of people were taken to a place called Dolia, where they were shot.

When asked by an Austrian journalist whether he knew anything about Operation Black, Waldheim replied, "I don't remember anything."

Moshe Mayuni, a Greek Jew who now lives in Tel Aviv, claims Waldheim, then a lieutenant, came to Yanina, his village in northwestern Greece, in early 1944 to supervise the detention and transportation of 1,860 Jews who lived there. Under his supervision, the Jews were forced to construct their own detention center in the town of Larisa, and from there most were sent to Auschwitz and other slave labor camps from which they never returned. Mayuni recalls that "Waldheim was the central figure and was obviously in charge."

Mayuni went on to tell Michael Ross of *The Los Angeles Times* that "I could never forget him because I saw him more than once." He added that Waldheim was particularly cold, and that he confiscated victims' valuables. "He had my brother and another man beaten on the head with a club" for not following an order immediately."

Another witness, Marco Matza, who is also an Israeli citizen, claims that he, too, was among the Greek Jews seized by Nazi troops in Yanina early in 1944 and sent to a detention center, from which he was deported. Like Mayuni, he said he recognized Waldheim immediately from the World War II photographs of him on Israeli television when the story of his Nazi career broke.

"When I saw his picture that had been taken in 1943 on television, the electricity went through my body, and I knew that I knew this man and that he was the commander there," Matza told *Los Angeles Times* reporter Ross.

Again, Waldheim has refused comment. Some historians believe the Greek accusers to be well-intentioned but not really able to identify Waldheim. Others are satisfied as to their truthfulness.

It is apparent from examination of captured Nazi documents, and evidence uncovered by Greek and Yugoslav historians, that Waldheim, the highly respected intelligence officer, was shuttling constantly between Greece and various parts of Yugoslavia at this time. In the early stages of his defense, efforts were made to convince his critics and the media that he could not have been in Greece because he was in Yugoslavia. Apparently, these efforts were aimed at anyone who did not have a map. The proximity of the towns involved and the description of his role in Nazi records makes it clear that he was in a position of authority in both areas at various times in 1943 and 1944.

Waldheim's personnel roster specifies that as an intelligence officer of the high command, his responsibilities included general staff briefings. His importance at Army Group E headquarters is indicated by the fact that he gave oral briefings to General Erich Schmidt-Richberg, general staff chief of the group's high command. Several Wehrmacht reports on such briefings found in the U.S. National Archives indicate that only three officers were present at these meetings: Schmidt-Richberg, Waldheim, and a First Lieutenant Frey.

In the first of three documents, dated May 20, 1944, Waldheim briefed the chief of staff, General Schmidt-Richberg, on "the situation in the Mediterranean, Italy and the Balkans." At the meeting, Schmidt-Richberg discussed the "effective" uses of hostages on a train in the Greek Peloponnesus "to insure the security of rail transport." (To discourage the Greek resistance from firing upon or sabotaging trains under German control, the Germans would round up Greek civilians and pack them into large cages, which were then attached to the front of the trains. Thus, the civilian hostages were exposed to any gunfire or explosive aimed at the trains by anti-Nazi partisans.)

Another document reports on a meeting of June 13, 1944, during which Waldheim provided an intelligence briefing to General Schmidt-Richberg, who, in turn, spoke on the use of civilian slave labor in Greece. Under the Nuremberg Tribunal's charter, the utilization of slave labor is a crime against humanity.

A third Nazi war document places Kurt Waldheim at a top secret briefing given by a senior German general after the attempted assassination of Hitler. "The Fuhrer has given orders that nobody must blame the officer corps for the [assassination] attempt," the document quotes the general. Dated August 4, 1944, it is stamped "secret command matter" and headed "Memorandum concerning discussions with the Chief." The document also shows Waldheim briefed the general on the situation in France, Italy, and the Balkans, and on local conditions. The "situation in the East" was reported on by Frey. It also reports on the discussions of Waldheim, First Lieutenant Frey, and General August Winter, who had been recently appointed chief of the general staff, on matters ranging from complaints about the poor quality of the Italian troops allied to the Germans to concern about how the currency crisis in Greece was affecting the Nazis' ability "to get out of the country what can be gotten." General Winter told the two intelligence officers that "only a very small nucleus of officers" attempted to kill Hitler in the explosion that wounded him on July 20, 1944. Winter conveyed instructions that "in the present tense situation," German officers must guard against anything that might affect the relationship between the troops and their commanding officers.

At the end of the meeting, the discussion turned to a long-standing dispute over responsibility for security matters between the Wehrmacht (army) and the SS. Winter reports that in his conversation with Himmler, the SS chieftain had resolved the dispute in favor of the SS.

"The relationship between the Wehrmacht and the SS-Police commander has now been definitely settled," Winter states.

On August 9, 1944, Waldheim briefed General Schmidt-Richberg on "the far west, Italy, France, and the situation in the Balkans." They also discussed the success of "Operation Viper," which subsequent reports by Waldheim's office reveal as a series of mercilessly executed anti-partisan "cleansing operations" in which entire villages were destroyed by Wehrmacht units subordinate to Army Group E. Thus an Ic/AO (intelligence) evening report of August 15, 1944, includes the following summary account: "XXII Mountain Corps: 'Viper': Further cleansing with destruction of all villages without important contact with the enemy." Army Group E High Command's daily report of the same date refers to the "destruction of Karpenission and of other bandit villages" in connection with "Viper."

Documents used at Nuremberg as evidence of Nazi war crimes in Greece include a secret report on Operation Viper signed by Waldheim.

His intelligence report of August 11, 1944, which details the status of the operation, including enemy deaths, was part of Nuremberg Document NOKW-935—a series of eleven captured reports used in the prosecution of twelve German officers charged with mass murder of hostages and the "reprisal" destruction of hundreds of towns and villages in the Balkans. They contradict Waldheim's repeated claims that he knew nothing about such deportations, including his cable to World Jewish Congress president Edgar M. Bronfman on March 7, 1986, in which he said he had "never been informed" about the deportation of Greek Jews and had never "served in army units linked with . . . the deportations of Greek Jews."

Documents located at the Federal Archives in Freiburg, West Germany, specifically one dated September 22, 1944, report on the instructions for deportations issued by the Ic/AO at Waldheim's headquarters: "Deportation of Jews: End of July 1944, deportation of Jews not holding Turkish citizenship in the entire command territory [of the Commander of East Aegaies] upon instructions of the High Command of Army Group E, Ic/AO." (Within the Ic/AO, Waldheim was the designated "03" officer. As 03, he "was the deputy of the chief intelligence officer . . . responsible for all operational intelligence and the control of the intelligence staff"—from the declassified study "Germany Military Intelligence," by the U.S. War Department's Military Intelligence Division, 1946.)

The Jews on Rhodes and Crete, numbering some 2,500 men, women, and children, were rounded up and stripped of their possessions during the final weeks of July 1944. They were shipped to the Auschwitz death camp, arriving there by mid-August, and nearly all were annihilated.

A second Nazi war document, dated August 11, 1944, describes the hostile reaction of the non-Jewish inhabitants of the Greek islands to the forced deportation. This intelligence report, sent to the Waldheim unit, notes that "the evacuation of the Jews from the area under command" was received by the Greek and Italian inhabitants there "with mixed feelings. In some cases the Germans were characterized as barbarians" by the Italians and Greeks.

Corfu, like the other Greek islands, was "under the complete control of Army Group E." On April 21, 1944, Waldheim's Ic/AO group sent a secret report to the German Army unit *Korpsgruppe Joannina*, with a copy to SS headquarters in Athens, detailing the numbers of Jews and foreigners on Corfu. A week later, in an April 28 letter stamped *secret*, the Korpsgruppe asked the Ic/AO group to request that the SD and security policy "bring about implementation measures . . . [f]or the purpose of settlement of the Jewish question" by "evacuating" the 2,000 Jews remaining on Corfu. Significantly, one of the listed responsibilities of Waldheim's Ic/AO group was "cooperation with SD, the Security Policy, Field Gendarmarie."

On May 12, according to an entry in the daily war journal of Army Group E, its commander-in-chief, General Loehr, agreed to a request that the group "furnish transportation for an accelerated evacuation of the Jews." The deportation began in early June. On June 17, 1944, the SS reported that 1,795 Corfu Jews had been "seized and transported from the island." Most perished at Auschwitz shortly thereafter.

Recently discovered documents disclose that on at least two occasions in 1944, Waldheim's reports to his superiors on partisan activity were followed immediately by reprisal measures taken by German forces under command of Army Group E. Indeed, Waldheim has acknowledged in his memorandum of April 6, 1986, that he knew operational decisions were being made by General Loehr and his chief of staff, Schmidt-Richberg, on the basis of his reports. More importantly, Waldheim knew when he prepared these reports precisely what kind of "operational decisions"—i.e., reprisal measures—were being ordered: Loehr had issued a directive on August 10, 1943, that partisan activity "must be retaliated in every case with shooting or hanging of hostages, destruction of the surrounding localities, etc."

This grisly pattern can be traced readily through the documentation:

(1) Iraklion: Waldheim's August 11, 1944, evening intelligence report identified the area south of Iraklion on the island of Crete as one in which "band activity" (partisan operations) had taken place. Two days later, German forces engaged in a "cleansing" operation in which, according to a subsequent report by Waldheim's office, "they destroyed two band villages" and "shot to death 20 hostages" in the area southwest of Iraklion.

(2) Between Stip and Kocane: Captured German documents obtained from the U.S. National Archives reveal that on October 12, 1944, Waldheim identi-

fied the area surrounding the road between Stip and Kocane as the key to partisan activity in Macedonia. In his morning and evening intelligence reports, he began his analysis of Macedonia by reporting a build-up of partisan activity on the road between the two towns. Within 48 hours, German forces set fire to three villages along the road—Krupiste, Gorni Balvan, and Dolnyi Balvan—and executed 114 civilian inhabitants. *Newsweek* (April 21, 1986) reported two survivors' accounts of these massacres:

> *One survivor, Petar Kovec, now 61, was just coming home to the village of Krupiste after working in the surrounding fields. German officers rounded up all the men of the village and arranged them in rows of ten. Kovec was in the first row—but he was the eleventh man so the officers pushed him out of the group at the last moment. "When I returned, I found only the walls of our house. Everything had been burned, even the livestock."*
>
> *Risto Ognjanov was another survivor of the Krupiste massacre. "They lined us up where the monument stands today," he told Nagorski, pointing to a small monument commemorating the town's forty-nine victims. "They ordered us to crouch on all fours." Ognjanov eighty-two, demonstrated the position until his son urged him back into his chair.*
>
> *"I just dropped when the shots started. Two dead bodies fell on top of me. After the shooting, the Germans began to check who was alive by shooting bullets into the feet." The bodies covering Ognjanov protected him. When the Germans left, Ognjanov and two others crawled from the bloody pile. "For me, October 14 is my second birthday," he said, breaking into tears. "It was the beginning of my second life."*
>
> *An order to fire: After Krupiste, the Germans moved on to Gorni Balvan. "They threw hand grenades into our village to announce themselves," remembers Arsov Stojic, sixty-two. "Suddenly the order was given to fire. I fell automatically at that moment; it was a reaction of fear. After that, the soldiers shot everyone who was moaning. Every soldier checked his victim. I just lay there. I don't know how I survived. It was pure luck.*

Waldheim subsequently reported on "enemy losses" for the month of October, disclosing the enormity of the atrocities committed that month by German forces subordinate to Army Group E. Waldheim calculated "bandit" losses at 739 dead and 94 taken prisoner. The telltale datum in this report is that these 833 people had only 63 weapons among them (13 machine guns, 49 rifles, and a submachine gun). Thus, it would appear that many, if not most, of those killed were unarmed civilians—presumably including the 114 people murdered in the October 14 reprisals.

When the Yugoslav War Crimes Commission charged Waldheim with involvement in war crimes in 1947, it referred to the testimony of Karl-Heinz

Egberts-Hilker, a captain in "Reconnaissance Battalion 22" of the Wehrmacht's 22nd Infantry Division, who was hanged in Belgrade in 1948 as a war criminal for his involvement in atrocities. Waldheim's intelligence reports, located at the U.S. National Archives in April 1986, represent important corroborative evidence supporting the testimony provided forty years ago.

On a variety of occasions, including press conferences, letters to officials, government memoranda, and formal submissions to the U.S. Department of Justice, Waldheim has denied the essence of each and every charge of knowledge and/or involvement in war crimes brought against him. He has said:

"I was never associated in any way with the Nazi Youth Movement." (Letter to Congressman Stephen J. Solarz, December 1980)

"I was never a member of these [Nazi] organizations." (March 4, 1986)

"I was not a member of the SA or any other organization of the Nazi Regime." (Telex to Edgar M. Bronfman, president of the World Jewish Congress, March 7, 1986)

"Naturally, I was in the riding unit of the Consular Academy which, in the hierarchy, was placed under the Nazi Cavalry Corp." (March 22, 1986)

"I had a lot of trouble finishing my studies. So I said to myself, I can participate, and that would keep me there without being attacked . . . And so I participated." (April 4, 1986)

"The knowledge that I was serving in the German Army was hard to bear. Deliverance from my bitter situation finally came when our unit moved into active combat on the Eastern Front in 1941. I was wounded in the legs and medically handicapped." (1977)

"I myself was wounded on the Eastern Front and, being incapacitated for further service on the front, resumed my law studies at Vienna University where I graduated in 1944." (Letter to Congressman Stephen J. Solarz, December 1980)

"I was an interpreter . . . It was not a very high position that I had so it was very natural that I did not know of those things [deportation of Jews]." (Reuters, March 5, 1986)

"All I did was to interpret between German and Italian commanders." *(The New York Times,* March 6, 1986)

"I was not an intelligence officer." *(Christian Science Monitor,* April 17, 1986)

The most comprehensive defense of Waldheim is the "White Book." Its authors say the book is a compilation of documents and an assessment that refutes all accusations that have been made against Waldheim. "None of the allegations has been substantiated," Ralph Scheide, one of the authors, declares. The "White Book" served as a starting point for the independent commission of military historians created by the government of Austria in the spring of

1987. That body's original mandate was to "examine and evaluate all material available in light of the serious charges against the Austrian president." On May 18, 1987, the Austrian chancellor empowered the commission to move ahead.

Three days later, Professor Hans Rudolf Kurz of Switzerland agreed to serve as chairman of the commission. The correspondence surrounding his appointment makes it clear that the commission was responsible for determining whether there was evidence of personal criminal behavior on the part of Waldheim during his war service. Kurz and his Austrian government advisors drafted an international panel of historians that included retired U.S. Army General James L. Collins, Jr.; the British historian Professor Gerald Fleming; Dr. Manfred Messerschmidt of West Germany; Dr. Jean Vanwelenhuyzen of Belgium; and an Israeli, Dr. Yehuda Wallach. A Greek historian, Dr. Hagen Fleischer, was added to the staff as permanent expert. Yugoslavia was asked, but declined to send, a member to the commission.

There was immediate suspicion around the world that the commission was a "stacked deck." First of all, it had been appointed by the government of Austria to investigate its own president. The government was not only paying the bill, but providing foreign office personnel to act as the staff for the commission. Second, the commission had no real tools for evaluating legal evidence, and without experienced trial lawyers, prosecutors, or members of previous war crimes commissions, it was highly unlikely that it could come to any substantive conclusions, even if it were inclined to do so.

The commission held meetings in Vienna on September 1-3, 1987, and met again for five days in October of that year, five days in November, and thirteen days in early 1988. In the interim, each member was assigned designated areas of research, and the group's final report claimed that there had been extensive communication among them.

The commission studied the Waldheim "White Book" to understand the position taken by the Austrian president on all the accusations against him. Members were then given volumes of documents that were readily available, but were denied access to other key documents because the U.S. government, the World Jewish Congress and, initially, the government of Yugoslavia refused to recognize the commission as having any independent standing.

But a shock lay ahead for Waldheim and all those who assumed that the commission's report would be a rubber stamp of the "White Book." The document files arrived for review labeled "Historical archive Salonika, Historical archive Crete, Yugoslav state archive Belgrade, Yugoslav military archive Zagreb, Historical reports Kozara," and so forth. But although the commission devoted only a paragraph in its final report to a CIA file dated April 26, 1945, this document may warrant volumes if we are ever to understand the real relationship between the U.S. and British intelligence agencies and the Nazi criminals who were allowed to go free and to prosper in business and government with Allied blessings after World War II.

The Historical Commission's final report read: "We've researched a CIA file of April 26, 1945, which, according to rumor, contains certain information concerning First Lieutenant Kurt Waldheim. Although access to this file was refused, since it is a document as yet classified, the extract which we were allowed to receive, and which we were assured was the only one concerning Waldheim, only contains a description of Waldheim as a person. This description is part of a list of numerous Wehrmacht officers."

We were able to learn in the course of completing this book that the still top-secret CIA file identifying Waldheim by name and by a detailed physical description was part of a document that came to the United States from British intelligence asking for assistance in capturing certain known Nazi officers. General James Collins, the American who served on the historical commission, told us, "The CIA showed me that extract which included Waldheim's name and description. It seemed to be a routine exchange of classified material between the Allies focusing on intelligence officers to be captured before the end of the war, if possible, or sought out after the war."

What is astonishing is that for seven years the Central Intelligence Agency denied that it held any information about Waldheim. That was the CIA position in official correspondence to Congressman Solarz and in responses to various petitions submitted under the Freedom of Information Act.

The intelligence agency finally acknowledged the document in a letter to the World Jewish Congress dated June 9, 1987; "We have received several earlier requests for information on Kurt Waldheim; the first one, under which the search was made, was for records in existence as of and through April 30, 1986. That request was completed in accordance with the Freedom of Information Act. The one document that was located, an OSS report dated April 26, 1945, was denied in total."

Following receipt of that letter, in a series of telephone conversations about possible appeal of the denied access, the World Jewish Congress was told that for "security reasons," the OSS files would not be released.

We've learned that the nature of that security clearance goes back to the basic agreement between the United States and friendly nations on the exchange of intelligence material. Since the document first came to the United States from British intelligence, U.S. officials cannot make it public without British consent. That consent has never been given.

Thomas Troy, a former CIA official and agency historian with expertise on events at the end of World War II said it was a "common practice to exchange such information about Nazis who should be hunted because of their special knowledge of Nazi plans." The British had compiled the list of senior intelligence officers, including Waldheim, by name, physical description, and duties, from captured German documents and information received from German prisoners of war.

The nagging question remains: why did the Central Intelligence Agency deny for so long that it had information about Waldheim? The even more irritating question is how did the United States, joined by Britain and other Allies, justify going along with the Soviet suggestion that Waldheim be chosen as secretary-general of the United Nations if, in fact, our archives contained detailed information about Waldheim's secret Nazi life.

The more documents that are studied, and the more former intelligence officers come forward, the clearer it becomes that there was either a massive "screw up" or an equally massive "cover up." The weight of evidence seems to lean toward the cover up. It is difficult to believe that the United States could lose track of evidence when considering the selection of the senior official at the United Nations. The U.S. ignored not only the 1945 file from British intelligence, but its own list of wanted war criminals, with Waldheim on it.

The Historical Commission boasted in its final report that it had examined a "wide field of documentation and tried to compile as faultless a record as possible," but it left the door open and hinted that other documents might turn up.

And when it decided to hear witnesses, including former German officers, voices of discontent were raised in the Austrian government. After all, these historians were just supposed to read the documents (paying particular attention to Waldheim's "White Book") and to issue a report that there was no evidence of personal involvement. However, they went further, and their conclusions shocked Waldheim personally, his Austrian supporters and opponents, and the worldwide audience of this bizarre tale.

Weeks before the commission filed its report, Waldheim ironically sought to disassociate himself from the group he had created by stating publicly that it was only an advisory body and that "I will not be bound by any of their decisions or recommendations." Since the "White Book" presented by Waldheim as the manifesto of his defense went beyond the war period in its content, the commission felt it also had a right to refer to events outside that period. Essentially, it concluded that Waldheim's defense that his duties did not affect the fate of prisoners or refugees was inaccurate. Analysis of his involvement with incriminating operations and orders showed various levels of knowledge, depending upon his proximity to the incident. For example:

The transmittal of interrogation protocols about the statements of allied commands was in close relationship with their later fate, which had been established in general terms by Hitler's order of October 18, 1942. Cooperation of this nature can be qualified as obedience to orders in clear knowledge of the fact that the order would result in crimes.

As 02 in West Bosnia, Waldheim was in immediate proximity of criminal actions, particularly in Banja Luka, where he must have been aware of the means of operation of the local IC. There can be no doubt as to the involvement of the IC-Division in matters of transport of prisoners and fugitives, even if little documentation is on hand. A concrete reference as to the involvement of Waldheim in questions of transport and problems of camps has not come to light until now.

As 01 in Athens, Waldheim knew of the practice of deportation of Italian prisoners/internees to Germany in September 1943, at a time, therefore, when there was no state of war between the German Reich and the Italian Kingdom. These unlawful acts, as well as numerous killings, were known in the higher staff echelons.

The commission went on to say that "From the mere knowledge of violations of human rights at the place of his own function, a certain guilt can result if the person concerned, for the lack of power or courage, violated his human duty to act against evil." The report accused Waldheim of passive acceptance of violation of human rights; in the press conferences that followed its release, commission members expanded upon this point. Despite the fact that they had avoided inflammatory language in the report, they felt he had lied repeatedly concerning the extent of his knowledge about the horrors around him and what he could have done to help prevent them.

Waldheim had referred in his defense documents to the fact that he was "bound by the law of unrestricted military performance of duty during his performance as a soldier." The Historical Commission refused to accept that justification. Citing German law, it said: "Legislation of the post-war years concerning the war period, particularly in the trials following Nuremberg, repeatedly established with all decisiveness that, even in war, military orders have no unrestricted validity. . . . The rejection of a blind 'cadaver obedience' was established in Paragraph 47 of the then valid German military code, which established that a subordinate, even if acting upon orders, would be culpable if the order in question evidently led to a crime or an offense. This principle of the guilt of fulfilling criminal orders, which is based on long-standing tradition in Germany, hardly enjoyed its full validity during the period of Nazi legislation—but it continued to exist as a moral fundamental."

In its research, the commission noted a number of cases in which officers took responsibility for circumventing orders that were against the law, or even acted against them, without considerable harm resulting to them. The statement "resistance against the instructions would have meant suicide" cannot be recognized in such a categoric fashion—although it must be admitted that nobody could be sure of escaping the revenge of the system.

At the end of its report, the commission, after hours of debate, resolved to tell the world that Waldheim had been an unmitigated liar with respect to his Nazi past. We've learned that there were a dozen drafts of that last paragraph and incredible pressure from the foreign office in Austria, including a threat not to accept the report if it were not watered down. Nevertheless, the commission cast aside its implied rubber-stamp status and spoke clearly: "Waldheim's description of his military past does not coincide with the conclusions of the commission in many points. He was intent on letting his military past be forgotten and, as soon as that was no longer possible, in making it seem harmless. This forgetting is so fundamental, in the view of the commission, that it could not obtain any clarification for its work from Waldheim."

As if to pay a final tribute to its sponsor, the commission, submitted in advance the questions to be asked of Waldheim during a brief interview "over tea," when he met with the members at the end of January 1988. This advance notice drew strong criticism from the U.S. Justice Department officials, British authorities and many in the Austrian government itself but it did nothing to change the outcome: Waldheim was unable to dissuade his own commission from condemning him.

Perhaps the best commentary on the commission's report was written by Dr. Jehuda Wallach, the Israeli member, for *The Washington Post.* Dr. Wallach said in part:

> *Even superficial reading of the commission's report will reveal that in almost every case investigated, Waldheim had adopted the tactics of first denying the facts and only gradually and reluctantly admitting things when confronted with documentary evidence that could no longer be denied.*
>
> *Until the present day, he tries to present his role on the staff of Army Group E in the Balkans as some kind of a minor "desk officer," moving colored pins on maps and dealing with routine paper work. The true picture appearing from the documentation is very different. Waldheim was . . . a well-informed officer who took part in consultations on the highest level. In his capacity as intelligence officer, he contributed to the decision-making process and, as the commission concluded, "he had an overall view that was not confined to tactical, strategic and administrative measures, but included in some instances actions and measures that were contrary to the law of war and principles of humanity."*
>
> *This leads to the obvious question, for which I have no answer: What led President Waldheim to initiate the appointment of a commission of inquiry manned by historians? As a former intelligence officer and experienced politi-*

cian, he knew there was and is a trail of incriminating documents bearing his signature or initials. Did he really believe that these would not be discovered?

In fact, his request to the Austrian government to establish a commission of military historians was triggered by publication by the World Jewish Congress of hundreds of relevant documents found in the U.S. National Archives and in the archives of the German Federal Republic. Did Waldheim and his supporters really expect that experienced and highly competent historians would interpret this documentary evidence in a way that would whitewash the president? I have been pondering this question from the moment I received from the Austrian Foreign Ministry the first packet of documents concerning the wartime activities of Lt. Waldheim. Honestly, I believe that as a historian I lack the proper tools to grapple with this question. This is probably a problem to be handled by psychologists. The latter will perhaps also be able to answer the question why this man now refuses to recognize the proper meaning of the historians' report and to draw the obvious conclusions from it.

After all, the dubious attempts made by the Austrian foreign minister, the Austrian media and the president himself to interpret the report as refuting the allegations against Waldheim were short-lived. Everybody reading the report understands that the findings of the commission by no means rehabilitate Waldheim. Quite the opposite is true.

In light of this report, the documentation in the U.N.'s Nazi war crimes archive, and the dossier of Waldheim's Nazi involvements, we carefully reviewed the circumstances that took him from a Nazi officership into the political arena without the punishment that many of his comrades faced. We have mentioned that after World War II, the policy of "looking the other way" with respect to war crimes was applied consistently in the case of scientists and researchers who could be of help to the United States and the Western Allies in dealing with future Soviet competition and threats. It would appear that Waldheim may have been the beneficiary of an extension of that policy to those who could, in the long run, be of political assistance to the West.

On May 7, 1945, Germany surrendered to the Allies, and records show that there was a short, mysterious period of internment for Waldheim at Bad Tolz, in Bavaria. American documents indicate that this facility was used by U.S. intelligence officers to debrief Nazi officers on a wide variety of plans about the German war effort. Those who believe that a deal was made between American intelligence and Kurt Waldheim point to Bad Tolz as the time and place when it would have happened.

We do know that Allen Dulles was then a senior official in the intelligence community, responsible for helping select those Nazi officials who would not be punished for their crimes when the war ended. We also know that when a request came to "check out" Waldheim because he was being considered for an important position in the foreign office of postwar Austria, that request reached Dulles. The fact that it came from his son-in-law, then secretary to Austria's foreign minister, thickens the plot.

Fritz Molden, who made the recommendation for Waldheim's appointment, remains loyal to him. Recently, we had an opportunity to ask Molden whether or not he had reviewed Waldheim's war record with his father-in-law, Allen Dulles, at the time he was "clearing" him with the United States. "It never occurred to me to do that," Molden says.

In addition to the Allies' knowledge of Waldheim's wartime activities, it is obvious that the Soviet Union, with access to all of the Yugoslavian files, was ready, willing, able, and certainly inclined to use the information they had garnered about him. As Waldheim was becoming a member of the Austrian foreign ministry in 1947, there were repeated exchanges of information between Yugoslav and Soviet intelligence officials. It is now claimed that documents were given to the Soviets on three separate occasions detailing Waldheim's personal activities in Greece and Yugoslavia when he served as a Nazi intelligence officer.

Anton Kolendic, the senior Yugoslav intelligence agent in Vienna in 1947 and 1948, told *The Washington Post* on October 30, 1986, he had planned to use the material in a "joint action" with Soviet intelligence to recruit Waldheim for future political benefits. Kolendic said that he turned over Waldheim's complete file to Soviet intelligence agents and that he had personal knowledge and was "absolutely certain" that the Russians had made the approach. A second senior Yugoslav official who talked to *The Washington Post,* on the condition of anonymity, confirmed the Kolendic story and indicated that after the records had been turned over to the Soviets, they said, in effect, that they would be responsible and that Waldheim was to be considered "Russia's man."

As Waldheim's diplomatic career flourished, and he became the number two man in the Austrian mission in Paris, then head of the foreign minister's personnel office in 1951, the Soviet Union refined its file on him. By the time he was sent to New York to head the Austrian mission to the United Nations in 1955, the Soviets had already made their awareness of his Nazi past known to Waldheim.

Members of Tito's personal postwar staff have confirmed that their government was aware of Waldheim's Nazi record and that the Soviets were equally aware. Mirko Milutinovic, Tito's chief of staff, said, "We knew that Waldheim had been compromised. We knew all about his presence at the time of the massacres."

In 1968, the eyes of the world were on Czechoslovakia, where brave freedom fighters were revolting against Soviet domination. One event there seems, in retrospect, to shed light on the unique relationship between Waldheim and the Soviets. Several leaders of the Czechoslovakian revolt asked for political asylum in the Austrian embassy in Prague in an effort to survive. This was not unusual, because Austria had a long-term reputation for granting such political asylum. The Austrian ambassador opened the door to the first few Czech leaders escaping from the Soviets. Then he wired his foreign minister, Waldheim, to advise him and request authority to shelter other leaders of the revolt at the embassy.

In a matter of hours, he had his response. Waldheim ordered the Austrian embassy closed and those Czechs who had been granted asylum ejected. The ambassador ignored the order but was never disciplined.*

Some of the Soviet diplomats who urged Austria not to intervene in the Czechoslovakian dispute later supported Waldheim's bid for the U.N. secretary-generalship. Some of Waldheim's critics suggest this is more than coincidence.

A ranking Austrian official at the United Nations today served in Austria's foreign ministry and knows Waldheim well. He believes that the Czechoslovakian incident was a clear-cut example of the Soviets' using what they knew and a promise of future support to secure favorable treatment, in this case, expulsion of the Czech leaders from their refuge. Several former senior Yugoslav intelligence officials have also confirmed that the records of Waldheim's Nazi past were used by their country as leverage to influence Waldheim's position in border disputes when he first served in the Austrian foreign ministry.

In preparing this book, we uncovered a Yugoslavian document dated December 12, 1947, and confirmed it to be an internal memorandum from the chief of the legal bureau, Uros M. Bjelic, to his ministry of foreign affairs. Its authenticity has been verified by two former members of the Yugoslav foreign affairs office and by a document examiner retained by the World Jewish Congress. It focuses on a border dispute pending between Austria and Yugoslavia:

From the Ministry of Interior, FNRJ—Bureau for War Crimes—File No. 1725 of 09/17/1947. We have received investigation material concerning certain German prisoners and other members of the HQ of the Army Group E, under the command of the convicted war criminal General LOEHR, in particular on the members of the intelligence and the so called Section Ic in this HQ.

---

* When Waldheim was interviewed by Ted Koppel and Pierre Salinger for "Nightline," the Austrian president was asked about his instructions to the ambassador. Waldheim was visibly flustered and gave a rambling, inconsistent answer. Then he was asked why no action was taken when the ambassador ignored his instructions. Again, Waldheim rambled.

Among the remaining most important members of these sections, whose leadership is presently in Germany and also in Austria and about whose criminal activities in our country during the occupation there exist data, there is also First Lieutenant WALDHEIM, whom a German witness/prisoner confirmed that he was involved in the reprisal decision-making process for executing hostages (current hostage affairs). Concerning the matter the following facts appear in the mentioned file:

"1st Lieutenant Waldheim, a long-time illegal national socialist, listed in the report as responsible for hostages, who had contact with V-Persons (collaborators) is today in Austria and not only as a free person but as a Secretary in the Ministry for Foreign Affairs (Legation Secretary). He is a member of the delegation of the Austrian Foreign Minister Dr. Gruber and was with him in London. This fact is also of not minor importance for our Ministry for Foreign Affairs."

We submit you this information in view of possible use, in particular with reference to the activity of the Austrian Minister for Foreign Affairs, Dr. Gruber, against our national interest.

Inform us if a decision should be made on Gruber's assistant Waldheim on the basis of which he would be registered at the UN War Crimes Commission. (It should be kept in mind that the last date for registration has been set for the end of this year.)

If, in fact, the Soviet Union had knowledge of Waldheim's Nazi past, and used it to secure political favors, and if both the United States and Britain also had information damaging to him, an unusual political irony may have occurred. By the time he became secretary-general of the United Nations, Waldheim may well have been in the position of a judge who is offered a bribe by both sides and must dance down the middle in making his decisions.

Despite the severity of the charges against Waldheim, there has been an ongoing search for the "smoking gun" that would transfer him from the list of suspects who have lied to that of active participants in war crimes. The World Jewish Congress, the Justice Department and most observers believe that the evidence already in place shows sufficient personal involvement not only to justify prohibiting his reentry into the United States, but to identify him as a war criminal. Yet a cadre of loyalists in Austria, and the Historical Commission itself, question whether or not there is enough proof to use that label.

As mentioned earlier, Miograd Cedic provided us with invaluable information on Waldheim's activities in Yugoslavia. In 1942 Cedic was seized by the Nazis with hundreds of others in his native village, twenty miles from Nis. He was taken to Zitkovac, where he was held for fifteen days as the Nazis arbitrarily decided who was to die, and when. "My uncle had been a local politician, and so he knew the German officers," Cedic said. "One of them was Kurt Waldheim. "I positively saw him there several times. He was a big shot. My family sent gold and jewelry to Waldheim and the others to spare me."

At a Washington, D.C. hotel, Cedic explained what had happened in detail to General James Collins, who served on the Historical Commission. We listened as Cedic explained to the general how he had been permitted to "slip out of the barracks each night and return each morning." (Those to die were selected at night.) Cedic had no witnesses to back him up, but he did pass two separate lie detector tests.*

After meeting with Cedic, Collins told us: "I am convinced that Cedic believes that he is telling the truth."

After his encounter with Waldheim, Cedic joined the Yugoslav resistance. In December 1944, he was hit by shrapnel in Bosnia and taken by his Nazi captors to a Czechoslovakian prison hospital. From there, he was moved to one of a group of camps in Linz, Austria. On May 5, 1945, the U.S. Army's 11th Armored Division liberated Cedic and thousands of other POWs from the camps.

Cedic shared with Collins a painful secret that he had carried to that Nazi camp. "My father was hanged and my uncle was shot because they paid Waldheim and the others to spare me," he said. "It was a common practice to try and save those in your family, but the Nazis made sure the partisans [anti-Nazi activists] found out, and so my relatives were killed by Yugoslavs who suspected them of collaboration."

Cedic recalls vividly what happened after he was freed and stayed on with many fellow countrymen to make a fresh start in Austria. He had no money, no family, and nowhere to go. He survived by doing odd jobs, but he never forgot his experience as a hostage and a prisoner—or his family's fate for paying the Nazis to spare him.

In 1948 Waldheim, now an up-and-coming member of the foreign ministry staff, visited Linz, where his former hostage was living. One day Cedic saw his photograph in a local newspaper and became incensed. "This Nazi who was responsible for killing our people and for the brutality in Yugoslavia was in government. I couldn't believe it," he said.

Cedic went to friends, including a local official, to share his secret, but they wouldn't listen. "They thought I was crazy for suggesting that an Austrian official could be one of the Nazi monsters," he recalled. "They ignored me."

Cedic arrived in the United States in 1951 as a displaced person. In Akron,

---

* The separate tests were administered by a private firm recommended by the police force in the city where he lives. The polygraph organization noted in its report that given Cedic's medical condition it would be easier than normal to determine evasiveness and none was deemed present.

Ohio, one of the families sponsoring Yugoslav immigrants had a daughter named Dorothy Sivchev. She and Cedic met, fell in love, and started a life together. Dorothy recalls that "he told me about Waldheim right after we met. When he tried to tell other people, even our friends, no one would listen. They thought he was confused."

As the years passed, Cedic and his wife relocated to Arizona. Meanwhile, the Austrian diplomat advanced, first to foreign minister and then to ambassador to the United Nations. It was in 1971 that he became secretary-general.

Cedic was visiting friends in Ohio on that evening when Waldheim appeared on television as the new chief international peacekeeper. To the world he was the Number One diplomat, but to Cedic he was a barbaric killer. Cedic knew he was "obsessed," but he felt there was nowhere to turn. If his friends didn't believe him, why would anyone else?

In October 1987, we appeared on "Good Morning America" with an official of the Austrian embassy and debated the issue of Waldheim the Nazi. Viewing the program, Cedic felt, "I finally found someone who will believe me and will help me." He called ABC-TV and traced us.

When we first talked by telephone, we were skeptical, but after two long meetings in Arizona, we went to Europe to try and find proof of Cedic's claims. It was uncanny. We could clearly place Waldheim where Cedic claimed he had been. We could prove Cedic's story about imprisonment. The missing link was the eyewitness who would corroborate everything that he had seen.

In November 1987, we got a call from a senior editor of *Wiener* magazine, which has the second-largest circulation among monthly news publications in Austria. He wanted an update, from an American viewpoint, on the Waldheim case, and he suggested the Cedic story. We wrote it and *Wiener* decided it was important enough to feature in a special insert in their December 15 issue, which was going to press.

Five hours after the magazines reached the newsstands, the Austrian state police, at the request of the president's office, confiscated every copy. The reason given was that our article "defamed the office of the president." There was no allegation that the article was untrue. We have since learned, in the court proceedings following the confiscation, that, unfortunately, truth does not guarantee a victory for the magazine. The judge has hinted that he may rule for the publication if he is totally satisfied as to Cedic's sincerity, but he is not obliged to. The first reaction from the president's spokesman at the time of publication was that Cedic did not exist. But the confiscation was a political blunder for Waldheim, as many of those who had remained loyal to him in Austria criticized the suppression.

There has been much confusion about the action taken by the U.S. government in barring Waldheim from the United States by placing him on the so-called Watch List. The investigation that led up to that action provides the clearest statement of Waldheim's Nazi career. We noted that it was the World Jewish Congress, leaning heavily on the Justice Department, that prompted the investigation and its results.

Neal Sher, Director of the Office of Special Investigations, quite properly declined simply to accept the documents stored in dusty files in Yugoslavia. His independent investigation was as thorough as any ever undertaken to prove or disprove Waldheim's involvement in war crimes. Six times, a law firm representing Waldheim submitted to the Justice Department massive documentation designed to disprove the allegations of war crimes. Privately, Austrian officials and their American lawyers expressed confidence that the U.S. government's finding would be favorable to Waldheim. On the contrary.

The report that justified placing Waldheim on the Watch List was drawn from a thorough review of the documents that surfaced in Yugoslavia, those at the U.N., and new information uncovered by an able team of lawyers, historians, and investigators. The official Justice Department conclusion states:

> The available evidence demonstrates that under established legal principles Waldheim, during his service with the German army in World War II, assisted or otherwise participated in the following persecutory activities: The transfer of civilian prisoners to the SS for exploitation as slave labor; the mass deportation of civilians to concentration camps; the deportation of Jews from Greek islands and Banja Luka, Yugoslavia, to concentration and death camps; the utilization of anti-Semitic propaganda; the mistreatment and execution of allied prisoners; and reprisal executions of hostages and other civilians.

Perhaps the definitive description of the meaning of the decision to ban Waldheim was printed in *The New York Times*, which added substantial background information to the Justice Department memorandum. In fifteen paragraphs, it exposed the secret life that made Kurt Waldheim the most disgraced senior diplomat of contemporary times, even as he retained full power and authority as president of his country:

> *"The evidence collected," a Justice Department spokesman said at a news conference, "establishes a prima facie case that Kurt Waldheim assisted or otherwise participated in the persecution of persons because of race, religion, national origin or political opinion."*
>
> *Sources familiar with the investigation said the Justice Department had found important new evidence against Mr. Waldheim both from the National Archives and through investigations in Yugoslavia.*
>
> *For example, Justice Department investigators were said to have learned*

that Mr. Waldheim, acting as a liaison officer with the Pusterian Division of the Italian Army in May 1942, had played a role in deporting 484 Yugoslav citizens in Bosnia to Norway for forced labor.

Documents found in Yugoslavia indicate that in 1942 Mr. Waldheim was working in villages from which Jews were being deported. Much of the other information found by the Justice Department added details that strengthened the case against him, sources said.

A Justice Department official said the broad outlines of the case against Mr. Waldheim had been discovered last year in the National Archives in Washington by the department and the World Jewish Congress, which conducted its own inquiry. In addition, more detailed information was found late last year when Neal Sher, director of the Office of Special Investigations, went to Yugoslavia to examine the archives there.

These were the activities in which the department said it found Mr. Waldheim had taken part:

—The transfer of civilian prisoners to the SS for exploitation as slave labor.

—The mass deportation of civilians—among them Jews from the Greek islands and the town of Banja Luka, Yugoslavia—to concentration and death camps.

—The use of anti-Semitic propaganda.

—The turning over of allied prisoners to a branch of the SS.

—Reprisal executions of hostages and other civilians.

In 1943, a department official said, Mr. Waldheim was responsible for assisting in "harsh Nazi policies aimed at terrorizing the Greek population through mass deportations and reprisal executions."

From late 1943 to 1945, he served in Greece and Yugoslavia with Army Group E, which officials said carried out Hitler's order that all captured allied commandos be shot or handed over to the security arm of the SS for interrogation and execution.

In that capacity, they said, "he was personally involved with two groups of prisoners, only one of whom survived," while the others were turned over to the SD.

The list Mr. Waldheim was put on today is an Immigration and Naturalization Service list called a Watch List, alerting agents at borders to watch for certain people.

The State Department announced that it was also putting Mr. Waldheim into its "automated visa lookout system," which alerts consular officials that he is not eligible for a visa to enter this country.

In a statement, the Justice Department said that its action was based on law that excludes anyone who under Nazi direction "ordered, initiated, as-

sisted or otherwise participated in the persecution of any person because of race, religion, national origin or political opinion."

The action placing Mr. Waldheim on the Watch List affects him as an "individual," Justice Department officials said. If he sought permission to enter this country for a state visit, as an Austrian leader, a decision on how to respond would have to be made by the White House and the State Department.

The Justice Department said that "efforts by a person to hide or otherwise distort potentially improper activities have routinely been regarded as significant" in determining whether to place a person on the Watch List.

On December 2, 1987, a letter from Neal Sher was delivered to the Historical Commission. It read: "I am aware that it has been suggested that the United States action in barring Kurt Waldheim from this country resulted from the fact that Kurt Waldheim was in the area where crimes and acts of persecution took place and that near proximity to such activities warranted a Watch List decision. That simply is not the case and we have never so represented. On the contrary, the findings are that there is sufficient evidence to implicate Mr. Waldheim personally, and in conjunction with the small functional units to which he was attached, in acts which clearly constitute persecution under legal precedent.

I would note that the evidence against Mr. Waldheim would undoubtedly come to life should he exercise the option of challenging the Watch List decision. He is aware that such opportunities exist under our laws."

Waldheim and spokesmen for him have constantly refuted the claim by the Justice Department that he has the right to appeal the Watch List decision. He has argued this point strenuously in media interviews. Unfortunately, his statements are inaccurate. The appeal procedure does, in fact, exist and would be set in motion if Waldheim were to request a visa to visit the United States. It would be denied because of his presence on the Watch List, and he would then have access to American courts to challenge it. However, once such a challenge was made, the Justice Department would be at liberty and, in fact, would be responsible for releasing all the documentation involved in the decision to bar Waldheim. Neither he nor those managing his survival campaign have any desire to see the damning documentation at the Justice Department made public to add to the voluminous material already on the record.*

---

* Three documents were key to the Justice Department's decision: a daily "war diary" kept by Waldheim's unit, a prosecution document from the Nuremberg trials, and a document detailing a critical message sent through Waldheim from a line officer to his superiors seeking permission to deport civilians and to destroy villages.

The diary shows that on August 8, 1943, Waldheim entered a directive from Adolf Hitler to execute captured Greek partisans, and that he immediately forwarded the or-

Canada joined the United States in barring Waldheim based on the evidence that was available, but most nations do not have a similar procedure. Their approach was to resist suggestions that Waldheim make official visits to their countries.

France, Japan, the United Kingdom, and Australia all avoided opportunities for visits from Waldheim, as did the Scandinavian nations. A few of the Arab states (if for no apparent reason other than to spite Israel) invited Waldheim to be a guest of honor.

No visit was so shocking to those who had discovered the reality of Waldheim's past as his welcome to the Vatican on June 25, 1987, by Pope John Paul II. It was Waldheim's first visit outside of Austria since his election, and it created an international furor. The media paid little or no attention to the fact that the government of Italy declined to welcome Waldheim as he crossed into that country en route to the Vatican. In other words, it was an official visit to Vatican City but not to Rome despite Waldheim's presence there.

Since that papal visit, there has been a definite shift in national opinion against Kurt Waldheim. Within Austria, the polls had shown repeatedly that the public supported the president despite the accusations against him and generally resented interference from other countries in their internal affairs. All that started changing late in 1987. By the 1988, leaders of both the political parties forming Austria's coalition government were seeking Waldheim's

---

der to field commanders. Specifically, the entry over Waldheim's signature said: "According to a new Fuhrer order, bandits captured in battle are to be shot. Others suspected of banditry, etc., are to be taken prisoner and sent to Germany for use in labor details." (At the time the German word for "bandit" was used to describe partisans.)

The Nuremberg trial document confirms transmission of the order to the German division that was operating against the Greek partisans in northern Greece. Waldheim's message read: "To the 1st Mountain Division: Reference Teletype Ia No. 959-43, Secret, of 7 Aug. 1943, concerning shooting of bandits. A new Fuhrer order is at hand, which will be transmitted. Bandits taken in battle are to be shot. Other bandit suspects etc. are to be arrested and evacuated for Sauckel labor service." (The latter refers to SS General Fritz Sauckel, who ran a network of slave labor camps. He was sentenced to death at Nuremberg, where the document was used as evidence.)

The third document relates to a series of radio transmissions that also passed through Waldheim. On August 15, 1943, he retransmitted a message between German army officers in the Balkans requesting the mass deportation of Greek civilians to labor camps. The document indicates the information was received by radio by Waldheim, who signed its transcription and forwarded it. The communication from a German army field officer was addressed to his headquarters, reporting "hope of success only if all male civilians are seized and deported." It also said "cleansing operations [destruction of villages] are deemed necessary."

All three documents were located in the U.S. National Archives in 1986 by World Jewish Congress researchers who turned them over to the Justice Department.

resignation. On the very day that this book was finished, more than 10,000 demonstrators had rallied outside the presidential palace in Vienna to demand that resignation.

Waldheim was to be guest speaker on March 13, 1988, when Austria solemnly observed the fiftieth anniversary of Nazi annexation. His speech was canceled. In fact, it was time for Austria to stop claiming that it had been the first victim of the Nazis and to admit its role as an ally of Hitler. The facts were clear, and the list was long of Austrians who had held command in Nazi forces and who dominated the concentration-camp roster of senior officers responsible for implementing the Final Solution.

Now the British government has reopened the Waldheim case to determine the truth about his involvement with British soldiers who may have been interrogated by his unit before they were sent to their deaths. Many believe that if Waldheim has been able to survive the accusations of his own Historical Commission, questioning by Ted Koppel of "Nightline," the magnifying glass of scrutiny by the world media, and the division in his own country this long, he will not resign.

To some, the shift in the attack must go from Waldheim to Austria itself. The country is beleaguered by falling tourism, a sagging economy, and a general depression that has caused intellectuals, academicians, students, business leaders, and politicians of all philosophies to ask—and in some cases to demand—that Waldheim step down "for the good of Austria."

There is no one in the world more hurt or more angry now that the full Waldheim story is known than Robert Rhodes-James, a distinguished member of the British Parliament and one of the more interesting men in his nation's public life. He is dapper, articulate, and not only knows what he is talking about, but has what it takes to make things happen. Rhodes-James is a historian who has worked with the United Nations. In fact, he was a key member of Waldheim's staff when he was secretary-general.

It was natural that when Waldheim's Nazi past became known, Rhodes-James was embittered. He spoke out forcefully and submitted a report to the British prime minister detailing the allegations against Waldheim that had been uncovered by the World Jewish Congress. Waldheim tried to convince Rhodes-James the reports were untrue in a letter dated October 31, 1986, with the salutation "Dear Robert": "I deeply regret that you, as my former colleague and friend at the United Nations, have made unfounded accusations. I regret this development not only because the allegations are completely false, but because it means a breach of friendship which I had highly treasured." Waldheim then provided Rhodes-James with a lengthy dissertation of his version of his wartime years, which differs completely from what is now known to be true. The lengthy letter concluded: "Along the same lines, a recent effort to identify Dr. Waldheim as being in a picture together with Adolf Hitler in 1940 in Paris has been proven false, and underlined the relentlessness by which Dr. Waldheim's critics will not stop before even the most far-fetched, absurd, and ludicrous efforts to burden him with a National Socialist past, or with involvement in war crimes or crimes against peace and humanity. There was no such involvement, and therefore, there can be no valid documents proving such claims. Dr. Waldheim and his family were known for their resistance against National Socialism, and his professional record with regard to the quest for peace, democracy and human rights speaks for itself." Nevertheless, Rhodes-James said on the floor of the House of Commons: "Waldheim is an unmitigated liar and is morally unfit to serve as president of Austria or to deal with responsible people anywhere." He went even further in a conversation with us. "I have examined the documents and they are real, . . . they are true, and we were all betrayed." This from a man who was both a trusted aide and a friend serves as a fitting endnote to the story of the unmasking of Kurt Waldheim.

★　★　★

In June 1988 Home Box Office in the United States in association with Thames Television in Great Britain produced and aired a worldwide mock television trial of Kurt Waldheim. While real trials seek justice, this one sought only television ratings. While real trials compel essential witnesses to testify and secure essential evidence, this one lacked many of those who knew the most relevant facts and functioned without the cooperation of the U.S. Department of Justice or the World Jewish Congress.

As entertainment it was boring. As a so-called trial, it had its moments of authenticity. But without the critical evidence, it was like swimming without water. The presentation against Waldheim was grossly incomplete despite the efforts of prosecutor Allan Ryan to win.

Some critics have pointed out a serious danger. Now that television cameras go into the courtroom, it is possible that in the future someone will remember that there was a "trial" of Waldheim and the TV cameras were there to record his acquittal.

Not so. Waldheim has been proved by his own hand-picked commission, the world press, his own admissions, and even in this TV trial to have been in the middle of the worst of Hitler's brutality. Waldheim has been shown again to have lied about his involvement in World War II. True, no one swears he pulled a trigger. But that is not absolution.

The Big Three

It was the winter of 1969-70, and Wolfgang Gerhard, a German living in São Paulo, Brazil, had a problem. For over a decade he had dedicated his life to protecting an old man living on a farm about 120 miles north of the Brazilian city. Now the farm owners were tiring of their lodger, and it seemed he would have to be moved. But where?

Gerhard was one of fewer than a dozen people who knew where the old man was—and, more importantly, who he was. And because of his identity, finding a new refuge for him would be no easy task. The old man was one of the most wanted fugitives in the world, with a million-dollar bounty on his head: Josef Mengele, the notorious "Angel of Death" of Auschwitz.

Gerhard began putting out feelers in the German expatriate community, seeking a new haven for his charge. He did not tell people on whose behalf he was making the inquiries, only that he was an "important person from the old days." That code was more than enough to convey what he was looking for. Many such "important persons from the old days" were in hiding in South America.

As if to prove that point, Gerhard received a call one night from an acquaintance with whom he had discussed his problem. The acquaintance had made inquiries and had discovered another important person, living in Bolivia, who might be willing to take in Gerhard's charge. The proposition was put to Mengele, who asked the identity of his new host. Discreet inquiries were made, and the answer came back: Klaus Barbie, the "Butcher of Lyon," and one of the few war criminals who was more wanted than Mengele. Mengele reportedly thought the offer over for several days and then declined. He was happy in Brazil and did not want to change countries again.

There is no evidence that Mengele and Barbie ever met; it is most likely that they did not. But the similarity of their stories is striking, especially during the postwar years and the ensuing decades in which the world searched fruitlessly for them. Only in their final chapters are their stories dissimilar. Barbie, who is now in a French prison where he will probably remain for the rest of his life, represents one of the great triumphs for Nazi hunters. Mengele, however, was never discovered, as he lived out his days in quiet, but not particularly happy, surroundings.

★   ★   ★

On Saturday, June 8, 1985, one of the most impressive panels of forensic experts ever assembled to work on a single case gathered in a brightly lit examining room of the São Paulo police department's forensic laboratory. Most were exhausted, having just arrived on planes from the United States. Among the experts filing into the room was Dr. Ellis Kerley of the anthropology department at the University of Maryland, a leader in the new field of skeletal identification through "electronic supraposition," which videotapes skeletal remains from various angles and feeds the results through a computer. Others there were Dr. Clyde Snow, a consulting anthropologist to the Oklahoma State medical examiner; Dr. Ali Hameli, medical examiner of the State of Delaware; Dr. John Fitzpatrick, chief of Radiology at Chicago's Cook County Hospital; Dr. Leslie Lukash, chief medical examiner of Nassau County, New York; and Dr. Lowell Levine, America's foremost expert in forensic dentistry.

This blue-ribbon panel had flown to Brazil to examine a pile of bones that had been exhumed the day before from a small cemetery in the town of Embu, about twenty-five kilometers from São Paulo. The bones were said to be the remains of an elderly man who had drowned some six years earlier while swimming off a São Paulo beach. The name on the grave was "Wolfgang Gerhard," and the experts had gathered to determine whether the bones under their microscopes were those of Josef Mengele.

In 1934 Mengele was a medical student at the University of Munich. By all accounts, he was not a brilliant student, but his professors esteemed him for his willingness to work unusually hard. Since coming to the university in 1930, Mengele had become progressively more fascinated with the origins and development of man, the theory of evolution, and genetics. Now, while continuing his medical studies, he was trying to obtain a Ph.D. in anthropology as well.

Mengele was also politically active. It was hard for a student in Munich during the years of the rise of the Third Reich to avoid politics. His father had joined the fledgling Nazi Party almost as soon as it was founded, and young Mengele had joined a Nazi student group as early as 1931. By the time he had started his clinical work at the university hospital, he was already a member of the Brown Shirts and the proud possessor of a Ph.D. in anthropology.

In 1936 Mengele was awarded his medical degree and began practicing at a local hospital. His real interest was still genetics and anthropology, and he soon grew bored with the day to day tasks of a young physician.

In January of 1937 came an event that changed Josef Mengele's life and, eventually, the lives of tens of thousands of unfortunates who came into contact with him years later at Auschwitz. He won an appointment to the staff of Professor Otmar von Verschuer at the Third Reich Institute for Heredity, Biology and Racial Purity at the University of Frankfurt. Von Verschuer was a leading proponent of the theories of racial purity that Adolf Hitler had embraced. At the institute, Mengele became one of the group that worked to develop theories on how a race could be improved through genetic inbreeding. Von Verschuer had a specific interest in twins, and his young protégé was soon working closely with him in this area.

Shortly after joining the institute, Mengele submitted his application for Nazi Party membership, which was quickly approved. Because of the work he was doing on theories of racial purity, he was recommended for membership in the SS. In May of 1938, he was approved for membership, after an exhaustive examination of his family's background going back six generations showed that there was no Jewish blood in the family.

Mengele was still at the institute when war broke out in 1939. Because of his work, he was not drafted immediately. In June 1940 he became a medical officer in the regular army, but he soon transferred to the Waffen SS. Because of his background in genetics, he was attached to the genealogical section of the Race and Resettlement Office, where he was one of many SS doctors assigned to examine the racial suitability of inhabitants of areas being occupied by the Germany army. His first posting was to the Ukraine section of Poland.

Meanwhile, von Verschuer, had become the head of the key Nazi research program into racial purity at the Kaiser Wilhelm Institute in Berlin. In January 1943, von Verschuer sent for his former student, and Mengele transferred to Berlin, where he was promoted to the rank of captain. Within weeks of his arrival, he received his first direct assignment from von Verschuer. After a long and exhausting train trip from Berlin, Mengele arrived at a huge enclave surrounded by barbed wire about an hour outside of Krakow. The place was called Auschwitz (in Polish, Oswiecim).

The Auschwitz that greeted Mengele was already the largest of the German extermination camps. It housed some 140,000 prisoners. At the heart of the camp were five gas chambers and crematories, which had the capacity to snuff out the lives of 10,000 people per day. It is believed that during its years of operation, more than 2.5 million Jews died at Auschwitz.

Mengele had two separate duties at the camp, one as a physician with routine medical tasks, the other, to carry forward the research of von Verschuer. The camp needed doctors, because disease was rampant. But it became clear that Mengele had a very unusual way of dealing with disease.

In a 1981 indictment, the West German prosecutor's office stated that in

May of 1943 Mengele was assigned the task of controlling a typhoid epidemic in a small section of the camp. The indictment shows that over a two-day period that month, Mengele sent more than 1,600 Gypsies suspected of having typhus to the gas chamber. The indictments indicate that later in the year, he used the same method to deal with another typhus outbreak, in the ajoining women's prison camp at Birkenau. In this case 600 women were put to death.

By the end of 1944, Mengele had taken charge of the 40,000 women housed in C camp at Birkenau. There was a major food shortage at the time, and he had been attempting to sustain the inmates on approximately 600 calories per day. Due to the food shortage he could not find enough to maintain even this allotment. The solution, again, was simple: if he could not feed them adequately, he would simply liquidate them. Over a period of ten days in November of 1944, Mengele had 4,000 women a night sent to the gas chambers.

Mengele had another duty at Auschwitz that was shared by all the SS doctors. Two were assigned to meet every train that arrived at the concentration camp. Using whatever means of examination they chose, the doctors were to separate the arriving inmates into two groups. Those considered too weak to work were sent immediately to their deaths. Those believed strong enough were allowed to survive so long as they could work the long hours at forced labor that faced them. By all accounts the SS doctors at Auschwitz hated this assignment. It was, after all, the absolute power over life and death. But as countless testimony has shown, at least one Auschwitz physician not only tolerated but reveled in the assignment: Dr. Josef Mengele.

Why did Mengele enjoy this assignment? He had become convinced that the only way to guarantee Aryan survival was to stamp out the Jewish race. Mengele believed that it was the only race that could challenge the Aryan. Thus he relished the ability to send Jews to their deaths.

But Mengele's real fame at Auschwitz revolved around a series of experiments he was conducting for von Verschuer. As every train arrived at the gates, Mengele would scan the arriving inmates in search of twins. Throughout 1944, he conducted many experiments on the twins whom he segregated. By any normal set of scientific standards, these experiments were both bizarre and barbaric. But after the war, when Allied doctors reviewed some of the voluminous results that had been sent back to the Kaiser Wilhelm Institute, a pattern began to emerge. It would appear that Mengele's research was aimed at trying to establish a way of creating twins through genetic engineering so as to increase the population of pure-blooded Aryans rapidly. He was also consumed by the quest to guarantee perfect physical qualities for these newborn members of the Aryan race. In a particularly infamous series of experiments, he attempted to change the eye coloring of prisoners by injecting dye into their eyes; fifty-one children were used in one of these series. When it became apparent that the dye was having no results except to cause infection and blindness, all fifty-one were sent to the gas chambers.

How many died at Mengele's hands at Auschwitz? Probably, we will never know. By most estimates it was surely in the tens of thousands—perhaps higher. Psychologists and psychiatrists who have examined his record at Auschwitz have concluded that for most of the time he was at the camp he was insane. Given to fits of irrational behavior, he would kill prisoners with his bare hands, sometimes in the most barbaric fashion. His hatred of Jews became progressively worse and would often come out at Jewish holiday seasons. In 1944 he ordered the deaths of 1000 young Jewish boys on Yom Kippur, choosing those who could not touch the crossbar of the soccer goal post on the camp field.

By December 1944, it became apparent that the tide had turned against Nazi Germany and it was only a matter of time before advancing Soviet forces would overrun Auschwitz. There is abundant testimony to the fact that Mengele became progressively more frantic in his effort to gather and preserve the records of his experiments, particularly those on twins. Reportedly, he boxed his medical records and on the night of January 16, 1945, as the guns of the advancing Red Army were heard in the distance, fled Auschwitz with several other SS doctors in a car whose trunk was filled with his notes.

It is not certain what happened to Mengele in the days and weeks immediately after his flight. By one account he became attached to a German army unit and spent several months in Czechoslovakia. We do know from later testimony by one of his former classmates that Mengele appeared at an army field hospital on the German-Czech border. The man remembers the date as being May 2, 1945, because a few minutes before seeing his old friend Mengele, he had heard of Hitler's suicide on the military radio.

In May 1945, some 25,000 German soldiers were confined to a small no man's land between the advancing Soviet army on the east and the Americans on the west. By mutual agreement, neither side advanced until June 15, when U.S. forces accepted the surrender of some 10,000 of the Germans. Mengele was among a group that attempted to escape, but he was soon captured by a group of American soldiers and brought to a prison camp in Weiden.

One fact of Mengele's capture remains in dispute—whether he used his own name or an alias. But U.S. Army records show that shortly thereafter he gave his captors his correct name and the information that he was a physician. However, he did not admit that he was a member of the SS. In fact, he denied it vigorously under examination, and his membership could not be confirmed, because he had not been marked with the usual SS blood-type tattoo. Thus he was allowed to remain in the camp as an ordinary prisoner.

Mengele then became the beneficiary of an extraordinary stroke of fortune. Even before the war's end, he had been identified as a major war criminal by prisoners freed from Auschwitz. In May 1945, he was added to the growing list of known war criminals who were being sought throughout the war zone. Although his name was prominent among the tens of thousands on this list, either the list never reached the small prison camp where he was held, or, if it did, no one bothered to read it.

Later it would be alleged that Mengele's release from the camp, despite his presence on this list of wanted war criminals, resulted from a complex conspiracy. But a thorough 1985 investigation by the U.S. Department of Justice's Office of Special Investigations failed to reveal any proof whatever. OSI investigators could not determine if a copy of the Watch List ever arrived at the prison camp; they concluded that, given the turmoil of the time, it was probable that the list had not arrived prior to his release in early September 1945.

Mengele eventually made his way to a friend's apartment in Munich and from there traveled to a rural agricultural area near the town of Rosenheim. For the next several years, under the name of Fritz Hollmann, he worked in the area as a farm laborer and was protected by at least one family who knew his background but sympathized with his Nazi service.

More confusion over Mengele's whereabouts ensued and played into his hands. From the moment that he had fled Auschwitz, Mengele's father had attempted to help him hide his trail. Several times when he was interrogated by U.S. authorities, the elder Mengele said that his son had died in the Soviet zone in the last days of the war. Apparently, he convinced American authorities that his son was dead, because in 1948, when an inquiry into Mengele's whereabouts began in Washington, the Nuremberg prosecutors reported back that an October 1946 investigation had revealed his death. That closed the books, at least for American investigators, on the notorious Dr. Josef Mengele.

By the summer of 1948, Mengele had tired of his life as a farm worker, but he knew that he had no future in Germany. Earlier in the year, the Allies had tried a group of SS doctors at Auschwitz and executed several for crimes much less severe than Mengele's. With his father, he decided that his future lay in South America, and they began laying plans for his escape to Argentina.

In September or October 1948, Mengele left the farm and returned to the Gunzburg area, where he remained hidden by his family until the spring of 1949, when he began the journey financed by his father. First, he traveled by train to Austria, then crossed the Italian border on foot. A series of trains took him to Genoa, where he was booked aboard the ship *North King,* which would land him in Buenos Aires. In Genoa, a friend of his father's brought him money, new identification papers, and, difficult as it is to believe, a suitcase filled with notes of his Auschwitz experiments.

One detail was left to the days before the ship sailed. An agent for his father, bearing false identity papers for Mengele, took him to the Swiss Consulate, where he obtained a passport in the name of Helmut Gregor. He had only two more obstacles to overcome, the first of which was relatively simple. He presented his new passport at the Argentine Consulate and obtained an entry visa. Now he had to secure an Italian exit visa—which almost proved to be his undoing. The only way he could get such a visa was by bribing an Italian customs official, but he went about it in such a clumsy manner that he found himself under arrest. He ended up spending three weeks in an Italian jail, but, in the end, additional bribes were paid and he was released.

Once again, his luck held. The *North King* had encountered mechanical difficulties and had postponed its sailing date for more than a month. On the day of his release from jail, he boarded the ship and two days later left Europe.

Mengele had chosen carefully in selecting Argentina as his first place of residence in South America. The country had a long history of pro-Nazi sentiment and had become a postwar haven for fleeing Nazis. Several weeks after landing in Buenos Aires, Mengele found his way to the large house of a known Nazi sympathizer who rented rooms to former Nazis. Years later it would become clear that Mengele supported himself in Argentina as a sales representative for his father's German farm machinery company.

In the early 1950s, Mengele reportedly traveled often to both Paraguay and Brazil on sales trips. He began to prosper, and several times during the decade moved to successively larger homes in Argentina. He also invested in several companies. Apparently, by 1956 he had grown bolder, confident that he was no longer being sought. The difficulties of living under an assumed name were becoming overwhelming, so he went to the West German Embassy in Buenos Aires, identified himself as Josef Mengele of Gunzburg, and asked for identity papers in his own name. On September 11, 1956, the embassy issued the papers. Evidently, no one there bothered to check any lists of war criminals; otherwise, they would have found Mengele's name on most of them. Armed with his new German identity card, Mengele went into an Argentine court and swore that Helmet Gregor and Josef Mengele were one and the same person. In due course, the Argentine government issued him a new identity card, and he returned to the West German Embassy, and, apparently with little difficulty, obtained a West German passport. Over the next several years, he made numerous business trips to other South American countries.

In July 1958, Mengele liquidated all his holdings in various small companies in which he had invested and, with two associates, founded a pharmaceutical firm for the manufacture of drugs and other medical products. The incorporation papers listed Dr. Jose (Spanish for Josef) Mengele as founding director. By the end of the year, Mengele was an established Argentine businessman who felt that only good lay ahead of him.

The ease with which Mengele obtained German identity papers and a passport showed that Germany was not very interested in the notorious doctor from

Auschwitz. But many in Germany and elsewhere still remembered vividly the atrocities he had committed and were determined to bring him to justice.

One such person was an Austrian, Hermann Langbein, who had been arrested by the Gestapo during the war for anti-Nazi political activities and had ended up as a clerk in the medical offices at Auschwitz. He could not sleep at night for remembering Mengele, and, in fact, had become obsessed with him. Langbein began to assemble a file of evidence against the physician, and eventually his investigations showed that Mengele had obtained a German divorce from his first wife in 1953, after signing a power of attorney in Buenos Aires by which a German lawyer could represent him at the hearing. Armed with this information, Langbein tried to convince German authorities that Mengele was alive in Argentina. As he sought a prosecutor in the German government, Mengele, apparently, for some unrelated reason, became very uneasy about prolonging his residence in Argentina and fled to Paraguay. He entered the country on a short-term visitor's visa on October 2, 1959.

During the years of the search for Mengele, it had often been alleged that someone in the German State Prosecutor's office in Bonn tipped off the Mengele family about Langbein's visit. It now appears that what triggered Mengele's flight from Buenos Aires was his arrest, some three weeks earlier, on suspicion of practicing medicine without a license. He was able to bribe his way to freedom, but he feared that he had become the target of official investigations in Argentina. However, it is also possible that word of the inquiries Langbein was making in Gunzburg reached Menegele's family, who warned him that an investigation was underway.

By 1959 Paraguay had become a haven for Nazi fugitives, and Mengele, using his own name, settled in a region known as the Alto Parana in southeastern Paraguay, near the Argentine border. So many Germans lived there that German rather than Spanish was the common language.

Meanwhile, back in West Germany, Hermann Langbein's efforts were finally successful. On June 5, 1959, a German court drew up an indictment of Mengele, seeking his arrest on seventeen counts of premeditated murder. A copy of the warrant was sent to the German Foreign Office, which contacted the embassy in Buenos Aires to begin extradition proceedings. But by the time the Argentine police were notified, Mengele was long gone to Paraguay, where he had applied for citizenship under the name Jose Mengele.

While the original search for Josef Mengele had been a one-man effort by Hermann Langbein, news of the indictment led other individuals and organizations to become involved. The World Jewish Congress began to gather witnesses—Auschwitz survivors—to testify in court so as to expand the indictment. At about the same time, the German ambassador in Paraguay received word that Mengele was in the country and made a formal request to the government to locate him. He indicated that if Mengele was, in fact, in the country, a request for his extradition would be forthcoming. On November 27, 1959, despite this information, a Paraguayan court issued a naturalization certificate to "Jose" Mengele. At the same time, it informed the German ambassador that any extradition request for Mengele would almost surely be rejected on the grounds that allegations against him were of a political nature.

For almost a year, Mengele remained in southern Paraguay, but he lived in great fear that the Israelis would come to kidnap him, as they had kidnapped Eichmann from Argentina. In fact, the Mossad's move against Eichmann, one of the most daring chapters in Nazi-hunting history, had thrown fear into the hearts of all former Nazis hiding in safe havens.

★   ★   ★

From the day the war ended, Eichmann had been the most-hunted. If any single individual can be said to be the architect of the Final Solution, it was Eichmann. He was not a personal killer, he was a bureaucrat. He did not personally shoot a gun or operate a gas oven, or stand guard over a prisoner. But, as head of the Gestapo's "Jewish Section," he was the man who put the entire system together and made it work. He took the crazed idea of attaining racial purity by genocide and turned it into a still more crazed reality. He built the camps, he organized the deportations of the Jews to them, he experimented until he found the quickest, cheapeast, and most efficient method of mass murder.

Eichmann was born in 1906 at Solingen, in the Rhineland. In 1914 he moved with his family to Linz, Austria, where his father had taken a job as an accountant with a power company. Later, the senior Eichmann went into business for himself, operating a mine that extracted oil from shale. Adolf Eichmann, who was not a good student, dropped out of technical school at the age of fifteen and went to work in his father's mine. He soon left to take a job with the power company, first as an apprentice and, later, as a salesman for a subsidiary oil company establishing gasoline service stations.

In 1932 Eichmann joined the SS. He was recruited by Ernst Kaltenbrunner, a young lawyer who was the son of a former business partner of his father's. Eventually, Kaltenbrunner became head of the SS: he was tried and hanged at Nuremberg. Eichmann was assigned to the Austrian Legion, in which he served in several quasi-military assignments until 1935, when he was transferred to Berlin and assigned to the office that oversaw the activities of Freemasons. Shortly after he arrived in Berlin, the SS set up the Office for Jewish Emigration, to which Eichmann was transferred. The new office was charged with formulating policies toward Jews and overseeing their implementation. After the *Anschluss,* Eichmann was assigned to the Vienna branch.

In October 1939, one month after World War II began, Adolf Eichmann issued a memorandum outlining the Reich's plan to transport Vienna's Jews to

Polish and Czechoslovakian "resettlements," establishing a separate Jewish Territory that would eventually contain the entire population of Jews under German control. The first transport of 1,000 Viennese Jews left on October 20, 1939, for Nisko, Poland. The Central Office in Vienna had gathered the city's Jews into one central organization, which was charged with the task of administering the transports. By assigning the task of running the transports to the Jews themselves, the Germans cleverly served their own ends while giving the operation an appearance of cooperation from within the Jewish community. The Nazi description of these "resettlements" was pure deception. The transports, ostensibly delivering the Jews to a new, autonomous homeland, actually discharged their passengers into a wasteland that offered little or no chance for survival. The Final Solution had begun.

After his success at running the Jewish offices in Vienna and, later, in Prague, Eichmann had been recalled to Berlin, where he was placed in charge of the Reich Center for Jewish Emigration. Later, at Nuremberg, his name was mentioned with great frequency. Several witnesses testified that they had been there the day Eichmann bragged, "I will leap into my grave laughing, because the feeling I have five million human beings on my conscience is for me a source of extraordinary satisfaction."

On May 23, 1960, Premier David Ben-Gurion announced to the world that Adolf Eichmann, the SS Colonel who had headed the Gestapo's Jewish Section, was under arrest in Israel and would stand trial for his life. Ben-Gurion made the announcement before the Knesset (Israel's Parliament) with what *The New York Times* called "dramatic understatement."

No information was given as to where, when, or under what circumstances Eichmann was apprehended and how he had ended up in Israel. When pressed, specifically about whether he had been captured by an agency of Israel or a free-lance Nazi hunter, Ben-Gurion would say no more than "Adolf Eichmann is already under arrest in Israel and will shortly be placed on trial here under the terms of the law for the trial of Nazis and their collaborators."

By the next day, May 24, canvasses of every nation had convinced the media that there had been no formal extradition from another country. Since it was impossible to believe that a repentant Eichmann had walked across the border and said "I'm here," speculation was that he had been spirited away from wherever he was hiding. Some said that he had been found in the Middle East, others speculated about various South American countries. The following day, with the mystery unresolved, a clean-shaven fifty-three-year-old Adolf Eichmann was arraigned before Chief Magistrate Yedidya Levy in Jaffa.

The judge said, "Adolf Eichmann, you are charged with causing the death of millions of Jews in Germany and the enemy-occupied countries in the years 1938 to 1945. Are you Adolf Eichmann?"

Eichmann turned pale, but remained calm and said in a clear voice, *"Ich vin Adolf Eichmann"* (I am Adolf Eichmann).

The Eichmann kidnaping has been imortalized in print and on film, but the complete story of how he was eventually caught has never been made public. Based on details that came out at his trial and later, and discussions we have had with former senior Israeli intelligence officers, we believe we now know most of what happened.

The first indication that Eichmann might be living in Argentina came to the Israelis via the West German secret service. A former Dachau inmate, living in a Buenos Aires suburb, had reported to Frankfurt prosecutor Fritz Bauer, a dedicated Nazi hunter, that a schoolmate of his daughter, one Nikolaus Klement, had been making violently anti-Semitic statements. The informant suspected that the boy's father, known as Ricardo Klement, a balding, middle-aged office worker who lived in the suburb of Olivos with his German wife and four children, might be a hidden Nazi.

The Israelis became very interested, because the suspect's name was so close to "Ricardo Clementi," an alias known to have been used by one of thirty major Nazis who had fled Europe through Italy and Spain, using Red Cross travel documents obtained through the Vatican.*

The Israelis did not realize immediately that the unimposing office worker in South America was Eichmann, the killer whom they wanted so badly, but they believed that he was an important Nazi. Israel had no extradition treaty,

---

* It would be learned later that Eichmann had been captured not once, but twice, by the Americans in 1945-46. In the spring of 1945, he had obtained identification papers for himself in the name of Adolf Barth, a Luftwaffe corporal. As the Reich fell, he made his way to Ulm with the false papers and was arrested by the Americans, who released him because they had no interest in low-level members of the regular German army. In early 1946 he was picked up again and sent to a POW camp at Weiden. This time he escaped before his identity could be established.

In March 1946, as Otto Heninger, Eichmann took refuge in Bavaria, where he worked as a logger. Over the next four years, he worked in northern Germany and in Spain, both as a logger, and, for a time, as a chicken farmer. In the spring of 1950, he traveled from Spain to Austria and crossed the Italian border. He obtained the Italian Red Cross displaced-person travel document issued by the Vatican in the name of Clementi.

In Argentina Eichmann worked as a surveyor for an engineering firm. Then he lived under various aliases in Brazil, Paraguay, and Bolivia, doing office work, managing a small laundry, and running a rabbit farm. In 1956 he moved back to Argentina, adopted the name Klement, and worked as a mechanic. Later he spent almost two years in the interior as a farm manager. Apparently, he had been back in the capital, working in a Diamler-Benz auto plant office, for only a short time before he came to the attention of the Germans and Israelis.

and only a tenuous relationship, with Argentina. But, with German help, intense negotiations with the Argentine foreign ministry were undertaken. Despite all that would be said later, high-level Argentine officials gave Israeli intelligence operatives permission to put Klement under surveillance.

Once the Israelis got a good look at the suspect, and took photographs that were flown back to Israel and Germany, they began to suspect that Klement was Eichmann. But they were not certain until March 21, 1960, when operatives watched Klement leave work and stop at a florist shop to pick up a large bouquet of flowers. They followed him to a new house that he had built, in which he had lived for less than a month, and saw him give the flowers to his wife, who greeted him at the door with a kiss. The watchers were convinced: March 21 was Adolf Eichmann's wedding anniversary.

The Israelis then consulted with German officials. The West German government wanted Eichmann badly, but its previous requests for extradition of Nazis from Argentina had largely been ignored. Despite the Argentine agreement to allow surveillance, the West Germans were not at all confident that a request for Eichmann's return to Germany would meet with success. Rather, it was likely that he would flee and go underground as soon as he learned he had been located. Israel decided that independent action was the only answer.

The Israelis considered assassination, but dismissed the idea. As Simon Wiesenthal has said, "if you kill an Eichmann, the world will never learn what he did." There had to be a trial once Eichmann was removed from Argentina. Initially, the idea was to return him to Germany, but it was decided at the highest levels of Israeli government to try him in Israel—if he could be captured.

Some kind of an excuse was necessary, and finally presented itself in the form of Argentina's 150th anniversary, to be celebrated in May 1960. Israel asked if a delegation headed by Minister of State Abba Eban could attend in order to improve relations between Israel and Argentina. When permission was granted, El Al Airline's New York station manager, Joseph Klein, himself a concentration camp survivor, flew to Buenos Aires to arrange for the landing of a special El Al flight carrying the delegation.

On May 11, Eichmann got off a bus and was walking home from work along General Paz Avenue when an automobile suddenly pulled to the curb and several men jumped out, grabbed him, and threw him into the back seat. It all happened so quickly and quietly that bystanders scarcely realized what had taken place. It turned out later that the abductors were part of a five-man unit of Israeli military commandos led by Yehudah Shimoni.

Eichmann was taken to a safe house, where he underwent a physical examination. He had the scar of an appendectomy, a scar above his left eyebrow, and an SS blood-group tattoo under his left armpit—all matching the German medical records. But the physical examination was only a confirmation: in their first interrogation of their captive, the Israeli commandos had asked his name. "I am Adolf Eichmann," was his prompt reply. "Are you Israelis?"

On May 20, the plane carrying the Israeli delegation landed in Buenos Aires. Within hours it had been refueled and had taken off again, with a reported destination of Rome. (The delegation was stranded, and another plane had to return a week later to pick them up.) Israel has never admitted that Eichmann was taken out on the first plane. In fact, he had been drugged and the Israelis had brought him aboard the plane in a wheelchair. They showed Argentine customs officials an Israeli passport and said that he was a wealthy Jew, near death, who wanted to die in the Promised Land; he was using the unscheduled flight to return there quickly.

Until June 6 Argentina protested continuously over the kidnaping of Eichmann from within its borders. Other nations were sympathetic to Israel's desire to try Eichmann, but, critical of its violation of Argentine jurisdiction. But perhaps the most bizarre story came out on June 6. when the Israelis told Argentina that Eichmann had left "voluntarily" to stand trial in Israel.

Foreign Minister Diogenes Taboada of Argentina released a note in which the Israeli government stated that Eichmann had been located by a "volunteer" group in Argentina, where he was living under a false name without the knowledge of Argentine authorities, and with the help of other Nazis. The message claimed that the volunteer group had approached Eichmann and asked whether he were willing to go to Israel to stand trial, upon which he asked for twenty-four hours and then agreed to go. According to the Israeli government, the volunteers then informed their foreign office that Eichmann was in Israel and prepared to face a court. The Israelis expressed regret for the infringement of Argentine sovereignty, but urged consideration of the fact that the man involved had been responsible for the killing of millions of Jews and others. They claimed that members of the volunteer group were survivors of the Nazi massacre of the Jews and that the Israeli government was certain that "the Argentine government will show understanding in the face of such historic and moral values."

After the initial charade of the "independent hunt" and capture of Adolf Eichmann, Israeli secret service officials admitted that they had coordinated the hunt for years and controlled the kidnaping from Argentina. This infuriated the Argentine government, which not only demanded the return of Eichmann, but called on the U.N. for assistance. On June 15, Argentina lodged a formal complaint with the Security Council that the "illicit transfer of Adolf Eichmann to Israel from Argentina had created an atmosphere of insecurity and mistrust incompatible with the preservation of international laws."

The nations of the world knew there would be rhetoric, and knew also that Israel was going to move ahead with its prosecution of Adolf Eichmann.

In one of the most controversial trials in judicial history Eichmann was found guilty of mass murder and was executed on May 31, 1961.

★   ★   ★

During 1960 and still in fear that he might be the subject of an Eichmann-style kidnapping, Mengele made several trips to Brazil, where he found several areas with extensive German populations in which he felt he could be comfortable. Reportedly, by November 1960, he had left Paraguay and was looking for a place to settle in Brazil.

He had met Wolfgang Gerhard when the latter visited Paraguay. Gerhard was a fanatical pro-Nazi, whose only regret was that he had been too young during the war years to serve in the SS or the German Army. By profession he was a real estate agent who specialized in finding Brazilian properties for northern Europeans who were relocating. One such couple was Geza Stammer and his wife, Gitta, who were moving from Austria to a German enclave some 200 miles north of São Paulo, where they had bought a small coffee plantation. Gerhard introduced Mengele to the Stammers, and they hired him as a farm manager. Over the next twenty years, Mengele would move several times, but Gerhard would remain his protector, and, in the end, it would be Gerhard's identity that he assumed in death.

For more than a decade Mengele had lived openly, but in relative obscurity, first in Argentina and then in Paraguay. Now he was suddenly the object of intense manhunts by several South American countries, the Israelis, the West Germans, and private Nazi hunters. For the first time, the West Germans offered a cash reward for a former Nazi: the price on Mengele's head was $20,000. Three times in 1962, the Brazilians thought they had found him. They even arrested a man who had considerable difficulty proving that he was *not* Mengele. Barely a week went by without some European or South American newspaper reporting another Mengele sighting. But in the midst of all this hysteria, Mengele continued to live on the Stammers' farm and in mid-1962 moved with them to a larger farm in Serra Nagra, about 100 miles north of São Paulo. As he had done previously, Mengele loaned the Stammers half the money required to buy their new farm.

In retrospect, one reason that Mengele was able to live undetected in Brazil for much of the next two decades was the certainty that he was still living in Paraguay under the protection of the country's dictator, Alfredo Stroessner. The Israelis searched for Mengele in Paraguay, private Nazi hunters made frequent trips to the country, and the West German government was so sure that Mengele was in Paraguay that, in 1963, German chancellor Konrad Adenauer offered Stroessner $4 million to extradite him. When Paraguay refused the money, the West Germans were even more certain that Mengele was there, and under Stroessner's protection. As pressure mounted on Paraguay, the Stroessner government began a more thorough internal investigation. In September 1964, it issued a statement admitting that Mengele had become a Paraguayan citizen but claimed that "he [had] departed four years ago." We know now that this statement was completely accurate, but at the time it was not believed. Even those few who were ready to believe Paraguay's denial that Mengele was still in the country criticized the Stroessner government for not determining where he had gone, if, in fact, he had left the country.

Probably the closest approach to finding Mengele in the early 1960s came through an event that took place not in South America, but thousands of miles away in Germany. Finding Mengele had become a top priority of Nazi hunter Simon Wiesenthal, who was convinced that wherever he was—and, for a long time, Wiesenthal was certain that Mengele, like Alois Brunner, was in Egypt or elsewhere in the Middle East—he was being supported by his family back in Gunzburg. In fact, Wiesenthal believed that Hans Sedlmeier, a long-time close friend of Mengele's and an executive in the family business, was acting as a conduit between the fugitive and his family.

Amazingly, as would be learned two decades later, Wiesenthal was completely correct. Sedlmeier had made trips to South America to meet Mengele, received letters and other communications from him, and even set up a secret visit between Mengele and his family in Switzerland in the mid-1950s—reportedly, the only visit Mengele made to Europe after he left Italy in 1949.

Wiesenthal convinced West German prosecutors that Sedlmeier had information that could lead to Mengele. Based on Wiesenthal's demands, a search warrant was obtained and a raid made on Sedlmeier's house. But Sedlmeier had been warned about the raid by a police employee who was in the family's pay, and had gathered up and destroyed all incriminating documents. Had Sedlmeier not been tipped off about the impending raid, there is little doubt that the prosecutors would have learned Mengele's whereabouts, and he would have been captured in a matter of hours.

While the world continued to search, and condemnation of Paraguay increased, we now know that Mengele continued to live quietly with the Stammers. He stayed with them for thirteen years, growing more dominant in the relationship. His family ended up financing much of the farm and its equipment, and even household expenses. And although she denies it vigorously, it is generally accepted by investigators from several countries that over the years Mengele developed a sexual relationship with Gitta Stammer that lasted for years. Apparently, the longer Mengele was with the Stammers and the more confident he became that he would not be found, the more he began to slip back into the authoritarian ways of his youth and his Nazi service career.

By the late 1960s, the Stammers had tired of Mengele and told Gerhard that he had to go. This led to the abortive attempt to link Mengele with Barbie. But Mengele would not move: he minimized the Stammers' discontent.

In 1969 Mengele's reluctant hosts decided to give up the farm and move closer to São Paulo, where Geza Stammer had taken a job. They bought a large house some twenty-five miles north of the city, in the town of Jardid Luciana, and Mengele and his family financed half the purchase. But within a few months, the relationship between the Stammers and Mengele had deteriorated again, and the couple renewed their demand that Gerhard find him another place to live. Finally, Gerhard introduced Mengele to a German couple, Wolf and Liselotte Bossert, with whom he could spend time as an alternative to the Stammers. Wolf Bossert had served in the German army and was a passionate pro-Nazi; he and Mengele hit it off at once. Not until several years later did the Bosserts learn who their new friend was—and then it did not bother them. As Wolf Bossert said later, "When I discovered who he was, I felt sorry for him. He was the most hunted and persecuted man in the world."

In 1971 Wolfgang Gerhard decided to leave South America and return to Austria. Upon his departure, he gave Mengele a priceless gift—his Brazilian identity card. In all his years on the Stammers' farms, he had never held proper identity papers, forcing him to live as a recluse. Now, armed with Gerhard's identity card, which he and Bossert altered, Mengele had papers that would stand up to casual inspection and he could travel within the country.

The identity card became even more valuable in mid-1972, when Mengele became seriously ill with a blockage of the intestines and had to be admitted to a hospital in São Paulo. The doctors became suspicious, because the card was for a forty-seven-year-old man, and Mengele was then in his sixties. However, the attending physician believed his explanation that the date of birth on the card was simply a typographical error that "Gerhard" had never bothered to correct.

Although he now spent most of his time with the Bosserts, Mengele was still living with the Stammers, but in mid-1974 their relationship finally reached the breaking point. In fact, several of Mengele's protectors, in both Brazil and Germany, worried that Geza Stammer was so angry he might turn Mengele in to the authorities. Finally, Stammer moved out of the house, vowing not to return until Mengele was gone. In November 1974, the Stammers sold the house and moved to São Paulo. Mengele stayed on for several months, until the new owner took possession, when he, too, had to move.

Both the Stammers and the Bosserts were concerned about where Mengele could go. Although Wolf Bossert had become his closest friend—in fact, his only friend—Bossert was unwilling to have Mengele move in with his family, because he had seen what Mengele's presence had done to the Stammers' relationship. Finally, Bossert and the Stammers got together and, with money from Mengele's family, bought a small house in suburban São Paulo, to which the former Nazi moved in March 1975.

While all this domestic interplay was going on, the hunt for Mengele continued. Some were convinced that he was still in Paraguay, despite constant statements from the Stroessner government that he had not been there for more than a decade. Simon Wiesenthal made several statements indicating that his sources and agents had identified Mengele as being in Paraguay and in Egypt. Once Wiesenthal stated that he had just missed finding Mengele on a visit to Spain. Other sightings of the fugitive were reported in Chile, Bolivia, Peru, Uruguay—in fact, in almost every South American country except Brazil.

By all accounts, the last years of Mengele's life were tragic. His health began to deteriorate, and his fear of capture progressed into deep psychosis. His financial state worsened as well, and he constantly implored his family for more money. He rarely left his small house, and almost his only contact outside his immediate neighborhood was Wolf Bossert, who visited him several times a week and took him on outings with the family and other friends. But Bossert became fearful of these outings as Mengele's mental condition deteriorated, because he began to revert more and more to ranting about fascism and the Nazi cause. He went into long tirades about the rightness of Hitler and his theories and decried what had happened to Germany since the end of the war.

If Wolf Bossert is to be believed, Josef Mengele died on February 7, 1979. It was the height of the summer, and there was an unusual heat wave. Bossert had convinced Mengele to come with him to a rented beach house about twenty-five miles south of São Paulo, in the town of Bertioga. In the late afternoon, Mengele and Bossert were taking a walk along the beach when Mengele decided to take a short swim. As Bossert later told a television interviewer, he suspects Mengele suffered a stroke while swimming, or perhaps the strong current was simply too much for the old man. Seeing that he was in distress, Bossert swam out and dragged Mengele back to shore, but by the time they reached the beach he was dead weight. Attempts to revive him on the beach by a doctor proved unsuccessful. The Angel of Death was himself dead.

Mengele's burial was a fairly easy matter, because of some amazing advance planning made by Wolfgang Gerhard. During the 1950s he had acquired a burial plot next to his mother's at Our Lady of the Rosary Cemetery in Embu, about twenty miles west of São Paulo. Mengele's body was taken from the beach to the local coroner, who signed the death certificate in the name of Wolfgang Gerhard, aged fifty-three. Within twenty-four hours Mengele was buried in the plot in a simple white coffin. In retrospect, that turned out to be a serious mistake for those who wanted to keep his identity secret. Mengele himself had asked to be cremated, and had his wishes been carried out, it is likely that the world would never have learned about his twenty-year life in Brazil.

Even in death, Mengele remained the target of almost every Nazi hunter.

On one occasion Simon Wiesenthal told reporters a very involved story about how Mengele was living in Paraguay as part of a network of Nazi fugitives known as *Die Spinne* (The Spider). Wiesenthal said that Mengele owned two large houses near Asunción and was always accompanied by a contingent of armed bodyguards; moreover, his agents had seen Mengele dining at the German Club of Asunción, where he frequently made his point in arguments by slamming his pistol on the bar. At one point, *The New York Post* even reported at great length that Mengele was alive and well and living in Westchester County, just north of New York City, in the town of Bedford Hills.

Perhaps the most elaborate confusion came in 1984, when two foreign journalists persuaded *The New York Post* and *Paris Match* that an old man living in Uruguay was Mengele. *The Post* flooded Uruguay with reporters and came away convinced that the man was, in fact, Mengele. They hired a group of photo identification experts to compare pictures of the two, and three experts concluded that photographs of Mengele taken during the war years as compared with those of the man in Uruguay were 90-plus percent similar in physical characteristics, such as shape of the skull, length of the nose, and distance between the nose and the lips. Upon learning that this identification had been made, the American television networks descended upon the unfortunate man, whose name was Señor Branaa. He spent the better part of two days convincing the reporters he was not Josef Mengele. Finally, by showing them school records and photo albums from his youth, and introducing friends who had known him for more than thirty years, he was able to discourage them.

But the Mengele hysteria continued, and more and more Nazi hunters came forward to claim that the fugitive was living in luxury somewhere in South America. Even the U.S. government made an official statement of its belief that Mengele was alive, and probably in Paraguay. In fact, the government was so sure of it that, under pressure from Congress, the responsibility for finding him was assigned to the Office of Special Investigations in 1985.

The intervention of the U.S. government into the worldwide search for Mengele seemed to galvanize international interest in the hunt. A few days after the announcement that OSI was becoming involved, the Israeli government announced its intention to make a major new attempt to find the former Nazi. This galvanized the West German government into a similar proclamation. Soon thereafter, a series of governments and individuals began to offer rewards for Mengele's capture. The Israeli government offered $1 million. Not to be outdone, Simon Wiesenthal announced that he too was putting up a million-dollar bounty, and West Germany increased its bounty to 1 million marks—about $400,000. Even the Reverend Sun Myung Moon entered the field with an announcement in his Washington-based newspaper *The Washington Times* that he, too, was offering a million-dollar reward for the capture of Josef Mengele. Various other private Nazi hunters raised the total to almost $5 million.

In May 1985, representatives from West Germany, the United States, and Israel gathered in Frankfurt to formalize their joint effort to find Mengele. The meeting was chaired by Hans Klein, the chief German prosecutor, and it was agreed that Germany would take the lead in the investigation, because if Mengele were found he would be tried that country. Klein did not tell the meeting that German investigators had been told that some months earlier, at a party, Hans Sedlmeier had let it slip that he had operated as the family's contact with Mengele. (Sedlmeier may have let it slip because he knew that Mengele was long dead, and he personally was growing tired of the game.)

Armed with this new information, Klein was able to persuade a German judge to give him another warrant to search Sedlmeier's house in Gunzburg. As they had twenty years earlier, German police swooped down on the house, only this time Sedlmeier had not been warned in advance. As the police conducted a thorough search, Sedlmeier tried to slip a small book from the pocket of a suit hanging in a closet. The police grabbed the book and found a series of phone numbers and addresses listed in code. They also found a cache of photocopies of letters that Mengele had sent to his family over the years. Sedlmeier apparently thought that the letters had been destroyed, but it turned out that his wife, who revered Mengele, had kept them surreptitiously.

One of the letters was from Wolf Bossert, stating that, "With deep sorrow I must announce the death of our common friend." To the German police, this seemed to confirm that Mengele was dead. They immediately contacted Brazilian authorities and São Paulo's police chief, Romeu Tuma, took charge of the investigation. The Germans supplied him with two addresses, one of which turned out to be the home of Wolf and Liselotte Bossert. The other was a post office box registered in the name of Geza and Gitta Stammer. Both locations were put under twenty-four-hour surveillance for four days. When no one resembling Mengele appeared at either place, police staged a raid on the Bossert house. Inside they found what amounted to a shrine to Mengele, including personal effects, hundreds of photographs, and some of his personal papers and writings. There were Christmas cards sent to the Bosserts regularly from the Mengele family in Germany, especially from Mengele's son Rolf. The Bosserts were arrested; after several hours of interrogation, they broke down and admitted their long-standing relationship with Mengele and the fact that his body could be found in the cemetery at Embu.

News of the discovery was closely held by Brazilian and German authorities, but on June 6, news leaked out to the German press. Immediately, the German government confirmed the story and notified both the Americans and the Israelis of their discovery. Both were furious that they had learned about the disclosure through the news media.

Meanwhile, the Brazilian government moved quickly to exhume the body. Simultaneously, the panel of forensic experts was formed in the United States by both OSI and the Simon Wiesenthal Center of Los Angeles. Less than 48 hours later, the experts had gathered in São Paulo to examine the pile of bones that had been removed from the grave.

They had one major problem. The detailed medical records that normally make such post-mortem identifications possible, especially dental records, were missing in the case of Mengele. But they did have his early SS file, which showed that he had broken a finger on his left hand and that he had suffered from osteomyelitis as a boy.

By June 21, the forensic experts believed they had an answer. It all matched up: the broken finger, the gap between the two upper front teeth that Auschwitz survivors remembered so well, the height of the body, determined by measuring the skeleton, and other physical characteristics. The experts gave their opinion that the body was undoubtedly that of Josef Mengele. Finally, Rolf Mengele came forward and admitted that the remains were those of his father. He gave details of Mengele's years in Brazil and of his death in 1979.

Skeptics were not convinced. They pointed out that the skeleton was longer than Mengele's known height by several centimeters: people grow shorter as they age, not taller. They argued that the forensic examination failed to reveal any indication of the osteomyelitis which Mengele had suffered from in his youth. Further, the examination had shown that the person buried at Embu suffered from a deformity of his left leg and hip, and no eyewitnesses or medical records of the Mengeles indicated such a condition.

It has not been previously revealed that since the initial June 1985 examination, several other teams of forensic experts have reviewed the results and re-examined the bones. No doubt remains that the man in the grave at Embu was, and is, Josef Mengele. The conclusion is that some of his early medical records, particularly of his height, were simply not exact, and experts have concluded that the osteomyelitis he experienced was not severe enough to leave lifelong traces. Investigators in the United States, West Germany, and Israel have closed the files on Josef Mengele, saying that they understand the feelings of those who want to believe that he is still alive, so that they can be avenged for his horrible deeds. But the scientific evidence is overwhelming. There can be no doubt that the Angel of Death is dead.

★   ★   ★

Josef Mengele eluded his pursuers for more than twenty years by living an invisible life on remote farms in Brazil. By contrast, for the last ten years of his exile, Klaus Barbie lived openly in Bolivia, often giving interviews to visiting journalists; he showed no embarrassment or repentance about his past. As Mengele had found safety in obscurity, Barbie found safety in the political protection of a series of Bolivian strongmen whose interests he served well.

Nikolaus Klaus Barbie was born October 25, 1913, in an area that is now a suburb of the West German capital of Bonn. His father was a teacher, and his youth was unremarkable. He attended a boarding school for several years and was an average student. Eventually, he returned to his family and continued his schooling.

Undoubtedly, a turning point in young Barbie's life came in 1933, when he turned twenty. Within a sixty-day period, first his younger brother, then his father, died. Only weeks before these tragic events, Barbie had joined the Nazi youth movement; afterward he threw himself into the organization, probably to compensate for his personal losses. He rose quickly in the organization, and by the end of 1933 was a leader of the local chapter in Trier, where his family had moved. The following year, he graduated from the German equivalent of high school with grades that were not good enough to gain him admission to a university, so he took a job with a public works organization. Barbie continued his activity in the Nazi youth movement and became the protégé of the local Party leader. It was this man who suggested to Barbie that he should apply for membership in either the Gestapo or the SS. Barbie was intrigued by the work of the Nazi Secret Service, and in September 1935 he applied for admission to the SS. He was accepted and inducted on October 1, 1935.

Barbie showed immediate enthusiasm for his new career. He was first assigned as a clerk to the main SS office in Berlin, then transferred to Dusseldorf in another clerical position. During this period he became a member of the Nazi Party and undertook basic military training. In mid-1939 he was promoted to the rank of *Oberscharfuhrer,* the equivalent of sergeant.

In October 1939, Barbie was assigned to SS regional headquarters in Dortmund, which would be his official assignment until the war ended. (His postings all over Europe were temporary assignments.) In Dortmund he received a series of commendations for his work in an SS section that gathered intelligence on individuals and groups suspected of harboring anti-state feelings and engaging in prohibited political activities. His superiors were sufficiently impressed that in April 1940, he was promoted again—to second lieutenant. This was unusual in that the SS rarely promoted enlisted men into the officer corps, which was traditionally limited to university graduates. Barbie had overcome his lack of formal post-secondary education.

In May 1940, Hitler launched his Blitzkrieg, and by the end of the month both Belgium and Holland had fallen. Immediately, Barbie was assigned to the SS office in Amsterdam with the unit charged with investigating those who might harbor anti-Nazi sentiments. Reportedly, his unit was also responsible for gathering information on the Jews of Amsterdam—intelligence that was put to use almost at once.

In early 1941, the Nazis moved forcefully against the Jews in Holland. In February, many young Jewish men were rounded up and shipped to the death camp at Mauthausen in the first act of the annihilation of the large Jewish-

Dutch community. By the end of the war, 75 percent of Dutch Jews—some 110,000 men, women, and children—were murdered. By the middle of 1941 Barbie had received his first medal, the Iron Cross Second Class, for his work in "cleaning out" Jewish ghettos. He was also promoted to first lieutenant.

In early 1942, Barbie was sent to an SS school in Germany for specialized training in anti-resistance and counterespionage activities, the field he would occupy for the remainder of his service. By May he had completed his training and received his first counterespionage posting, to the small town of Gex, on the Swiss-French border. His assignment was to break up a Soviet spy ring operating in the area. Eventually, he succeeded, although most of the ring-leaders were able to escape. Then, in November 1942, he received his first command. At the age of twenty-nine, he became the commander of SS Section IV—counterespionage and intelligence—in Lyon, France. His assignment was simple: to stamp out the active French Resistance movement in the area by any means he chose.

Barbie plunged into his new assignment with an enthusiasm and ferocity rarely matched by SS officers anywhere. As a French court would find later, during his career in Lyon, Barbie was guilty of deporting more than 8,000 people to their deaths, of participating personally in more than 4,000 murders, and of supervising and participating in the torture of more than 15,000 suspected members of the Resistance.

However, these bare statistics don't begin to tell the story of Klaus Barbie. Hundreds of witnesses have come forward to tell how, hour after hour, and day after day, Barbie personally beat and tortured them, trying to extract information about the Resistance. Many of the torture methods he favored dated from the days of the Inquisition. He had a torture chamber built in the basement of the prison at Fort Montluc, a 19th-century military facility in the center of Lyon that he converted into a prison for Resistance suspects. More than 3,000 died at his hands, or on his orders, in this prison.

Although Barbie's main task in Lyon was to root out and destroy the French Resistance, he also took an active interest in "Jewish affairs." The French in the area had worked very hard to try to protect Jews, especially Jewish children. Near Lyon was the small farming village of Izieu, a community of fewer than 100 people, almost hidden at the end of a small valley. There, in a farmhouse, more than forty Jewish children had been gathered in what amounted to a small orphanage. Barbie learned of their existence, and in April 1944 he drove to the farmhouse with two trucks, into which he loaded the children and their teachers. Several of the teachers were executed immediately, and all of the children were sent to Auschwitz, where they died in the gas chambers.

By the summer of 1944, things were going badly for the Germans in France. It was clear that Lyon would have to be evacuated, and Barbie embarked on a final round of destruction. He began to clear his jail cells the simple way—by executing their inhabitants. In July he supervised the massacre of several hundred civilians at the village of Villars les Dombes. Now, with Allied troops approaching, information on the Resistance was no longer a priority, so Barbie was transferred from intelligence to an active combat unit. In August, the Germans all but abandoned Lyon, leaving behind groups of commandos to slow advancing Allied forces. Barbie was given command of one such unit assigned to capture or assassinate General Henri Giraud, who was leading the French Army unit approaching Lyon from the South.

Barbie planned to ambush Giraud, but his unit was surprised by local guerrillas who attacked from the rear. On August 28 he was severely wounded. His unit escaped, and Barbie was taken to a nearby German hospital, where he was operated on for leg wounds. He was then evacuated to the German military hospital in Baden-Baden. In November he was promoted to the rank of captain and awarded the Iron Cross First Class for his activities in Lyon.

Barbie remained in the hospital until February 1945. It was clear that Germany was falling, and every able-bodied soldier was drafted for the final stand. Barbie was assigned to a combat unit in Essen, in the Ruhr Valley. On April 1, 1945, the Allies began their final push into the valley. On April 18, Barbie and a few of his men barely escaped capture. He knew that SS officers had been targeted for immediate arrest, so, as many other SS officers were doing, he burned his arms to cover the tattoos he bore as a member.

The months after the war ended saw a widespread search for Klaus Barbie, whose deeds in Lyon were only then becoming public. But, as soon as members of the Resistance in western France were questioned, he moved into a position high on the wanted list of Nazi war criminals. However, his training in anti-resistance activities saved him, as he employed many of the same tactics used by the French Resistance to avoid capture. For almost six months, he worked as a farm hand in the village of Coassonnette, using forged papers supplied by an organization of former SS members. Barbie himself soon became a leader of this organization and eventually provided false identity papers for almost 500 SS fugitives from justice. Near the end of 1945, he was arrested for black-market activities and jailed in an American prison in Darmstadt. Despite his position on the list of most-wanted war criminals, apparently—as in the case of Mengele—the list had not reached the prison, or it was never checked. His black-market activities were considered minor transgressions, and within two weeks he was released.

Barbie then traveled to Marburg, Germany, where he rented a room under the name of Klaus Becker. Using this name, he shuttled among several towns in the area early in 1946. During this period, he became a key member of another organization of former SS officers, most of whom had been involved in intelligence activities. He was able to obtain falsified military discharge papers that enabled him to live openly with his wife and two children in the town of

Kassel. The papers identified him as a former enlisted man in the German Army rather than an SS member.

In August 1946, Barbie was almost captured again. He had come to the attention of U.S. Counterintelligence Corps (CIC) officers who had captured a former SS officer who bore documents implicating others in the area. Barbie was arrested, but as he was being transported to CIC headquarters, he escaped by leaping from the jeep and eluding his pursuers in a hail of gunfire.

Several months later, Barbie and two other members of the underground SS organization traveled to Munich, where they hoped to pick up new sets of identity papers being forged by the Nazi underground. But they stumbled into an elaborate "sting" operation undertaken by a British intelligence unit. On November 12, Barbie and his companions were arrested at a cafe in downtown Hamburg and taken to a cell at British Secret Service headquarters. That same night, they staged a truly extraordinary escape through a combination of sheer luck, aid from other former Nazis, and the fact that their lone guard fell asleep.

By now, Barbie's group had become the target of U.S. counterintelligence. Twice, Barbie narrowly escaped capture again in CIC raids, once by jumping from a hotel bathroom window as agents poured through the door of his room. By February of 1947, he had become the object of a major manhunt and moved to the Munich region, where he thought he could remain safely.

Now Barbie's postwar existence took a sharp turn from that of Mengele, who had taken shelter in obscurity. Barbie remained free by becoming an agent for the CIC. By 1947 the United States was concerned about its ability to control its section of Occupied Germany. One response was to recruit former Nazis, especially intelligence officers, as informants on Nazi underground and Soviet activities in the area. A key informant was Kurt Merk, formerly a young captain in the German Army's counterintelligence corps, the *Abwehr*. During the war, Merk had been assigned to a counterintelligence unit in France, and in this capacity had worked with Barbie on several assignments. Barbie learned of Merk's involvement with the CIC and sought him out in the town of Memmingen. Through Merk, he met American CIC officer Robert Taylor, who recruited him to work under Merk. In some ways the situation was extraordinary. While Taylor was recruiting Barbie for his CIC team and offering him its protection, Barbie was being sought by the CIC in another part of Germany as a war criminal.

Reportedly, Barbie's first job with the CIC was to set up a network of informants to develop information about what French intelligence was doing in their zone of occupation. This assignment would become a major factor later, when the CIC began to deal with the French over Barbie. Within months, Barbie and Merk were running a network of some seventy agents that extended throughout southern Germany and into Eastern Europe. It was one of the most active and successful operations run by the CIC in Germany. By one account, the Merk-Barbie network was supplying 70 percent of the intelligence being sent from the area to CIC headquarters in Frankfurt.

By the end of 1947, Barbie's dual role as a CIC informant and a wanted man had come to the attention of the CIC brass at headquarters, and an order came down from Frankfurt for his arrest. What ensued can only be described as a major bureaucratic war. The CIC in Region IV, where Barbie was operating under under the code name Becker, considered him perhaps their most valuable agent and strongly resisted the arrest order. The battle raged for months, but finally, in December 1947, Barbie was arrested and brought to the main CIC interrogation center in Frankfurt.

Much of what we know about Barbie during this period is contained in the report on a 1983 investigation undertaken by the Office of Special Investigations when it was directed by Allan Ryan. The "Ryan Report" dealt harshly with U.S. complicity in hiring and protecting Barbie, and, as we will see, in spiriting him out of Germany to South America.

Amazingly, Ryan concludes that in December 1947, Barbie was arrested not because of his SS past in Lyon, but for fear that he had retained his ties to the Nazi underground and was acting as a double agent. Although he remained in custody in Frankfurt from December 1947 until May 1948, interrogation records seem to indicate that his captors were never aware that he was on several wanted lists as a war criminal. In fact, they had him listed as serving in an entirely different SS unit, one that was not involved in war crimes.

Eventually, those CIC members who believed Barbie was more valuable as an operative won out. On May 10, 1948, he was released and installed in a CIC safe house in Augsburg with Merk and the latter's mistress. They were supervised by Erhard Dabringhaus, a CIC civilian agent who is now a professor at Wayne State University in Detroit.

Barbie was developing some of the most valuable intelligence flowing into CIC headquarters. One of his greatest coups was in learning the details of Soviet use of a uranium mine in its occupation zone, which gave the CIC early information on the Soviet atomic bomb program. Some intelligence officers still argue that this piece of information alone justified Barbie's continued employment as a U.S. intelligence agent.

At about the same time, the French finally learned that Barbie was in the American zone and under CIC protection. A French military war crimes tribunal had twice issued arrest warrants for Barbie in 1945, and now the French sought American cooperation in serving them. Several times the CIC gave the French access to Barbie for questioning, but he remained under close CIC protection. Strangely enough, according to many who sat in on these interrogations, the French did not seem interested in Barbie's activities as a war criminal. They were concerned mainly with his early CIC activities in setting up the network for penetrating French intelligence in the U.S. occupation zone.

One of the major contradictions in the story of Barbie as a CIC agent is the point at which the CIC first became aware of his actions in Lyon. The Ryan Report puts the date at May 14, 1949, when several newspaper accounts of the Nazi occupation of Lyon and the extermination of the French Resistance there were published. According to the former CIC operatives, they had previously believed that although Barbie had been a counterintelligence officer in Lyon, he had undertaken his duties in a "professional" manner. They claim that it was not until the summer of 1949 that they became aware of his savagery and brutality in the French city.

This account, however, is sharply contradicted by Dabringhaus, who says that he began to learn the nature of Barbie's actions in France from Merk in the fall of 1948. He claims that he passed this information to his superiors, who expressed revulsion. But, at the same time, they could not discount the importance of the information that they were receiving from Barbie. Dabringhaus says that they decided to retain Barbie as long as he remained useful, then turn him over to the French.

Even if you accept May 1949 as the date when CIC officials learned about Barbie's true role in Lyon, they continued to shield him. Eugene Kolb, a U.S. Army colonel who commanded the CIC in Region IV, in 1949, defended Barbie strongly in several long communications to his headquarters. Even in the 1980s Kolb maintained in interviews that he did not believe all the accusations against Barbie. Kolb drew a sharp distinction between the killing of French Resistance fighters, whom he considered soldiers killed legitimately in a war, and the killing of Jews. He maintained he never knew Barbie had been involved in the deportation of Jews and when the French government demanded Barbie's return, it did so based only on his activities against the Resistance.

During the summer and fall of 1950, the French increased their efforts to extradite Barbie. The United States kept throwing up roadblocks, including a requirement that had been imposed in 1947—aimed mainly at the Soviets— that no extradition could take place unless the requesting country supplied the exact location of the wanted criminal. As the CIC moved Barbie constantly, the French were unable to meet this stipulation.

But, by the year's end, Barbie had become a major embarrassment to the organization. The CIC had many problems, apparently including the concern that if it turned Barbie over to the French, he would tell them about the activities aimed at France—something better left unknown, in the CIC's opinion. According to former CIC agents, a small meeting was held in the winter of 1948-49 to decide what to do with Barbie. Three alternatives were proposed: turn him over to the French, cut him loose to fend for himself, or kill him. As extraordinary it seems, there was strong support for the idea that killing Barbie was preferable to turning him over to the French: the embarrassment would have been too great for all concerned.

Reportedly, the meeting broke up without reaching any conclusions. Shortly thereafter, however, some CIC members began to formulate still another plan. A small detachment of CIC officers had been established for the sole purpose of funneling embarrassments to the group out of Germany. This "Operation Ratline" involved a clandestine escape route through Austria and Italy to destinations in South America, where former Nazis could disappear into the German enclaves of several countries. Apparently, late in the winter of 1950-51, it was decided to insert Barbie into Ratline for escape to South America. He would simply disappear from the face of the earth.

In February 1951, "Klaus Altmann" was born from an alias that Barbie had sometimes used in his CIC activities. Travel documents were provided, including a new passport, an Austrian visa, and the documents needed to pass through Italy. On March 9, Barbie and his family left Southern Germany as the Altmanns, and transited through Salzburg to Genoa, where, on March 23, they boarded the Italian vessel *Corrientes*, bound for Buenos Aires. As far as the CIC was concerned, Klaus Barbie had ceased to exist.

In late April 1951, Barbie and his wife and two children arrived in La Paz, Bolivia. After arriving in Argentina several weeks earlier, they had boarded a train for the Bolivian capital, Barbie using the name Klaus Altmann Hansen. Bolivia was a perfect choice for him. The country was under military rule with fascist undertones, and had a sizable and powerful German community. This community strongly supported the military government, which, in turn, offered protection to many new arrivals.

Over the next several years Klaus Altmann (Barbie soon dropped the surname Hansen) engaged in various businesses. He settled in La Paz and sent his children to a German school. Within the German community, he never denied that he was a former SS officer. According to several who knew him, he even bragged of his activities, including tortures inflicted in Lyon.

In 1964 Bolivia underwent another shift in military leadership, led by Air Force General Rene Barrintos Ortuno. The coup was supported by the German communities in most of the big cities, and individual Germans, including Klaus Altmann, offered assistance to the new regime.

During his years in Bolivia, Barbie had established valuable contacts with other former Nazis in several other South American countries. Like him, they had become men of wealth, power, and influence. These contacts had evolved into a kind of semiofficial organization of hidden Nazis—a very real organization, but one neither as formal nor as powerful as many Nazi hunters believed, especially Simon Wiesenthal, who put its membership in the thousands and described its power as staggering. Barbie made use of these contacts to provide the new Bolivian government with weapons and other needed materials. He rose quickly in favor through his dealings with the new military government and was placed in charge of Transmaritima Bolivia, S.A., the nation's official shipping line. (The fact that Bolivia had a shipping line is somewhat remarkable, since the country is landlocked, but, as is the case with many such countries, its desire for a port was all-consuming.)

One of Barbie's first actions was the purchase of a cargo ship, which soon became a source of national pride, despite the fact that it had to use a Chilean port. Barbie moved quickly, and within a matter of months Transmaritima had opened offices in Chile, Panama, and West Germany. The latter office, in the port of Hamburg, was operated by Barbie's son.

In the period 1969-71, using a Bolivian diplomatic passport, Barbie traveled all over the world as Altmann, setting up activities for Transmaritima. U.S. immigration records indicate that he made at least half a dozen trips to the United States and an equal number to Europe. It is even believed that he visited Paris once, despite the fact that he was still high on the French list of wanted Nazi war criminals.

Klaus Altmann was now an important person in Bolivia, and under the direct protection of the minister of the interior and the president. He continued to supply the new government with desperately needed arms. Even when Transmaritima Bolivia collapsed into bankruptcy in 1971, Barbie-Altmann stayed above the ensuing furor through ample protection by Bolivian officials. However, the failure of its shipping company was an embarrassment to the Bolivian government, and by mutual consent, Barbie moved to Peru, where he began to lead a quiet life as a businessman in October 1971.

It seemed as if the world had largely forgotten Klaus Barbie, but one who did not was Beate Klarsfeld, a German Protestant whose father had been a regular army soldier during the war. In 1960 she met and married a Jewish-French lawyer, Serge Klarsfeld, and settled down in Paris. Before her marriage, Beate Klarsfeld had no real understanding of what had happened in the Holocaust. However, the stories she heard from her husband of how his father had been dragged away and sent to his death at Auschwitz, and from her husband's friends of the many deaths in their families, changed her radically. By the mid-1960s, she and her husband had dedicated themselves to bringing escaped Nazis to justice and focusing public attention on the horrors of the Holocaust.

Barbie came to Beate Klarsfeld's attention in early 1971, when a Munich prosecutor dropped a case against him that had been brought by a group of Jewish survivors. The case interested the Klarsfelds, because if the dropping of the case remained uncontested, it represented a precedent that could be devastating to other potential Nazi prosecutions. Beate Klarsfeld began to research Klaus Barbie, and became aware of the extent of his activities in Lyon. She went to the city and launched a major press effort, aimed originally not so much at bringing Barbie to justice as at getting the German prosecutor to re-open his case. As the campaign spread to various French newspapers, and through news services to Germany, Klarsfeld learned from a source in the prosecutor's office in Munich that it was possible that Barbie was in Bolivia. The prosecutor had come into possession of a 1968 group photograph of a number of German-born businessmen living there, and experts in his office believed that one of them might be Barbie. Of course, they were correct.

Klarsfeld showed the photograph to a number of survivors of the French underground in and around Lyon, and they identified the man with near certainty as being Klaus Barbie. With this information, Klarsfeld turned to the Parisian newspaper *l'Aurore,* which on January 19, 1972, published a major front-page exposé running photographs of Barbie alongside those of "Klaus Altmann" under the headline "Former Nazi Klaus Barbie Has Just Taken Refuge in Peru After a Long Stay in Bolivia. Will France Demand Him?" The newspaper's reporters had tracked Barbie from Bolivia to his new hiding place.

Even as the Paris newspaper was gathering its evidence and preparing to publish, Klarsfeld had assembled a thorough dossier on Barbie. She had obtained eyewitness accounts of many of his crimes, including tortures, murders, and the deportation of the children of Izieu, the Jewish orphanage outside Lyon. As Klarsfeld was preparing to fly to Peru, Barbie-Altmann was arrested there by the Peruvian Ministry of the Interior. He denied everything, and, without any evidence to the contrary, the Peruvian government released him. Immediately, he and two bodyguards began to drive back to Bolivia, where he knew he could find sanctuary. At almost the same time Beate Klarsfeld was landing in Lima, Barbie was crossing the frontier from Peru into Bolivia.

Klarsfeld was met at the airport by a huge crowd of reporters. Over the next several days, she gave interviews to every news organization in Lima, and the media seized upon the Barbie story. The Peruvian government reacted quickly. It learned that Barbie had departed and gave Klarsfeld the information. She took off immediately for La Paz, where her reception was very different from what it had been in Lima. Not only did she receive no assistance from the government, the Bolivian police warned her flatly that if she continued to make public statements against Altmann-Barbie she faced immediate expulsion from the country.

Klarsfeld's presence in La Paz did have one positive effect. After she met with the French Ambassador to Bolivia, he went to the Interior Ministry to demand Altmann's arrest and extradition to France. In fact, it was learned later that Altmann became so concerned that he might be assassinated or kidnapped that he had himself arrested and placed in a military prison—more as an honored guest than as a convict. Believing she had done all that she could, Beate Klarsfeld returned to Paris. But within two weeks, she had returned to La Paz to renew pressure on the Bolivian government for Altmann's prosecution.

After returning to Paris she continued to press her case against Barbie, and the French government stepped up its pressure on Bolivia. Finally, almost a year later, in March 1973, Bolivia arrested Barbie. He remained in a Bolivian prison for 235 days while the supreme court considered the French extradition request. When the court reached a decision, it ruled that Klaus Altmann had become a naturalized Bolivian citizen; as such, he could not be extradited to France since the two countries had no extradition treaty. Additionally, said the court, a Bolivian statute of limitations ruled out any prosecution for crimes that had been committed during the era in question.

No one doubted that the Supreme Court's decision was more a case of repaying Barbie for past services to the Bolivian government than a decision based on the legal merits. But the effect was the same—as long as this military government remained in power, Klaus Altmann-Barbie was as safe as Alois Brunner was in Syria.

During the next decade, Barbie lived openly but quietly in the city of Cochabamba, about 250 miles south of La Paz. He was protected around the clock by private bodyguards and members of the Bolivian National Police. As the years passed, he became more active in advising the government in security matters, and it is reported that he was instrumental in setting up for Bolivia an external intelligence network that encompassed South America and extended into North America and Europe. This network was geared to providing the government with information about communists and insurgent activities within Bolivia and their contacts with left-wing groups in other Latin American countries and Europe.

Was Klaus Barbie protected in Bolivia in part by the United States because he was supplying much-needed information on leftist activities in South America? This charge has been, and continues to be, stoutly denied. The OSI investigation of Barbie that was completed in 1983 concluded that he had never been employed or funded by the CIA. Moreover, the so-called Ryan Report concluded that Barbie had never even met with or spoken to any member of the CIA during this period in Bolivia.

However, there is substantial evidence to dispute this claim. Barbie almost surely did have contact with the CIA during this period—both in obtaining information from that agency and in sharing information that he had obtained. The contact need not have been direct, nor need it have been recorded in CIA records in the archives at Langley. It is most likely that Barbie traded information with the CIA through a "cutout" in the Bolivian Interior Ministry who was in regular contact with the CIA station chief at the U.S. embassy.

But did this mean that Barbie was being protected by the CIA? The French thought he was. Documents including internal memos of the *Direction de la Securite Militaire*—French military intelligence—detail the French belief in links between Barbie and the CIA and West German intelligence through the Bolivian Interior Ministry.

As Klaus Altmann, Barbie continued to live his quiet life in Bolivia, but he was not averse to giving interviews to the local or international media. While admitting who he was, he continued to deny stoutly that he was guilty of any acts that could brand him a war criminal. His favorite phrase was simply "War is war, and in a war everyone kills." He insisted he had done only that which any other soldier in similar circumstances would do. Clearly unrepentant, he announced that he would not change anything he had done. He also consistently stated his belief that France would never seek him, or try him, because the knowledge he possessed was too explosive. "I could topple French governments with what I have to tell," he once said to a French television crew.

Throughout the 1970s, Beate Klarsfeld continued to focus world attention on Barbie, but in 1978 his protection became even more secure when General Juan Pereda overthrew the Banzer government. Over the next two years, four additional military regimes came to power, with each successive leader more closely allied with Barbie and more dependent upon his intelligence network. Finally, in early 1980, General Luis Garcia Meza seized power in still another coup. Garcia Meza had close ties with Barbie, and, reportedly, the former Nazi helped organize paramilitary troops for the new Garcia government and involved them in producing cocaine paste, which was sold to drug traffickers. Although there is no proof that Barbie was directly involved in drug trafficking, the evidence is overwhelming that he did establish the mechanism that allowed higher-ups in the new government to become involved in the drug trade.

The beginning of the end for Barbie came on October 10, 1982, when socialist Hernon Siles Zuazo swept into power over the succession of military governments that had controlled Bolivia for more than two decades. The new government was decidedly unfriendly to previous regimes and their supporters, including Klaus Altmann-Barbie.

Seeing an opportunity, Beate Klarsfeld moved quickly to push the French government into renewing its extradition request; through the media, she returned public attention to Barbie. Under this pressure, Altmann-Barbie fell back on the strategy he had used to protect himself years earlier—he arranged for his own arrest.

It was a mistake. The new government was in no way interested in protecting Klaus Altmann-Barbie, but it was in a quandary as to what to do with him.

West Germany had requested his extradition in 1976 based on an 1899 treaty between Bolivia and Germany. The succession of military governments had ignored the request, but it had never been withdrawn. A meeting was held in La Paz between Bolivia's new interior minister and the French and West German ambassadors. The Bolivians told the German ambassador that he was welcome to Barbie, but that the fugitive had to be removed from the country immediately. The ambassador cabled Bonn for instructions and received word that Germany would take Barbie, but not immediately: it was the fiftieth anniversary of Hitler's accession to power, and feelings were running high in some parts of the country. The Germans asked for six months, and the Bolivians refused. The interior minister threatened to simply take Barbie to the nearest frontier and release him, and the French said No—give him to us. Thus matters began to become extralegal. The ministry did not want the case to go back into the Bolivian courts. It simply ruled that when Klaus Altmann had applied for Bolivian citizenship more than a decade earlier, he had made false statements on his application. Further, there was a ten-year residency requirement for Bolivian citizenship, and when Altmann-Barbie received his in 1957 he had only been in the country for five years. This nullified his Bolivian citizenship and meant that Barbie could not afford himself the protection of the Bolivian courts. He was subject to expulsion.

On February 4, 1983, Altmann-Barbie was taken to a military airfield near La Paz and placed aboard a military transport that had been flown in the day before. He had no idea where he was being taken. As he left the prison, he had been told that he was being sent into exile in Paraguay, which, of course, would have been wonderful news if true, but he didn't believe it. He thought he was going to be sent back to Germany, partly because a West German television crew accompanied the flight. "How much does a razor cost in Germany these days?" he asked a reporter.

When the seven-hour flight landed, Bolivian police escorted Barbie from the plane to a group of French-speaking officials. The plane had landed in Cayenne, French Guinea, where Barbie was to be turned over to French authorities. Barbie was thunderstruck. He turned to one of the Bolivian police and reportedly said, "My life is lost."

A French military jet stood nearby, and Barbie was transferred to it. Twelve hours later he landed in Lyon.

Shortly after midnight on July 4, 1987, Klaus Barbie was brought in chains into a courtroom in Lyon. For eight weeks a court of three judges and nine jurors had heard testimony against him and the spirited defense put forward by his team of three lawyers. His defense had finished its final arguments only six hours earlier. But the panel had already reached a verdict.

A majority of eight votes out of twelve was necessary for conviction. For more than half an hour, the seventy-three-year-old Barbie listened with head bowed and no sign of emotion as presiding judge Andre Cerdini read the specifics of the charges against him. Then came the climactic moment: Guilty on all counts. His sentence, the harshest possible under French law, was life imprisonment without hope of release. That verdict has since been upheld by France's Criminal Appeals Court which rejected a list of fourteen separate arguments as to why a new trial should be ordered.

The trial climaxed four years of legal maneuvering in several French courts. Barbie could not be charged with the many tortures and executions he had carried out against the French Resistance during the war years because he had twice been tried in absentia for those crimes: in April of 1952 and November of 1954. He was found guilty on both occasions and sentenced to be executed if captured. However, under French law, an execution not carried out within twenty years of conviction becomes void. Nor could he ever be retried for those crimes.

In 1983, shortly after Barbie's return from Bolivia, a new indictment had been drawn up. Among its eight counts were:

— the deportation to death camps of the Jewish children from Izieu.

— ordering the last train convoy, which sent 651 Jewish and Resistance prisoners to their deaths in extermination camps, even as the Nazis were abandoning Lyon.

— ordering the roundup of Jews at headquarters of the General Union of Israelites in France on February 9, 1943, and sending eighty-four of them to death camps, from which most never returned.

— taking part personally in the arrest, torture, and deportation of individual Jews and members of the Resistance, including the 1942 execution of twenty-two hostages in retaliation for an attack on two German policemen; personally torturing nineteen prisoners in 1943; and executing seventy-three Jews in the town of Bron in 1943.

It was finally decided to try Barbie on the basis of this indictment, and, in case his lawyers argued that too much time had elapsed since the crimes, to try him also for "crimes against humanity"—crimes so heinous that they have no statute of limitations. (A law covering such crimes had been passed by the French National Assembly in 1964.)

The trial opened on May 10, 1987. Barbie's defense team was led by sixty-two-year-old Jacques Verges, a controversial lawyer of French and Vietnamese descent known for his defense of radicals and their causes. With him were Algerian lawyer Nabil Bouaita and Jean Martin M'Bemba, a West African lawyer from Brazzaville, the Congo. The prosecution team was led by fifty-seven-year-old Pierre Truche, a soft-spoken former magistrate, assisted, as allowed under French law, by Michel Zaoui, a private attorney representing Barbie's Jewish victims and their relatives, and, in an altogether fitting gesture, Serge Klarsfeld, representing the children of Izieu.

The defense strategy was apparent immediately. Verges would meet the specific charges against Barbie head on, while Bouaita and M'Bemba would attempt to put both France and Israel on trial for alleged "crimes against humanity." In the odd way of French trials, Barbie was the first witness. He spent two days on the stand denying everything. By his own description, he had been a minor officer in Lyon who had nothing to do with deportations or "the Jewish question." Rather, he said, he had been a soldier fighting the Resistance. Then, on the trial's third day, Barbie suddenly announced that he would have nothing more to do with it. He charged that his expulsion from Bolivia, of which he still claimed to be a citizen, was illegal. For the next eight weeks he refused to come to the courtroom. He would appear only four times more: twice when witnesses against him were asked to identify him, then to make a final statement, and, finally, to hear the verdict.*

The most dramatic evidence against Barbie came from a series of women who had been active in the Resistance and who testified that he had tortured them for days on end. Their experiences were remarkably similar. Barbie would usually strip them naked, suspend them from hooks, and beat them or apply electric prods to various parts of their bodies. Sometimes he would nearly drown them in a tub of water repeatedly—a form of medieval torture that he apparently favored.

The most damning piece of physical evidence presented at the trial was a telex that had been uncovered by Beate Klarsfeld. Signed by Barbie and addressed to his superiors in Paris, it detailed the roundup of the children at Izieu and specified how they would be transported to Auschwitz.†

When it came to the defense, Verges attacked the telex as a forgery and claimed that Barbie had not been in Lyon on the day of the Izieu raid. Bouaita charged that even if Barbie were guilty, his actions were no different than those of Israelis toward the Palestinians in the Lebanese refugee camps of Sa-

---

* French fears that Barbie would release damaging information about former Resistance fighters who had collaborated never materialized, perhaps because Barbie absented himself from so much of his trial.

† The April 6, 1944, telex signed by Barbie read in part: "The Home for Jewish Children, 'Child Colony,' at Izieu (Ain) was raided this morning and a total of forty-one children aged from three to thirteen were apprehended." It went on to detail how they would be transported to death camps and to apologize that in the roundup, no significant valuables had been found and confiscated.

bra and Chatilla, South Africa's oppression of blacks in Soweto, or French actions during the Algerian civil war. "We share the grief over the children of Izieu, but we do not ignore the deaths of Algerian children. The children of Izieu, the children of Sabra and Chatilla, and the children of Soweto: we do not separate victims in death." M'Bemba recounted what he called French massacres of black civilians in colonial Africa. "Blacks," he said, "want their place recognized alongside Jews as victims of crimes against humanity."

In his summation, Prosecutor Truche recalled the more than 100 witnesses who had appeared to testify against Barbie. It was no accident, he said, that their accounts were so similar. As for Barbie's contention that he hadn't known about the Final Solution, Truche scoffed: "How could a man trained in intelligence services suggest he did not know? How could Lyon have been different from any other place?"

The trial's most dramatic moment came just before the jury retired to reach a verdict. Barbie, in chains, was led back into the courtroom, his first appearance in several weeks. Did he have any final statement? Judge Cerdini asked . "Yes, I have a few words to say in French," he replied softly. "I did not order the roundup of Izieu. I never had the power to decide about deportations. I fought the Resistance, which I respected, in a hard manner. But, that was the war, and the war is over."

The arrest, extradition, and conviction of Klaus Barbie represents one of the great triumphs of postwar Nazi hunters, an achievement on a par with the kidnapping, trial, and execution of Adolf Eichmann. It represents especially a personal victory for Beate and Serge Klarsfeld, and proves that the tenacity and dedication of even one or two persons can overcome the roadblocks thrown up by governments who would protect or forget the perpetrators of the Holocaust. During the long years that Barbie sat in his two-cell suite in St. Joseph's Prison, while French courts fought over whether he would be tried, and on what charges, many predicted it would never happen. They believed that Barbie simply represented too great an embarrassment to the government of France, and that it would simply wait for the elderly man to die as Josef Mengele had—of natural causes, without ever facing the world and his victims to answer for the horrors he had perpetrated.

But Beate and Serge Klarsfeld never lost faith. From the day Barbie was returned to Lyon, they continued to state their belief that he would be tried and made to pay for his crimes. Thus it was right and just that Serge Klarsfeld had the final words on the fate of Klaus Barbie. Asked by reporters what the verdict meant to him, he replied, "That the children of Izieu will not die. For me, that's a satisfaction." He added, "The French people do not forget. They have condemned all the crimes committed by the Nazis. They have not forgotten."

The Child Killer

Although it had happened more than thirty years earlier, it was a scene that Anna Singur would never forget. Anna, then thirteen, was walking with her brother, taking a cow to a neighbor's house. As they were passing through the town square, she saw a young policeman emerge from the police station. He was dragging a very small girl by her hair and the back of her neck. They recognized the child immediately as Monica Zinger, the daughter of a prominent Jewish doctor in the town.

"With his right hand he held either the neck or the hair: from the back I did not see exactly. She was the daughter of the Jewish doctor Zinger. She was three or four years old. She was dressed in a coat, without a head cover. The girl was crying and saying in Polish, 'Mother, he is taking me to kill me, I want to live.' These words I remember well. I do not forget them after thirty years."

Anton Vatseba also remembered the scene as if it were yesterday. As a seventeen-year-old he was walking through the square with friends as the policeman emerged dragging the little girl.

"I saw that he carried the child into the yard and put her next to the foundation of the police station, not far from the well. The girl was saying something to him in Polish, but I was too far away to hear her words; she was surely pleading with him to spare her. He put her down, stepped back several paces, drew his pistol, and killed her with two shots."

The scene took place in 1943 in the village of Lisets (Lysiec), Poland not far from the small city of Stanislau and about 100 miles east of Czechoslovakia and 60 miles north of Romania. The region of Stanislau is currently known as Ivano-Franckovsk. Prior to 1939 the area was a part of Poland. But, a month after Hitler and Stalin signed their nonaggression pact in August 1939, Poland was divided. The Stanislau region, the Polish part of Galicia, was annexed by the Soviet Union into the Ukraine. Thereafter, western Poland was controlled by Germany and eastern Poland by the Soviets.

Then, on June 22, 1941, Hitler broke the nonaggression pact and invaded the Soviet Union. The initial push was toward Moscow, but on July 19, against

155

the advice of his general staff, Hitler ordered the advance deflected south toward Kiev. Galicia was one of the first areas to fall as the invasion swung south. At the time there were approximately 500,000 Jews living in Galicia. The city of Stanislau, with a population of 50,000, was about half Jewish.

Almost as soon as they controlled the area, the Nazis began a program to render the area *Judenfrei*—free of Jews. Initially, this was through deportations to camps in other parts of Poland, camps whose names are now all too familiar—Auschwitz, Treblinka, Majdanek, Rava-Ruska. By the middle of 1941, the German orders had changed. The camps were filling up. Now, the Final Solution was to be handled locally. It is estimated that in the Galicia region of the Ukraine, 60,000 Jews were gassed or shot between 1941 and 1943.

The Germans had a second problem. They did not have enough troops they could spare from front-line duty to staff the region's *Judenfrei* effort and "pacify" the population. So by order of Heinrich Himmler, "protection units" *(Schutzmannschaft)* were organized, comprised of local ethnic collaborators. In reality, these were German-commanded paramilitary police units, staffed entirely by volunteers who received good pay, good food, clothing, and free medical care. (This latter fact will become critical to the case at hand.)

At the time, Lisets had twenty to forty Jewish families among a population of about 2,000—perhaps 10 percent. It also had a *Schutzmannschaft* unit of from five to twelve members under one or two German officers.

Villagers remembered well the policeman who killed little Monica Zinger. His name was Bogdanus Kosij. He was young—about twenty—tall and thin, with blue eyes and light hair. He had arrived in the village from the town of Pukasiwci to the north, which was just outside of Halicz, now known as Galich. He was the son of a wealthy farmer there, and the family was well known. At first he lived in the police station, but later he moved into the house of the village bailiff (mayor) Wasyl (Vaslij) Ostapiak, probably the town's wealthiest man, after he married Ostapiak's sixteen-year-old daughter, Yaroslava. They had met as students in a private school.

The villagers remembered other heinous acts committed by the young policeman Kosij. Ivan Pashkevich detailed the death of seven-year-old Liusia Roziner. Police were executing Jews in the nearby town of Ivano-Frankovsk, and they left Liusia for dead. But she had only been wounded in the arms, and villagers bandaged her wounds and hid her in a barn in Lisets. Kosij learned the child's whereabouts and went to the barn carrying his rifle. "Kosij came from the police station with his rifle. The barn door was wide open. I saw him shoot twice. The first shot missed. With the second he killed her. The barn door was wide open and I saw the girl when Kosij was shooting at her."

Josif Il'kovskii remembered a scene of horror in the town cemetery. He was walking by with friends when he saw a banker named Bredgolts, his wife, and their two daughters, aged about ten and seven, being led toward the cemetery by Kosij and a group of policemen. He witnessed Bredgolts' wife begging for mercy, watched the couple being forced to kneel next to their standing children, and saw the four of them shot to death by the policemen, including Kosij. He remembered that Bredgolts was a tall, heavy man. After being shot once he fell to the ground, but had enough strength to stand again. He had to be shot several more times before he finally fell dead.

Maria Il'kovskii, Josif's aunt, recalled Kosij well: "Best than any other policeman, I remember Kosij because he was everywhere." She witnessed several different scenes played out at the village's small cemetery. She remembers watching Kosij march a twelve-year-old boy who tended cows outside the village to the gates of the cemetery and then shoot him to death. She watched a prominent Jewish family, the Kandlers, being placed in a truck. The eldest son, Bernard, broke away and tried to run. He was shot down by Kosij.

Maria Il'kovskii recollected going a few days later with some other villagers to the cemetery to see "the shot people." There, stacked up inside the gates, were the nude bodies of the Kandler family, including the banker, his wife, two daughters, the eldest son, his wife, and their child; Dr. Zinger's daughter; and a teenaged boy. Villagers including Il'kovskii's father were ordered to bury the bodies by Kosij's father-in-law. But before the burial, Maria remembers that Bailiff Ostapiak's son took a photo of Kosij in front of the pile of bodies.

★   ★   ★

West Palm Beach, Florida in September 1981 could not have been more removed in time, distance, or mood from that remote village of Lisets in the war-torn Ukraine. But in the quiet courtroom of Federal District Judge James C. Paine, the shocking and tragic events of Lisets would hold center stage in a new drama. The U.S. government intended to prove that Bogdanus Kosij, Nazi collaborator and Jew killer of Lisets, was now Bohdan Koziy, immigrant, respected Fort Lauderdale motel owner, and model U.S. citizen.

If the government could prove that Koziy was Kosij, and in "clear and convincing fashion" that he took part in the persecution of persons based on race, religion, or national origin while working with or for Nazi Germany, he would be stripped of his U.S. citizenship and made subject to deportation. It was in this federal courtroom in West Palm Beach that Bohdan Koziy was finally being called to account for his actions during World War II.

Although the subject of the trial was murder and persecution, the legal action was not a criminal trial, but rather a civil action under the terms of the Immigration and Naturalization Act of 1952. It was what is called in legal terms an "equitable action." The concept was built around the legal theory that citizenship, through the process of naturalization, is not a right but a grant—a gift, if you will—from the government. As early as 1913, the Supreme Court had ruled in a landmark decision *(Luria v. U.S.)* that a suit seeking the revocation of citizenship is legally indistinguishable from, say, a suit to cancel a patent or title to public lands.

The loss of citizenship, in the legal sense, is not a punishment, because it is alleged that the person had no right to it in the first place. So the courtroom would not be the scene of a criminal trial, with its strict rules of evidence and the right of the defendant to be judged by a jury of his peers. Rather it would be a nonjury civil trial, carried out under the federal rules of civil procedure. Additionally, courts had ruled over the years that there is no statute of limitations on denaturalization suits and delay does not violate due process; previous court decisions in naturalization cases, even under similar sets of facts, do not bind the present court under the theory of *res judicata*; and subsequent appeals courts are not bound by the lower court's determination of factual issues.

But in some ways the action was quasi-criminal, in that eyewitness identifications, especially those in a photo line-up situation, would be subject to the same tests applied in criminal proceedings; that the government was bound only to introduce evidence that applied to issues raised in its original complaint; and that the government must prove its case through the use of "clear, unequivocal and convincing" evidence. The United States was trying to prove that Koziy had undertaken acts, and was a member of organizations, that, had immigration authorities been aware of his memberships in them, would have denied his application to emigrate to this country and to become a citizen.

Bohdan Koziy was one of hundreds of thousands of Eastern European refugees who had come to this country under the provisions of the 1948 Displaced Persons Act. After the war, the Allies, led by the United States, took responsibility for resettling over eight million displaced persons living in Germany, Austria, and Italy. As of 1948, seven million had been repatriated under arrangements agreed upon by Roosevelt, Churchill, and Stalin at Yalta. However, one million refugees remained displaced.

The United States, as a first step toward resettling these European refugees, joined fifteen other countries in adopting the Constitution of the International Refugee Organization (IRO) which provided international standards for the resettlement of refugees. Congress implemented the IRO by adopting the Displaced Persons Act of 1948. The act defined "displaced persons or refugees" by reference to the IRO Constitution, which specifically excluded from the category of "displaced person" eligible for resettlement:

1. *War criminals, quislings, and traitors.*
2. *Any person who can be shown:*
   (a) to have assisted the enemy in persecuting civil populations of countries; Members of the United Nations; or
   (b) to have voluntarily assisted the enemy forces since the outbreak of the second world war in their operations against the United Nations.

In 1950 the DPA was amended to reflect more closely the IRO standard. The 1950 amendment also excluded from displaced person status "any person who advocated or assisted in the prosecution of any person because of race, religion, or national origin or. . . any person who has voluntarily borne arms against the United States during World War II."

A "Displaced Persons Commission" was charged with the responsibility of conducting an investigation, and submitting a written report, evaluating each visa applicant's character, history, and eligibility. The act provided that "any person who shall willfully make a misrepresentation for the purpose of gaining admission into the United States as an eligible displaced person shall thereafter not be admissible into the United States."

As previously noted, Koziy was actually being tried under the terms of the 1952 Immigration Act, which sets up three categories of persons encompassed by the term "displaced person":

(1) persons who forcibly were brought into Germany, Austria, or Italy during World War II;

(2) persons residing in Germany or in Austria who fled out of fear of persecution and who later returned, but did not settle permanently in either country; and

(3) persons who fled to the west due to the advance of Soviet armies.

It also established dual grounds under which citizenship can be subsequently revoked: "illegal procurement" and procurement by "concealment of a material fact or by willful misrepresentation." These two grounds were further divided into four categories:

(a) individuals who seek to procure, or who have sought to procure, or have procured a visa or other documentation, or who seek to enter the United States by fraud, or by willfully misrepresenting a material fact;

(b) individuals who before entering the United States were convicted of a crime involving moral turpitude, or who have admitted to having committed such a crime;

(c) individuals with past or current membership in, or affiliation with, any totalitarian party, its affiliates, or predecessor or successor organizations;

(d) individuals who on their entry into the United States were excludable under existing laws such as the Displaced Persons or the Refugee Relief Acts.

Koziy later would argue on appeal that the 1952 law did not apply to him because he had entered the United States in 1949, before its passage. But the court would rule that section D made it clear that the 1952 law does apply even to those entering before its adoption.

The Supreme Court in 1960 *(Chaunt v. U.S.)* set up a test to determine whether a concealed fact is material: *would it have been sufficient, had it been known, to deny citizenship; or might it have been useful in an investigation which would have led to the uncovering of further information that would have led to a denial of citizenship. Subsequent decisions modified this second test to one requiring the government to show that possession of this concealed fact would have led to an investigation that would have definitely resulted in a denial of citizenship.*

Now the Supreme Court has further modified *Chaunt* in a confusing decision made public in May 1988, as this book was in the final stages of preparation. In *Kungys v. U.S.* (see page 42) a split court tried to further define "material" as it relates to the concealment of a fact and the denial of citizenship.

Altogether, the court voted 6-2 (Justice Anthony Kennedy took no part in the decision) to remand the case back to the Third Circuit Court of Appeals for further review to determine whether facts concealed by Kungys on his visa and citizenship applications were material. The two dissenting justices, Byron White and Sandra Day O'Connor (who actually dissented only in part) thought the appeals court correct in determining that what Kungys concealed was material. The other six justices thought the appeals court should take another look at the case, but they could not completely agree among themselves as to exactly what "material" meant.

Justice Antonin Scalia, writing from himself and Chief Justice William Rehnquist and Justice William Brennan (and in part for Justice O'Connor) said the test of whether a misrepresentation or concealment of a fact is material is whether "they can be shown by clear, unequivocal and convincing evidence to have been predictably capable of affecting, i.e., to have had a natural tendency to affect, the Immigration and Naturalization Service's decision."

Justices John Paul Stevens, Thurgood Marshall, and Harry Blackmun agreed that the Third Circuit should look again at the facts in the Kungys case. But they seemed to come up with a slightly different test of what is material concealment. For the three, Stevens wrote: "A misrepresentation is material . . . only if it is capable of influencing the decision whether to confer citizenship. . . . The only statements that are capable of influencing the outcome are those that conceal disqualifying facts or that prevent or hinder the discovery of disqualifying facts. To demonstrate citizenship was 'procured by' a material misrepresentation, the government must demonstrate by clear, unequivocal, and convincing evidence that it relied on the misrepresentation in deciding whether to confer citizenship."

The entire majority also agreed that immigration law permits denaturalization if the misstatements demonstrate lack of good moral character but again disagreed on exactly how serious those misstatements would have to be so as to demonstrate such a lack of character.

The fact that the trial was held in West Palm Beach was simply the luck of the draw, so to speak. The action against Koziy was filed in federal court of the southern district of Florida; West Palm Beach is one site of courts within the district. Trials are assigned to judges within the district on a rotating basis and in this case, Judge Paine's name came up.

Georgia-born Paine, fifty-seven, was new to the federal bench. After graduating from the University of Virginia Law School in 1950, he had settled in West Palm Beach, where he was a top trial lawyer for almost thirty years before accepting a federal judgeship. He had been on the bench less than six months when the Koziy trial started: it was his first major trial.

A long, tortuous road had brought Bohdan Koziy and the federal government to this point of confrontation on a warm Florida morning. Evidence showed that in 1944, as it appeared that the Soviets would reoccupy Galicia, he and his family, and the family of his father-in-law, had fled to Germany one step ahead of the advancing Soviets. They settled in Heide, where Koziy spent the rest of the war as a farm worker. Afterward, he settled in a refugee camp in Nordenheim, Germany. Like so many other displaced persons, the family was looking for a place to settle far from war-torn Europe.

Koziy's answer came in the form of a newspaper advertisement in a Ukrainian paper published in Germany. The ad had been placed by a Ukrainian Catholic parish in Rome, New York—a factory town on the Erie Canal—that sought to sponsor, under the generous terms of the Displaced Persons Act, expatriate Ukrainians seeking a new life. Koziy answered the ad, and in 1949 he, his wife, and their son and daughter landed in New York.

On his entrance visa application, filed December 17, 1949, Koziy was asked to list in detail his activities during the war years. He said that when the war broke out, he was a student in Stanislau. Later he became a tailor's apprentice and was a farm worker before emigrating to Germany *after the war*. He made no mention of ever having been in the village of Lisets. In the crush of arrivals, his application was given only a cursory examination and he was welcomed to the United States with open arms.

Koziy's first job was pumping gas in a service station. Shortly thereafter, he was managing the station. Then he became a machine operator and later leased his own service station at a New York Thruway exit. He continued to work hard, to save his money, and eventually he bought a motel in nearby Clinton, New York.

In 1955 Koziy attained the dream of most immigrants by becoming an American citizen in a ceremony in Utica, New York. On his citizenship application, he repeated the same history he had listed on his immigration visa form. In answer to the question on his citizenship application as to whether he had ever belonged to any organizations, Koziy listed only one: "Boy Scouts." To the question as to whether he had ever committed any crime involving moral turpitude, Koziy answered "No." Finally, he swore and affirmed that at all times in his life he had been "a person of good moral character."

In 1973, with his son and daughter grown, Koziy decided to move to Florida. At first he worked in hotels; later he bought his own motel on Orton Avenue in Fort Lauderdale, about three blocks from the beach. It was an old-fashioned, two-story motel of the kind that still proudly advertised "color televisions, air-conditioning and telephones" in every unit. Koziy turned one unit of the motel into an apartment for him and his wife. He continued to work as the manager of an oceanside hotel while operating his newly acquired motel. His living room wall was decorated with family pictures: his son Jerry in his Army uniform while serving in Vietnam, his daughter Vera's wedding picture, taken just before she and her new husband moved to Italy.

To all outward appearances, Bohdan Koziy was a model citizen, the kind of successful immigrant who for generations has been the bedrock of America—a man who was well liked and respected in the community. But storm clouds were gathering on his horizon.

In 1977, several months after Koziy had taken over the motel, he was called into the Miami offices of the Immigration and Naturalization Service and questioned about his wartime activities. Had he ever been a policeman in the town of Lisets, he was asked. "No," he answered. He admitted that his wife was from that town and that he had been there briefly at the time of his wedding. However, they had met at school in Stanislau, where he had spent most of the war years, first as a tailor's apprentice and then as a farm worker. He stuck absolutely to the history he had listed on his visa application almost thirty years earlier.

Koziy returned to Fort Lauderdale and heard nothing more about the charges that he had been a Ukrainian policeman involved in Jewish murders and persecutions until one evening in April 1978, when a reporter from *The Miami Herald* showed up on his doorstep. Koziy, described by the reporter as being "a trim, tan, vigorous man with silver hair, blue eyes and a softly accented voice," sat with his wife, both of them in bathing suits, watching television.

The Herald had obtained copies of statements given in August 1976 to a Soviet assistant prosecutor in Lisets by eight villagers, outlining the crimes they had seen the policeman Kosij commit. The interviews had been conducted in Ukrainian and Polish, and the statements had been translated into Russian. The newspaper never revealed the source of the documents, but reportedly they came from Koziy's file in the Miami immigration office and were leaked to the newspaper by an INS employee who was angered by the organization's slow, almost invisible pace in investigating the charges.

Yes, Koziy said, he had been born in that area and had spent a little time in Lisets, where he was married. But he swore, "I never killed a Jew. Never." He was very angry that the INS would "take such lies seriously."

Now, interestingly, he changed his story for the first time. He did not say he had been a tailor's apprentice and a farm worker. He told the reporter that from 1941 until 1944 he had been a member of the Ukrainian underground, fighting both the occupying Germans and the Ukranian's traditional enemies, the Soviet communists. As he now told the story, he had been a student in 1939 when the Soviets took over the Ukraine. He had immediately joined the underground to fight the communists and did so until the Germans invaded in 1941.

"In June 1941, the Ukraine declared independence. Women threw flowers when the Germans came, and we had tears of joy. I went back to school. But it was all an illusion. Our happiness ended in two or three weeks. The Germans started putting our leaders in concentration camps and I was ordered back underground."

Koziy told the reporter he had spent the next three years fighting for the partisans in a forty-five- to fifty-mile radius of Stanislau. He had lived with his wife and in-laws in Lisets for three months in 1943, and his wife had returned there in June 1944 for the birth of their first child. But he could not have killed any Jews there, because when he moved there in 1943 "there weren't any Jews left there. There were no Jews in Lisets."

"I never killed a Jew," Koziy said. "I had nothing against Jews. The partisans helped save the Jews. We told the Jewish doctors we would save them and they would take care of us in our hospitals. When I was shot in the leg a Jewish doctor took care of me."

"Anything I did in my past life in my country in Europe I am proud of. When I have the chance, I would do it again and again. However long I will live, I will fight any communists and Nazis and dictatorships," Koziy told the reporter. He was proud, he said, to be an American and to be a Ukrainian.

The Herald published its story and it created a short-lived flurry of interest. Koziy repeated his denials to one and all, but nothing further happened. But in Washington, D.C., something was happening that would change Bohdan Koziy's cozy life in Florida. As we will see in greater detail under intense pressure from Congress, a new Nazi-hunting unit had been established within the Department of Justice—the Office of Special Investigations. The OSI culled the files it had inherited from the Immigration Service and by late November felt it was ready to file its initial complaints. The first, filed in Philadelphia on November 20, charged that Wolodymir Osidach, then seventy-five, had been not the dairyman he claimed to be during the war years, but rather the commandant of the Ukrainian militia in the town of Rava-Ruska and the Nazi collaborator who had organized and carried out the Final Solution for the Nazis in that region. (Osidach died of natural causes while appealing his denaturalization.) A day later the second case was filed in Miami: its target was Bohdan Koziy.

It alleged that from 1942 to 1944, Koziy, as a uniformed member of the Ukrainian police, "engaged in crimes involving moral turpitude, in that he knowingly and willingly participated in cruel and inhuman acts against unarmed civilian men, women and children including arrests, beatings, shootings and killings, thereby assisting German authorities in persecuting civilian populations during World War II." Further, the complaint alleged, Koziy "willfully misrepresented and concealed his residence and employment by the Ukrainian Police in Lysiec, Poland, to gain entry into the United States and citizenship."

The complaint alleged that Koziy had been a member of the Organization of Ukrainian Nationalists (OUN), "an organization which collaborated with and assisted German occupation authorities." This charge would become critical at Koziy's trial. Defense witnesses, mainly from the Ukrainian emigré community, would testify at length that the OUN was a resistance group that fought both Germans and Russians with equal verve. But government witnesses, experts on Poland and Eastern Europe in the war years, would testify that many in the OUN were nothing more than German collaborators who did much of the Nazis' dirty work in the Ukraine. More importantly, after the war the OUN had been listed officially as a subversive organization by Immigration authorities. Had Koziy, or any immigrant, admitted membership in the OUN, he or she would have been barred from entering this country under the terms of the Displaced Persons Act. The complaint also noted that the defendant had often spelled his name Kosij when he first arrived in this country and apparently did not change the spelling consistently until he applied for citizenship under the name Koziy. Because the action was civil in nature, Koziy was not arrested. Instead, he was served with a copy of the complaint and was given sixty days in which to respond.

In 1979 the Immigration Service had lost a highly publicized war crimes trial in Chicago, *U.S. v. Frank Walus,* because of misidentification (see chapter 7). The new OSI vowed that this would never happen again. Virtually all the witnesses in its trials would be people still living behind the Iron Curtain: they could not be brought to the United States, so Justice Department lawyers would travel to their countries to get their testimony on videotape. These interviews would also include photographic line-ups, in which the witnesses would be asked to identify defendants from groups of photographs taken during the war years. Defendants would be allowed to send their attorneys to these overseas examinations and to cross-examine the witnesses at any length. The government was prepared to pay all the travel expenses of the defense lawyers and for them to hire interpreters of their choosing.

Twice during early 1981, Justice Department lawyers traveled to Eastern Europe and the Soviet Union on the Koziy case. In January, they went to Warsaw and several other places in Poland, and in March to Lisets and other locations in the Ukraine. On both occasions, they offered to allow Koziy's chief counsel, Miami immigration lawyer Phillip Carlton, and co-counsel Steven Jugo, to accompany them at government expense. Koziy would not allow it. "It was our client's decision not to go abroad," Jugo would explain. "It was Mr. Koziy's belief that everything that was to be said over there would be lies and he did not want us to participate." Koziy called those who would testify against him "Slaves who will say anything their communist masters want them to say."

First in Warsaw, and then in Lisets, the American investigators questioned several of the individuals who had given oral statements to the Soviet assistant prosecutor in 1976. They also questioned other villagers who had since come forward. All were able to identify a photo of Koziy from among a montage they were shown. The investigators used a copy of Koziy's photo from his 1949 entry visa application. The witnesses repeated at length the stories of the killing of Monica Zinger and of the Kandler and Bredgolts families and reported other atrocities in which they claimed that Kosij had participated. These videotaped statements would become the heart of the government's case against Bohdan Koziy.

In May 1981, Koziy and his attorneys were recalled to the Federal Building in Miami for a deposition in the complaint. Now Koziy told a story very different than the one he had given to the INS investigators when they questioned him in the same building almost four years earlier. This time his recollection of the war years was more in line with what he had told *The Miami Herald* reporter that night in 1978: He had spent the war years fighting the Germans and the Russians as part of the underground, not collaborating with them. "I never finished school. I ran away. I joined the underground. I fought both the Germans and the Russians. For us they were both the enemy."

He repeated that he had never killed a Jew. "Our aim was not to destroy the Jews, but to help them and to save their lives." Yes, he had lived in Lisets for a few months in 1943 at the time he was first married, but by the time he had arrived no Jews were left in the town: the Germans had removed them all.

What about the charges being made against him? "Pure fabrications," he answered. "Everything against me is a fabrication. I am a man of honor. I am a man of principle. You will never make me what you think I am. I feel hurt, disappointed. I am a model citizen of this country."

The charges had been trumped up by the KGB, Koziy claimed. They were determined to silence him "because I am living propaganda telling the American people and American friends the truth about communism. They are very clever. They are experts. They are making a mockery out of the American justice system." This would be his defense when his trial started.

Bohdan Koziy's trial began on the kind of warm and humid September morning that makes Floridians very thankful for air-conditioning. Before that September 15 was over, Menachem Begin's visit to Washington would end; an assassination attempt against a U.S. Army general in Germany would fail; Egyptian president Anwar el-Sadat would expel the Soviet ambassador, his staff and almost 1,000 Soviet technicians; and Ronald Reagan would threaten to veto an appropriations bill with what he considered too high a spending level on social programs. But in south Florida, all eyes were focused on the small federal courthouse in downtown West Palm Beach.

Judge Paine's courtroom was packed, as it would be for the next two weeks. The ten long wooden benches for spectators were filled, every one of the 500 seats taken. Many in the audience were death camp survivors. But there were also a large number of Ukrainian emigrés who had come from as far away as Canada to show their support for Koziy and to protest what they called the U.S. government's role in what was clearly a Soviet plot to discredit the vocal anti-communist Ukrainian community.

At one side of the courtroom, behind a heavy wooden table, sat Koziy with his two attorneys, Carlton and Jugo. Seated on the other side behind a similar table were four government attorneys: OSI prosecutors Michael Wolf, Jovi Tenev, Kathleen Coleman, and Neal Sher, all down from Washington. Between the two tables sat what was to become the star of the trial—a Panasonic videotape machine and videotapes that represented most of the evidence to be presented against Koziy. The tape player fed three large monitors placed around the courtroom, including one on the raised bench of Judge Paine.

But two documents would also play a critical role in the trial, and they were the subject of much controversy before and during the proceedings. The first was a pink insurance application (anmeldung) dated April 1, 1942, for one Bogdanus Kosij, newly recruited member of the Ukrainian police command. It allowed the new recruit to receive the same health benefits as any Reich policeman. The second, a white form (abmeldung), dated almost two years later, January 31, 1944, testified to the severance after good service of police officer Bogdanus Kosij. Both carried the official stamps of the Ukrainian police command and the Ivano-Franckovsk District Archives in the Soviet Union. And that was the crux of the problem: that the two critical documents had been provided by the Soviets. Moreover, they demanded that the documents be kept in their possession at their embassy in Washington. When they were needed for trial, or for examination by either side, they would be sent down to Florida by diplomatic courier. Koziy and his attorneys branded them as forgeries and demanded that they be barred from evidence. After a long and bitter closed-door meeting, Judge Paine ruled that the documents could be admitted, but the government would have to provide expert testimony as to their authenticity, while the defense was free to provide witnesses to question any such evaluation. Had this been a criminal trial, Paine might have been forced to rule differently on the documents issue—and a number of other issues that would come up during the trial. But under the more relaxed rules of a civil trial, the documents were admissible.

The trial opened with OSI attorney Wolf asserting that it was the government's belief that Koziy could be stripped of his citizenship simply by showing that he had lied on his visa application about membership in the OUN and other inconsistencies in his sworn statements. But, he said, the government would go much further: it would prove that Koziy had murdered at least ten Jews and that he "personally murdered several Jews who were hiding Polish citizens and arrested Polish citizens who were hiding Jews."

Carlton countered in his opening statement that the defense would show that the government was completely mischaracterizing the nature of the OUN. He argued that they were partisans who fought both the Russians and the Germans, and that Koziy was twice wounded by the Nazis while fighting them. He said the proceedings would be a "political trial," pitting the might of the Soviet Union against Ukrainian patriots. He would also prove, he said, that people saw Koziy in a policeman's uniform because that was a disguise he frequently wore as a member of the underground. "He often dressed as a woman, too," Carlton told the court. "We will show he fought for what he believed in. He fought for a free Ukraine. And here he is accused of atrocities."

With the stage set, the government's first witness was Professor Raul Hilberg of the University of Vermont, author of what is considered the definitive work on Eastern Europe under the Nazi occupation. Because of a scheduling conflict, he was allowed to testify on videotape, and his testimony consisted of what was to all intents and purposes a three-and-a-half-hour lecture on the methods of the German occupation. As he spoke, his 790-page *Destruction of the European Jews* sat on the prosecution table.

At one point, Professor Hilberg read from a memo written by a German commander to his superiors in Berlin describing the situation in the Galicia area. "The Ukrainians are absolutely friendly," the German told his superiors, "the Poles are depressed and the Jews are in despair."

The government's second witness told a particularly poignant story. Maria Teichberg, then eighteen years old, remembered the pounding on the family's door in Stanislau, Poland, one Sunday morning in October 1941. Her father answered the door and was pushed back by a German officer who was accompanied by several Ukrainian policemen. One of the Ukrainians punched and kicked her father and then ordered the entire family out of the house. They were herded into the center of town, where hundreds of other Jews were cowering in the square. Soon trucks pulled up, and they were all ordered aboard. The Ukrainian police kicked and beat anyone who delayed. Teichberg and her father were on one truck when, for an unknown reason, a German ordered her to get off. The trucks pulled away. She never saw anyone in her family again.

No, she said, she had never seen or heard of Bohdan Koziy. But she was there to give witness to the activities of the Ukrainian police. She was very familiar with them, and their blue uniforms: she still saw them in her nightmares.

Then the government moved to present the first of the seven videotaped statements by Lisets villagers. Carlton objected on the grounds that the witnesses were not physically present in the courtroom and thus he was deprived of the opportunity to cross-examine them. Wolf countered that Carlton had been given the opportunity of accompanying the government lawyers to Lisets at taxpayers' expense, but had declined, thereby waiving any right of cross-examination. (In a criminal trial, the accused has the right to confront his accusers in person except in the most extraordinary circumstances, but civil trial rules are less rigid, and the judge is given more discretion.) Judge Paine quickly agreed that counsel's refusal to accompany the government lawyers to Europe did constitute a waiver of their limited right of cross-examination in a civil proceeding, and he allowed the videotaped statements to begin.

Josef Jablonski, a heavyset, balding construction manager from Warsaw, was the first witness to appear on the videotape. He sat upright in a heavy leather chair and spoke haltingly in Polish of his youth in Lisets, where he was born and lived until 1946. He would stop every few seconds to let an interpreter catch up. He said he knew Koziy on sight, because he had gone to school with Yaroslava Ostapiak, knew her well, and knew that she had married Koziy.

"Did you ever personally see Koziy kill people during this period?" Jablonski was asked.

"Yes," he answered without hesitation.

"Did you see this on one occasion or on more than one occasion?"

"I saw it on two occasions," he replied, again without hesitation.

Jablonski then related how on an autumn afternoon in 1943—he thought it must have been October—he saw Koziy "and a fat German officer" leading a group of seven women down the back stairs of the Lisets police station into the courtyard. He said that he was standing about fifty meters from the back gate of the courtyard and could see everything. He recognized one of the girls as a classmate from school and another as her sister. He said that he saw Koziy level his rifle at the group, and the officer his pistol, and the firing started. When one of the women approached Koziy and begged for her life, "Koziy pushed her away and kept firing."

When the seven women had been killed, Jablonski testified, he saw Koziy and the German go back into the police station to emerge again moments later with two men. "One of the two men was trying to escape," Jablonski related. "Koziy was running back after him and caught him. He led him back and then took out his pistol and put it to his head and shot him." Jablonski said the man Koziy shot was Bernard Kandler and the two girls he recognized, his sisters.

Jablonski then related how several days later he had witnessed the killing of four-year-old Monica Zinger. His account of her shooting was the same as that of other witnesses, with the exception that he remembered Koziy dragging her into the courtyard by her arm and not by her hair or neck. Later he picked Koziy's photo out of the line-up.

The courtroom was silent throughout this riveting testimony. Koziy sat without expression and apparently unmoved, watching Jablonski. His passive demeanor and seeming lack of interest would not change over the next three days, as he and the others in the crowded courtroom watched the videotaped testimony of six more witnesses.

Next Josif and Maria Il'kovskii repeated the statements they had made to the Soviet prosecutor years before about the events they had witnessed at the town cemetery. Both picked Koziy's picture out of the photo line-up. Then Max Kandler wept as he remembered how his family had been murdered. "I am the only one left. Only me," he repeated, as he said that he was certain it was Koziy who had sprayed the family with machine gun fire.

Next came Anton Vatseba, who echoed much of what Josef Jablonski had said. He, too, related how he had witnessed the killings of both Bernard Kandler and, several days later, little Monica Zinger. He called Koziy a "bloodsucker who had so much blood on himself that it was almost running out his ears." Still Koziy sat expressionless.

Karol Koluszko testified that he was absolutely certain it was Koziy who had pedaled his bicycle out to Koluszko's farm one day in October of 1943 and arrested his uncle and grandfather for hiding Jews. He said he knew it was Koziy because he had been a guest at his wedding to Yaroslava and that she had introduced them. He correctly picked Koziy's picture out of the photo line-up.

Finally, housewife Yadwiga Spilarewicz said that it was Koziy who had discovered where seventeen Jews were hiding and who had led a force of police that rounded them up and loaded them on trucks. None were ever seen again, and all were presumed killed. She also related that it was she who had been hiding Monica Zinger and that the police had learned of this. "They led us to the police station. A policeman took the child out of my arms. The child started screaming 'Mommy, Mommy!' I was crying. He pushed me through the door and closed the door. They took the child and I never saw her again." She said she was later sent to prison for harboring the child.

Of the seven videotaped witnesses, six testified that they had personally seen Koziy wearing a Ukrainian police uniform and four said they had personally witnessed him killing Jews.

Following the videotaped testimony, a parade of government witnesses came forward to testify over the course of the next several days. Some were document experts who attested to the authenticity of the two Soviet-supplied documents. Others were former bureaucrats who testified on the procedures and policies in force when Bohdan Koziy had arrived in the United States in 1949 and applied for his entry visa. William Carmody, who had worked on many postwar immigration cases, testified that the OUN was a "proscribed organization and anyone who was a member was ineligible [for admission to the United States]." To bolster that claim, the government presented a list of former OUN members who had been denied entry visas.

Michael Thomas, a former employee of the International Refugee Organization (IRO) in the postwar period, testified that in his long experience any refugee seeking admission to the United States at that time who had been a member of the underground was quick to list the fact, because under the Displaced Persons Act such persons were accorded a preferential status that all but guaranteed their quick admission. He said the commonest problem was not people fearful of revealing they had fought with the partisans, as Koziy had stated he had, but people falsely claiming they had fought the Germans.

Persons seeking to come to this country under the Displaced Persons Act had to be certified admissible by the IRO. Under IRO regulations in place in 1949, any persons who voluntarily left their home countries to travel to Germany before the end of the war were not considered displaced persons or refugees, and thus were not qualified for the IRO certification for admission to the United States under the terms of the Displaced Persons Act. Thomas testified that in his experience, had the fact that Koziy fled Lisets to escape the Soviets in 1944 been known to the IRO when it sought to certify him, he would have been disqualified for admission to the United States.

Then the original copies of Koziy's entry visa and citizenship applications were entered into the record. Finally, after eight days of testimony, the government rested its case.

Now it was attorney Carlton's turn. He had promised in his opening statement that he would produce witnesses who would "detail, bit by bit, tear by tear, what went on in this good man's [Koziy's] life."

His first witness was Yaroslava Koziy. She told Judge Paine that as a sixteen-year-old bride, she did not know what her new husband was doing during the war. He would disappear for months at a time on his work for the underground. She did not know where he went or what he did. "I wasn't supposed to know," she testified. "I didn't want to even know."

She did know, however, that her husband was never at any time a policeman, nor did he ever do any work for the Ukrainian police in Lisets. But she did see him in a police uniform from time to time. It was one of many disguises that he wore. These disguises included beggar's and women's clothing. But it was all in the name of the resistance.

Yaroslava Koziy also testified that she did not recognize any of the seven witnesses who had testified against her husband via the videotape, nor did she even recognize their names. She gave this testimony despite the fact that the village was very small, with a total population of less than 2,000: most of the witnesses against her husband were the same age as she, and two had said they were her classmates at school. One, Karol Koluszko, had claimed to be a guest at her wedding and stated that she had introduced him to her husband.

Then came Koziy's father-in-law, Wasyl Ostapiak. He called the testimony against his son-in-law "complete lies," adding that he would never have allowed his daughter to marry a Ukrainian policeman.

Next came a woman originally from Stanislau to offer an eyewitness alibi for Koziy. Maria Kolodij, from Toronto, testified that she knew him at school. In the fall of 1943, at about the same time the videotaped witnesses said he was engaging in a killing spree in Lisets, she remembered visiting her boyfriend in a small hospital some distance away. While she was there, she said, she saw Koziy, who was also a patient.

"I say hello," she testified. "I shake hands. I see that his left arm is bandaged. I said a couple of words and that is all." She said she understood from her boyfriend that Koziy had been wounded in the resistance. She also said she had seen him about a year earlier when he had appeared to be a student.

At first Kolodij said that she had never discussed the denaturalization case with Koziy. But under tough cross-examination from government lawyer Jovi Tenev, who produced a transcript of a taped interview Kolodij had given government investigators two years earlier, she admitted that Koziy had called her in Canada to ask her to testify for him.

"Koziy phoned me, yes, and told me about the troubles and he said maybe I be a witness. He told me that the Jewish put him in this trouble. I say okay, because I knew you from my country and what can I say bad for you?"

The next witness was Mykola Ostapiak, a distant cousin of Yaroslava's. She testified that she had met or seen Koziy several times during the occupation years, but had at no time seen him in a police uniform. She added that she remembered being told he was active fighting in the underground. Finally she testified that she had a number of relatives named Vatseba, but none lived in or near Lisets. "I am 100 percent certain there were no Vatsebas in Lisets. I would have known if I had a relative in Lisets." (Anton Vatseba, you will remember, was one of the government's primary witnesses and said he had personally witnessed Koziy killing Jews.)

Now came the most controversial of Koziy's defense witnesses. Petro Mirchuk, a round-faced retired professor, has written more than twenty books on the Ukraine during the war and his own experiences in the OUN and in a Nazi concentration camp. He had received two Ph.D.s from Ukrainian-related universities in Europe.

Carlton sought to have Mirchuk ruled an expert witness. Wolf introduced two letters Mirchuk had written to the OSI about the Koziy case in which he had called the Department of Justice's investigation into Koziy's past "a KGB-Jewish plot." He also pointed out that when Mirchuk had testified in a denaturalization case in Philadelphia, the judge had ruled that his pro-Ukrainian bias was so pronounced that it "weighed heavily" against his credibility.

Mirchuk himself responded. "He thought that as a Ukrainian I could not be objective. That is like saying as a Jew, you cannot be objective. No one can be objective. No one in the world."

Judge Paine allowed Mirchuk to testify as an expert. Mirchuk then proceeded to detail over eight-plus hours of testimony how, he, too, was a member of the OUN, fighting both the Russians and the Nazis, until he was captured one day by the Germans and sent to Auschwitz. Thrusting his bare arm forward to show his concentration camp tattoo, he said "there were so many of us in Auschwitz it was the best place to learn what was going on in the Ukraine."

He called the case against Koziy, and similar cases, "a holy Jewish inquisition." He said that all the cases against Ukrainians were part of a KGB plot, and that the Justice Department was cooperating with the Soviets for some reason. He testified at length that Ukrainians never helped Nazis and had never killed civilians, and that the Nazis had persecuted Ukrainians. "We fought against the communists and the Nazis," Mirchuk said firmly.

"AND AGAINST THE JEWS!!" came a shout from the back of the courtroom. The seething animosity between many of the Jewish and Ukrainian spectators in the courtroom had finally erupted. After Judge Paine restored order, Simon Goldberg, a retired dressmaker and Auschwitz survivor, told reporters that the Ukrainians in the camp "were worse than the Nazis. They were there because of their politics and we were there because of our religion. These people he defends are 100 percent guilty. I know. I was there. I know what these people did. It is not as he is saying."

Later, during a break in his testimony, Mirchuk left to go to the restroom. He came running back into the courtroom to say he had just been assaulted. "I have been attacked in the toilet by a Jew!" he exclaimed. Pointing his finger at a spectator, he shouted, "He attacked me in the toilet! He called me a liar and a murderer!" Federal marshals investigated immediately and found that several spectators had followed Mirchuk into the restroom and had accosted him. The assault had been entirely verbal.

Finally, on the fourteenth and final day of trial, Bohdan Koziy took the stand in his own defense. For more than seven hours he told the court in no uncertain terms that the charges against him were "lies, all lies."

"It is a lie, what they say," he swore under oath. "We never, never collaborated with the Germans or anybody else. We are too proud.

"You try to make me what I never was, what I am not now, and what I can never be. I feel sorry for you, Mr. Wolf."

He described his wartime years as a constant fight against both the Russians and the Nazis. At one point he rolled up his left sleeve and left pants leg to exhibit scars—the results, he said, of a German machine gun that was turned on him during a "partisan raid" against a German supply depot at about the same time in 1943 that the government contended he was a policeman in Lisets. He also said that he had lost parts of six fingers when a grenade had exploded prematurely.

"Twice I was wounded by the Germans fighting them. Twice they shot me. I was their enemy, not their friend."

Wolf tried to show that the wounds were incurred in 1944, after Koziy had left the police and when he was fighting not Germans, but Soviet-leaning partisans, or the advancing Soviet army.

How did he explain away the testimony of the seven witnesses on videotape? "They are all dupes," he said confidently. "They will say whatever their communist masters tell them to say. If I were living under the communist heel, I am not sure that I would not do the same."

Why, he was asked, had he not listed his membership in the OUN on his citizenship application instead of simply listing "Boy Scouts?" He did not understand the meaning of either "membership" or "organization," he answered. He had not considered the OUN an organization according to his less-than-perfect knowledge of English, and he did not consider himself a "member" as he understood the term at that time. He had considered himself a sympathizer, not a member. Now, years later, he realized he had been incorrect, and he would have listed the OUN if he were filling out the application today.

At one point Koziy picked up the two Ukrainian police documents and waved them in his hand. "These are forgeries, clear forgeries," he asserted. He pointed to the documents and showed that each had several small holes in it. "We did a better forgery job in the underground without modern machinery," he said snidely.

When Koziy finished his denials, the government asked to put on a single rebuttal witness for a few questions. Judge Paine granted the request. The witness was Antonio Cantu, a chemist and documents expert with the Treasury Department. Dr. Cantu, a Ph.D., had been the government's expert witness, who had testified to the authenticity of the insurance forms.

Did he know anything about the holes that Koziy had so triumphantly pointed out? Yes indeed, was Cantu's answer: he had made the holes himself when he removed samples of the documents for microscopic examination of the inks and paper fiber—part of the process by which he had concluded that the documents were genuine.

Thus, after fourteen days in the courtroom, the trial of Bohdan Koziy came to a a low-keyed close. Since it was not a criminal trial, there were no dramatic summations for a jury. Neither government lawyer Wolf nor defense counsel Carlton strutted around the courtroom as lawyers in television dramas are wont to do. Instead, Judge Paine said simply that the two should submit written briefs of the legal issues within a month and that he would rule on the case sometime thereafter.

The lawyers packed up their bulging briefcases, Koziy went back to the small apartment into which he had moved after selling his motel to pay his legal expenses, and the spectators went back to their homes, all of them to await Paine's eventual ruling.

The decision did not come for almost six months. But on March 29, 1982, Paine ruled that the government had made its case that Bohdan Koziy had made material misrepresentations on both his visa and citizenship applications—misrepresentations of fact which, had they been known, would have probably disqualified him from citizenship, or even admission to the country in the first place. As a result, Paine ordered: "That the order of February 9, 1956, of the Supreme Court of New York, County of Oneida, admitting the defendant to citizenship is revoked and set aside and the Certificate of Naturalization No. 7115205 shall be canceled."

Paine wrote in the thirty-page opinion that "Bohdan Koziy's citizenship must be revoked. He procured his naturalization by concealment and willful misrepresentation of material facts." He then listed those misrepresentations:

> The defendant's employment in the Ukrainian Police made him a member of and participant in a movement hostile to the United States and thus ineligible for a visa under Section 13 of the Displaced Persons Act.
>
> The defendant's active participation in the Organization of Ukrainian Nationalists (OUN) also made him a member of and a participant in a movement hostile to the United States and thus ineligible for a visa under Section 13 of the Displaced Persons Act.
>
> By reason of his employment with the Stanislau Kommando of the Ukrainian Police, defendant assisted Nazi Germany in persecuting civilians.
>
> By reason of his employment with the Ukrainian Police defendant voluntarily assisted the enemy forces of Nazi Germany.
>
> By engaging in military actions against Soviet partisans and by training others to fight Soviet partisans defendant voluntarily assisted the enemy forces of Nazi Germany.
>
> For each of the independent grounds enumerated . . . above, defendant was ineligible for a visa under Section 2(b) of the Displaced Persons Act.

This was all Paine was required to do: to find that Koziy had made material misrepresentations. But he went further, much further. He said pointblank that he believed Koziy was a murderer. He said he had found the Polish witnesses who appeared on videotape believable, and their identifications of Koziy from the photo line-up "reliable when considering all the circumstances. . . .There was no evidence that the photographic spreads were either suggestive or in some other way tainted." He also found the captured Nazi documents to be authentic. At the same time, he found none of the evidence that Koziy had offered in his defense to have been at all credible.

"The defendant personally and single-handedly murdered the young female child of Dr. Zinger," Paine concluded. "As the child was pleading to be spared, the policeman shot and killed her at pointblank range." Paine also said the evidence had convinced him that Koziy "actively participated in the murder of a Jewish family named Kandler in the fall of 1943, particularly one Bernard Kandler."

Thus, the judge concluded, "by reason of his personal acts of persecution and murder of civilians while employed as a Ukrainian policeman in Lisets, defendant assisted Nazi Germany in persecuting civilians. . . . Both Mr. Koziy's employment with the Ukrainian Police and his participation in acts of persecution and murder of civilians each demonstrate, independently of the other, that he totally lacked the good moral character required for [United States] citizenship."

Phillip Carlton, Koziy's counsel, said he was disappointed in the decision, but added that "this is clearly but the first step in a long legal road." Carlton could not have known when he made this statement how long that road would be, or in what courts the legal arguments would be made.

The initial court battles, however, were predictable.

Carlton brought in Thomas A. Willis, a Miami appeals specialist, and together they petitioned the Eleventh Circuit Court of Appeals that Judge Paine's decision be reversed. They based their appeal on four of Paine's rulings and actions.

First they contended that Paine had committed "reversible error" (an error so serious as to either negate the verdict or require a new trial) in his finding that Koziy was a member of either the OUN or the Ukrainian Police Force. Second, they argued that he had erred in admitting as evidence the two Ukrainian police documents—the insurance form and the severance statement. Third, they said Paine erroneously refused to allow Koziy's defense to present two witnesses, an expert in the Displaced Persons Commission and a documents expert because the defense had failed to list them as witnesses until well after a court-appointed deadline for filing a list of potential witnesses.

Finally, they raised a constitutional issue. Koziy was stripped of his citizenship because of what is called "illegal procurement"—that is, he hid material facts and thus obtained the citizenship through an illegal act. But illegal procurement was not a specifically proscribed act at the time Koziy obtained his citizenship; it was added to immigration law at a later date. Koziy's lawyers argued that to apply it to his case would be to violate constitutional provisions against the use of ex-post facto laws—laws passed after the date of the commission of an offense. For these reasons, they argued, Paine's ruling should be thrown out and Koziy's citizenship restored, or, alternatively, he should be granted a new trial.

The appeals court did not agree. On February, 27, 1984, Circuit Judge Joseph W. Hatchett, writing for a unanimous three-judge panel, rejected every one of Carlton's points and affirmed Judge Paine's ruling. Judge Hatchett wrote: "To prevail in a denaturalization proceeding, the government must prove its case by clear, convincing and unequivocal evidence, and leave no issue in doubt. The District Court [Paine] held that the government had fulfilled its burden of showing Koziy's membership in the Ukrainian police. It found that Koziy was ineligible for a visa under the Displaced Persons Act and was never lawfully admitted to the United States. The District Court held therefore that Koziy had illegally procured his citizenship because he had failed to fulfill a statutory condition precedent to naturalization. . . .The District Court's factual findings concerning Koziy's affiliation with the Ukrainian Police are not clearly erroneous. . . .Unless the District Court's findings are clearly erroneous, we are compelled to abide by them."

As for Paine's ruling that Koziy's two witnesses could not testify, the appeals court found that he had had more than two years' warning that documents would be introduced into evidence and that the workings of the Displaced Persons Commission would be at the heart of the government's case. "His failure to obtain [the two witnesses] before the Court's deadline displays bad faith," the appeals court decided, and not reversible error on Paine's part for refusing to allow them to testify. Similarly, the two Ukrainian documents were properly admitted into evidence. The government had presented enough evidence as to their origin and authenticity to allow them to be made a part of the trial's record. It was then up to the defense to present evidence attacking their credibility. It had offered none.

Finally, the appeals court ruled, "the government's utilization of illegal procurement as a basis for revoking Koziy's citizenship did not violate Koziy's constitutional rights. It only deprived Koziy of his ill-gotten gains."

In summary, the three appeals judges concluded: "for the reasons stated above, we find the District Court committed no error in the proceedings. Accordingly we affirm the order of the District Court." Now four judges had carefully studied Koziy's case and concluded he was guilty of war crimes.

Carlton, the lawyer handling Koziy's appeal, went further. First he reappealed to the Eleventh Circuit, asking that the entire court rehear his appeal. On April 2, 1984, it refused. His next stop was the United States Supreme

Court. On October 1, 1984, the Supreme Court, without formal comment, refused to hear the case. Koziy had run out of places to appeal. Judge Paine's ruling would stand. Koziy was no longer a United States citizen, and as such was now subject to deportation.

Even as the appeals process continued, the Office of Special Investigations faced the problem of what to do with Bohdan Koziy, assuming the appeals courts upheld his denaturalization and a subsequent deportation action was successful. The problem was one common to many of the actions that had been and would be brought by OSI against Latvian, Lithuanian, Estonian, and Ukrainian emigrés. They were former citizens of countries that no longer existed. In some cases, they might be guilty of crimes that took place within the borders of what is now the Soviet Union, Poland, or Czechoslovakia. But unless they were among the few who had been tried and convicted, in absentia, after the war, they could not be deported to those countries unless extradition was requested.

Under treaties signed after the war, what is now West Germany was given jurisdiction to try war criminals in its courts system, even if the defendants were not German citizens and the crimes they were accused of committing did not occur on what was then, or is now, German soil. Then, too, from time to time, Israel had asserted jurisdiction over a war criminal, but these occasions were usually confined to a "big fish," and few of the prosecutions being brought in the United States fit into this category.

Usually, in these circumstances, the denaturalized person was allowed to go where he wanted to, so long as a given country was willing to accept him. As we will see in later chapters, a number have gone to West Germany, several to Austria, and others to various South American countries like Paraguay, which were actually their first stops after leaving Europe and whence they subsequently came to the United States.

But the idea of Bohdan Koziy going to some safe haven deeply angered and offended prosecutors. Far from being some concentration camp guard who simply followed orders, regardless of how heinous those orders might have been, this was a man they believed had killed women and children in cold blood, and with obvious relish. This was a man whom they believed should not go free burdened only with the need to file a change of address form with the Fort Lauderdale Post Office. So they vowed to do what they could to see that he was really brought to justice.

Their first stop, based on the treaties giving German courts jurisdiction over such cases as Koziy's, was the government of West Germany. On November 4, 1982, the Justice Department, on behalf of the OSI, working through the State Department and the U.S. embassy in Bonn, forwarded to the German Foreign Ministry a formal request that the West German government seek the extradition of Koziy for the purpose of placing him on trial for murder and other crimes committed in and around Lisets. Accompanying the request was a copy of pertinent parts of Koziy's trial record and Judge Paine's decision, in which he stated that the evidence of Koziy's crimes was overwhelming. On March 28, 1983, West Germany replied. It refused "to initiate extradition proceedings in this case." (The German reasoning was extraordinarily complex and is described in full in chapter 12.)

OSI then tried to interest Israel in asserting jurisdiction over Koziy. But as the Demjanjuk prosecution has shown, such a trial in Israel is extremely complicated and expensive. The Israelis want to limit such trials only to major war criminals, and Koziy simply did not fit that description, so the Israelis refused.

This left the Soviets, since Lisets and the Ukraine are now part of the Soviet Union. Prosecutors were frankly reluctant to turn to Moscow, even though the crimes were committed on what is now Soviet soil, because U.S. judges are often loath to order deportations behind the Iron Curtain, and because forcing denaturalized emigrés back to Eastern Europe only gives ammunition to those critics who charge that the whole Nazi-hunting process is a communist plot being abetted by the Justice Department. But in Bohdan Koziy's case, they felt it was their last hope that he would ever face any real punishment for killing Monica Zinger and the others, so the request was made to the Soviet Foreign Ministry. The Soviet Union did not have any of the problems that the Germans did. They readily agreed to try Koziy under Soviet law for his crimes. In April 1985 they requested his extradition. But, as we shall see, unknown to the Justice Department, by the time the Soviet request came through, Bohdan Koziy was long gone.

On March 18, 1985, Koziy was due in the federal courthouse in Miami to appear before an immigration judge to start what the government expected to be a protracted process of hearings and appeals that would lead to his eventual deportation. Koziy did not show up. Phillip Carlton said that he had last heard from his client in a letter he had received January 2, postmarked Fort Lauderdale, in which Koziy said he had "gone away," but did not say where. Carlton believed he had left the country. That, he argued, would render the deportation question moot. He asked the judge for a sixty-day postponement to give him time to prove that his client was no longer in the United States.

OSI lawyer Wolf insisted that the process begin, and the government submitted a copy of the nine-volume, 9,000-page record of Koziy's trial and appeals as its evidence that he should be deported. Within a month Immigration judge Henry Watkins formally agreed. In a twenty-page opinion issued on April 12, he ordered Koziy's deportation.

Carlton said that the order had no force or effect because, as far as he knew, Koziy was no longer in the United States. "I'm taking the position that this case is at an end. You can't deport someone who isn't here." Wolf said that he did not know where Koziy was either, but that he would seek an arrest warrant, so that if he was found to be in the country, he would be deported to the Soviet Union—which by this time had sought his extradition for the purpose of trial.

Still nothing was heard from or about Bohdan Koziy. Then in August, acting on a tip it had received, NBC News reported that Koziy was living in luxury in the Central American nation of Costa Rica.

With a population of slightly over two million, Costa Rica, a country smaller than the state of West Virginia, is blessed with a tropical climate, the most stable democratic government and economy in the region, and perhaps the highest standard of living in Central America. Although the country still has an agriculture-based economy, it has long wanted to establish itself as a major retirement center, especially for North Americans eager to live out their days relatively cheaply, and in comfort. Thus the government has established a special category of quasi-citizenship called *rentista,* which carries with it a higher status and more rights than those of a mere visitor or tourist, yet is less than full citizenship which, for an American, would carry with it the automatic loss of U.S. citizenship and the possible loss of that monthly Social Security check. To qualify for *rentista* status, a foreigner need only show that he or she will have monthly income of at least $300 from some established foreign investment, government, or private pension (including Social Security).

However, this easy quasi-citizenship, which carries with it numerous protections under Costa Rican law, has also made Costa Rica a haven for international fugitives. Financier Robert Vesco, wanted in the United States for massive frauds, lived there from 1972 to 1978 as a *rentista.* Mexican drug kingpin Rafael Caro Quintero—wanted for ordering the death of a U.S. Drug Enforcement Administration agent—was living there openly when he was finally arrested and extradited to Miami.

The exact sequence of Koziy's flight to Costa Rica can now be pieced together. By the late spring of 1984, it was clear to Koziy that he would not be able to overturn his denaturalization. Although his appeal was still pending before the Supreme Court, the court had already ruled for the government on another "Nazi" denaturalization case and his case not very different: presumably, the Supreme Court would rule against him also. Therefore, he had to find a country that would take him in—one where he would have some measure of legal status and protections, and above all, one that did not have an extradition treaty with the Soviet Union and which, he hoped, was anti-communist without enjoying good relations with the Soviets. Costa Rica was perfect.

In May the Koziys made what would be the first of three visits to the Costa Rican consulate in Miami. There they received progressively more detailed information about the country and about the procedures for emigration. In August, Yaroslava went to the Federal Building in Miami and applied for a United States passport. Despite her husband's denaturalization, her status had not changed: she was still a United States citizen in good standing, and the passport was issued in due course.

Yaroslava made at least two and possibly three visits to Costa Rica as a tourist over the next sixty days. On at least one of those trips, she is believed to have met her daughter Vera and her Italian husband. They found a lawyer and bought a house in which the Koziys would live. On a four-day visit in early September, Yaroslava applied to the Costa Rican Institute of Tourism for *rentista* status, indicating that she would receive her required $300 a month in foreign income from an investment that had been set up by her son-in-law in Italy.

This was an important step. The Koziys' main problem was that Koziy was, at this point, a man without a country. He had been stripped of his U.S. citizenship and had no other. Valid foreign citizenship is required to apply for *rentista* status in Costa Rica, so he could not, but Yaroslava, a U.S. citizen, could.

It appears that Yaroslava moved permanently to Costa Rica about the second week in October. On October 26, she was issued her official *rentista* status. Two nights later Bohdan Koziy went to Miami International Airport and boarded the evening LACSA Airways flight to the Costa Rican capital of San Jose. He had no passport, but he did have a current and valid visitors' visa for Costa Rica as a tourist that enabled him to board the flight. Apparently, he had gone to the Costa Rican consulate in Miami several weeks earlier and presented a document entitled "Declaration of Intention to Become a U.S. Citizen," which had been issued in New York in 1950 as part of Koziy's citizenship process. The document listed his occupation as a "tailor" and his nationality as "Ukrainian." Although the face of the document stated "Invalid for any purpose seven years after the date hereto," the Costa Rican consul charged Koziy thirty dollars required to "authenticate" the document and issued a tourist visa listing his citizenship as Ukrainian— although the Ukraine, as a country, does not exist.

On the night of October 28, Bohdan Koziy landed in San José, where he was met by Yaroslava: he entered the country without difficulty. Several days later, he and Yaroslava went to the Costa Rican Institute of Tourism and applied to make his status permanent under a legal provision that allows *rentistas* to be accompanied by dependents. In short order, he was issued a permanent resident card as a dependent of his *rentista* wife.

The Costa Rican government was deeply embarrassed when it became known in August that Koziy was living in the country, but officials there said they were unsure what could be done about it. To begin with, no country was seeking Koziy's extradition. Unlike the Vesco and Caro Quintero cases, where warrants were outstanding, none was pending on Koziy. The U.S. government sent a federal marshal to San José to confirm that Koziy was there, but once that fact had been established, it took the position that its proceeding against him had always sought only to revoke his U.S. citizenship and to oust him from the country. With his move to Costa Rica, that had been accomplished. The United States didn't want him. The Soviet Union had finally indicated that it would seek his extradition if and when he was held deportable from the United States, but it had made no such request of Costa Rica and, in fact, Costa Rica has no extradition treaty with the Soviet Union.

Said Costa Rican Minister of Public Security Benjamin Piza-Carranza, "There is no charge against him, nor is there any country asking for his extradition. It is a difficult situation. We are a democratic country and we can't detain him. We have no charge."

Yaroslava Koziy was asked to come in for an interview. She complied, telling reporters afterward, "I just want to live in peace, that's all. I want to forget everything. I want to let it be, so let me alone, please."

But there was one irregularity that Costa Rican Solicitor General Ismael Antonio Vargas's office could find. Costa Rican immigration law did require valid citizenship as a requisite for obtaining permission to enter Costa Rica even as a tourist. Since there was no such thing as Ukrainian citizenship, they believed Bohdan Koziy was in the country illegally and announced that they would seek to expel him on that basis. However, they admitted that if they succeeded, they did not have the slightest idea where they would send him, since no one seemed to want him. Bohdan Koziy was ordered to present himself to Costa Rican authorities and did so several days later.

After questioning, Koziy made his first public statement since arriving in Costa Rica: "Fighting the American injustice for four years, I lost faith in American justice. I decided since they did not want me I would go away from their country." He announced that he would fight any attempt to be deported from Costa Rica. "I believe in Costa Rican democracy," he said. So the battle moved into the Costa Rican courts.

The first of what would be several contradictory rulings by the Costa Rican courts came on August 24, 1985, when the Court of Justice ruled that Koziy could remain in the country because once in, regardless of the validity of his tourist visa, his status as a dependent of a *rentista* superseded any other questions. And in Koziy's case, since no country was seeking his extradition, there was no legal reason to question his legal status.

This changed in early 1986, when the Soviet Union formally requested Koziy's extradition to stand trial for his crimes. In August, Deputy Interior Minister Alvaro Ramos announced that the Costa Rican government would begin proceedings to seek Koziy's extradition to Russia. The case moved through the courts, and on March 11, 1987, Judge Ligia Maria Gonzalez ordered Koziy's extradition to the Soviet Union, but he placed several conditions on this order. Under Costa Rican law, no one can be extradited to face a possible death sentence, capital punishment having been declared unconstitutional in Costa Rica. Therefore, the judge ruled, Koziy could not be turned over to Soviet authorities until they guaranteed that he would not face the death penalty and the Costa Rican Foreign Ministry certified that it believed the guarantee valid. However, he did order Koziy's detention pending receipt of the necessary guarantees from Moscow. Koziy's lawyer managed to turn the order into one of house arrest on grounds that Koziy was too sick to be jailed, so Judge Gonzalez ordered him to remain in his home pending examination by government doctors. When Koziy had not made himself available for the medical examination by April 3, Gonzalez ordered his arrest. This led to the enactment of a bizarre drama at the entrance to Koziy's villa, outside San José.

Plainclothes police agents arrived to arrest Koziy, but he refused to open the gate of the high iron fence surrounding his home. When the police threatened to force their way in, he drew a pistol from his belt and stood in the doorway with a pistol to his head threatening to kill himself rather then go back to the Soviet Union. A tense thirty-minute standoff resulted. At one point Koziy shouted in Spanish "I will die here in a free land, in Costa Rica. I will never go back to communism."

The police were convinced that he was serious and conferred with superiors back in San José. Finally, they decided to allow him to remain at home for the time being. But several hours later, the authorities reversed themselves. Vice-Interior Minister Alvaro Ramos said that police would return to the house the next day to take Koziy into custody. "If he does not come, we will use force."

This led to hours of frantic negotiations between Koziy's lawyer and the police and prosecutors. Finally, after receiving a guarantee that Koziy would not be turned over to the Soviets pending the outcome of further appeals in the Costa Rican courts, he did surrender to authorities.

Koziy was held for less than sixty days. On June 26, Judge Gonzalez reversed himself and ordered him freed. The judge ruled that despite the fact that the Soviet government had submitted the requested guarantee that Koziy would not face the death penalty, this guarantee had not come from a Soviet authority of sufficient standing. He also ruled that his second condition had not been met when Costa Rican Foreign Minister Rodrigo Madrigal refused, in the absence of any formal extradition treaty, to guarantee the Soviet promise. A frustrated Soviet ambassador to Costa Rica, Yuri Pavlov said about the decision, "short of having Mikhail Gorbachev come to San José and stand on the steps of the courts building I don't know what more we can do."

Koziy, with fatigue lines etched deeply into his face, emerged from the San

Augustin minimum security prison at Heredia to the applause of a crowd of supporters. Koziy had developed a broad base of support among stridently anti-communist Costa Ricans, to whom he had become a symbol, and others who saw him as a poor old man being hounded for something that had happened a lifetime ago and half a world away.

"I am happy to be free," a subdued Koziy told his supporters. "I am the victim of a Russian political conspiracy. I am a very unlucky man. I just want to go home."

Costa Rican authorities said that Judge Gonzalez's decision ended, once and for all, any possibility that Koziy would be deported to the Soviet Union. But, they said, there was still the matter of whether his entry into the country was "irregular," and they would seek some final court ruling as to the correctness of his status. If the courts ruled that he should be expelled, he would be. But they admitted that given the confused state of affairs, they did not have any idea where he would be sent.

That is no longer an issue. On September 11, 1987, Costa Rican Minister of the Interior Ronaldo Ramirez ruled that Koziy and his wife could remain in Costa Rica as long as they break no national law. In making his ruling, Ramirez said that in his opinion "His [Koziy's] authorship of crimes against Jews has not been demonstrated. He has broken no laws in Costa Rica and is therefore free to stay." He reached this conclusion despite the fact that three separate U.S. courts had reached contrary conclusions and the United States had agreed to make available all the evidence in its possession of Koziy's crimes. He did say that Koziy's visa was subject to periodic reexamination, but only to determine whether he had broken any Costa Rican laws.

Bohdan and Yaroslava Koziy live today in a large Spanish colonial hacienda amid the coffee fields of Alajuela Province, fifteen miles west of San José. It is said to be one of four properties in Costa Rica owned by their daughter and son-in-law. Neighbors say that they live a quiet life, spending most of their time tending their large gardens. They are said to keep mainly to themselves.

The American Nazi Hunt

In an indirect way, the strong movement against war criminals hidden in American society that would finally blossom in the late 1970s had its beginning in one of America's most heavily Jewish communities—Brooklyn, New York—more than a decade before the rise of the Third Reich.

The year was 1920. Warren Harding swept into the White House and brought with him a Republican congressman from a strongly Democratic district with its center in Flatbush. Two years later, the Democrats had a little trouble finding a candidate to take on the incumbent. Finally, a young lawyer, thirty-four-year-old Emanual Celler, came forward and, in something of a mild upset, defeated the incumbent.

Manny Celler would be reelected again and again. Twenty-four times he would go before the voters, and twenty-four times he would be returned to Washington for another two years. He would become one of the most powerful men in the Capitol, on a par with such congressional greats as Sam Rayburn, Carl Albert, and, more recently, Thomas P. "Tip" O'Neill.

By 1972 Manny Celler's reelection was almost a reflex action in Brooklyn. Few seemed to have noticed that Celler, at eighty-eight, had become the oldest member of the House. Brooklyn's Democratic leadership was not about to challenge him. As long as he thought he could serve, they would back his reelection. But a tough, no-nonsense young lawyer named Elizabeth Holtzman, whose only political credential was her membership on Mayor John Lindsay's staff decided that enough of Manny was enough. She stepped forward to take him on in the primary.

Holtzman's youth contrasted sharply with Celler's doddering age. She found a major issue in their ethnically changing district in the Equal Rights Amendment, which Celler had kept bottled up in his Judiciary Committee for almost twenty years. On election day, she shocked everyone by edging him out for the Democratic nomination: her victory margin—611 votes. In Brooklyn, the Democratic nomination was tantamount to election. And, after an easy general election victory in November, Elizabeth Holtzman was on her way to

Congress. Had Manny Celler not hung on for so long while retaining so much power that no "establishment" Democrat would run against him, Elizabeth Holtzman would probably never have been elected.

When Holtzman arrived in Washington, her priority was a seat on the House Judiciary Committee, so she could fulfill her campaign promise to move the Equal Rights Amendment out of committee to a floor vote. She attained her goal, and was assigned to Judiciary's Subcommittee on Immigration, Citizenship and International Law. She had come to Congress with no particular background in, or even interest in, the Nazi war crimes issue. But during her first term, she began to hear from her largely Jewish constituency about their concerns in the matter. With the active assistance of her subcommittee chairman, Representative Joshua Eilberg, a long-time congressman from Philadelphia, she began to look into the Immigration and Naturalization Service's handling of allegations about suspected Nazis. What she found appalled her.

The INS, circa 1970, was a slightly disorganized and highly decentralized operation. Policy was made in Washington, but the regional offices where that policy was implemented were almost autonomous, and it was regional administrators who decided what policies should be pursued, and with what degree of vigor. The investigations against immigrants were actually handled at a district level and, even within district offices, individual investigators had great leeway in deciding which cases they would actively pursue. It was up to the individual investigators to decide whether allegations of war crimes, or any other immigration violation, would be followed up. As later investigations would reveal, war crimes allegations often sat uninvestigated on agents' desks, because they were too busy with other matters or simply uninterested.

Sam Zutty, an old New York INS investigator, was eventually given the task of centralizing investigations of suspected Nazis. In 1978 he testified before Eilberg and Holtzman's subcommittee about the way allegations of Nazi war crimes were being handled in most INS offices:

> When the allegation came in, it was handed to an investigator just like a prostitution case or a fraud case or any other case. It was not given any special consideration. It was handled as a case involving a possible deportation or denaturalization charge. The investigator who handled it had to make his own determination as to the extent of the investigation and how much effort was going to go into it. . . . The investigator was often hard pressed to find the means of how to investigate. We had no liaison with Russia or Israel. Local witnesses were practically unobtainable, so what was he going to do . . . ?

One inevitable result was that very few cases were investigated and even fewer were brought to trial. In the 1950s, only five cases involving war crimes were prosecuted by the INS. Amazingly, the first three were all brought against Jews who were accused of collaborating with the Nazis while prisoners. Jakob Tencer was accused of abusing his fellow prisoners while in charge of a forced-labor brigade at a German ammunition factory in Pionki, Poland. Jonas Lewy was accused of abusing fellow Jews as a *kapo* in the Polish ghetto in Lodz. Heinrich Freidmann was also accused of abusing fellow Jews as the head of a forced-labor battalion at the Luftwaffe plant in Mielec, Poland. None of the three cases was related except in the similarity of the allegations. All three resulted from former inmates meeting the accused on the street, recognizing him, and contacting the INS with the charges.

As it turned out, the testimony received from witnesses in all three cases was also remarkably similar. Some evidence was heard in all three cases that the accused had committed abuses. But there was also considerable testimony that, in many instances, the three had acted heroically to protect and save Jewish lives, and that they had worked hard to improve the general conditions under which those in their charge were forced to live and work.

Tencer's case was thrown out by the immigration judge who handled the original trial. He stated that the evidence was so contradictory and the evidence that Tencer had done good acts so overwhelming that he could not, in conscience, order him deported. The original judge in Freidmann's case ordered him deported, ruling that Freidmann had entered the country illegally because he had taken part in the persecution of those in his charge. However, on appeal, another immigration judge ruled that Freidmann had simply done what he had to survive under the conditions that existed, and that his actions did not amount to persecution. He reversed the first judge and dismissed the case.

Lewy had a more difficult time. In 1955 an immigration judge found against him and ordered him deported. That decision was upheld in an initial appeal, but further appeals dragged the case into 1958. At that point, Lewy was ordered deported to Poland, and an inquiry was made of the Polish government to see if it would accept him. Poland simply refused to respond for five years. It was not until 1962 that an official response came—Poland refused to accept him. INS did not know what to do with him. He then filed a new appeal and in 1964 still another judge ordered the whole case reheard because of procedural errors in the original hearing. But many of the original witnesses could no longer be found, and finally, in 1965, the INS decided not to proceed with the new hearing. Lewy eventually died in New York City in the 1980s.

Perhaps what convinced the INS that proceeding with Nazi war crime cases was simply too involved and too complex was the case against Andrija Artukovic. The former interior minister of the Nazi puppet state of Croatia, Artukovic was accused of being responsible for the executions of tens of thousands of Jews and Serbs. The INS brought a deportation proceeding against him in 1951, and before it ended three decades later, it had become one of the longest, costliest, and most complex cases of its kind ever heard in U.S. courts.

The INS had known exactly who Artukovic was and what he was charged with doing for some time. It had done its best to ignore him, but the INS was forced into action when columnist Drew Pearson broke the news that Artukovic was in the country. Pearson's columns were quickly followed by a demand from Yugoslavia that he be extradited. Actually, not one, but two separate actions were brought against Artukovic in 1951. One sought his extradition to Yugoslavia at its request, the second his deportation. The actions were separate, but they would become hopelessly entangled as the years passed.

Artukovic was taken into custody in connection with the extradition action. But in September 1951, his lawyer got him released on bond, pending a ruling on an initial appeal he had filed against extradition based on the fact that at the time no valid extradition treaty existed between the United States and the Tito government in Yugoslavia. A combination of legal maneuvering and INS indecision kept the extradition request from even being heard for almost eight years. But, in the meantime, the separate deportation action against Artukovic did go forward. After an eight-month hearing, on June 27, 1952, a hearing officer ordered him deported. That action was appealed, and, in April 1953, the Board of Immigration Appeals (BIA) upheld the deportation order. Many thought the case was over now—that Artukovic would be deported to some third country, which in turn would probably extradite him to Yugoslavia, where he would face trial for his many crimes. But the reality was that the battle had only just begun.

The INS initially delayed in trying to enforce the deportation order, assuming that sooner or later the extradition matter would be settled. But, when several additional adverse rulings came down against them in the extradition case, the INS decided, in 1956, to go forward with the deportation. It sent Artukovic an official notice that if he did not voluntarily leave the United States within thirty days to go to any country of his choice, he would be deported to Yugoslavia. But in so informing him, the INS had to give Artukovic legal notice that he could appeal the deportation order if he could show that in Yugoslavia, he would face the possibility of "physical persecution."

Given this opportunity, Artukovic's lawyers responded and a whole new series of legal battles ensued. Then Artukovic got a lucky break. In what was clearly a political decision, the INS ruled that no person could be deported to Yugoslavia because of its communist government. The ruling stayed in effect for more than a year, until it was thrown out by the U.S. Supreme Court in 1958. This brought the Artukovic deportation matter back to the front burner. But now INS made still another decision. It decided not to proceed with the deportation until the extradition case, which appeared to be heading for trial at last, was settled.

On June 16, 1958, the extradition hearing finally began in a courtroom in

Los Angeles. It dragged on for months, and not until January 1959 did the immigration judge hand down his startling ruling. He dismissed out of hand all evidence offered by the Yugoslavian government as to the crimes committed by Artukovic. He termed them politically motivated and turned down the extradition request.

That brought the deportation case back into question. So much time had passed that it had to be, in effect, reopened. This occurred in another hearing that started in April 1959. The problem was where to deport Artukovic. He could not be sent to Yugoslavia, and no other country seemed to want him. Attempts to get Ireland and Switzerland to accept him had failed. The judge stopped the case until INS could find a country that would accept him. For all intents and purposes, the Artukovic case was ended.*

While the Artukovic case was making its slow way through initial proceedings, the INS undertook proceedings against three others accused of hiding war-crimes pasts. In 1955, Antanas Spokevicius, a Lithuanian, was accused of participating in the liquidation of more than 20,000 Jews in the Kaunas ghetto as a member of the Lithuanian police auxiliary. On his visa application, he had claimed that he was a schoolteacher during the war, and now INS proposed to deport him based on that falsehood. The case seemed open and shut. After a relatively short hearing, an immigration judge agreed that Spokevicius had lied on his visa application and ordered him deported. But the Board of Immigration Appeals saw it differently. It agreed that Spokevicius had lied on the visa, but believed his argument that he had done so "out of fear of being repatriated to his former homeland," where he thought he would face persecution. It reversed the judge, and ordered that Spokevicius be allowed to remain in the United States.

The second case was against another Lithuanian, Felix Krasnauskas, who claimed on his visa application that he had been a farmer throughout the war. The INS had clear proof that, far from farming, Krasnauskas had spent much of the war as chief of police of the Gestapo-supervised auxiliary police force in his district, and as such had probably participated in any number of atrocities. As with Spokevicius, the trial judge quickly ruled against Krasnauskas and ordered him deported. But again, the BIA overturned the ruling, stating that

---

* By 1980 the U.S. attitude toward Yugoslavia had changed considerably and deportation proceedings were begun again by OSI. After numerous court rulings, appeals and re-appeals including several trips to the U.S. Supreme Court, Artukovic was finally extradited to Yugoslavia in 1986, thirty-four years after he was originally ordered deported. In 1987 he was tried and convicted of war crimes and sentenced to death by a firing squad. He is still appealing that ruling.

there was no evidence that Krasnauskas had ever participated "in a movement hostile to the United States." Effectively, this meant that the BIA was defining the Gestapo as an organization not hostile to the United States.

The third case involved Laszlo Agh, a Hungarian who was accused of beating and mistreating members of a forced-labor detachment of Hungarian Jews whom he had supervised. At his 1959 hearing, eleven eyewitnesses appeared to swear that Agh was the man who had beaten and persecuted them during the war years. Agh produced an equal number of witnesses who swore to his good character and the fact that they had never heard him say anything anti-Semitic. But none had known him back in Hungary—only since he had been in the United States.

Again, the immigration judge ruled quickly that Agh should be deported and, the BIA overruled him. Despite the eyewitnesses who had identified Agh as the man who had persecuted them, the BIA said that the government had not proved its case by "reasonable, substantial and probative evidence." The BIA reversed the trial judge and ordered that Agh be allowed to remain in the United States.

The lessons of these three cases, and of the Artukovic case, were not lost on INS investigators at all levels. As the Artukovic situation was proving, cases based on war crimes allegations were difficult and complex. And as the three reversals showed, even when they were won, the likelihood was high that the Board of Immigration Appeals would reverse the rulings, if for no other reason than it did not have the heart to send people back to Eastern Europe and communist rule.

Before Elizabeth Holtzman and Joshua Eilberg began to focus on the question of former Nazi war criminals in this country, only two persons had ever been expelled from the United States because of war crimes accusations. The first case bordered on the bizarre. Ferenc Vajta had been a pro-Nazi newspaper editor in Hungry and was involved in planning the deportation of Hungarian Jews during the war. After the war, he went to work for the OSS and was also involved with the U.S. Army's Counterintelligence Corps in Italy. He eventually found his way to the United States, thanks in part to a letter that had been written on his behalf by the CIC. He entered the country, not as a perspective permanent resident, but on a six-month visitor's visa.

Vajta had been extremely well known in Hungary, and almost the first Hungarian he met in America recognized him. Within a matter of weeks, Walter Winchell, the influential columnist, had gotten wind of the story and published an article. Immediately, the INS ordered Vajta arrested, and he was summarily ordered deported since he was only in the U.S. on a visitor's visa. He appealed the case for almost two years, but, in February 1950, he was deported to

Colombia.* Vajta was the only man deported from the United States for past Nazi dealings before 1973.

One other case stands out in this era, and it resulted in the only other explusion from this country of an individual with a Nazi past. Hermine Braunsteiner had been a legend at several death camps in Poland. She personally beat and tortured hundreds of prisoners as an SS officer and prison camp guard. After the war she had been incarcerated for a short time and then released. Eventually, she made her way to Canada, where she married an American, Russell Ryan, whom she had met in Germany. In April 1959, the Ryans moved to the United States and settled in New York City, and in January 1963, Hermine Ryan became an American citizen.

She was uncovered by Simon Wiesenthal. Information supplied by Wiesenthal to *The New York Times* resulted in a series of stories about the former SS camp guard. Because of the newspaper stories, the INS began an investigation, but the case presented a unique problem for them. It was the first case presented to them in which accusations of a Nazi past had been made against a person who had already been naturalized. While they could proceed on a deportation case internally, a suit to strip someone of citizenship had to be filed by the Justice Department in federal court.

For almost two years, the case bounced back and forth between INS and the Justice Department over the question of whether a 1957 Austrian amnesty given to certain former Nazis covered Ryan and thus eliminated the requirement that she state her past on her citizenship application. Four years after INS opened the investigation, the Justice Department finally decided that it would prosecute; in August 1968, it filed denaturalization charges. Ryan's lawyers then filed a series of motions which took almost three years to dispose of. Finally, the Ryan case was scheduled for trial in July 1970, seven years after the original *New York Times* story appeared. But the case was never tried; Hermine Ryan agreed voluntarily to relinquish her citizenship.

Now that she was no longer a citizen, Ryan was again the subject of INS interest. They began a deportation investigation that culminated in a hearing on February 7, 1972. As often happened in deportation hearings in the 1960s, the case would go for several days and then stop for several months, by fits and starts. By March 1973, the hearing had never actually ended. But then the

---

* How Vajta ended up in Colombia is itself a fascinating story. While working with the CIC in Italy after the war, he apparently developed close relationships with higher-ups in the Curia at the Vatican. When he was ordered deported, Spain and Italy refused to take him back, and the INS did not want to deport him to Hungary. So the Vatican stepped in and arranged for Colombia to accept him, and for a small Catholic college there to employ him. He spent the rest of his life in Bogotá as an economics professor.

West German government, which was about to start a complex war crimes trial against a group of guards from the same prison camp in which Ryan had been a guard, requested her extradition to stand trial with the others.

Ryan was arrested immediately, and on May 1, 1973, was ordered returned to West Germany. An appeal was denied and, in August 1973, she was turned over to German police. In February 1975, the trial against her and fourteen others began—a trial that would last for more than six years. In 1981 she was convicted of multiple murders and was sentenced to life in prison.

By 1973 Elizabeth Holtzman and Joshua Eilberg were beginning to make waves. They complained bitterly to the INS about the way Nazi accusations were being handled and the INS looked for some way to respond. At about the same time, Dr. Otto Karbach, of the World Jewish Congress, sent the INS a list of fifty-nine names that he believed to be those of Nazi war criminals living in the United States. Rather than simply sending the names out to individual district offices, as would have been done in the past, the INS decided to respond to criticisms of its handling of such cases by establishing a "Project Control Office" in New York to review accusations against Nazis and to gather evidence in such cases. Sam Zutty was assigned to head the office.

It became clear rather quickly that the Project Control Office was really nothing more than a public relations gesture. Zutty *was* the office. He had no staff, no budget, and no authority to seek the help of any other U.S. agency in gathering evidence. Nor could he contact foreign governments to seek evidence on any case unless three separate committees of his superiors reviewed it and agreed that there was sufficient evidence to make such a request.

When it became clear that Zutty had been given a mission but no authority, Eilberg and Holtzman stepped up the pressure. Eilberg approached Gerald Ford and got the president to put pressure on the State Department, which, for the first time, began to cooperate with the INS on accusations of Nazi crime. The State Department had long maintained that it did not believe foreign governments would be interested in helping the United States identify former Nazis living in this country. But to pacify Eilberg, U.S. ambassadors in Germany, Israel, and the Soviet Union raised the issue with the governments there and were surprised to learn that all three were very willing to cooperate in any way they could.

As a starting point, the State Department took the list of fifty-nine names that had been provided by the World Jewish Congress' Karbach and gave it to the West German government. Within ninety days the Germans had reported back that they had some information on sixteen of them. Eventually, the Germans were able to provide substantial information on more than half the names on the list. At the same time, an approach was made to Israel, where the governmental unit charged with hunting war criminals said it would comb its files for information on the fifty-nine and would also attempt to find witnesses who could substantiate the accusations against them.

Compared to the past, progress was being made, but it was very slow. By mid-1976, three years after Zutty's Central Control Office had been established, the INS had brought only one case against an accused former Nazi, Archbishop Valerian Trifa of the Romanian Orthodox Episcopacy, and then only after a series of newspaper stories had identified him as a probable war criminal.

Eilberg and Holtzman had waited patiently to see what the new INS initiatives would amount to. When it became apparent that it was little or nothing, they began a new battle. Eilberg announced that hearings would be held, and Holtzman began to threaten new legislation. Shaken by the prospect, the INS tried to respond quickly. Within a few weeks it filed one case, and by the end of the year had filed four more.

Over the next year, INS would file almost fifteen cases, including six denaturalization cases. As each case was filed, it was accompanied by a public relations release trumpeting the proceeding and repeating how tough the INS was going to be against accused Nazi war criminals. And as each case was filed, the INS dispatched a congressional relations specialist to the Hill to brief Eilberg and Holtzman. The only problem with all this activity was that these cases would have to be tried in court, and not in the newspapers. The INS was woefully ill-prepared to try any of them. They were only beginning to establish the kinds of relationships with Israel and West Germany that might result in finding witnesses and documents to support the accusations, and the State Department was still refusing to approach the Soviet Government officially for help.

Now, with all these cases on its hands, INS was faced with the realization that it would soon have to go into court and start trying them. Its response was to form a Special Litigation Unit within its General Counsel's office to handle all Nazi war crime cases. At the same time the New York Control Office was disbanded.

By any measure, the Special Litigation Unit was a disaster. In more than two years of existence, it did not bring a single new case. It did attempt to try five of the cases that had been brought to appease Eilberg and Holtzman, but the results were horrendous. Only one was successful, and one dragged on for more than two years until broken off by INS lawyers desperate to find a way to salvage it. The remaining three were lost outright—one when a key piece of evidence was lost and could not be introduced in the trial and another when, as was learned later, key material in the government's file was not introduced into evidence. The third case lost was the one that has come to be known as the case of "the Nazi Who Never Was," Frank Walus.

In 1976 Simon Wiesenthal, in Vienna, had gone public with charges that a Polish emigré living in Chicago, Frank Walus, had been a collaborator involved in persecuting Polish Jews, including women and children, as part of a Gestapo-led auxiliary police unit. Walus, charged Wiesenthal, "performed his duties with the Gestapo in the ghettos of Czestochowa and Kielce and handed over numerous Jews to the Gestapo."

Armed with charges from such an "unimpeachable" source as Wiesenthal, the INS began to move. They turned to Israeli investigators, providing Walus's name and a photograph from his entry visa into the United States, and a statement of the charges being brought by Wiesenthal. Some of the details of Wiesenthal's charges became confused. The Israelis apparently thought they were being asked to verify that Walus had been a bona fide member of the Gestapo, and not simply a collaborator: they wrote up their report based on this misunderstanding. When the report came back to the INS, no one caught the error and Walus had been transformed into a member of the Gestapo.

The Israelis took out newspaper advertisements seeking survivors of Czestochowa and Kielce to come forward and perhaps identify a war criminal from their past. Eventually, forty-four did come forward and were shown a photo line-up of eight pictures, including a blow-up of the small picture of Walus from his naturalization application. As an appeals court would say later, the picture blow-up was so bad—to say nothing of the fact that it was taken almost twenty years after Walus was said to have committed his crimes—that the person depicted was all but unrecognizable. Nonetheless, seven of the forty-four said that they could recognize the picture as that of a Gestapo officer whom they remembered as being called Frank. (It would come out that all eight had been told before seeing the picture that agents were trying to locate a former Gestapo officer named Frank.)

Upon learning from the Israelis that several witnesses appeared able to identify Walus, and under even greater pressure from Holtzman to begin prosecutions, several INS investigators flew to Israel. They confirmed what the Israeli investigators had previously learned, although they did not repeat any of the photo line-ups. Back in Washington, INS officials were trying to decide how to proceed when Israeli sources leaked to a Chicago newspaper the names of more than eighty alleged Nazi war criminals living in the United States. Among them was one identified as "Fritz Wulecki" with a Chicago address. The result was headlines: "Nazi Jew Killer Living on SW Side?" The INS had to move, because the real name would be discovered quickly. Less than a week later, formal denaturalization proceedings were begun and Walus was served with the papers. He had sixty days in which to answer charges that he should lose his U.S. citizenship because he had hidden his war crimes when applying for admission to the United States in 1959.

Walus claimed he was innocent—claimed that he had never been a member of the Gestapo and that he had not even served in the military. Yes, he admitted, he was from Kielce, but he maintained that throughout the war he had been a civilian worker on various German farms. His story was dismissed out of hand.

Walus finally found a lawyer who was willing to take his case—no easy matter, because he had been all but tried and convicted in the newspapers already. But Bob Korenkiewicz, a local attorney, agreed to take the case and even paid out of his own pocket for a trip to West Germany. He had had his suspicions before he left, but what he found there convinced him that his client was innocent.

From the Berlin Documents Center, the repository for all Nazi military records, he received a statement showing that there was no record of any Frank or Franz Walus having served in the Gestapo. From the office that administers the German national health insurance program came a statement that Frank Walus had been insured from 1940 to 1945 while working on farms in southern Germany (just as he said he had). In southern Germany, Korenkiewicz found witnesses who were willing to swear that Walus lived among them all through the war. From Poland he received affidavits from individuals who had known Walus before the war and who swore he had not been in Poland during the war. Even the parish priest in Kielce swore that to his knowledge, Walus was not a member of the Gestapo or a collaborator.

But when Korenkiewicz returned to the United States armed with what he considered irrefutable evidence that his client could not have been the man remembered by the survivors of the Kielce ghetto, he could not get the INS to accept the documents, or even to interview the witnesses he had found. By now the case had developed a kind of momentum of its own. The newspapers were full of it, and the INS had told Congress repeatedly that the case exemplified the kind of strong prosecution they would be bringing. To abandon it now was unthinkable, no matter what evidence Korenkiewicz had uncovered in Germany. A kind of Nazi-mania had developed. The INS was going ahead with the trial, and Korenkiewicz could bring any witnesses he wanted to Chicago, at his expense.

Walus came to trial in March 1978. The presiding judge was Julius Hoffman of "Chicago Seven" fame. Even before the trial, Hoffman announced that the matter was repugnant to him. He ran the trial with an iron hand and an eccentricity that bordered on the bizarre. He allowed government witnesses great latitude, while limiting severely Korenkiewicz's cross-examination of them. When Walus himself testified, Hoffman limited him almost entirely to simple yes and no answers.

Eleven witnesses brought from Poland and Israel said that it was Walus whom they had seen committing various atrocities. Their testimony, however, often disagreed, especially in physical descriptions of the man in question. Some testified that they were sure Walus was the perpetrator, but the man they described was years older, inches taller, and many pounds heavier than Walus had been at that time or any other.

Walus could afford to bring only six witnesses to Chicago. Two testified to the accuracy of the health insurance records that placed Walus on various farms throughout the war years. Three witnesses confirmed this, including one who said that Walus had lived on his farm during much of the period. Another witness, an expert in Nazi military affairs, testified that although Walus had been brought up in Germany, he was born in Poland. That made him a Pole in the eyes of the Germans, and Poles could not serve in the Gestapo. Moreover, he had been three inches shorter and fifty pounds lighter then the minimums required for Gestapo service.

In the end Hoffman said he simply did not believe the documents that Walus had gathered, or the witnesses he had presented; he was persuaded by the government's witnesses. As for the discrepancies in size and age, Hoffman dismissed them, saying that a man in uniform often looks larger and older than he actually is. Hoffman ordered Walus stripped of his citizenship, and the INS was elated: it had a victory.

Even as an appeal was being prepared by Walus's lawyers, new evidence came to light supporting his plea of innocence. A French Jew who had been a forced laborer on a farm during the war read about the trial and contacted the U.S. embassy in Paris. He had known Walus during the war, he said. They had worked on the same farm. Other persons who knew Walus in Poland came forward to swear to his innocence. Finally, additional documents were uncovered in Germany that added more proof of Walus's occupation as a farm worker all during the war.

The new evidence was presented to Hoffman, and he was asked to reconsider. He refused. Then a formal appeal was filed. The process took almost two years, but in February 1980, the court ruled. It threw out Hoffman's verdict and ordered Walus retried. In making the ruling, the court said that it appeared the government's case against Walus was "weak" but that Hoffman's handling of the trial had been so biased that it could not evaluate the evidence properly. Thus, it stopped short of reversing Hoffman and acquitting Walus. It would be up to the government to review the evidence and to decide how to proceed.

By now the INS had been replaced by the Office of Special Investigation (OSI). OSI personnel reexamined all the evidence against Walus, traveling to Poland and Germany to reinterview the witnesses who backed Walus. The reinvestigation took almost a year, but the result was all but preordained. In addition to substantiating almost all the testimony of Walus's witnesses and corroborating the authenticity of the documents, OSI investigators found additional witnesses who placed Walus on German farms throughout the war years. One new witness was the local parish priest from the area where Walus said he had spent the war. The priest said that young Walus had attended mass every Sunday during the war. The conclusion was absolutely inescapable: Walus was innocent.

No one doubted the sincerity of the eleven witnesses who had testified against Walus. Undoubtedly they had seen the horrors in the Czestochowa and Kielce ghettos to which they had testified. But it now seemed completely clear that the man they accused of the atrocities could not have been Frank Walus. And, given the differences in physical description, there was almost certainly more than one person involved. It was decided not to retry Walus, and the court was petitioned to allow the government to withdraw the denaturalization.

Judge Prentice Marshall, who had inherited the case, agreed. But, recognizing the deep emotional involvement in the case of the sizable Jewish and Eastern European emigré communities of Chicago, he did so with an unusual written opinion: "In granting the government's motion, we do not forget the abominable atrocities inflicted at the hands of the Nazis on those and the families of those who testified against the defendant. But those outrages cannot be undone, and certainly not by an unjust conviction of the defendant. Indeed, we are confident that those who survived the atrocities and seek vindication in the memory of those who did not would not want their honor stained by a conviction which would not withstand careful dispassionate scrutiny."

Only later was the source of the "evidence" against Walus that had reached Simon Wiesenthal identified. Walus had bought a two-family duplex when he came to Chicago. In the early 1970s, he rented out the second unit to a tenant with whom he eventually had a fight. Walus evicted the tenant, who then started telling one and all how his former landlord used to sit around and reminisce about the atrocities he had committed against Jews in the good old days. Apparently one of the groups to which he told the story was a Jewish refugee agency in Chicago, which passed the information along to Simon Wiesenthal.

In a way, this is perhaps the most amazing prosecution ever undertaken against an accused Nazi in this country, and a total condemnation of the way INS was operating. The evidence of Walus's innocence even before the trial was overwhelming. The entire Nazi-hunting effort in this country was placed under a cloud and, although it had not brought the case originally, the Office of Special Investigations was embarrassed. However, said OSI, in the long run it may have been fortunate that the Walus case did occur, because it forced the government to reexamine its methods and motives and brought to the OSI a new degree of professionalism that has proven vital to its success in the intervening years.*

Allan Ryan, Jr., the OSI director who decided not to retry Walus, has said that if the original case against the Chicagoan had been brought under the safeguards that now exist, he has no doubt that that case would never have been filed. But while the Walus case may have been a valuable learning experience, it has had one unwanted side effect in that it created a martyr. Frank Walus is, understandably, a bitter man. He has become an activist—an anti-OSI activist. In almost every prosecution of an accused Nazi in this country, he will show up as a defense witness. He will testify about what happened to him, and the defense will raise the question that it could be happening again. In fact, the Walus case represents just about the lowest point in U.S. Nazi-hunting efforts.

Eilberg and Holtzman had become convinced that the INS was hopelessly disorganized and ineffectual: the only solution they could see was to take the matter out of INS hands. Early in 1978, Eilberg wrote Attorney General Griffin Bell to say that "there is a general feeling [in Congress] that the government attorneys assigned to prosecute the various denaturalization and deportation cases are incompetent and ill-prepared." This gives rise, he pointed out, to the fear that future war crimes cases "will not be diligently investigated nor will they be properly and expeditiously prosecuted." Something had to be done.

The two representatives then turned their attention to closing a semi-loophole that had been opened when Congress passed the Immigration and Naturalization Act of 1952. The law had established four classes of persons who could be excluded from admission to the United States, or who could be deported should they be found to have entered the country. Former Nazis undoubtedly fell into more than one of these classes, but they were not specifically excluded. Eilberg and Holtzman closed that loophole by pushing through

---

* Among the reforms that Walus forced on the OSI was the manner in which photo line-ups were conducted, the manner in which documentary evidence, such as the German insurance documents, is treated, and the wording of newspaper advertisements seeking witnesses. No longer would the advertisements contain the name of the individual being sought or, for that matter, his physical description. Both had been done in the Walus case and had clearly predisposed the witnesses who came forward. Moreover, an important new procedure was instituted. Walus's lawyer had asked both the Polish and West German governments for certain war crimes documents and for a search of their files, but he was turned down because he requested the information as a private citizen. Henceforth, the OSI decided, if a defense lawyer wanted a record check or a document, he would forward his request to OSI, which would transmit it to the government involved through official State Department channels, thus guaranteeing a response.

Congress the act of October 30, 1978, that amended the 1952 Immigration Act by making excludable any alien who "during the period beginning March 23, 1933, and ending May 8, 1945 . . . under the Nazi government of Germany . . . ordered, incited, assisted, or otherwise participated in the persecution of any person because of race, religion, national origin or political opinion."

This was the last victory Eilberg won in Congress. He was defeated for re-election in November 1978 and, when the new Congress convened in January 1979, Holtzman took over his Immigration subcommittee chairmanship. She was also a rising power on the full Judiciary Committee. Immediately she made her intentions clear. If something was not done right away about the Nazi situation, she intended to make life miserable for the Justice Department on the Hill, and she had the power to make good on that threat.

This was a fight that Attorney General Griffin Bell did not want, so he and his staff huddled with Holtzman. On March 28, 1979, they announced a solution. A new unit would be established within the Justice Department whose only function would be to investigate war crimes charges and to bring prosecutions. It would be called the Office of Special Investigations and would have its own staff and budget. Although the cases it would bring would be civil in nature, it would be a part of the Department's Criminal Division. The decision was implemented by Bell's successor, Benjamin Civiletti, who, on September 4, 1979, ordered the transfer of the Special Litigation Unit from the Immigration and Naturalization Service to the Criminal Division of the Justice Department via Attorney General's Order No. 851-79.

The head of the Criminal Division in 1979 was Assistant Attorney General Phillip Heymann, who had been a prosecutor and now was a Harvard Law School professor on leave. Heymann regarded the mission of the new division as what he called "a moral imperative." He immediately persuaded Walter Rockler, a former Nuremberg prosecutor, to take a six-month leave from his Washington law firm to organize the new division, hire its staff, and begin to bring some order to the disorganized mass of data inherited from the INS.

By late fall, OSI's team had been assembled. The team took possession of the INS files, began to sort the material, and planned its initial activities. But Heymann was pressuring Rockler for some positive action that would show that the new office was functioning and aggressive. He wanted to have the OSI file its first cases before the end of the year. Thus Rockler told his deputy, Allan Ryan, Jr., a former assistant solicitor general who had been employed with the understanding that he would eventually succeed Rockler, to cull the INS files for strong cases that could be filed immediately. Ryan reported back that there were several. On November 20, the Office of Special Investigations filed its first two complaints, as we have seen—one against Wolodymir Osidach, the other against Bohdan Koziy.

Shortly thereafter the fledgling OSI decided that its next priority was one major piece of unfinished business. Although the State Department was now more willing to help in war criminal investigations, and had helped the Immigration and Naturalization Service establish relations with both West Germany and Israel, it had enlisted only limited Soviet help in Nazi-hunting efforts despite its efforts. Upon specific U.S. request, the Soviets agreed to supply brief statements from witnesses as to events or suspects, but these limited statements had little or no value as evidence in court. If it were to do its job properly, the OSI needed greater cooperation from the Soviets, including independent access to witnesses in a manner that would result in testimony admissible at trial.

Rockler and Ryan confronted the problem head-on and approached Attorney General Civiletti for help. He, in turn, contacted the Soviet ambassador in Washington and asked for assistance in setting up meetings in Moscow. Within weeks, Rockler's and Ryan's applications for visas had been approved, and the two flew to Moscow.

Ryan remembers that neither of them knew what to expect. They had requested a meeting with the Soviet Union's top legal officer, the procurator general, who is analogous to the U.S. Attorney General in some ways, but much more powerful and autonomous within the Soviet system. However, they had received no assurances before leaving Washington as to who would meet with them, or whether they would be well received. They had come to Moscow hoping to make an agreement that would allow Soviet citizens to be brought to the United States to testify in deportation and denaturalization trials. The alternative, should the Soviets be unwilling to let their citizens travel to the West, would be to win Soviet approval for videotaped depositions taken on Soviet soil which defense counsel would be allowed to cross-examine.

The three-day meeting went better than either American had dreamed. At the outset, they were ushered into a large ornate meeting room where high-ranking officers of the proctorate were seated around the table in their quasi-military uniforms. There was an empty seat at the head of the table. A few minutes later, the aging procurator general, Roman Rudenko, walked slowly into the room.

General Rudenko had suffered a stroke and was visibly weak. He stayed only a few minutes, but set the tone of the entire series of talks. He began by remembering the Nuremberg trials, where he had served as the chief Soviet prosecutor thirty-five years earlier. He noted that in the interim, the Soviet Union had continued its efforts to bring former Nazi war criminals to justice, while the United States had let the issue drift. But he expressed his pleasure that the United States appeared to be getting serious about the issue and said that the Soviet Union was willing to do all it could to assist: just tell us what you want. After a round of pleasantries, Rudenko left, turning the meeting over to his chief deputy, Aleksandr Rekunkov,* who would negotiate the details of what became known as the Moscow Agreement.

Rockler and Ryan left Moscow with an agreement whereby the United States could ask a Soviet citizen to testify in the United States; if that citizen was willing and in good health, it would be allowed. In cases where the witness was either unwilling or unable to travel to the United States, depositions would be videotaped in Moscow, with defense counsel present to cross-examine. Moreover, the Soviets would attempt to provide more documentary evidence for the use of American prosecutors and would open their archives to U.S. investigators. Finally, and to an extent most importantly, matters would be handled directly between the OSI and the procurator's office—no going from OSI to Justice, to State, to the U.S. embassy in Moscow, to the Soviet Foreign Ministry, to the procurator's office: they would communicate directly. Rockler and Ryan came home with everything they had hoped for and more.

Over the next several years, OSI took testimony from over 100 Soviet witnesses relating to about half of the two dozen cases it filed between 1980 and 1983. But it became apparent quickly that although the Soviets said they were willing to let their citizens travel to the U.S., in practice, this was not the case. As Ryan would describe it in his book *Quiet Neighbors*: "In the first few cases we requested that the witnesses be allowed to travel to the United States for trial, but, if that was not possible, we would take depositions. The Soviets responded by scheduling depositions. After a while, we decided to request depositions at the onset."

With the office established and functioning, Walter Rockler returned to private law practice and Ryan took over as director. During the next few years he began hundreds of investigations, filed a dozen new cases, tried those that had been filed but left untried by the INS,† pursued appeals, and put together the staff that would eventually emerge as perhaps the most expert Nazi-hunting force in the world. Probably the best account of these early years is Ryan's own in *Quiet Neighbors*:

---

* Rudenko died a short time later, and Rekunkov succeeded him. Rekunkov himself would become a major target of conservatives and others challenging the OSI's relationship because he was in charge of the program of internal exile of Soviet dissidents and "refuseniks." A full discussion of the Soviet evidence and witness situations is contained in chapter 9.

† Ryan also dismissed several cases that had been brought by INS. We have seen the Walus case, wherein OSI investigators actually helped find key witnesses of whom the defense was unaware and who bolstered Walus's claim of misidentification.

The INS had also brought a case in 1977 against Mykola Kowalchuk, a Ukrainian-born Philadelphia resident accused of helping the Nazis persecute Jews as a member of

OSI had a first-rate staff of people: twenty lawyers, seven historians, four investigators, and a phalanx of researchers, analysts, paralegals, and secretaries, fifty people in all. None of the lawyers or investigators had any detailed knowledge of Nazi war crimes before we came to OSI; the historians, on the other hand, were experts. But the lawyers, thrust into complex investigations and trials, came to have a very respectable knowledge of the Nazi period after a very short time. And we made generous use of experts from academia in the United States and Europe.

We were a diverse group of people, but we worked closely and soon came to fit together well. One reporter noted, "The atmosphere in [the] busy office is distinctly bullish, and there is a strong sense of camaraderie" as we went about our work.

Some of the people were Jewish, some were not; it made no difference to me in hiring and I never bothered to count. I received many resumes from lawyers whose families had been directly affected by the Holocaust; they were survivors, or they had lost close relatives, or both. Some of these applicants emphasized to me that they felt a deep and burning commitment to track down the perpetrators of the Holocaust.

Such entreaties made me uneasy, and while I could sympathize with their commitment, I turned down several applicants whose zeal struck me as excessive for a prosecutor. I needed lawyers who could be objective in appraising evidence, and in presenting cases in court. We were federal prosecutors, not personal representatives of those murdered by the Nazis; I could not afford the risk that a staff member's moral commitment might be so consuming as to subconsciously affect his objectivity. If the evidence in a prospective case was weak, we had to know it, and to know where and why it was weak, so that we could strengthen it, and if we could not strengthen it, close it. A prosecution, like a seawall, is only as strong as its weakest point; all the evidence in the world of Nazi persecution means nothing if our evidence against the prospective defendant himself is uncertain.

---

the Ukrainian police in Lubomyl. During 1942 some 6,000 Lubomyl Jews were slaughtered by Nazis with the help of the local police. The INS had let the case languish, and when the key eyewitness died before a deposition could be taken, Ryan dismissed the charges against Kowalchuk. This, perhaps more than any other case, shows the cautious—some might say overcautious—approach taken by OSI. Although it could not prove a specific crime, it could clearly show both membership in a prohibited organization and the fact that Mykola Kowalchuk had lied on his visa application. There was also enough evidence to pursue the case against his brother, Serge Kowalchuk, filed by INS in 1977. Serge Kowalchuk was also a member of the Ukrainian police in Lubomyl. He was eventually stripped of his citizenship, and when ordered deported left voluntarily for Paraguay.

> *Before I approved the prosecution of any case, therefore, I required a detailed memo setting forth the basis for the charge, the expected testimony of the witnesses (and assessments of their credibility), the documentary evidence, the anticipated defenses, and our responses to those defenses. I could not personally interview the witnesses in every case before it was filed; I had to rely on the objectivity and honesty of the attorneys, historians, and investigators who did and who gave me the prosecution memo for decision. I soon recognized those attorneys who were objective and those who took liberties with the evidence, those who dealt honestly with weaknesses in cases and those who tried to conceal them.*

During the early days, a series of court rulings helped shape the OSI of today. Many of the rulings were favorable; a few were not. In fact, at times, according to OSI lawyers who were there during these years, it often seemed like the fledgling office was taking two steps forward and one step back.

What may be described as the two key cases in this period dated back to the days of the INS's Special Litigation Unit. The first was that of Boleslaus Maikovskis, a resident of Mineola, New York. Before it was finished, it became one of the most complex war crimes deportation actions ever pursued by the OSI.

Maikovskis entered this country in 1951, but never became a citizen. He was accused of persecuting Jews and others while serving as police chief of Rezekna, Latvia, during the war years. The original charges against him were filed in 1976, and a deportation hearing was begun in October 1977 but discontinued because the immigration judge ruled that depositions could not be taken behind the Iron Curtain.

Had that decision been allowed to stand, many of the cases brought by the OSI today could not be carried forward; one of its first acts was to appeal the ruling. The Board of Immigration Appeals, in a marked departure from some of its earlier rulings, overruled the judge and allowed for depositions to be taken in the Soviet Union—a landmark victory for the OSI.

OSI investigators traveled to the Soviet Union and the depositions were taken in May 1981. The deportation hearing resumed in 1982. On July 30, 1983, immigration judge Francis Lyons ruled that although the OSI had proven that Maikovskis had participated in mass arrests and the burning of the village of Audrini, and that he had concealed his SS collaboration when he applied for a visa to enter the United States, the government had failed to prove that concealment of his past was "sufficiently material" to invalidate the visa application. Nor did the acts of which he was accused show the necessary "level of depravity" to warrant deportation. Judge Lyons ruled that Maikovskis was not deportable.

A precedent like this would have meant that OSI was all but out of business, so a new appeal was made to the BIA. In another landmark ruling, the BIA overturned Judge Lyons and ordered Maikovskis deported to the Soviet Union, where he had been tried in absentia in 1965 and convicted of war crimes. Maikovskis is still appealing this ruling in the federal courts, but the BIA's decision, coupled with subsequent court rulings, established the framework in which OSI could get on with its business.

During this same period, OSI undertook a second key case and one that became among its most famous. Like the Maikovskis case, it had been started by INS, which ran into big trouble. Feodor Fedorenko was a Waterbury, Connecticut, resident who came to the United States in 1949 and was naturalized in 1970. A Ukrainian, he was accused of participating in the persecution of Jews as a guard at the Treblinka death camp in Poland. Treblinka was one of the smaller camps in Poland, some sixty miles north of Warsaw. It was staffed by about thirty SS officers and noncoms and some 200 Ukrainian auxiliaries, including Fedorenko. The camp housed about 10,000 prisoners, most of them Jews, about 70 percent of whom perished.

Fedorenko admitted his service, but claimed it was never voluntary. He said that he had been conscripted into the Russian army in 1941 and was captured shortly thereafter by the Germans. Interned at a prisoner-of-war camp at Zytomer, he claimed, he was held under conditions as bad as those he would encounter at Treblinka. At this camp, he said, he had been again conscripted, this time by the Nazis, to serve as a camp guard, and it was clear that if he had refused, he would have been killed. "They'd shoot you like a dog," Fedorenko testified at his trial.

Further, he attested, he had never taken part himself in any persecutions at Treblinka, where he claimed to have served for only a short time in 1942 1943. He declared that after a prisoner uprising at Treblinka in early 1943, the Germans moved additional regular troops into the camp and he was transferred first to a labor camp at Danzig, then to a prisoner-of-war camp at Poelitz. He also said that the guards at Treblinka lived under conditions only marginally better than those whom they were guarding.

However, camp records showed that during his service at Treblinka (which was for a longer period than he had claimed), Fedorenko had received a series of promotions and commendations for the caliber of his service. Such promotions and commendations would have been impossible, the government argued, without his being integral to the camp's main mission of executing Jews.

Denaturalization proceedings began in 1977, and the next year the court found for Fedorenko, on grounds that he had convinced it of his claim that he was operating as a guard under duress. Again, had this ruling been allowed to stand, it would have prevented many OSI victories, because almost any defendant could argue that he had been forced into taking criminal actions. OSI appealed,* and in 1979 an appeals court reversed the trial court, throwing out the defense of duress and ordering Fedorenko's citizenship revoked.

Fedorenko then took his case to the U.S. Supreme Court. It was the first Nazi war crimes case the court had heard, and therefore a victory was vital. Not only was the court ruling on the duress issue, but it was ruling indirectly on the process by which OSI sought to strip accused war criminals of their citizenship based on the fact that they had lied on their visa or citizenship applications.

---

* The story behind the decision to appeal the Fedorenko case may be one of the most interesting sidebars in the history of American Nazi hunts, and is still a matter of some contention. It is important because the case ended up in the Surpreme Court decision which set the grounds on which OSI was able to move forward, and the government lawyer involved became OSI's director.

After the case was lost at the trial court level, a decision had to be made on whether or not to appeal. All federal appeals are prepared by the office of the solicitor general, and Fedorenko's was assigned by lot to a young attorney in that office—Allan Ryan.

In *Quiet Neighbors*, Ryan says: "By the time I read the transcript and the judge's decision, I was convinced that the case could be won on appeal, and the solicitor general agreed." But other published reports paint a very different picture of the decision to appeal. In a memo, the authenticity of which Ryan apparently does not dispute, he recommended to Solicitor General Wade McCree that the case not be appealed. The memo, dated September 12, 1978, said in part: "I thus think we are at a dead end in this case. To be sure there is a very limited category of cases where appeal, even if foredoomed, must be taken to show the flag and to demonstrate the government's indignation at the judgment below and its determination to reverse even when the chances of reversal are almost nil. If we had extra-judicial evidence that Fedorenko was in fact a war criminal such appeal might be worthwhile. But we do not. The fact is we do not know. . . . He may be. Or he may be the unfortunate victim of innocently mistaken identification. Or indeed, he may be the target of a group of Treblinka survivors who saw family and friends slaughtered and are determined to bring vengeance on any Treblinka guard. We simply do not know."

Ryan maintains that this first memo was written only on the basis of the judge's decision and before he had a chance to read the entire trial transcript. Within two weeks, he claims, he had read the transcript, changed his mind, and began pushing for the appeal. But in the interim, the American Jewish Congress, fearing the precedent if the case were allowed to stand, had written to McCree demanding the appeal be made. A group of Jewish leaders had set a meeting with Attorney General Griffin Bell to denounce the way the case had been handled at trial, and Representative Eilberg also wrote to Bell to blast the conduct of the case.

Reportedly at the meeting with Jewish leaders, Bell announced that the case would be strongly appealed. Whether the decision to appeal was political and over Ryan's objection or was based on the legal merits of the case is now largely irrelevant: the result was the same. Ryan wrote the brief, argued the case, and won a landmark reversal. In the process, he became so interested in the subject of Nazis that he ended up as the OSI's first permanent director.

In 1981 the Supreme Court ruled in favor of the government, upholding the ruling by which the Fifth Circuit Court of Appeals had invalidated the duress defense and confirmed Fedorenko's denaturalization order.* Interestingly, the majority decision was written by Justice Thurgood Marshall, the court's leading liberal. Lined up on the other side were several of the court's conservatives, led by Justice Byron White. The majority ruled that the procedure being undertaken by the government to revoke citizenship was legal and proper. It rejected the duress defense on grounds that the Displaced Persons Act barred from admission to the United States "all those who assisted in the persecution of civilians." The crux of the majority decision was that based on this language, a defendant's motive for committing acts of persecution was immaterial and inadmissible. The fact of service as a concentration camp guard was in and of itself, "as a matter of law," grounds to have denied entry. And if it can be demonstrated by evidence that is "clear, unequivocal and convincing," and would not leave "the issue in doubt," any showing that entry was gained by lying about the fact is grounds for denaturalization.†

It was a victory as complete as the OSI could have hoped for. The decision has formed the basis for almost everything that has come since, and will continue to do so. But, during the same period, the OSI did not get several changes in federal law that would have made its job much easier. As we have seen, it is not at all uncommon for a case to drag on for years, even decades. Ryan and OSI believed that two changes in the law would expedite handling of Nazi war crimes cases. The first was to consolidate denaturalization and deportation actions into a single trial. As things stood, if you were seeking to oust a former war criminal who had become a citizen, you had to strip him of his citizenship first. This required a trial and perhaps a series of appeals within the immigration court structure; then the defendant still has recourse to the federal appeals

---

* OSI began deportation proceedings against Fedorenko in 1981. An immigration judge ruled Fedorenko deportable in 1983. That judgment was upheld by the BIA in 1984. Fedorenko was deported to the Soviet Union on December 21, 1984, after the Supreme Court refused to block the deportation order. He was tried and convicted in Russia for war crimes in 1986. He was executed in July 1987, becoming the first man ever executed in Russia for war crimes after being deported from the United States.

† A key passage of the decision written by Marshall is contained in a footnote (34): "Thus an individual who did no more than cut the hair of female inmates before they were executed cannot be found to have assisted in the persecution of civilians. On the other hand, there can be no question that a guard who was issued a uniform and armed with a rifle and a pistol, who was paid a stipend and was regularly allowed to leave the concentration camp and visit a nearby village, and who admitted to shooting at escaping inmates on orders from the commandant of the camp, fits within the statutory language about persons who assisted in the persecution of civilians.

courts and the Supreme Court. Only when the defendant has been stripped of his illegally acquired citizenship can deportation proceedings start—then they have to be started from scratch. The entire case has to be proven again as though nothing had happened before. Combining the actions would cut the time in half.

If this was not palatable to Congress, OSI had an alternative suggestion—a law that would make a fact established in the denaturalization phase of a case automatically accepted, as a matter of law, in the deportation phase of the case.

Ryan and OSI believed these two changes to be simple and straightforward, but Congress would not buy them, despite several attempts.

When the OSI was formed in 1979, Neal Sher was a young Justice Department trial attorney. A second-generation Jewish-American from New York City, Sher found the prospect of Nazi-hunting exciting and transferred to the newly formed OSI. When Rockler returned to private practice and Allan Ryan assumed the helm, he chose Sher to replace him as chief deputy. In 1984, when Ryan left for private practice, it was natural for him to turn the directorship over to Sher.

In his three-and-a-half years at the head of OSI, Ryan had built the group into a model Nazi-hunting operation and had enjoyed unparalleled success in the courts. From 1979 through July 1, 1984, forty-eight cases—either undertaken by OSI or inherited from the INS Special Litigation Unit—were prosecuted. Thirty were denaturalization cases and eighteen deportation proceedings including six that were brought after citizenship had been stripped from defendants in denaturalization proceedings. Of the sixteen denaturalization cases that were tried, fourteen were won, and all were upheld on appeal. Of the other fourteen denaturalization cases, seven were awaiting trial, four defendants had died, and three had been dismissed by OSI. Results in the deportation actions were slower in coming. Two had been lost, two had been won, and the rest were awaiting trial or were on appeal. In sum, it was an admirable record for any prosecutory unit—even more so given the complexity of the litigation involved and the fact that the actions were brought on cases almost forty years old.

Four years later, Sher has built upon what he inherited and what he helped build as chief deputy. The investigatory process has become faster, more sophisticated, more refined. Today, nothing angers him more than the charges often aired by groups opposed to OSI's work—that the organization is only a front for either hate-filled Jewish organizations or the Soviet government, bent on doing injustice to staunch anti-communist groups. Upon being asked about these charges by a reporter on one occasion, Sher replied in what the newsman described as angry tones:

Simon [Wiesenthal] . . . sends us evidence all the time. We also get allega-
tions from people on the street and from non-Jewish organizations. But, the
vast amount of cases we find on our own. If people think we sit here and wait
for allegations, that's a lot of nonsense. Nothing infuriates me more than the
accusations that we are puppets . . . controlled by the KGB or the Jewish orga-
nizations or anybody else.

We get archival materials from all over the world. For instance, we get a list
of guards from Auschwitz and Dachau. And then we compare those lists with
the immigration files. We have submitted tens of thousands of names. And if
we get a match, we are well on our way to a good case

Sher says that his biggest help is the fact that the Nazis were meticulous
recordkeepers. Rosters were carefully updated, even in the face of advancing
Allied armies. If someone on an auxiliary police force got paid or received insurance benefits (as in the case of Bohdan Koziy), it did not go unrecorded.
Not only were careful rosters kept at concentration camps, but daily logs listed
in excruciating detail what transpired every day. Guards came in to report
their actions so as to get commendations and extra leave time. The OSI has collected copies of these documents, many of them obtained from the Berlin Documents Center, others from Allied governments which captured them in the
war's final days, as the camps were liberated. At Mauthausen, for example, a
daily "Death Book" logged every prisoner who died an unnatural death, the
date when he or she was killed, and the perpetrator of the killing. Complete
duty and pay rosters for most of the concentration camps are in OSI hands, as
is a complete roster of the Lithuanian *Schutzmannschaft.*

OSI has also developed a complete data base on those who entered the United States during the period when most of the accused war criminals arrived.
Information has come from manifests of ships that carried displaced persons to
this country after the war, immigration and naturalization records, and lists
maintained in the postwar years by the Red Cross and the International Refugee Organization (IRO).

Using a sophisticated computer program, OSI investigators match lists of
concentration camp guards or *Schutzmannschaft* members with the lists of
those who arrived in this country: the program, designed by OSI, will even
seek a match based on Anglicized names. When a hit occurs, additional factors
are scanned: age, physical description, and others. When the two sources appear to identify the same person, a check is made to determine whether that
person is still alive and still in the United States. If the answer is yes, a file is
opened.

But this is only the starting point. Technically, the OSI need prove only proscribed organizational membership and its concealment on a visa or citizenship

application. In practice, however, the courts have held that the government must prove not only concealment of material facts that would have disqualified a person for admission, but specific acts committed while serving the Nazis in whatever capacity they are alleged to have served.

At this point, the OSI may go to a foreign nation in search of specific evidence, or to one of the Nazi-hunting organizations to seek help in securing witnesses. They may also turn to the mountain of data already in-house, or to the many witnesses they have already identified, at home or abroad, who survived the Holocaust and have provided testimony or information in previous cases. The process may, and often does, take years. But it is not until investigators have assembled enough hard evidence—evidence that would stand up to the strict scrutiny of a criminal court even though the process is civil—that a case is actually filed. That is why OSI has such a large proportion of open files and ongoing investigations compared to the number of suits it has actually brought. And why people who work for OSI get so upset when they are accused of shooting from the hip and bringing cases based on misidentifications or lacking in iron-clad evidence.

During Neal Sher's tenure as the head of OSI, his victories have been many, his defeats few and far between. OSI has brought twenty-four new cases under his leadership. He has won seven of eight cases tried, and the one lost at the trial level was reversed in favor of the government on appeal. So meticulous is OSI's investigation and preparation that you can be almost sure that when it brings a case, that case will be won. This is shown by the fact that more and more defendants in recent years are unwilling to see their cases adjudicated. They either flee the country outright or make settlements in which they renounce their citizenship and leave the United States. Sher sees situations like this as clear-cut victories. "What we are trying to do is to strip these people of their ill-gotten citizenship and deny them the United States as a safe haven. If we can accomplish this without a long and costly trial, so much the better. I'm not trying to extract the price of a public trial and a public humiliation of these people. I just want them out. If that happens, no matter how it happens, we have won."

The OSI has also begun to bring cases against several different classes of defendants. It was successful in its prosecution of Vladimir Sokolov, the Yale faculty member and former Nazi propagandist, and Sher says there will be more actions like this in the future. He has also brought the first action against a Jew since the very early days of INS proceedings in the 1950s. Jakob Tannenbaum, of New York City, was accused of collaboration with Nazis and taking part in persecutions while serving as a *kapo* at the Goerlitz concentration camp from September 1944 to May 1945. In a plea-bargaining arrangement, Tannenbaum, who lost his wife, child, and nine other family members in the Holocaust, voluntarily relinquished citizenship in exchange for a guarantee that he would be allowed to remain in the United States without fear of deportation. The settlement spared all concerned what would have been a long and emotionally wrenching trial.

How long will the Office of Special Investigations remain in business? When Allan Ryan turned the reins over to Sher in 1984, both of them guessed perhaps five more years. Now, with the five years almost up, and more than 500 files still open, with others being opened daily, Sher no longer speculates about the time frame. How long will OSI continue? "As long as anyone accused of Nazi war crimes is alive and living in the United States" is his simple reply.

A Paperclip Coverup?

One of the major unanswered questions about the treatment of war criminals by the United States concerns the almost complete failure to investigate accusations against war criminals and to prosecute those against whom the accusations seemed valid during the 1960s and in the early 1970s. Was it simply the result of lack of interest, inefficiency, and simple bureaucratic inertia—the reasons most commonly given? Or was there a much more sinister explanation: some kind of widespread conspiracy rooted in the fear that if broad-based investigations were undertaken, it could lead to the disclosure that war criminals had been brought to the United States under programs designed to funnel former Nazi scientists into American defense and space programs?

The fact that the United States had such organized programs has been well documented since the early 1970s. From the earliest days of the war, the U.S. Office of Scientific Research and Development based in London housed an ever-growing number of scientific intelligence officers and agents whose purpose was to develop information about a wide range of German scientific advances and the men and women who were developing them. It was recognized by both the Americans and the British that in almost every technological aspect of warfare, except communications and radar, the Germans were well ahead of the Allies. Their technological superiority in weaponry was even more starkly evident when the V-2 rocket bombs began to fall on Britain. German industrial technology was also considered very advanced.

Early in the war, the Office of Scientific Research's intelligence arm had the mission of uncovering German secrets through espionage or evaluation of captured equipment. But as the war progressed, and eventual victory became apparent, that mission changed. By 1944 Allied planners had realized that the West would face dual problems in the postwar era. The first was how to prevent Germany from remilitarizing and repeating the cycle that had followed World War I and led inevitably to World War II. The second was the growing realization that America's next great competitor would be the Soviet Union and that, consequently, it must be prevented from getting too great a share of the spoils of war, which might eventually to be used against the West.

Part of the solution was political: the division of Germany among the Allies until stability had been established. On the technological and scientific side, initial plans called for a ban on all such research in Germany for some period after the war. But that plan was discarded as impractical, because it had been tried unsuccessfully after World War I. German scientists had simply traveled to neighboring countries, continued their research, and then returned to Germany en masse to join the Third Reich. Many U.S. officials, especially those in the War Department, believed strongly that the answer lay in a program to bring German scientists to the United States. As British author Tom Bower has documented thoroughly in his recent book *The Paperclip Conspiracy,* by March 1945 several U.S. industries, particularly the chemical industry, were petitioning the War Department to allow it to bring top-flight German chemists to the United States. Simultaneously, sections of the War Department had their eyes on detailed lists of German scientists, including many who had been the backbone of the German rocket program and those responsible for innovations in shipbuilding and metallurgy.

It should be recalled that in the spring of 1945, while the war in Europe was winding down, the war in the Pacific looked as if it might continue at great cost for some time. So the initial proposal to bring German scientists to the United States involved those who could be of immediate use in the continuing war against Japan. There was also a climate of fear that many of Germany's industrial secrets had been passed on to the Japanese, and it was hoped that these scientists could evolve countermeasures to possible developments by the Japanese based on German technology. The most immediate need for German assistance seemed to be the U.S. rocket program. U.S. Army Intelligence, G-2, had received information that the blueprints for V-2 rockets had been passed to Japan.

Since 1943 Colonel Gervais Trichel, head of the rocket branch of U.S. Army Ordnance, had been preparing for the day when he could bring German experts into his program. In May 1945, Trichel presented to Robert Patterson, Undersecretary of War, a detailed plan to bring up to fifty German rocket scientists and technicians to America to be housed in facilities remote from public eye. The plan was approved on May 28. In a letter from Patterson to Trichel—uncovered by Bower—Patterson said in part: "These men are enemies, and it must be assumed that they are capable of sabotaging our war effort. Bringing them to this country raises delicate questions including the possible resentment of the American public." Patterson said that they could be brought to the U.S. only with the greatest secrecy.

A week later the Joint Chiefs of Staff informed the British that approval had been given for such a program. As Bower notes, "The British were assured that the scientists would be screened to 'eliminate war criminals and undesirables,' and were asked to agree quickly." The British did respond positively, upon two conditions: that only Germans who would be useful in the war effort against Japan would be recruited, and that a committee would be set up between the two countries to eliminate any competition for the services of these German scientists and technicians. (At the time, the British were laying their own plans to bring in Germans for much the same purposes.) While the Americans had their eyes on German rocket scientists, top priority in Britain was given to German maritime experts, especially those from the Nazi's technologically advanced submarine program.

On July 19, 1945, the Joint Chiefs of Staff gave tentative approval to the program, which had been labeled "Operation Overcast." As approved, up to 350 German scientists and technicians would be brought to the United States on paid six-month contracts that could be renewed for a single six-month period. The Germans would come without their families, and it was intended that upon fulfillment of their contracts, they would be returned to Germany. The approval specified that the Ordnance Department could bring in up to 100 German rocket scientists and technicians immediately, and Ordnance indicated that it was prepared to do so within six weeks.

Then something unforeseen happened. The atomic bombs were dropped on Japan, and the war in the Pacific ended abruptly. This threatened the newly approved program, whose rationale lay in using German expertise to fight the Japanese. But the War Department regrouped quickly, and emphasis on the program shifted from fighting the Japanese to the original idea of preventing the remilitarization of Germany and the use of its technological superiority by the Soviet Union. The justification was accepted by the Joint Chiefs who reapproved the program on August 14, 1945, and they gave the go-ahead for Operation Overcast. They labeled the program *top secret* to keep it from public knowledge.

In granting formal approval, the Joint Chiefs laid down certain guidelines: every German admitted under the program must be certified as "indispensable to the successful accomplishment of the most vital military research programs"; all would be employed under contract only for the six-month period previously agreed upon; and the Joint Intelligence Objectives Agency (JIOA), which had responsibility for administering Overcast, would have to make detailed background investigations of all potential "employees" to exclude former war criminals.

By early 1946, an undetermined but sizable number of German scientists and technicians had already been brought to the United States; they probably numbered at least 150. What had become abundantly clear, even in the short period that had elapsed, was the invaluable nature of their expertise. This was particularly true in the rocket area: within a few short months, German scientists had effectively taken over the program's development. Other experts at work included those in the chemical and metallurgy industries; specialists in aviation medicine, aircraft design, and tank design; and an unspecified number of theoretical scientists including chemists, mathematicians, and physicists.

Proponents of the program were now convinced that the short-term employment envisioned by the original Overcast approval was simply not in the long-term interests of the United States. They began to push for a change in the program, so that those already in place, and others to come, could be admitted permanently and given long-term contracts. On March 4, 1946, the War Department's most powerful body, the State-War-Navy Coordinating Committee (SWNCC), put forward a proposal to allow for the long-term employment and permanent admission of German scientists and technicians. By now the operation had become "Operation Paperclip," so named because U.S. investigators would tag the files of those proposed for admission by placing a paperclip on the front cover

Under the SWNCC proposal, stringent background checks would be required. The policy statement stipulated that "No person found by the commanding general, United States Forces, European Theater, to have been a member of the Nazi Party and more than a nominal participant in its activities, or an active supporter of Nazism or militarism shall be brought to the U.S. hereunder." But the statement also recognized that many German scientists had been compelled to join the Nazi Party and had received Nazi honors for their scientific work. It was noted that recipients of "honors awarded a specialist under the Nazi regime solely on account of his scientific or technical abilities" would not be grounds for disqualification. On September 6, 1946, President Harry Truman signed the new policy, and Operation Paperclip became a top-secret program of the War Department

By early 1947, the former limit of 350 German scientists had been exceeded: Paperclip contained no such limitation. However, one of its provisions did cause great concern to those running the program: JIOA would have to undertake reinvestigations of all those already in the country before they could be certified for permanent resident status.

It has long been believed that if some Nazi war criminals did slip into the United States through Operation Paperclip, it was because of simple mistakes or bureaucratic foul-ups. However, the pioneering work of American freelance journalist Linda Hunt has revealed that this is far from the truth. Many German scientists and technicians who could never have passed the most routine of background checks were brought into the country with the full knowledge of the Joint Intelligence Objectives Agency, which systematically doctored applicants' personnel files to remove materials that would have invalidated their petitions.

Hunt's years-long investigation of Paperclip has revealed that on February 26, 1947, JIOA director Bosquet Wev submitted the first forty personnel files of scientists and technicians already in the United States to the State Department for certification for long-term residence. Reportedly, Samuel Klaus, the State Department's representative on JIOA's governing board, was aghast at what he saw in the files. Many of them indicated that the persons in question had not only been ardent Nazi supporters, but some had actually taken part in programs that used slave labor or involved human experimentation, usually on Jewish prisoners. Several of the names, in fact, were on war crimes lists that had been developed for Nuremberg.

The State Department sat on Wev's initial group of applicants, and by early summer 1947, State and JIOA were involved in a bitter battle over the clearance of Paperclip applicants. Wev wrote General S. J. Chamberlin, the War Department's Director of Intelligence, that "the most positive and drastic action possible [must] be taken in order to break the impasse which currently exists. . . . The best interests of the United States have been subjected to the efforts expended in 'beating a dead Nazi horse.' . . . These scientists are proving to be an asset to the scientific research and development programs of the United States. The return of these scientists to Germany would present a far greater security threat to the U.S. then their retention in this country."

The State Department remained intransigent, so JIOA came up with the obvious solution. If State would not accept the dossiers they had submitted, they would "reinvestigate" and resubmit the applications. Thus a two-pronged effort began: JIOA had first to go back to existing files and sanitize them by deleting information that could make an applicant ineligible for inclusion under the Paperclip guidelines. The second effort was to ensure that no new application being compiled would contain negative information that might disqualify an applicant.

On December 4, 1947, JIOA forwarded to the Office of Military Government-U.S. (OMGUS, the U.S. occupation command) previously completed background reports on fourteen individuals, asking that they be "reviewed" and that new security reports be submitted "where such action is deemed appropriate." At least that was what was said formally. The underlying directive was that OMGUS should prepare new reports containing no information that would cause the State Department to deny the applicants.

As Linda Hunt's investigation has shown, among that initial set of fourteen reports returned to OMGUS was one on Wernher von Braun, the man who became the "Father of the American Space Program" and probably the person most responsible for putting a man on the moon. Von Braun had been one of the key German scientists targeted by the Americans for inclusion under Overcast. He was among the first seventeen to arrive in this country, and he and his German rocket team were considered vital to the future of the American space program.

Von Braun's original security report had read in part, "He was an SS officer but no information is available to indicate that he was an ardent Nazi. Subject is regarded as a potential security threat by the Military Governor." OMGUS now "reinvestigated." Suddenly it found all kinds of people who were willing to say what a fine fellow, and lukewarm Nazi, von Braun had been. A new OMGUS report was duly issued deleting the security-threat classification. Hunt has reviewed more than 150 OMGUS "reevaluations" made for JIOA. In every case, the reports were changed to eliminate security-threat classifications.

What sort of war criminals entered the United States as part of the JIOA whitewash? Three stand out: Arthur Rudolph, Walter Dornberger, and Hubertus Strughold.

Rudolph was a key member of the Nazi rocket program, the production manager of the Mittelwerke V-2 rocket assembly plant. The Mittelwerke factory was attached to the Nazi's Dora-Nordhausen slave labor/concentration camp, one of the most infamous operated by the SS during the war. Some 60,000 prisoners were housed at Dora, in unspeakable conditions, and used as slave laborers to build and maintain the elaborate rocket-bomb factory beneath an adjoining mountain, in tunnels dug as deep as a half mile into the earth.

Abundant evidence shows that the prisoners of Dora were brutalized both by the SS and by the civilian German missile technicians, and literally worked to death. They were required to work fourteen-hour shifts, seven days a week, under conditions that made even visiting SS officers physically ill. It is estimated that more than 30,000 died at Dora, most from starvation, illness, and overwork. Several thousand, however, were executed by the SS or the civilian German workers for even the slightest transgression against the stringent work rules. Usually, these executions were carried out in view of all the other workers to encourage discipline. When the U.S. Army liberated Dora and the adjacent Mittelwerke factory in 1945, they found only a few starving survivors and 2,000 unburied bodies. (The head of the Mittelwerke plant was Georg Rickhey, who had been brought to the United States under the Paperclip program in the summer of 1946. But less than ninety days later, when the conditions at Mittelwerke were discovered, he was returned to Germany immediately and tried as a war criminal.)

Eventually, Rudolph was admitted to the United States, but it took some doing and substantial rewriting of history. The first background-security report conducted on him had been devastating. Dated June 13, 1945, it listed him as a possible war criminal, suggesting that he had perpetrated atrocities against the civilian population—the slave laborers of Dora. In a handwritten "Remarks" section appeared the following notation: "100% Nazi, dangerous type, security threat ... suggest internment."

When it started to become clear how valuable Rudolph might be to the U.S.

rocket program, JIOA asked for a reexamination. As expected, a subsequent (March 4, 1946), evaluation had a different conclusion. Rudolph was "not a war criminal, but was an ardent Nazi." Better, said JIOA, but still not good enough. OMGUS was asked to reevaluate Rudolph's case again. Finally, understanding dawned, and OMGUS got it "right" the third time around. This report stated that the background investigation had found "nothing in his records indicating that he was a war criminal, an ardent Nazi, or otherwise objectionable." Arthur Rudolph had been born again, and had been made acceptable to the State Department

Rudolph ended up being almost as valuable to the U.S. rocket program as von Braun. From 1951 to 1960 he was project director of first the Redstone Arsenal and then the Pershing missile programs and was chief engineer on the Saturn 5 project, the booster that sent Neil Armstrong to the moon. He retired from NASA after the successful moon flight and was awarded its highest honor, the Distinguished Service Medal. He then became a highly paid consultant living in California.

In the only case undertaken to date against a Paperclip subject, the Office of Special Investigations notified Rudolph on November 28, 1983, that it was starting a denaturalization procedure against him (he had become a U.S. citizen in 1957). Rudolph struck a quick deal. Rather than go to court for a public airing of the charges, on March 27, 1984, he voluntarily left for West Germany, where he renounced his U.S. citizenship and remains today.

Walter Dornberger, a Wehrmacht major general, had been instrumental in organizing the entire German rocket program. In the 1930s he had recognized the potential displayed by such young geniuses as von Braun and had worked with von Braun to assemble the team of almost 800 scientists and technicians that became the heart and soul of the V-2 program

Early in the war the team under Dornberger worked at Peenemunde, on the Baltic. A large contingent of slave laborers was held at the base. Then, in 1943, the installation came under Allied air attack, which showed the Germans how exposed and potentially vulnerable their rocket program was. The result was the decision, agreed to by Hitler in September 1943, to construct the underground Mittelwerke plant at Dora-Nordhausen.

Time was of the utmost importance, since the longer the program was centered at Peenemunde, the greater the potential that it could be destroyed. Dornberger helped negotiate the agreement with the SS by which the workforce at Camp Dora was increased enormously; he also supervised the crash program to build the missile plant.

Dornberger's efforts were successful. In February 1944, at the cost of thousands of workers' lives, the plant was ready to go into production. In great secrecy, a special train carrying almost 600 scientists and technicians and their families left Peenemunde for Mittelwerke. It was not a moment too soon, because in the interim the Soviet Army had made great advances in the Baltic: as the train pulled out, the sound of Soviet heavy artillery could be heard clearly.

In June 1945, Dora-Nordhausen fell to the Americans, but the area would soon be turned over to Soviet control. When the first American officers in scientific intelligence arrived at Mittelwerke, they found Dornberger and von Braun ready to negotiate for the services of the rocket team. The group had decided to stay together and go to the highest bidder. They played the Americans off against the Soviets and the British, and the Americans won the bidding contest. Soon afterward 118 members of what was called the "Peenemunde Group" arrived at El Paso, Texas.

However, Dornberger did not get to America immediately: he had too wide-ranging a knowledge of the German rocket program and its personnel. The United States agreed to "lend" him to the British so they could debrief him as part of a program similar to Overcast, called "Backfire." He was flown to London, but there something unexpected happened. The British were looking for someone to blame for the V-2 bombing raids on their nation, and Dornberger looked like the perfect choice. He was arrested in London, and taken to an interrogation center to be charged as a war criminal.

The United States was outraged. It had long suspected that Britain was out to scuttle Overcast, which was spiriting to America scientists whom the British coveted. Dornberger's arrest seemed to confirm this suspicion, and the United States demanded his release. The Americans used an interesting argument— interesting in light of Dornberger's eventual resettlement in the United States with a cleansed war record.* They argued that Dornberger could not be held responsible for the use of the V-2 bombs on Britain. He was neither a scientist nor an officer in the German rocket forces. He was, they said, an administrator, whose main function was to act as a link between the SS and the factory staff.

For almost two years Dornberger languished in a Wales prison for war criminals while the bureaucratic battle raged on. Finally the British decided that Dornberger was simply not worth the effort and released him to the Americans. He was flown immediately to Texas.

Initially, Dornberger worked in the Army Ordnance's rocket program, but in 1951 he became an official of Bell Aircraft in Buffalo, New York, and a special CIA consultant. Eventually, he served on the board of directors of several aerospace companies. He died peacefully in his sleep in Buffalo while under investigation by the OSI.

Hubertus Strughold had been very important in the development of Ger-

---

* Much was made of the fact that Dornberger was not "even" a member of the Nazi Party. As an Army general, under Nazi military rules, he had been ineligible join the Party.

man aviation medicine. By the end of the war, he had risen to the position of director of the Luftwaffe Medical Research Center in Berlin.

One reason why Allied air forces had enjoyed early success against the Luftwaffe was the ability of U.S. and British planes, both fighters and bombers, to fly at higher altitudes than could German fighters. It became essential that the Luftwaffe find some way to allow its pilots to attain higher altitudes, and it fell to Strughold and the physicians and scientists under him to devise the methods. Eventually, they succeeded, and in so doing Strughold became one of the world's foremost experts on high-altitude physiology.

It was only after the fall of France that the Allies began to learn how the Germans had begun to close the gap on high-altitude performance capability. Wide-ranging human experimentation on the effects of high altitudes on body and mind had been carried out on the prisoners at Dachau. At least 100 Dachau inmates died in pressure chambers as their final agonies were filmed for review by Luftwaffe doctors, including Strughold.

By any measure, Strughold was one of the most successful Paperclip importees. He became the chief medical scientist of the U.S. Air Force and a special consultant to NASA. Many of the advances of the last two decades in aviation and space medicine are attributed to him. The OSI has had an open investigation file on him since the early 1980s, but despite the abundant evidence of his knowledge of and complicity in the Dachau experiments, Strughold continues to live in retirement in San Antonio, Texas.

At times, the Paperclip process seemed to approach the level of farce. If the JIOA file on an applicant contained no derogatory information, the State Department simply accepted what it was given at face value and sought no independent verification. One of the more outrageous results was the case of German general Dr. Walter Schreiber, who came to the United States in 1948 and eventually became one of the mainstays of the Air Force School of Medicine in San Antonio. Schreiber's background was extraordinary. He had been responsible for the construction of some of Germany's most essential arms factories in underground complexes. The process had been a triumph of engineering but had resulted in the deaths of tens of thousands of slave laborers, as had been the case at Dora-Nordhausen. Schreiber had also been one of the instigators behind the Nazi human experimentation programs and had assigned doctors to concentration camps and supplied them with the money and equipment they needed to carry out their experiments.

After the war Schreiber had fallen into Soviet hands, and he appeared at the Nuremberg trials as a Soviet witness against a number of defendants. He himself was then the subject of a denazification court proceeding at Nuremberg, which found him guilty of being an important and ardent Nazi and sentenced him to two years in prison. But Schreiber's talents were in great demand by the U.S. Air Force. Instructions were sent to JIOA to find some way of getting him included in Paperclip. The resulting security investigation duly reached the following conclusion: "There is no evidence to indicate that Schreiber believed in or fostered any Nazi principles which advocated or condoned atrocities or inhuman treatment of persons or armed aggression." The State Department never bothered to check independently even public war crimes trial records. They accepted at face value what OMGUS had said through JIOA, and Schreiber came to the United States to sign a Paperclip contract.

Then, in 1952, investigative columnist Drew Pearson revealed the facts of Schreiber's background and the additional fact that Nuremberg prosecutors had recommended his prosecution for participation in the medical experimentations. Even after the Pearson columns were in print, JIOA continued to insist that allegations against Schreiber were not supported by the evidence. However, in May 1952 it arranged for him to leave the United States and resettle in Argentina, where his daughter was living.

The State Department's refusal, or unwillingness, to check even the most readily available public sources also allowed Konrad Schaefer to come to the United States under the auspices of Project Paperclip. Schaefer had been one of the doctors involved in the medical experiments at Dachau. He had been an assistant to Dr. Hermann Becker-Freysing, who was involved in trying to make sea water palatable so that downed pilots could survive in the ocean. In a series of experiments, Dachau inmates were deprived of all food and fresh water and forced to exist on sea water that had been treated with various chemical compounds. Many died.

After the war Schaefer was one of the twenty-three tried at Nuremberg in what has become known as the "Medical Case." He was acquitted because, while it could be shown that he was involved in the planning sessions and in evaluating the results of the sea water experiments, it could not be shown that he had been personally involved in them. Despite his acquittal, his participation in the planning and evaluation of human experimentation clearly excluded him from Paperclip, but in 1949 he landed at Randolph Field under its auspices. The OMGUS background report stated that a thorough investigation of records "failed to disclose any record of previous arrest." Again, the State Department did not even bother to check listings of Nuremberg defendants— about the most readily available record of war criminals. In 1951 Schaefer's background became public knowledge and he was repatriated to Germany.

It is impossible to say with certainty how many war criminals immigrated to the United States by way of Paperclip. Between 1946 and 1955, over 750 such individuals arrived and a similar number probably came in under like programs such as "Project 63," aimed at keeping German scientists out of the hands of the Soviet Union. Most of the Germans eventually became U.S. citizens, although many of them were probably excludable under various provisions of Paperclip, particularly those who had been members of organizations like the SS, which had been defined at Nuremberg as criminal conspiracies. It *is* certain that a bare minimum of several hundred benefited from the sanitization of their records by JIOA. The question of how many were actually guilty of war crimes is still the subject of bitter debate, but they number at least in the dozens, if not in the hundreds.

And are they all home free now, so to speak? The answer, regrettably, is probably yes. The OSI has open files that may number in the dozens on persons who came to the United States as part of Paperclip. But, say the prosecutors, it is unlikely that they will be able to proceed against most or even any of them.

In 1979 the OSI began a denaturalization case against Tscherim Soobzokov, a New Jersey resident accused of being a member of the Waffen SS, the German Army North-Caucasian Legion, and the Tachtamukai Town Police. The court threw out the case after it learned that although Soobzokov had lied on both his visa application and his citizenship papers, documents in the CIA's files showed that the State Department had been aware of his memberships. Soobzovok had admitted his memberships to a State Department investigator shortly after the war and before he had applied for a visa to emigrate to the U.S. under the Displaced Persons Act. It was held that even though the INS had no knowledge, and Soobzokov had deliberately withheld the information, the "U.S. government" did have the knowledge, thus negating a "failure to disclose" prosecution.*

So it is with the Paperclip people. As we have seen, in many cases wherein wartime activities might now disqualify an individual from citizenship, the likelihood is very high that OMGUS and JIOA knew of the person's background and sanitized the records. As it did in the Soobzokov case, that prior knowledge will now preclude denaturalization based on grounds the applicant lied on his admission or citizenship applications.

What OSI is left with might be a general case based on a theory that the individual's wartime record reflects the lack of the requisite "good moral character" necessary for citizenship. Apparently, it was ready to make that argument in the Rudolph case. But, under almost any criteria, Rudolph was an exception. Whether any of the other Paperclip imports were war criminals of his magnitude is doubtful. There is also the argument that if the government knew

---

* Soobzokov was killed in 1985 when a pipe bomb placed on his front porch exploded in his face. No one ever claimed responsibility for placing the bomb, and police were never able to find a motive or to say whether it was connected to his Nazi past.

of a subject's past when he was admitted under Paperclip, it must have found him to be of sufficient moral character, because it did not object. To bring a case now would be to argue, in effect, that the government had changed its mind about the person's character. This will be an almost impossible basis for prosecution, unless it can be shown that at no time did the government realize the extent of a subject's former crimes.

★ ★ ★

Several government investigations have tried to determine whether there was some kind of conspiracy to protect Nazis in this country in the 1960s and early 1970s. Two were undertaken internally by the Immigration and Naturalization Service—one, in 1975, by its Internal Investigations Unit and another, in 1977, by a private outside consultant. Both reviews produced similar results. The Internal Investigations Unit concluded that there had been no conspiracy, no "roadblocking," nor any other "improper" activities on the part of INS personnel. The independent consultant reached the same conclusion, although he noted that recordkeeping was so bad and most case files so poorly handled that it was difficult to form any judgment in the matter.*

INS investigator Anthony Devito was working in the New York office in 1972. Devito had been assigned to the Hermine Braunsteiner Ryan case (See Chapter 7). First, he found that the case file was lost and searched for it to no avail. Then he received a tip from another INS employee and found the file buried in a cabinet in the Detroit office. For some inexplicable reason it had apparently been there for more than six years. And when he finally began to investigate, Devito claims, he ran into all sorts of problems. He was denied travel funds to interview witnesses in Europe or to bring witnesses to the United States, although such funds were readily available and routinely given to investigators on other cases. He says that witnesses whom he did interview confidentially suddenly began to receive threatening phone calls, as did his wife. He believed that information from his investigation was being leaked to Ryan's lawyer. His office was broken into and documents in the case file were removed. Then, while he was on vacation, the chief investigator of the New York office removed the case file and refused to return it for almost three months, until a *New York Times* reporter threatened to write a story. When the file was finally returned, several critical documents had been removed. A subsequent investigation investigation by the FBI found no evidence of wrongdoing, but

---

* Former OSI director Allan Ryan, Jr., says he, too is sure that no conspiracy existed. In his 1984 book Ryan stated, "Based on my own experience as the Director of the Office of Special Investigations, I can state that INS's failure to pursue Nazi investigations vigorously was a matter of neglect, not corruption or conspiracy."

Devito is still convinced that his superiors in the New York office of INS did not want the Ryan case pursued. He also believes that INS undertook a coverup after he went public, and that the FBI investigation was perfunctory at best.

The only significant investigation undertaken to determine whether there was a conspiracy to block investigation of alleged Nazis was done by the General Accounting Office, the investigatory arm of Congress. The request for such an investigation was made on January 13, 1977, by Representative Joshua Eilberg, in his role as chairman of the Judiciary subcommittee on Immigration, Citizenship and International Law. Eilberg asked the GAO to ascertain "whether the Immigration and Naturalization Service had deliberately obstructed active prosecution of alleged Nazi war criminals or engaged in a conspiracy to withhold or quash information in its possession."

This type of inquiry to the GAO by a subcommittee chairman is rather routine, but the investigation turned out to be anything but. As Victor Lowe, director of the General Government Division of GAO would later testify, the investigation was one of the most difficult and time-consuming undertaken by GAO during his long tenure.

The main problem was the initial lack of cooperation GAO received from INS and other agencies that might have information on suspected or accused Nazis. Because INS files on potential Nazi war criminals contained information from other agencies, particularly the State Department, the FBI, and the Central Intelligence Agency, either approval had to be obtained from them to review the files, or the so-called third-agency documents had to be removed from the files before the GAO was allowed access to them. Despite intense pressure from Eilberg, including a face-to-face meeting with Justice Department, State Department, and CIA officials in April 1979, the GAO was still denied access to the files. Finally, after agreements were laboriously reached between the GAO and the various agencies, GAO investigators were allowed to review the files after removal of documents that the other agencies did not want seen.

When it finally examined the files, the GAO investigators found an almost unbelievable record of ineptness, lack of interest, neglect, and inactivity. What was not clear to the GAO investigators is whether all this constituted a conspiracy. By May 1978, the GAO believed it had gone as far as it could in trying to make this determination, and effectively threw up its hands and issued its report. Its central finding: "It is unlikely that a widespread conspiracy existed, but GAO cannot absolutely rule out the possibility of undetected, isolated instances of deliberate obstruction. GAO's investigation was hindered by the effect of passage of time, the availability of information, and limited access to agencies' records. In any event, the inherent difficulty in establishing the existence of a conspiracy must be recognized."

GAO investigators looked at case files on ninety-four persons who had been accused of having Nazi ties. Forty of the cases dated from the period before 1973—a significant date because INS had then established the Central Control Office for such cases in New York City. The investigators found that prior to 1973, the INS had received complaints against fifty-seven individuals. Most of the allegations came from private sources, either newspaper stories, articles, or books. Several, though, had come from other government agencies, including the FBI, the CIA, and the Department of State. GAO was able to find sufficient information for an adequate review in forty of the fifty-seven cases. It concluded that INS had conducted investigations in only half of these cases. Of the twenty cases not investigated, initial inquiries by INS had revealed in five cases that the subjects had either died or left the country. In one case the subject had diplomatic immunity, and in another, an inquiry to another federal agency had produced no information and the matter was dropped. In the remaining fourteen cases, no investigation whatever had been made, and the GAO could find no reason why it had not been undertaken.

Of the twenty pre-1973 cases that were investigated, GAO concluded that five had been investigated thoroughly in a professional manner and prosecutions begun. In the remaining fifteen cases, none of which had led to a prosecution, GAO classified the investigations as "deficient or perfunctory."

Taking these forty pre-1973 cases as a whole, GAO concluded that INS was simply inept and uninterested in processing them. It said that it could find no clear evidence that the INS was "involved in any deliberate effort to obstruct either investigation or prosecutions of these cases." GAO noted that prior to 1973, the INS was putting most of its efforts into the investigation of subversive cases and of rooting out suspected communists in the United States. "INS investigative priorities before 1973 did not include war crime," was the conclusion reached.

After 1973, GAO reported, INS handling of suspected Nazi war criminal cases improved significantly. In the period between 1973 and 1978, 252 allegations of Nazi involvement were received by the INS. Eighty-one of these cases, INS reported, were not investigated either because the individual was deceased, had left the country, could not be located, could not be identified with the allegation, or the allegation itself was not sufficient. One hundred sixty-nine cases were assigned for investigation, of which twenty-one were recommended for legal proceedings. GAO selected a sample of 54 of these 169 to review. It concluded, based on the review, that "INS has substantially improved its handling of such cases."

The GAO finally concluded that while additional improvements still had to be made, INS had come a long way in improving both the method by which it investigated these charges and the attitude that it brought to the inquiries. But the GAO investigation had one glaring omission: it was based on files possessed by the INS. Thus it was able to conclude that problems experienced by the INS were the result of ineptness rather than a deliberate conspiracy. But the unanswered question is why there were so few files opened on persons who had been brought to the United States under any official program, including Paperclip.

The GAO noted that of the 111 files that it started out with only three represented "individuals . . . assisted in entering the United States by federal agencies." One of those three had been brought to the United States by the State Department because he was an expert on the Soviet Union, had remained here for several years, and had then returned to Europe—all long before any allegations had been received that he might have a Nazi war-criminal background. One of the other two had been given employment by the Department of Defense.*

The more telling question might be why there were so few such files in existence. It is likely that if any conspiracy existed, it was designed to ensure that the INS did not begin proceedings against any of the war criminals who might have arrived under Paperclip or one of several other similar projects.

The GAO seemed to realize this when it reported, "No information was found in the files of the service [INS], the CIA, the FBI, Defense, or State, to indicate these or other agencies engaged in a conspiracy to withhold or quash information in their possession, or to obstruct prosecution deliberately. Nevertheless, a number of factors, such as lack of assurances that GAO saw all documentation, and the passage of time, prevent GAO from being assured of the validity of the above conclusion."

---

* The third has never been publicly identified but he is widely believed to be a Ukranian emigré in New York City who was also identified as "Subject D" in another GAO investigation of the government's use of former Nazi collaborators for postwar anticommunist work. Reportedly, he was brought to this country in 1952 by the CIA under an assumed name and because a U.S. citizen in 1957. The OSI has had an open file on this individual for many years.

A Russian Plot?

The people who run the Office of Special Investigations are fond of pointing out how generally noncontroversial their efforts are within the U.S. government and the level of support they enjoy on Capitol Hill. Year in and year out, OSI's budget is quickly approved, and Congress has not bothered to hold an oversight hearing in many years—a sure sign that it is happy with the program. But there has been, and remains, one cloud on the horizon. There is, in fact, one issue that is sufficiently divisive to make it potentially damaging to OSI's future, either by swaying public opinion, lessening congressional support, or, more probably, by judicial intervention in the form of adverse decisions. The issue is the continued use of, and in some cases almost total reliance on, Soviet-supplied evidence and witnesses. It is a significant issue and thus worth a separate, although brief, look in this volume.

The Demjanjuk investigation is a case in point. John Demjanjuk, a Ukrainian, came to the United States in 1952 and settled quietly in the middle- class Cleveland suburb of Seven Hills. For almost thirty years, he worked as a mechanic at the Ford Motor Company plant outside Cleveland. He became an American citizen in 1958.

Demjanjuk's story of how he spent the Second World War is straightforward. As he tells it, he had been conscripted into the Soviet Army shortly before Hitler invaded the Soviet Union in 1941. Wounded in the early fighting, he spent several months in the hospital. When he recovered, he was sent back to the front and later captured by the Nazis in the Crimea in May 1942. From that point, he says, he was sent to a series of POW camps, first Rovno, and later Chelmno, both in Poland. In the summer of 1944, when the Nazis were desperate to stop the advancing Red Army, they began recruiting anti-communist Ukrainians from their POW camps to form Nazi-led Ukrainian fighting units. Demjanjuk says he joined such a unit and ended up fighting in Austria and, eventually, in the final defense of Prague. At war's end, his unit surrendered en masse to the Allies.

The government says that it doesn't believe Demjanjuk. Yes, they will accept his chronology up to the point when he was captured in 1942. But rather than being interned in a series of POW camps, the Justice Department says that Demjanjuk volunteered for Nazi service, was trained at the SS training camp at Trawniki and then served at the Sobibor and Treblinka death camps. At Treblinka, the government says, Demjanjuk's job was nothing less than to run the gas ovens; he was known there as "Ivan the Terrible."

It is not our purpose to argue the merits of the Demjanjuk case.* That is properly the subject of another book, and unquestionably will be the subject of many. Rather, we bring up the case because it has become for many the symbol of the use of Soviet evidence in Nazi war-criminals trials in this country.

In April 1987, the World Jewish Congress released a well-documented report showing that more than thirty Baltic, Ukrainian, and other Eastern European groups in the United States, Canada, and Western Europe were engaging in "an intensive and shocking campaign aimed at undermining the Justice Department's Nazi prosecution program." Specifically, the report cited the fact that legal defense funds had sprung up for accused Nazis who were utilizing every delaying tactic known to the American judicial system to avoid the ultimate confrontation and inevitable result of deportation. At the same time, these organizations were openly anti-Semitic in articles written for various publications and had started a congressional lobby, Americans for Due Process, to push for the shut-down of the Office of Special Investigations because of its cooperative relationship with the Soviet Union.

"The critical thing is that the OSI is trying to deport people to the Soviet Union," Rasa Razgaitis, vice-president of the New York-based Americans for Due Process, recently argued to a reporter. "Our own State Department has admitted that there hasn't been an acquittal in a political trial there since 1917. In effect, you are administering the death penalty." Paul Zumbakis, a Chicago lawyer who has twice defended men accused of being Nazis and who works

---

* Demjanjuk's denaturalization proceeding was begun in 1977. After many starts and stops, and after a long and very bitter trial, his citizenship was ordered revoked in June 1981 and the decision was affirmed the following June. OSI began deportation proceedings on July 2, 1982, and when Demjanjuk failed to appear, an arrest warrant was issued. He was arrested July 14 and jailed, becoming the first ex-Nazi since Hermine Ryan to be imprisoned as part of a denaturalization or deportation process. Deportation hearings were postponed until July 1983, when Demjanjuk was ordered deported. But where? When he refused to name a country to which he wanted to be deported, the OSI named the Soviet Union. Then Israel asked that he be turned over to them for trial. The United States agreed, and in 1986, after all appeals including two to the Supreme Court had failed, Demjanjuk was extradited to Israel, where, in 1987, his long and highly publicized trial began. In April 1988, after a thirteen-month trial, he was found guilty and was sentenced to death. He has since appealed that verdict and the sentence to Israel's highest court.

with the Lithuanian World Community, an international organization highly critical of the OSI's efforts, says simply the OSI is a KGB dupe: "The KGB is working directly with the Department of Justice." He adds that the OSI "should be run out of Moscow where they've been smearing various ethnic groups for forty years."

These Eastern European emigré groups are united in their fervent anti-communism. Therefore, they have found natural allies among the American conservative movement, especially those on the far right of the political spectrum. A particularly effective champion is Pat Buchanan, conservative commentator and writer, and former White House Director of Communications. In September 1986, Buchanan caused a firestorm of reaction by writing a very long Op-Ed article in *The Washington Post* defending the innocence of John Demjanjuk and castigating the prosecutors and for their reliance on Soviet-supplied evidence. It is worthwhile to reprint some portions of the article, because it sums up so well what many believe.

NAZI BUTCHER OR MISTAKEN IDENTITY?

Within days, the Butcher of Treblinka, the sadistic Ukrainian who operated the gas chamber at that Nazi death camp in occupied Poland will stand trial in Israel. So we are told.

The man to be prosecuted as "Ivan the Terrible," the barbaric guard of Treblinka, is John Demjanjuk, a naturalized American who came to the United States in 1952 as a displaced person, a church-going family man from Cleveland and retired auto mechanic for the Ford Motor Co.

Until the late '70s, Demjanjuk had seemed the very model of the solid citizen. It was then that the newly formed Nazi-hunting Office of Special Investigations at the Department of Justice opened its Demjanjuk file. Two years later, Justice Department lawyers strode into a Cleveland courtroom for a denaturalization hearing, and in February 1981 had John Demjanjuk stripped of his American citizenship and declared a Nazi war criminal who had lied his way into the United States. Following five years of failed appeals and incarceration in federal prisons, John Demjanjuk this year was extradited to Israel to be put into the dock as an accused mass murderer in the most famous Nazi war crimes trial in Jerusalem since Adolf Eichmann's.

Four years ago, while a columnist, I read a news report of the infamous "Nazi butcher" still living in Cleveland. It quoted his lawyer as insisting that Demjanjuk was a victim of mistaken identity. After a phone call to that lawyer, subsequent calls, radio interviews, correspondence with Demjanjuk's family—and amassing a file of clippings, correspondence and court records sent by the handful of believers in John Demjanjuk's innocence—I have come to believe with them that John Demjanjuk is not the bestial victimizer of men, women and children of the Treblinka killing ground, but a victim himself of a miscarriage of justice. Hence, this article.

... The evidence of Demjanjuk's guilt appears at first glance to be irrefutable. Five eyewitnesses, all survivors of Treblinka, identified Demjanjuk—from two wallet-sized photographs of 30 and 40 years earlier—as Ivan the Terrible. In 1980, the Soviets unearthed an identification card placing Ivan Demjanjuk at the Trawniki camp in Poland where the SS trained prison guards for the Sobibor and Treblinka charnel houses. (When the card arrived in January 1980 at the Department of Justice with the photograph of Demjanjuk, Ryan exulted: "You son of a bitch. ... We've got you.")

Yet, there are reasons why that handful of Americans—and a growing number of Israelis—believe the 66-year-old man in the dock this coming month in Jerusalem is innocent—a decent and honest family man whose life has been destroyed by Soviet malice and American gullibility.

Could it be that five survivors of the Holocaust are as mistaken in identifying Cleveland's John Demjanjuk as the Butcher of Treblinka as 11 Holocaust survivors—and even Simon Wiesenthal—were in identifying Chicago's Frank Walus as the Butcher of Kielce, Poland? For six years, Walus' life was a living hell because of the testimony of such "eyewitnesses." Finally, overwhelming proof turned up that all were dead wrong, that Walus had spent the entire war in Germany as a farm laborer, that he was too short (5 feet 4), too young and of the wrong nationality (Polish) even to belong to the Gestapo.

Here are some of the grounds for doubting Demjanjuk's guilt. ... In brief, as many Treblinka survivors claim "Ivan" was killed in 1943 as say he survived the war. And the number who do not identify Demjanjuk as "Ivan" far exceeds the number who do. Upon such testimony, should this man be sent to this death?

Finally, the Soviets, the source of the charge that John Demjanjuk was a Nazi collaborator, never even suggested he was at Treblinka. They still insist he was a camp guard at Sobibor, 100 miles distant.

But what of the identification card from Trawniki, with Demjanjuk's photograph on it? Is that a KGB forgery?

Consider. First, one expert who examined the card found that an "umlaut" was missing on a word on the ID card, and that the card used, instead of a separate letter, a combination of letters not common in German until about 1960. Second, the former paymaster at Trawniki claims he never saw a card like this at the camp: "Missing is the date of issue, missing is the place of issue, missing is the officer's signature." Third, the photograph of Demjanjuk on the card has been tampered with; parts are blocked out. Demjanjuk—from a blowup of the photo—is wearing a Russian tunic. Fourth, the photograph was obviously stapled to some other document before being placed on the card. Fifth, the seals on the card are misaligned—as though separate documents were placed together. Sixth, the ID card gives Demjanjuk's height as roughly 5 feet 9; he is actually 6 feet 1. Seventh, we have no card. The Soviets have only provided a photostatic copy.

. . . Why would the KGB go out of its way to frame an auto worker for the Ford Motor Co. who was neither an outspoken anti-communist, nor a leader in the American-Ukrainian community? Cui bono? Who benefits? Excellent question.

This is what Demjanjuk's defenders believe to have happened: Several years after he settled in the U.S., Demjanjuk's wife went to see his mother in the Ukraine, to tell her her son was alive, that she had grandchildren in America. Word spread through the village: Ivan Demjanjuk survived! Which came as a shock to Soviet authorities—who had been paying a pension to the mother for her son missing in action in The Great Patriotic War. The KGB came to the house, confiscated all family records and photographs—and took away her pension. Within two years, News from the Ukraine—the same publication the KGB used in an effort to frame another Ukrainian-American, Ivan Stebelsky of Denver, as a Nazi war criminal—charged that John Demjanjuk, living in Cleveland, was a Nazi collaborator.

When the Office of Special Investigations was organized in 1979, it took custody of the records from the Immigration and Naturalization Service, including the News from the Ukraine charge against Demjanjuk and the reports from Israel that several Treblinka survivors had identified him as Ivan the Terrible after viewing a single wallet-size photo of Demjanjuk from his 1951 visa.

At that point, Ryan, in the opinion of Demjanjuk's defenders, played directly into the hands of the KGB. As Ryan himself writes in Quiet Neighbors, Norman Moscowitz—assigned to the Demjanjuk case—asked Moscow for help: "Moscowitz sent a cable to our embassy in Moscow. Did the Soviets have records of Trawniki? Did any mention a man named Ivan Demjanjuk?"

Months later, Ryan got the answer he had been praying for. By an incredible coincidence, not only did the Soviet Union have old forgotten files of Trawniki; they had found a training camp identification card of the very Ivan Demjanjuk about whom Ryan had inquired. With Demjanjuk's picture on it! Ryan was exultant. And why not?

The KGB, which had first fingered Demjanjuk as a war criminal, had now—guided by the brilliant investigator-prosecutor Ryan—gone back and found in its dusty files from World War II precisely the documentary evidence Ryan suggested might be there. And it had taken only six months to find the ID card. Or, as skeptics contend—only six months for the KGB forgery factory to create one.

Thus far, the Soviets have refused to turn over the original card to Israel for *the prosecution of Demjanjuk. Why? Unless the card is a KGB forgery that would blow the seven-year Demjanjuk case to smithereens—and turn press attention upon those who forged it, and those taken in by it.*

In the last nine years, John Demjanjuk's life has been utterly, totally, destroyed. He has been humiliated, disgraced, vilified as virtually no other American of his time; bankrupted, imprisoned, extradited to stand trial in the same cage as Adolf Eichmann. A stigma has been placed on his family and name forever. He is going down in history as one of the great sadistic monsters in one of the greatest mass atrocities in human history. If John Demjanjuk is "Ivan the Terrible" he deserves it all. If he is not, then—in this writer's judgment— John Demjanjuk may be the victim of an American Dreyfus case.

(Patrick Buchanan is an assistant to the president. He notes that the views, analysis and conclusions above are his own, and not necessarily those of the Reagan administration.)

Buchanan did not directly attack the Office of Special Investigations in his article. But his feelings on the subject were, and are, well known. As he once put it to another reporter: "I don't think there is a need for OSI. If you have a case that comes to light of a Nazi war criminal here, the Justice Department can handle it. I am utterly against collaboration with the KGB, which is the Soviet version of the Gestapo. My view is there ought to be a congressional investigation of OSI on their clandestine collaboration with the Soviet Embassy."

When talking about Soviet help—and the term "Soviet help" is a kind of catch-all phrase to include help from other Eastern Bloc countries, especially Poland—you are really talking about two completely separate issues: Soviet-supplied documents, and witnesses who are Soviet or Eastern Bloc citizens.

"Soviet" documents is something of a misnomer. We are talking about captured German war records that today sit in Soviet or other Eastern Bloc archives. Just as documents captured by the United States are either in the Berlin Documents Center or the National Archives in Washington, documents and records captured by the Red Army are stored in a series of about a dozen archives in Moscow or spread across the Ukraine and Latvia into Poland and the other Bloc countries. Because they operated in territories that were recaptured by the Red Army, most of the documents pertaining to service in the Ukrainian, Latvian, and Lithuanian auxiliary units are today in Soviet archives. Some of the concentration camps were liberated by the Red Army: Their records are also in Soviet-controlled archives.

In the Demjanjuk case, the key document has come to be known as the "Trawniki Card." It is an identification card kept in the personnel records of the trainees at the SS training center at Trawniki, where the government contends Demjanjuk was sent to learn to be an SS guard. The card in question was issued in the name of one "Iwan Demjanjuk" and the government contends that the picture of the young man on the card is the picture of a young John Demjanjuk, known in those days as Iwan Demjanjuk.

Remember the trial of Bohdan Koziy? In that case the key documents were the insurance application and mustering-out papers. In other cases documents supplied from Soviet archives have included identity cards, pay and insurance records, camp and unit daily logs and journals, and copies or records of messages, reports, and orders either relating to an accused or signed by him.

In some cases, the documents have been supplied directly by the Soviets at the request of OSI. Other records, though, have been found by U.S. investigators who have been given rather free access to rummage through some of the collections. Even some private Nazi hunters have been given such access.

Canadian Nazi hunter Sol Littman has made several trips to Soviet-controlled archives in his quest to learn more about one particular auxiliary division, many of whose members emigrated to Canada. Littman told us that in his experience, some of the archives are highly organized and professionally maintained. The materials in these tend to be well indexed and, as a result, easy to access and use. Others are not well maintained. Not only are their contents not indexed, but much of the material seems to have been untouched since the day it was thrown into boxes in 1944 or 1945. Obviously, it is much more difficult to find relevant materials stored under such haphazard conditions. But Littman says that he has been given relative freedom and good levels of cooperation from local authorities, and from Moscow, in exploring and researching in these archives.

Opponents of OSI say simply that the documents supplied by Moscow or Warsaw are clever KGB forgeries. They claim that KGB forgers are the best in the world, that their technology is light years ahead of anyone else's, and that these documents represent the best of their work.

A somewhat exasperated OSI responds that this is nonsense. Neal Sher points out that every document received from Moscow undergoes the most rigorous examination in FBI laboratories. If there was any doubt on the part of the FBI, documents in the past have been sent to the CIA labs in Langley, Virginia. Then, too, the OSI has on its roster of consultants some of the best-known documents experts in the private sector and academia. They are often called in to examine specific materials.

Then, says Sher, "if we still have any doubts, we do not use the document. And I don't mean that in the past we have found what we believe are forgeries. On the contrary. We have not found a single instance where we believe we have found a deliberately forged document. We have received some whose history is unsure or unclear, and others that did not match what we have come to know as the style or substance of what was the norm for others that are similar. In these cases, and there have been only a few, we will not use the document at trial."

And once the documents are introduced into evidence, the defense has an opportunity to examine them with its own experts.* Then, at trial, the government puts its experts on the stand to testify as to authenticity and the defense has the opportunity to do the same. It is then up to the judge to accept the document as genuine or to reject it. There has not been a single case on appeal where an appeals court has reversed on the basis of documents that a trial judge has believed genuine, nor has there been an instance where a trial judge has branded any documents introduced into evidence a forgery. Opponents say that this points out only that the KGB is very good at what it does and that the OSI is either a dupe or a willing accomplice in this KGB attempt to discredit anti-communist Eastern European emigré communities by branding its members Nazi war criminals.

But if the United States is being duped, or is playing along with some kind of KGB plot, then so, too, is the government of West Germany. If Soviet-supplied documents have been used in several dozen U.S. prosecutions, they have been used in hundreds of West German actions over the past forty years. Currently, as we will see, the British Parliament is considering changing British law to allow accused war criminals living in Britain to be tried. They recognize that if they do, they, too, will face this problem of Soviet-supplied documentary evidence. So they asked the West German prosecutors for their opinion of the reliability of such evidence. West German Justice Minister Hans Engelhard replied to a parliamentary committee in a letter dated June 27, 1987, which stated in part: "Copies of captured German documents from World War II, and the testimony of Soviet citizens and reports of Soviet commissions of inquiry regarding war crimes proceedings against Germans and their collaborators, have been made available. . . . *There is no known case in which any Ger-*

---

* The "Trawniki Card" of Iwan Demjanjuk may, by now, be the most-scrutinized document in recent history. Demjanjuk supporters have long argued that he was not given an adequate defense by his original attorney. They say he did not have experts examine the card properly or question and challenge the methods of authentication that had been performed by U.S. experts. But in the course of Demjanjuk's Israeli trial, literally dozens of the world's foremost document experts have examined and reexamined it. A few, testifying for the defense, have branded it a highly sophisticated forgery, one calling it "the best I have ever seen." But most of the defense witnesses have been intelligence experts who have testified generally about the KGB's abilities as forgers, and not about the card in question. On the other hand, almost a dozen documents experts from the United States, Europe, and Israel, including the Mossad's top man, have testified that they believe the document is genuine and that the picture on it is that of a young John Demjanjuk.

man judicial authority or any expert has ever cast doubt on the copies of any German document conveyed by the Soviet Union."

The matter of Soviet and Eastern Bloc citizens as witnesses is another story entirely. The problem here is not really one of veracity. Although defendants always challenge the truthfulness of such witnesses, and they have from that first OSI-run trial of Bohdan Koziy down to the present, the real problem is procedural or, more properly, how to obtain these statements in a way that American judges will find uniformly acceptable.

We must go back to that original three-day session in 1980 when Walter Rockler and Allan Ryan hammered out their agreement with First Deputy Soviet Procurator-General Rekunkov. Rockler stressed the need, if the depositions were to be videotaped on Soviet soil, for cross-examination by defense counsel to take place. Rekunkov agreed readily. But Rockler suspected that Rekunkov didn't really understand the process of cross-examination within the American system and how adversarial—how downright nasty—it can become. He spent a considerable time trying to explain, even to the point of exaggeration. The Soviets simply replied that it would not be a problem. But to a great extent, where this kind of evidence is necessary, it has been.

Under the system that evolved from that meeting, and after it became clear that the Soviets, despite what they had said initially, were not going to let their citizens travel to the West, videotaped depositions now are usually taken in the town in which the witness resides. The U.S. government pays for the travel and living expenses of defense counsel and for the defense counsel's own translators to attend these sessions and makes all arrangements for travel documents.* The examinations are conducted in a session at which someone from the procurator's staff serves as a quasi-judge.

Rockler's suspicion that the Soviets simply did not understand the concept of cross-examination has been borne out. Often the procurators are appalled at the tactics that defense lawyers employ. At times they will cut off questioning that they think is aimed at impugning the credibility of the witness. At other times they will limit questioning to the official statements made by the witnesses to Soviet authorities. Occasionally, they will forcefully interject themselves into the questioning, almost browbeating witnesses if they are giving answers at odds with statements they had made previously.

And there are times when defense counsel goes out of its way to be disrup-

---

* The Soviets also agreed to allow any defendant to accompany his counsel so he himself can confront witnesses head-on. They agreed to give a written guarantee that the person would be allowed to enter and leave the Soviet Union unfettered. The offer still holds, and is routinely made to all defendants, but none has yet accepted.

tive. Old hands at OSI remember one early case when a lawyer representing a defendant apparently decided to be so nasty and so disruptive that the presiding procurator would end the examination. The lawyer could then go back to the American judge and claim that her right to cross-examination had been denied in an effort to get the case thrown out.

During the first morning session, the lawyer did everything she could think of to anger the judge. She denigrated the witness, the Soviet Union, the Soviet justice system, and the procurator himself. During the lunch break the irate and indignant official took OSI lawyer Neal Sher aside to complain and to say that he would no longer tolerate her conduct. Sher explained what was going on and what the lawyer was trying to accomplish. The slightly bewildered Soviet understood and allowed the proceeding and the lawyer's conduct to continue. But he said he found bizarre and degrading a system of justice that would condone such conduct in the name of trying to find the truth.

Edgars Laipenieks is a San Diego resident who entered the United States in 1960. After the war he had emigrated to Chile and had become a Chilean citizen. He has never become an American citizen. In 1981 the OSI began deportation proceedings against Laipenieks, charging that he murdered and beat civilians, including Jews, at the Riga Central Prison while a member of the Latvian Security Police. At his deportation hearing, he admitted beating communist prisoners "with my bare hands to encourage them to talk." But he denied ever beating or persecuting Jews.

The most damaging evidence against Laipenieks was contained in the videotaped statements of eight former Riga prisoners, now Soviet citizens, who all swore that Laipenieks had beaten them. But in June 1982, immigration judge John Williams threw out the eight statements and ruled that without them the government had failed to provide sufficient evidence that Laipenieks had personally persecuted anyone on the basis of religious or political belief. He dismissed the case.

Williams thought that the very fact that the Soviets cooperated with the American government in finding the witnesses and setting up the cross-examination made the entire process suspect because of the Soviet Union's long history of attempts to discredit the anti-communist and anti-Soviet Latvian communities in the West. He was even more concerned with the role the Soviet procurator had played in the proceeding. He noted that the procurator, who is a significant and feared figure in Soviet society, kept referring to "the war criminal Laipenieks" whenever he mentioned the defendant. This, Judge Williams believed, could easily have prejudiced the witnesses into believing they had to make statements against the defendant. He was also bothered by the fact that the procurator had limited cross-examination in some areas. Finally, he said that OSI attorneys had been too deferential to the procurator.

OSI appealed the case, and the five-member Board of Immigration Appeals reversed Williams. They stated in a very long written opinion that they believed the cross-examination fair under the rules of civil procedure and that they found the testimony of the eight Latvians credible. They ordered Laipenieks deported back to Chile. But then a three-member panel of the Ninth Circuit Court of Appeals sided with Williams's assessment of the procedure in a badly split 2-1 verdict. The two-judge majority said they found the same problems with the process as had Williams, and they agreed that the videotaped evidence of the eight must be discarded. They went even further; ruling that such Soviet-supplied testimony cannot be considered unless the witnesses are physically present and subject to cross-examination. They decided that they agreed with Williams's decision that not enough other evidence had been presented by OSI to warrant a deportation.

The third judge on the panel disagreed. In a stinging dissent, he wrote that the majority had too easily dismissed what he called the "scholarly" unanimous decision of the five-judge BIA. He thought the BIA reversal correct, and that the deportation order should be allowed to stand.

Appeals are still pending in this case.

Then there is the complex case of Juozas Kungys, the Clifton, New Jersey, resident accused of taking part in the 1941 massacre of more than 2,000 Jews in the ghetto in Kedainiai as a member of the Lithuanian 2nd Battalion. The case came to trial in September 1983.

As in the Laipenieks case, the heart of the government's evidence was contained in a series of videotaped Soviet-citizen witnesses. And just as Judge Williams would, District Judge Dickinson R. Debevoise had serious problems with the manner in which the statements were obtained. He was especially concerned with the chilling effect the presiding Soviet official might have had and took special note of the fact that each Soviet witness was forced to swear that his testimony would be in accordance with Soviet law and subject to Soviet perjury-like penalties. To Judge Debevoise, this gave rise to the possibility that the witnesses thought they had to say what Soviet officials wanted them to say.

Debevoise wrote:

None of the foregoing established conclusively that Soviet authorities did in fact unduly influence the testimony of the deposition witnesses in this case. It does establish that there is a very grave risk that they may have done so and that there has been a totally inadequate opportunity to investigate this question.

. . . The government elected to collaborate in the prosecution of this case with the Soviet Union, a totalitarian state. . . . Knowing the nature of the Soviet legal system the government has an obligation to make every effort to ensure

that the testimony it received under the auspices of the Soviet authorities was not tainted, given the known Soviet practices designed to obtain the desired results in a particular case even at the expense of the truth.

. . . The government has not fulfilled its responsibilities in this case.

Then, as Williams would do in the Laipenieks case, Debevoise ruled that without the deposition testimony the government had failed to provide enough other evidence that Kungys had personally persecuted anyone and he ruled in his favor.

In June 1986, the Third Circuit Court of Appeals overturned Debevoise. But in so doing the appellate court completely ducked the issue of the witnesses' statements videotaped inside the Soviet Union. The court ruled, simply, that even if the statements were not accepted into evidence, the government had presented enough collateral evidence to make its case. The court ordered Kungys stripped of his citizenship.

As we noted in chapter 6, the Supreme Court has now ruled in the Kungys case. But in its May 1988 ruling it, too, ducked completely the question of the video-taped Soviet witnesses. Instead its decision was that the Third Circuit Court should again review the case to determine whether false statements Kungys made on his visa and citizenship applications were sufficiently "material" to have resulted in the visa or citizenship being denied.

Actually, the Kungys case has other precedents. By and large, on the occasions—and they have been relatively few—that appeals courts have faced the issue of the admissibility of witnesses' statements videotaped behind the Iron Curtain, when they have found for the government they have done so without facing squarely the issue of the statements. In each case they have held that enough evidence was present, even without the statements, to side with the government. But in the cases where the court has ruled directly on the issue of admissibility, it has thrown out the statements.

Another set of defense attorneys has raised what amounts to a corollary issue on the U.S.–Soviet relationship in Nazi cases, but one that goes to the heart of how the Justice Department obtains witness statements in the Soviet Union and an issue that could have a wide-ranging impact on how OSI operates.

Lawyers for two Massachusetts men, Matthew Katin and Vytautas Gudauskas, accused in 1984 of being Lithuanian *Schutzmannschaft* members, demanded that any depositions taken in their cases in the Soviet Union be taken only at the U.S. embassy or a U.S. consulate and with an American official presiding. A Soviet procurator could be present, but could not preside. The district court judge agreed and issued an order. After waiting for almost two years, OSI asked the judge to reconsider the order arguing simply that the Soviets would never agree and that such an order if it were allowed to stand would end OSI's ability to obtain the depositions of Soviet citizens. But the defendants' lawyers showed the judge that the safeguards they were demanding are virtually identical to agreements for deposition-taking in war crimes cases that have been made between the Soviet Union and the governments of both Canada and Australia. The judge refused to change his order and OSI has announced it will appeal the order to the Court of Appeals.

Most of the matters we have discussed here have not been finally adjudicated. So far, there have been only partial decisions, or decision are still being appealed. If the courts, and especially the Supreme Court, ever face the issue and rule against the government, at the very least the United States will have to renegotiate its relationship with the Soviet Union in witness situations.

There are, in fact, seemingly simple solutions. The most obvious would be for the USSR to live up to the letter of the 1980 Moscow Agreement and allow Soviet citizens to travel here and give live testimony. Another answer would be to send U.S. judges to the Soviet Union with government lawyers and defense counsel to preside at the depositions.

Finally, OSI often finds itself under fire from the left. Civil libertarians are continually upset that the denaturalization and deportation actions that OSI brings are civil in nature and not criminal, and that defendants do not have the expanded rights they would have in a criminal trial. But to change this would take a major turnaround in U.S. immigration law. Suspected war criminals are treated in exactly the same way as other violators of immigration laws. Some exceptions would have to be carved out for suspected war criminals to allow them a new set of expanded rights—a not very likely prospect—or there would have to be a change in the laws and regulations to give all immigration law defendants expanded rights (even more unlikely).

In Washington today there is a great hue and cry about the way Cuban detainees, the Mariel boat people, have been handled. Their rights are about the same as the rights of those accused of being war criminals and of being in the United States illegally because they allegedly lied on their visa applications. There is considerable feeling that some exemption should be inserted into immigration law to give them expanded rights. But the Reagan administration has made it clear that it has no intention of doing so, and Congress shows no inclination to back the idea of changing the immigration laws for them. (And the Mariels represent a much more sympathetic group than do war criminals.)

Neal Sher has little time for this argument that accused war criminals are somehow deprived of their rights. Noting the case of Karl Linnas, who was deported to the Soviet Union where he died of heart problems while awaiting trial, Sher points out that during the seven years the case was in litigation, there were fourteen separate proceedings before federal or administrative tribunals, including three separate reviews by the Supreme Court. "How much greater safeguards are necessary?" asks Sher.

Canada and Australia

Any discussion of the hunt for hidden Nazi criminals in Canada, or, more properly, the lack of any hunt for so long, must begin with a a look at Canadian demographics. Geographically vast, Canada—in relative terms—is sparsely populated. Its 1981 census put the population at 25 million. The country is one of ethnic diversity, and Canadians are justly proud of this fact, and believe it is a strength that has shaped Canadian culture and continues to do so.

Of the population of 25 million, more than half a million—529,000 plus—are Ukrainian. A comparable number are from other East European stock, and many of these are postwar arrivals, or the descendants of post-war arrivals.* These groups are closely knit and form a potent political force that is arduously courted by both provincial and federal politicians. Without meaning to slight or condemn any group, it's obvious from the U.S. experience that many of those suspected of having war crimes in their past come from the East European ethnic groups. To a very great extent, the history of Canada's inactivity in pursuing war criminals, and the probable future of any Nazi hunt in Canada, must be viewed with this sizable population and its political clout in mind.

Perhaps thee most complete collection of data on suspected war criminals living in Canada is housed in a small, two-room office in in downtown Toronto. The fact that it is not a government office speaks volumes for the state of the Canadian Nazi hunt. The office is the Canadian branch of the Simon Wiesenthal Center, and the base of Sol Littman, former print and television journalist, author, and now one of the world's most dedicated Nazi hunters.

If six years ago you had told Sol Littman that he would end up a full-time

---

* In the years following the war more than 180,000 immigrants were admitted into Canada, more that a third from refugee camps in Europe with no papers to speak of. Initially, there was almost no screening of these arrivals. Later in the process, in 1948-1949, the Royal Canadian Mounted Police (RCMP) were given the assignment to screen, as best they could, those who were still arriving in waves. But as we will see, the screening process turned out to be so ineffectual as to be almost nonexistent.

Nazi hunter, he probably would have laughed. But that was before he covered—on assignment from the Canadian Broadcasting System—the 1982 trial of Helmut Rauca, the only accused war criminal who has ever been tried in Canada.*

In 1961, a West German war crimes court sentenced in absentia, for mass murder, one Helmut Rauka, a notorious German-born SS officer who had served in Lithuania and who was accused of participating in the deaths of more than 10,000 Jews in the ghetto in Kaunas. The court suspected that Rauka was in Canada, and requested his extradition on several occasions. Each time, the Mounties were given the request, and they have said that they searched for him diligently. The Mounties may always get their man, but in this case, for more than two decades, they didn't.

Even after the West Germans figured Rauka might have made the slight change in the spelling of his name to Rauca, and issued a new request under both spellings, the RCMP still couldn't find him. Using the alternative spelling they did locate an old ship's manifest showing that a Helmut Rauka had arrived in Canada in 1950, and they went to his address. But "Rauka" had moved years before, and no one at the old address had ever heard of him. It probably never occurred to them to check the Toronto phone book. He was listed. In the mid-1970's, after still another request from Germany, the RCMP ran a driver's license check under both spellings. It came back blank. The license had been issued under the name Albert Helmut Rauca, his full legal name.

In 1981, in an attempt to appease the Canadian Jewish community, which was getting progressively more vocal about the lack of activity in searching out Nazis, the Mounties were told to pull out their few Nazi files and have another go at it. Corporal Wayne Yetter (now a sargeant and one of Canada's chief official Nazi hunters) was given the Rauca file, and, as part of a series of routine checks, asked the Canadian passport office if it had ever issued one in the name of Helmut Rauca or Rauka. Yes indeed, was the prompt reply. After twenty years, the Mounties had gotten their man.

After a long trial, Rauca was ordered deported to West Germany. On October 29, 1983, he died of natural causes in Germany while waiting to be tried.

After the Rauca trial, Littman decided to write a book on the case. As he researched the subject, he became progressively more fascinated with the topic of hidden Nazis. Finally, the book was finished, but he was hooked. He had found a new calling: Nazi hunter.

---

* Rauca came to Canada in 1950 and became a Canadian citizen in 1956. He settled in Toronto and worked until retirement. He had a driver's license in his own name, a library card, government health insurance, and eventually, a government pension check that arrived every month.

We now move ahead to November 1985. Sol Littman has become the Canadian representative of the Los Angeles-based Wiesenthal Center. The hunt for Josef Mengele was just reaching fever pitch when the center received a batch of documents from the U.S. archives obtained under a freedom-of-information filing. Included was a rather strange set of messages back and forth between U.S. authorities trying to answer a 1962 request from Canadian visa control officials seeking background information on Mengele. The request was of the usual type checking on someone seeking a visa to enter Canada. The question was obvious: Had Mengele come to Canada in 1962? Might he, heaven forbid, still be in Canada?

Littman tried to find out. He went to the man whose name was on the 1962 request. The official said that he did not remember the situation, nor did he know who Mengele was. (This Littman found strange given the fact that at this time Mengele's name was in the headlines almost daily.) Littman tried the RCMP, but they could not find any record whatsoever of the 1962 request. Having done all that he could, Littman wrote Prime Minister Brian Mulroney to request that the government make a full investigation to determine whether Mengele had ever come to Canada. When he didn't get a reply, he went public in January 1986. At almost the same time, the Wiesenthal Center in Los Angeles made the same documents available to both *The New York Times* and *The Toronto Star*. They did the same checking that Littman had done and met the same stone wall. They published stories at about the same time Littman held his press conference to ask why the prime minister had not responded.

The result was a wave of negative publicity that was politically unsettling to Mulroney. It brought to the surface, once again, all the stories about war criminals in Canada. The government decided to do something about it once and for all. Two weeks later, on February 7, 1986, Justice Minister John Crosbie rose in Parliament to announce the formation of a Commission of Inquiry to look into the question of whether any Nazi war criminals were still living in Canada and, if so, how many, and what options Canada had for dealing with the problem. The commission would be led, Crosbie announced, by the Honourable Jules Deschenes, former chief justice of the Superior Court of Quebec. Crosbie also said he was sure that the inquiry would discover at most maybe only "thirty to forty" war criminals living in Canada as opposed to much higher figures that were being spread around in the media.

The Deschenes Commission was more like a U.S. presidential commission than a simple, one-man operation. It had a sizable staff, outside consultants, and a budget of more than $4 million. It held public hearings and took testimony, and, most importantly, investigating every allegation that an individual might have a war crimes past. But in the end, the commission's report, and its myriad conclusions both as to what Canada can and should do, and what specific individuals should be investigated as war criminals, was the sole effort of

Deschenes. He wrote or approved every word of its 900-plus pages, he set himself up as the final and sole arbiter of every decision about the guilt or innocence of an accused, and he personally made every critical recommendation.

★　★　★

At the risk of getting ahead of our narrative, one of the best ways to trace the history of Canadian Nazi hunting is through the work of Dr. Alti Rodal. Ms. Rodal, who holds a doctorate in European history from Oxford, and a top-secret security clearance that allowed her access to all kinds of governmment documents, was hired by the Deschenes Commission to trace the history of Nazi hunting in Canada. It appears that what the commission expected was a typical academic's work—dry, dull, heavy on the footnotes. What they got was a truly extraordinary document, more than 600 pages in length—a document that more than anything serves as an absolute condemnation of Canada for serving as a haven for Nazis during much of its postwar history.

The report almost failed to see the light of day. By all accounts, Rodal plunged into her work after getting the assignment but on the date her report was due, she was still far from finished. She went to the staff directors of the commission to ask for an additional six months and was told no, because they did not have the money. So she worked on without pay until she was finished. (In fairness, Deschenes himself later intervened to get her paid for the extra half-year of work.) Rodal has said that if she had quit when they wanted her to, her final product "would have been about ninety pages long." But, she adds, "I felt it was critical to put all this into a historical perspective that will outlive whatever prosecutions there are going to be. One day all the potential defendants will be dead, and something from this commission should live on."

Rumors about the so-called the "Rodal Report" quickly began to circulate after she turned it in. But it was announced that the report was an internal document of the commission and would not be released. Its contents would be reflected in the commission's final report. But the actual document was meant as background for Deschenes, and, as such, was not for publication.

After the release of the Deschenes Commission's final report, the media and interested observers began to bombard the government with demands that Rodal's work be released. Finally, after seven months, and then only through a suit filed under Canada's Access to Information Act, it was. And it was instantly apparent why the government had not wanted it released.

Rodal's research had uncovered not simply a forty-year history of inactivity and inattention to the question of war criminals entering Canada, but, much more ominously, a pattern through successive governments of actual protection of war criminals for political reasons. Some examples:

—In 1947 the Royal Canadian Mounted Police allowed twenty men with SS blood-type tattoos to come into Canada after all had denied even having served in the German army. "Despite expressing doubts about the truthfulness of at least four of the men regarding service with the Nazi armed forces, there was little further probing about their background," Rodal wrote. She said records indicated the RCMP investigators were worried about the possibility of "negative publicity" should the twenty who represented various East European ethnic communities be turned away. Several of the men said they had obtained the tattoos "by accident." More than half had attempted to remove them. Rodal used the incident as an example of how "thorough" the RCMP had been in screening immigrants.

— Former Canadian prime minister Louis St. Laurent (1948-57) and his aides actively communicated with alleged Nazi war criminals living in Quebec and ended up helping the worst one of them to get away. "St. Laurent and his aides were personally involved in communicating with the alleged war criminals, their protectors, and those who would have had them expelled from the country," Rodal wrote.

The alleged war criminals were all Vichy French collaborators, who Rodal said had been allowed to enter the country with the government's full knowledge. All had been tried in absentia by the French government and found guilty of collaborating with the Nazis. The RCMP eventually found out about the group's arrival, but, says Rodal, by the time this happened, "they had succeeded in establishing themselves amidst Quebec's religious and social elite and could count on its support." Rodal found that St. Laurent, a native of Quebec, allowed most of them to stay in Canada: his cabinet finally passed an order-in-council allowing the collaborators to remain as "political refugees." Moreover, St. Laurent's office tipped off the most notorious—Count Jacques de Bernonville—to flee before he could be deported. De Bernonville, twice convicted in absentia and sentenced to death, was the former chief aide to Klaus Barbie. He had arrived in Canada disguised as a priest. He fled in 1951, after fighting several attempts to deport him, after—as Rodal discovered—receiving a letter from Pierre Asselin, one of St. Laurent's private secretaries. De Bernonville fled to Rio de Janeiro where he was found strangled in 1972.

— Former Prime Minister Pierre Trudeau was personally opposed to proceedings against accused war criminals. In early 1981, during a flurry of public comment over war criminals in Canada, Justice Department lawyer Martin Low issued an opinion that short of enacting legislation to try alleged Nazis in Canada, there was nothing the government could do. (This has been Canada's official position ever since.) The opinion apparently set off a bitter dispute within the upper reaches of the Trudeau Cabinet that was eventually settled by the Prime Minister himself, thereby quashing any attempt to move forward.

Rodal attempted to detail instances wherein Trudeau had showed opposition to taking action, but the government deleted that portion from what was made public. "I knew they would censor it," Rodal said in an interview. "I had included a footnote that provided instances where Trudeau was opposed."

— In 1983 two alleged Nazi war criminals who arrived in Canada were allowed to enter by a RCMP investigator who believed sufficient time had passed since the war as to make the war crimes issue irrelevant. "It is noteworthy," Rodal wrote, "that this officer is described by another RCMP officer as a 'quite right-wing German who regards the war criminals issue as blown all out of proportion.'"

— Canadian officials worked with both the CIA and British intelligence to bring in known war criminals whose pasts were too hot to allow them to stay in Britain or the United States. Some had been employed in Operation Paperclip, and others for intelligence purposes, but they had to be moved once their histories became known. Rodal called Canada a "dumping ground" for these types, who were allowed into the country in the guise of Soviet defectors. Rodal indicated that the plan may have been in operation for as long as ten years.

★   ★   ★

On March 12, 1987, leaders of both the Ukrainian and Jewish communities were called to Ottawa for a tense morning briefing.* Almost three months earlier, on December 30, Judge Deschenes had turned his final report in to Justice Minister Ramon Hnatyshyn (who had succeeded Crosbie). In the interim, it had been closely held as cabinet ministers studied it and decided how to respond. There were also reports that Deschenes had rewritten, or at least heavily edited, large portions of the report at Hnatyshyn's request. Now it was to be released to the public and leaders of the two communities had been called to get an advance briefing so that they would be prepared to react.

As Hnatyshyn began to detail the report's findings and recommendations, both groups had reasons to be elated. Yes, wrote Deschenes, there were Nazis living in Canada. No, there were not thousands or even hundreds of them. He said that his investigation had revealed enough evidence to make a prima-facie case of war crimes against twenty individuals. In addition, enough questions remained on 218 additional cases to warrant further investigation.

An extraordinary amount of time and space in the final report was given over to the question of numbers. The commission staff, from a variety of sources—including Jewish groups, Nazi hunters, and foreign governments—established a "Master List" of 774 "suspects." Eventually, another 38 names were added

---

* There has been, and continues to be, a great deal of criticism of the whole Deschenes process as one pitting the Ukrainian and Jewish communities against one another. Obviously, they have nearly opposite concerns about the hunt for former Nazis in Canada, and it seems clear that the government has played one off against the other.

and then a third grouping of 71 German scientists and technicians who might have come to Canada either directly or via the United States and Great Britain. Each and every person on that list was investigated except those against whom, in Deschenes' words, the charges were "clearly spurious."

Then, using generally unspecified criteria, Deschenes either cleared the individuals, or put them into one of his two categories. Apparently, the criteria Deschenes used turned on the question of whether there was prima facie evidence that a particular individual committed a specific crime against a specific victim. Some observers believe that Deschenes used a test of guilty beyond a reasonable doubt before he included anyone in his group of twenty, and a test of "almost certainly guilty," based on the immediately available evidence, to include a person among the 218.

The bulk of the final report was given over to a recitation of Deschenes' findings in each case. For hundreds of pages it went on case by case, 711 individual opinions concerning names on the original Master List followed by an additional 38 decisions on names subsequently added to the commission's list. In every case, a decision to close the file, order further investigation, or brand the subject a probable war criminal was indicated.

In many of the cases, it is impossible to argue with or question Deschenes' decision. In 341 of the cases, he concluded that the person in question had never landed in Canada.* In another 21 cases, the person did come to Canada but had since left. The only possible argument with these judgments is that the Deschenes staff did not do a thorough job of trying to find the individuals. And this is open to considerable debate, because much of the Deschenes Commission's investigation used essentially the same methods that for twenty years had been so ineffectual in locating Helmut Rauca. There can be no argument over 86 files that were closed because of the subject's death. In each of these cases death certificates were obtained.

The real arguments began over a group of 154 cases that were ordered closed because, in Deschenes's words, "the Commission could find no prima facie evidence of war crimes." It was in these cases that Deschenes set himself up as judge and jury and decided that the person should not be investigated further because there was no information currently in hand to show his guilt. The case summaries contained in the final report were very heavily censored. Many took the form: "This individual, reputedly a member of a police force of

---

* Why did Deschenes spend so much time investigating people who never came to Canada? He himself asked the same question sarcastically in the final report. But his Master List contained many names that had been forwarded to Canada years before by Simon Wiesenthal. Included on that list were the names of the entire officer corps of the Galicia Division (see page 248) because Wiesenthal was not sure where they were. Of the 217 named, 196 never came to Canada.

an Eastern Bloc country, is alleged to have killed a civilian." It then states that the commission checked the Berlin Documents Center and other German archives and, finding no information on the subject, ordered the file closed.

The commission claims that heavy censorship was necessary to protect the privacy of the individual, an entirely reasonable proposition. But it also has the effect, intended or not, of making it very difficult to double-check the quality of the investigatory work done by the commission. Which brings up the subject of the commission and the Soviet Union.

Early in the commission's life, Deschenes announced that he would be going to the Soviet Union to work out an agreement for access to Soviet-held records. This brought an avalanche of protest from Canada's East European emigré communities and from their representatives in Parliament. The trip was postponed and then postponed again. Finally, Deschenes submitted a long list of "conditions" that the Soviets would have to meet before he would go. Negotiations went back and forth. The original deadline for his report was December 31, 1985. It had been extended to June 30, 1986, and it was now June 2. Deschenes said simply would not have time to go to the Soviet Union.*

The problem is that many of the subjects Deschenes was investigating are men accused of persecuting civilians while members of Ukrainian, Lithuanian, or Latvian police or auxiliary units. The Berlin Documents Center and the other German-maintained Nazi military archives are almost devoid of information about these units. The fact that German-based record centers do not have information on a suspect is meaningless, not exculpatory. The commission knew this full well because it had been told so by both a score of private Nazi hunters and OSI investigators with whom it had conferred. Yet in many cases this is used as justification for closing files.

Sol Littman has little good to say about the quality of the commission's investigations. He calls them "inept, amateurish, hasty and incomplete." The problem, he believes, was Deschenes' unwillingness "to consult with agencies with the background and skill in war crimes research, and the staff's unwillingness to follow advice offered by those they did consult with." He focuses on one single case that he feels serves as an example. Case No. 252.1 was ordered closed after simple record checks in Canada failed to show that the individual had ever entered the country, and a check with the Berlin Documents Center found nothing on the individual named. Littman says that there is enough identification given in case No. 252.1 for him to recognize it as one of the names

---

* Critics say Deschenes made the announcement that he had run out of time knowing that he had asked for and been granted another six-month extension (to December 31, 1986) and had been promised additional extensions if necessary. We have learned also that by mid-May the Soviet Embassy in Ottawa told Deschenes that it would meet every one of his conditions.

that he gave the commission—a person believed to have taken part in the killing of 40,000 Jews as a member of an SS auxiliary unit. "This is a case I have studied for some considerable time," says Littman. "I am reasonably sure that the man did enter Canada. They didn't find any trace of him using exactly the same techniques that didn't uncover Rauca for years. Isn't is reasonable to believe that he might have changed the spelling of his name, either anglicizing it or changing only a few letters? And I could have told them—in fact I did tell them—that they would find little or nothing in Germany on this unit. But I know there is substantial information on the unit in Soviet archives because the OSI has used it in several cases."

Littman and others believe that fully three-quarters of the names on the commission's Master List represented Eastern Europeans on whom little or no data is available in Germany. In a few cases, Deschenes recommended that subjects be placed among the 218 pending until research could be done behind the Iron Curtain. But it is believed that these are situations in which damning information is already available. Littman and others believe that hundreds of the commission's cases should have remained open until Soviet-controlled archives can be checked.

However, even the limited admission that there are twenty war criminals living in Canada, and another 218 on whom more investigation is needed, elated the Jewish observers, because it marked the first time ever that Canada officially had admitted that it was home to war criminals. The other groups present were also pleased, as was the government, because Deschenes's numbers reduced the problem to a manageable size: one that could be handled without disrupting large segments of Canadian society.

Deschenes gave considerable space in the report to a nasty discussion of whether Josef Mengele had ever been in Canada. Why he found it necessary to devote two sections of his final report to a subject long closed seems a mystery until you realize that Deschenes was using the charge originally raised by Littman* as an example of how wrong Nazi-hunting organizations can be.

---

* Shortly after making his original charge about Mengele, Littman finally learned what had actually happened in 1962. He wrote to the prime minister and the commission to say that it was not worth the commission's time to investigate the matter. He also made the fact of his error public.

The story behind the 1962 request from the Canadian government to the United States for background information on Mengele is a fascinating sidebar that says much about the Nazi-hunting history of Canada. Within a matter of weeks of Littman's disclosure, the RCMP called him to say they had learned what prompted the 1962 inquiry: a source that turned out to be "unreliable" had told a local provincial constable in Washington, Ontario, that he suspected a rather mysterious German living at a nearby farmhouse might be Mengele. The man, who used the name Joseph Menke, was said to

As for what to do, Deschenes presented in his report a range of alternatives: extradition, trial in Canada under Canadian law, or deportation. He was quite taken by the simplicity of the American approach. He said that Canada could undertake similar actions to revoke citizenship through existing immigration laws and ship accused war criminals back to their places of origin—the approach he strongly recommended. He even offered suggestions for updating and streamlining Canadian immigration law to make the whole process easier.

Deschenes had clear reservations about extradition because of the potential of sending people to the Soviet Union or to other countries with the death penalty. This made the East European emigré communities happy: they had argued long and hard against any such solution.

Finally, as Deschenes saw it, the least attractive alternative was trial in Canada. But, he said, should the government choose this alternative, it was constitutionally possible given the passage of new legislation.

He then addressed two major concerns of the East European emigré communities. He recommended strongly against the formation of a Nazi-hunting operation modeled after the OSI that would be both investigator and prosecu-

---

be a doctor, and this led to the somewhat obvious conclusion that he could be Mengele. Littman was told that as part of the investigation the U.S. government had been queried for background information on Mengele. There was never any visa application from Mengele or from anybody who could possibly have been the infamous Nazi physician.

Subsequently, Littman was to learn much more about the Menke episode and his eventual source was none other than the "unreliable" informant who had originally brought the tale to the provincial constable in 1962. It turned out that the informant—who Littman describes as "a respected, educated member of his community"—was told by a local practicing physician, a German, that a famous war criminal was hiding on a local farm. The informant became curious and went to the farm, but discovered it was more like a small estate hidden behind imposing locked iron gates. He tried to enter but was turned away by several burly men who were armed with pistols. He got into a shouting match with them, and two other men emerged from the house. The informant says he did not get a close look at them but thought one did resemble photographs he had seen of Mengele. He then reported his suspicions to a constable in the the the Woodstock Detachment, and what ensued is an amazing case study in bureaucratic bungling and buckpassing.

As files now show, the constable duly reported what he had been told to his superiors. The report finally reached the federal government—both the departments of justice and external affairs. Over the next three months, a series of memos was exchanged and meetings were held. The informant had originally voiced his suspicions to the constable on January 14, 1962. On April 19 the RCMP finally reported back to the Ontario provincial police that it would investigate the matter. (It was during this investigation that the request was made to the United States.) Finally, in July 1962, someone thought of actually going to the farmhouse to see who or what was there. When they arrived it was boarded up and deserted. There can be no doubt that Josef Mengele was never at that farmhouse. But in the light of what we've learned about Nazi war criminals, it is interesting to speculate about who this mysterious guest may have been.

tor. He said that these functions should remain separate and that decisions to prosecute a specific case should not be in the hands of those who had investigated it, and that prosecutions should be undertaken only by the federal government and not by provincial prosecutors.

Deschenes also gave a dual victory to both Jewish and Ukrainian observers. He reviewed the experience of both West Germany and the United States with Soviet-supplied evidence and concluded that nothing in Canadian law, or in the German-U.S. experience would prevent Canada from utilizing Soviet-provided evidence. But, he said, he had been too busy to travel to the Soviet Union himself, so he could not speculate on the details of a system for obtaining such assistance, which would probably involve long and difficult negotiations. In addition, he spelled out "safeguards" that should be applied before acceptance of Soviet-supplied documents and statements, including access to the original German documents, not copies; use of independent interpreters; access to original interviews and to previous statements by witnesses; the right to interview witnesses according to Canadian rules of evidence and videotaping of them.

Deschenes's next observation overjoyed the Ukrainians in his audience: the Galicia Division should not be indicted as a group. "Charges of war crimes against members of the Galicia Division have never been substantiated," said the report, and "in the absence of evidence of participation in or knowledge of specific war crimes, mere membership in the Galicia Division is insufficient to justify prosecution." The fourteen *Waffengrenadierdivision der SS,* also known as the Halychyna Waffen-SS Division or simply as the Galicia Division, was formed with Ukrainian volunteers in 1943. About 8,000 members surrendered en masse to the British in 1945, and were interned in a British camp in Italy. Given a chance to return to the Ukraine, they naturally declined.

In 1948 the British were desperate for farm labor, and division members were brought to England and put to work. In 1950 their labor was no longer required, so the question of what to do with them arose. Britain did not want them to remain, and Italy did not want them back. The answer was to let them emigrate to Canada. About 2,000 did, of whom some 600 are still living in the country. Former members of this unit have remained very close and, in fact, have their own fraternal association, "The Brotherhood of Veterans of the 1st Division of the Ukrainian Army in Canada." They are a major force within the Ukrainian community and, in fact, asked the commission for standing as official "observers" (meaning that they would have been allowed to attend some commission meetings not open to the public and their lawyers would have been allowed to question witnesses at public hearings in a way analogous to cross-examination). The question of whether the division as a whole committed war crimes remains unresolved. Division supporters argue that by the time the unit was formed, almost all the Jews in the Ukraine had already been killed. Further, the division was "SS" in name only: in reality, they argue, it was a simple army unit formed to fight the Soviets, their traditional enemies.

Many Nazi hunters, including Simon Wiesenthal, brand the division as nothing more than a band of war criminals. Members are accused of participating in the ruthless suppression of the Warsaw ghetto uprising, of widespread actions against other civilian populations, and of serving as concentration camp guards. Critics also charge that many members were recruited from the auxiliary police forces that committed acts of persecution from 1941 to 1943.

What's the truth? Historian Alti Rodal devoted considerable space and time to the subject of the Galicia Division in her study. She traced its history and both sides of the argument, then concluded: "While allegations that the Division as a unit may call for further exploration, substantive evidence to support these allegations has to date not come forward. A more pointed, if difficult, avenue of investigation would focus on the background of individual members of the Division prior to joining the Division."

The Ukrainian community was elated that the division as a whole had been cleared, but critics asked a pointed question. What about the likelihood that members of the division came from the notorious police auxiliary units? If so, on what basis did Deschenes exclude all 600 living members?

After presenting the report's conclusions, Hnatyshyn announced the government's response: Canadian war criminals were Canada's problem, and it would not ask any other country to deal with them. The problem he said, "should be dealt with here in Canada, and every case must be resolved in a manner consistent with Canadian standards of law and evidence." Legislation would be introduced to change Canadian law, and war crimes trials would be held.*

---

* Hnatyshyn made it clear that the government had made the decision that trials in Canada would be the only acceptable option. Yet, just as this book was being finished, the government seemed to have reversed itself, at least in one case, although it steadfastly refuses to acknowledge that it has changed pace.

Jacob Luitjens has lived in Vancouver since 1961 and has recently retired from a teaching career. Luitjens came to Canada from Paraguay, where he fled after the war from Holland. The Dutch had accused him of being a major Nazi collaborator during the war and directly responsible for murder and persecution. Holland has tried him in absentia in both a war crimes and a civil court.

Since 1961 Holland has tried repeatedly to get Luitjens extradited, but Canada has refused because the charge that Luitjens was convicted of is treason, which is not an extraditable offense under the Canadian-Dutch extradition treaty. (At one point Canada suggested that Holland retroactively change the crime for which Luitjens was convicted from treason to murder, because murder is an extraditable offense under terms of the treaty, but Holland has maintained that it could not retroactively do so.

Suddenly, in March 1988, Canadian authorities arrested Luitjens, saying that he

Hnatyshyn also announced that the government had informed the twenty people on the initial "hit-list" that they were the subjects of an investigation and should obtain counsel. This made experienced Nazi hunters in the audience wince. As one put it, "I'm going to be very surprised if any of the twenty are still around when the government gets around to filing an action."

Since the Deschenes Commission report came out, the Canadian government has organized its Nazi hunt. It has formed a forty-man Federal War-Crimes Unit under Assistant Deputy Justice Minister William Hobson. The Canadian Parliament has passed the new legislation required to prosecute war crimes, and Foreign Ministry officials have announced that Canada has signed an agreement with the Soviet Union by which investigators may obtain documents and witness statements. The Canadian-Soviet agreement is the first of eight that will probably be signed: similar agreements are being negotiated between Canada and the governments of Poland, Romania, Czechoslovakia, Hungary, West Germany, Israel, and the Netherlands.

At this early date, it is very difficult to put the Deschenes Commission report and Canada's response to it into meaningful context. If five years from now a sizable number of war criminals have been identified, tried, and imprisoned, it will be clear that Canada has courageously and forthrightly faced up to its problem and overcome it. In fact, we will have to admit that Canada has more courage than does the United States, which, in fact, does wash its hands of war criminals, sending most of them off to pleasant exiles. But at this writing we tend to agree with critics like Sol Littman who view the Deschenes report, and the whole process, as essentially "political" and the government's response as likely to result in the fewest possible war crimes prosecutions.†

---

would be held pending a deportation proceeding. In announcing the arrest, a spokesman for Hnatyshyn restated that the government does not believe it has the option of extradition, nor does it believe it can try Luitjens in Canada. But it does believe it can order him deported, and will so proceed. The spokesman refused to speculate whether the government might attempt additional deportations, or whether it considers it considers the Luitjens case unique.

One problem in all this is that under Canadian law, someone who is ordered deported must be sent to the country of his or her choice, unless the government specifies a country in the charge. So far the government has not indicated whether it will see to deport Luitjens to the Netherlands, which wants him badly, or will let him choose a country, possibly Paraguay.

† We agree with *Toronto Star* editorial board member Harold Levy, who wrote: "In sum, the government appears to be stressing the approach that will take longest to realize and is least likely to succeed. ... It also means that it is almost inconceivable that there will ever be a conviction in a Canadian court for a war crime related to the Holocaust. ... The government's stated preference for the approach least likely to succeed is a hollow attempt at allowing an embarrassing political problem to wither away."

As Sol Littman observes in a critique of the commission report: "All in all, the Deschenes Commission provides the government with what it wanted most—a small, controllable war crimes problem. Unable to deny any longer that a significant number of criminals had found shelter in Canada, the government prayed for a solution that would require a minimum of resources and would promise a minimum of political repercussions. . . . This is why there is so much emphasis on numbers in the report—particularly in keeping the numbers down and attacking the credibility of those who offer higher figures."

The government will probably choose a test case, possibly that of Imre Finta (See page 39). Lawyers for the defendant will certainly challenge the constitutionality of the new statute. That appeals process alone could take years to resolve. Then comes the actual trial and the appeals that will follow it. Only then, and only if the government has won at every step of the way, would the next prosecution begin. Thus we would not be surprised if in the next five years, only this one case will actually be tried before the courts. When you consider the ages of many of the potential defendants, a five-year delay is tantamount to a pardon. And what if appellate courts decide that Deschenes was wrong and there is no constitutionally sound basis for trying war criminals in Canada, the conclusion reached by the United States years ago? Will the government then throw up its hands and withdraw from the effort?

Recently, the Wiesenthal Center sent a new list of twenty-one suspected Nazi war criminals living in Canada to the Justice Department in Ottawa. On it were Lithuanians and Byelorussians accused of persecuting and killing Jews during the German occupation, and included the former commander of the Dimitrava concentration camp near Kretinga, Lithuania; the governor of Kretinga district; a captain and a lieutenant of the Lithuanian security police; and a chief of Lithuania's Siauliai security department. "Some of them certainly are dead and some of them certainly have moved on elsewhere," said Sol Littman, "but the government has the best machinery for locating them and identifying them." Nazi hunters want to believe that Canada has turned the corner on this issue. But there's too much history that says it hasn't.

★ ★ ★

The parallels between Nazi-hunting in Australia and Canada are uncanny. First, the decades-long lack of attention given the possible presence of Nazi war criminals in the country and now a flurry of activity. It even seems as if Australia is going to opt for the same course.

After the war, the Australian government agreed to accept 170,000 displaced refugees, including 50,000 from the Baltic states and 50,000 from Germany. Given the relatively small Australian population in 1945, this was a considerable number. Ever since this influx, rumors have been rampant that a number of war criminals were included among the immigrants. But through a succession of governments—left, center, and right—over more than forty years, Australia has managed to ignore any such rumors.

Then, in early 1986, a series of broadcasts by reporters from the Australian Broadcasting Company, using evidence compiled by private Nazi-hunters, spotlighted former Nazis living quietly in all parts of the country. The government of Prime Minister Bob Hawke felt that it had to respond, and did so by appointing Andrew Menzies, a retired official from the Department of the Attorney-General, to head up an investigation.

After an intensive five-month investigation, Menzies reported back. No, he said, he had found no indication that there was ever any official government policy to admit Nazis, or any official knowingly admitted a war criminal or to protect one once he had reached Australia.* But yes, said Menzies, there are war criminals living in Australia and something had to be done about it.

Menzies had assembled a list of about 200 possible suspects. After eliminating those who were dead, had left Australia, or were clearly innocent, he listed about 70 who warranted a fuller investigation than his meager resources allowed. He said he believed it was possible that these 70 might have been guilty of war crimes under the expanded definition formulated at Nuremberg.

In many respects, the Menzies investigation was much more straightforward than was Deschenes's in Canada. Certainly it was simpler, much less formalized, more low-key. And it was not nearly as visible or as susceptible to political pressures. Perhaps most importantly, Menzies did not take it upon himself to act as judge and jury. He understood his limitations and gathered as complete a list as possible of potential defendants, eliminated the obvious, and then told the government which ones it should be investigating. In essence, however, Menzies' bottom line was the same as Deschenes's: there are Nazi war criminals among us and we should do something about it. It was one thing for journalists or Jewish Nazi-hunting organizations to say it, but now—as with the Deschenes Commission—an official government investigation was saying it, and the government had to respond.

The Hawke government did respond. In 1987, it established its own equivalent of America's Office of Special Investigations—the Australian War Crimes Investigation Unit—headed by Robert Greenwood, who had recently retired from the National Crimes Authority. All of the 250 names that had been compiled by the Menzies Commission, as the results of its initial investigations were turned over to the new unit.

---

* Menzies did find, however, ample evidence of overt anti-Semitism in the policies of post-war Immigration Minister Arthur Calwell. A firm quota of no more than 15 percent Jews was imposed upon any group of immigrants, and this policy lasted until well after the initial influx of displaced persons. The same anti-Semitism prevailed during the war years, explaining why so few Jews fleeing Europe settled in Australia.

During the unit's year-and-a-half of existence, Greenwood has traveled to the United States, where he held lengthy meetings with both OSI officials and investigators from the Simon Wiesenthal Center. They gave him additional names of possible former Nazis living in Australia. He has traveled to Europe and to Israel to establish relationships with governments who might help Australia in the future and has gone behind the Iron Curtain, where the Soviets gave him additional names and agreed to cooperate.

Recently, Greenwood told us that he now has more than 200 active files,* culled from a list that had grown to almost 450 names. Reportedly, this does not even include many who were quickly removed from Menzies' original list. Obviously, this is a much larger number than Menzies had estimated, and represents, in part, names supplied by Nazi hunters from other countries who are happy to help, given some indication that Australia wants to act.

While Greenwood has been about his business, the government has been trying to figure out what to do with these cases once they are ready for action. The influence of the Deschenes Commission report is seen in the decision to depart from the OSI model of investigator and prosecutor. In any case, the Special Investigation Unit's final product will be a legal brief (with supporting documents and witness statements) to be forwarded to Director of Public Prosecutions Ian Temby, who will then make the final decision as to whether to move forward with a given case. But the mode of procedure is still unresolved at this writing. Australia has made the basic decision—and it is extremely controversial—that like Canada (and probably Britain, as we will see)—war criminals will be tried in Australia for the war crimes they are accused of committing, as opposed to simply trying to denaturalize them and then deport them or oust them as does the United States. But, unlike Canada, Australia has not completely ruled out extraditing war criminals to countries who demand them for trial. The Soviets, for instance, have told the Australians they would prefer to try particularly serious offenses themselves. But legislation has been introduced into Parliament to prohibit any extraditions to a country where the death penalty is possible. Australia has done away with its death penalty.

A bill not unlike the Canadian bill has been introduced into the Australian Parliament, but it has been the subject of fierce debate. The problem for many is that the proposed statute is simply too broad. Numerous position papers have demonstrated that under the bill's provisions, Australian soldiers might be charged, especially airmen who took part in the "carpet bombing" of Euro-

---

* Sources tell us that the total is closer to 275. Reportedly eliminated from the larger number were those who had died, left Australia, or could not be located and thus are presumed not to be in the country. In a policy decision that might prove controversial, others whose crimes were considered "so minor" as not to warrant pursuit were also eliminated.

pean cities. Such bombing raids had civilian populations as their target, and such raids were in violation of the Geneva Convention.

Another section of the bill that has drawn fire uses the word "omission" in defining war crime. A serious crime would be defined as "being by act or omission, in any way directly or indirectly, knowingly concerned in, or party to, the deportation of a person so mentioned." Many believe that Jews who either assisted in or did not actively oppose the segregation of fellow Jews into ghettos and their eventual shipment to death camps could be charged as war criminals.

In his report, Andrew Menzies made one recommendation that in great measure has set the tone for the what-to-do debate in Australia during the last several years. Menzies noted that the crimes involved had been committed more than forty years before. Most of the seventy names on his list represented men (reportedly, no women were named) who were now well along in years, some, in fact, quite old. Almost all, he said, seemed to have lived exemplary lives since emigrating four decades before. So, he said, we should consider prosecuting only those clearly guilty of "major" criminal acts; the others should be allowed to live out what few years they have left in peace.

Certainly more than Canada, and perhaps more than any other country currently debating this issue, Australia has been caught up in this "let the old boys alone" syndrome. Respected columnists and editorials in established journals have raised the specter of wizened old men, barely able to shuffle up to the dock, being dragged into court to answer for offenses committed thousands of miles away on distant shores and so long ago that few can remember them.

Typical of this viewpoint was an early 1988 column by David Barnett in *The Bulletin,* a respected national newsweekly. It read in part: " The War Crimes Bill proposes to recreate in Australia the Nuremberg hearings 43 years after VE Day, with so far some 250 elderly migrants who came to this country 40 or more years ago as potential defendants. . . . And what happens if Temby gets his convictions? What will [Australian Attorney-General Lionel] Bowen do with these white-haired septuagenarians? Will he really send them to jail? Asking around last week one concluded that certain people would prefer to let them go."

The debate continues in Australia, but it seems clear that at some point soon legislation will be passed allowing Australia to try war criminals in its courts, and Bob Greenwood's Investigations Unit will have its first test case ready. What will happen after that is only conjecture and will undoubtedly take a year or more to sort out. It is hoped that Australia will become an aggressive pursuer of war criminals in its midst, but that remains to be seen. Nazi hunters around the world are watching what is transpiring "down under."

Her Majesty's
Less Than Finest Hour

In order to discuss the hunt for Nazis by the United Kingdom—or the lack thereof—it is necessary to begin at 6:25 P.M. on August 10, 1942. It can now be documented that at precisely that time a telegram arrived at the British Foreign Office in London from the British consul general in Geneva. He was passing along a message from Gerhard Riegner, an official of the World Jewish Congress, addressed to a member of Parliament, Sidney Silverman. It is not uncommon for private organizations and, occasionally, individuals to ask diplomats to pass along sensitive messages to members of government. What was unusual was the content of the telegram—an accurate report of the beginning of the horrors of the Holocaust. The telegram read:

> *Receiving alarming reports stating that in the Fuhrer's Headquarters a plan has been discussed, and is under consideration, according to which all Jews in countries occupied or controlled by Germany numbering three-and-a-half to four million should, after deportation and concentration in the East, be at one blow exterminated, in order to resolve once and for all the Jewish question in Europe. Action is reported to be planned for the autumn. Ways of execution are still being discussed, including the use of prussic acid. We transmit this information with all the necessary reservation, as exactitude cannot be confirmed by us. Our informant is reported to have close connections with the highest German authorities, and his reports are generally reliable. Please inform and consult New York.*

The message was received by a lawyer in the Foreign Office, who knew that there had been a wide variety of reports on the persecution of Jews throughout Europe and on instances wherein civilians were dying because of lack of food or exposure to the elements. In his notations on the telegram, he wrote, "The German policy seems to be rather to eliminate useless mouths, both to save able-bodied Jews and others as slave labor . . . I do not think we should be wise to make use of this story in propaganda to Germany without further confirmation. . . . We should not help matters by taking any further action on the basis of this rather wild story." (Had that "wild story" been taken seriously at once by those in power, perhaps millions of lives might have been saved.) The next day, Silverman, a member of the Labour Party in Parliament, was given the telegram but forbidden to telephone Rabbi Stephen Wise, the legendary head of the World Jewish Congress in New York.

Silverman asked for a debate in Parliament on German atrocities. The reaction of Anthony Eden, then Foreign Minister, showed the skepticism of the British government with respect to allegations of a Final Solution. The parliamentary record in England shows that Anthony Eden stated, "I don't see why the House of Commons should have any debate."

The message that originated in Geneva in August 1942 finally made it to America on August 28, nearly three weeks later. But the U.S. State Department, after conferring with its British allies, would withhold for three months the content because of the "unsubstantiated nature of the information." At the time, Sumner Welles, Undersecretary of State, talked with Wise and demanded that the World Jewish Congress leader not publicize the contents of the message until U.S. agents were able to get some kind of confirmation.

Three months passed before the world was told about that message. By that time, the Final Solution was being actively carried out by Eichmann and others, and Radio Berlin was boasting about the deportation of Jews.

Those in power in London, and their counterparts in Washington, were not cruel or stupid, but in 1942 there seemed to be a naive unwillingness to accept the Nazis for what they were. No one believed yet that World War II was to be a war in which the enemy reached levels of brutality and horror beyond the wildest dreams of even the most imaginative observer.

If authorities did not accept the potential horror, there was no obligation to find solutions, but evidence was mounting from around the world. By late 1942 the Allies began to realize that the Final Solution was a reality and, despite their previous skepticism, something had to be done. Historians are frustrated because they cannot understand why it took so long, based on the evidence, for the British and U.S. governments to accept what so many refugees and independent observers were saying—that the extermination of the Jews, and the killing of thousands, indeed millions, of other innocent persons was actually happening.

By the time the telegram from Geneva had been made public, the United States and Great Britain had agreed to establish some type of commission to deal with war criminals. Finally, as we have seen in chapter 1, President Roosevelt announced that "punishment shall be meted out to the ringleaders responsible for the organized mass murder of thousands." The United Nations War Crimes Commission was born.

In Great Britain there were debates in the House of Lords and the House of

Commons over what the commission's work would be. The British government concluded that the commission should focus on crimes against humanity committed against the Allies, gather as much testimony as possible, and identify the criminals as best they could. It was understood that it was essential to collect the evidence as quickly as possible while it was still fresh, even if nothing could be done about it for years to come. But there was a major difference in the attitude between the United States and Great Britain toward the War Crimes Commission and the ultimate disposition of war criminals.

The basic American and British policies were so different that after the war ended, some victims of de-Nazification benefited, depending upon whether their cases were heard by American-supervised or British-supervised courts. While all the Allies were committed to destroying the German military machine, there was much disagreement with respect to the German economy.

As the U.S. perceived "victory," Roosevelt wanted a harsh, total settlement. The Americans believed that you should punish not only the soldier who used the gun, but the businessman who supplied it. They were angry at the use of slave labor in factories and felt that those behind the scenes were as guilty as those on the front lines.

Great Britain, ever mindful of Europe's economic interdependence, did not want to destroy totally the German economy. The only possible explanation seems to be a hesitancy on the part of the British government to see a postwar Germany too dependent on other countries for economic support. British anxiety about Soviet aggression in Europe was on the rise. At the same time Britain wanted in the postwar period to take full advantage of the Allied victory to regain political stature, despite the inevitable shrinking of the British Empire around the world. Britain was seriously concerned with the ominous events in Greece and the Slavic nations, and intimately involved in the economic direction that Europe would take after World War II. As a result of these many factors the British developed no particular national program of dealing with Nazis who survived and found their way to Great Britain. In fact, after the main Nuremberg trial, the British government prepared an official document in 1948, voicing opposition to further war crimes trials. That document referred to efforts by World Jewry to continue a hunt for escaped Nazi war criminals.

Prior to 1988, the British government had never set up a specific organization to deal with the investigation of Nazi war criminals in its territory. The nation seemed far more concerned with rebuilding itself economically and finding a place for itself in the leadership in the European community.

When the debate began over whether to open the United Nations War Crimes Commission archive in 1987, Britain took a relatively soft position. While the British delegation to the United Nations did not oppose opening the files, the members expressed a concern that access to the files be limited.

Finally, after considerable political pressure from the World Jewish Congress and from Jewish leaders in the United Kingdom, Britain moved forward more aggressively. It went along with opening the files at the U.N. to the world and, ultimately, has begun investigations into known Nazis living in the UK.

Some say it was Margaret Thatcher's commitment to law and order and the fact that she personally represents a constituency with a large Jewish population that forced the turnaround.

Due to the efforts of a handful of hunters who have relentlessly pursued personal investigations, we know the identities of at least several of the Nazis living in Britain. It is their continuing pressure on the British government that is primarily responsible for official investigation finally being launched which may lead to prosecutions.

The British situation is a clear-cut case of how we crossed over from being chroniclers of the hunters and became hunters ourselves. On October 22, 1986, in Los Angeles, a messenger from the Simon Wiesenthal Center for Holocaust Studies delivered to the British consul general, a dossier of seventeen suspected Nazis accused of horrendous war crimes. All were believed to be living in the United Kingdom. The degree of evidence varied, but, in each case, the basic information had originally come from the Soviet Union; however, much of the data had been independently corroborated through Red Cross records and witnesses traced throughout the world.

The list of seventeen was among half a dozen such lists that the Wiesenthal authorities delivered to various governments. At the time Rabbi Hier, administrator of the Wiesenthal Center, said he hoped that the British government would properly investigate those seventeen names and take serious action. First, the British would have to determine how many were still alive, and, then, how provable the case against each of them was. Finally, there would have to be some logical course of action.

The latter represented a problem, because Britain does not have an extradition treaty with the Soviet Union and most of the crimes were committed in territory now under Soviet control. As a result, lacking a place to which to extradite, it could look only to its own laws for prosecution. There is currently nothing in British law that allows for the prosecution of a crime committed outside of that country. In short, first the Nazis had to be hunted down and the case proven against them, while, at the same time, laws would have to be changed to enable the British government to take some formal action.

In early November, Greville Janner, a member of Parliament and a highly respected Jewish leader in England, wrote to Prime Minister Margaret Thatcher to verify that she had received the Wiesenthal Center list. We talked with Janner the next day, by which time he had obtained a copy of the list. He and several of his colleagues were intent on determining how many of the seventeen were alive, where they were living, and what could be done about them.

Janner wouldn't tell us the names, but made it clear (as did Rabbi Hier) that if, after a reasonable interval, the British government took no action he would "do what he had to do." We took this to mean that the list might be released to the media if the British home secretary failed to take action of any kind.

Four days later Mrs. Thatcher contacted Janner and wrote a letter stating, "we are considering this matter urgently and I shall let you know our conclusion as soon as I can." But there were leaks. While most of the names were not known to us, we did learn the name of one man, and we were not alone. Some energetic British television reporters had also discovered the identity of Mr. Antanas Gecas who lived in Scotland, as mentioned earlier. When Gecas was named and accused on British television, only the naive were shocked.

On November 20, 1986, Greville Janner rose in Parliament and asked the prime minister about the allegations against Gecas, who had been identified as a commander of a unit of the Lithuanian *Schutzmannschaft* battalions. He was charged with responsibility for the mass murder of thousands of civilians in Lithuania and Byelorussia. The Thatcher administration did not respond.

As a result of the exposé of Gecas and the fact that the government did not initiate a full-scale investigation of the list of seventeen names provided by the Wiesenthal Center, Janner and a handful of others met on November 24 to form the All-Party War Crimes Group. Its purpose was to determine whether any former Nazis were living in the UK and to do whatever had to be done to bring them to justice. They selected Merlin Rees, a former home secretary, as their chairman and spokesperson.

On December 9, 1986, the group met for the first time. In addition to the chairman, they elected Stefan Terlezki, John Wheeler, and Greville Janner, all members of Parliament, as officers. Each was committed to the cause and willing to speak out in Parliament and in the community to help achieve the goal. Martin Gilbert, a Holocaust historian, and Gerald Draper, a former war crimes prosecutor and professor of international law, agreed to help the group with its research because, in addition to hunting Nazis, the group wanted to have a full understanding of the laws of extradition, deportation, and denaturalization.

On January 13, 1987, the All-Party War Crimes Group met to discuss the fact that the prime minister had not yet replied to the list of seventeen Nazis provided by the Wiesenthal Center. Merlin Rees wrote to her and asked for clarification of the government's position. (Whereas in the United States someone might simply call a press conference or raise hell because the White House was failing to respond, the British resort to the more elegant exchange of communications. Only after many such formal exchanges produce nothing does anyone "goes public" with his complaint.

On January 28, 1987, Merlin Rees received a letter from the prime minister in which she outlined "important issues and difficult questions of law." She assured the group that "we are looking into this matter urgently and carefully and hope to have a response in the near future." Janner was frustrated. He just didn't believe that the government's investigations were happening fast enough. And, on January 29, he raised a question officially in the Parliament.

On that very date, Scottish television aired a thirty-minute documentary called "Britain: A Nazi Safe House?" which showed repeated instances of British government inaction over war criminals. Members of the All-Party War Crimes Group, former United States officials, and the alleged war criminal, Antanas Gecas, were interviewed on the program. That program was seen throughout the United Kingdom and highlights were shown all over the world.

Had the British government ducked its responsibilities? If so, why? No nation was more committed to the Allied cause than Great Britain. Was it merely protocol and complicated legal procedures that had prevented successive British governments from joining the hunt and finding Nazis in its own country? Some have suggested that the answer is the embarrassment of taking a magnifying glass into the wartime past. Too many mistakes were made, and there was too much indecisiveness on the part of British prime ministers right after World War II. "It would not be healthy" for British morale, they say, to refocus on what was left undone.

Finally, on February 11, 1987, after all of the publicity surrounding the Scottish television broadcast and continued pressure by the All-Party War Crimes Group, the prime minister released a letter sent to Rees, which totally discounted any possibility of prosecution of Nazi war criminals in British courts. It said that there was absolutely no British law that would enable such prosecutions, regardless of the amount of evidence that might be available. War crimes, the letter went on to say, are extraditible offenses, but there were major difficulties in extraditing these individuals. The offenses that had been committed would, under normal circumstances, warrant sending perpetrators back to the Soviet Union or whatever country the crimes might have been committed in. Because of the lack of an extradition treaty between the two countries, the prime minister's office admitted to being frustrated.

On February 19, 1987, *The Paperclip Conspiracy* by Tom Bower was published. It caused an immediate sensation in Britain. On February 24, 1987, a significant meeting took place in the office of the home secretary, Douglas Hurd. Merlin Rees, Greville Janner, and other officers of the All-Party War Crimes Group were present. Hurd shared with them the results of an investigation by the government into the seventeen names on the list that had been provided by the Simon Wiesenthal Center.

Hurd told them that the British government had been able to identify at least six persons who were currently living in the UK. He said the investigation was continuing, and, while they knew that some of the accused were dead, they were not sure how many. He explained that there was no way to get around the extradition problem with respect to the Soviet Union, but a procedure whereby identifiable Nazis living in the UK could be stripped of their citizenship and deported providing some nation would take them had been discussed..

By that time, we had obtained all seventeen names and a considerable amount of evidence against each of them. We had located seven who were alive—putting us one ahead of the British government. British journalists were also hot on the trail of another four.

On February 26, 1987, another list was given to the home secretary by the Wiesenthal Center. The list contained thirty-four names of war criminals who had committed offenses in the same area as the seventeen on the original list. Some of the names were leaked to the media. Labour Party leader Neil Kinnock spoke in Parliament that day and asked the British government what their intentions were with respect to the original seventeen and the new names.

We arrived in Britain on March 1, 1987, on one of six trips we made there that year. The next day, a vitally important meeting was scheduled in the office of Douglas Hurd. Rabbi Hier of the World Jewish Congress met with the British government to discuss the disposition of the cases against the accused Nazis. We were not permitted to attend the meeting, but in London, as in Washington D.C., there are leaks. We were close enough to learn what happened moments after the meeting, ended and to find out what the home secretary told the Jewish group from the United States. The home secretary said that the investigations of the seventeen on the original list were continuing, and that immigration files were now being examined. He acknowledged the documentary evidence from the Wiesenthal Center and said that the British government would formally request access to Soviet files if it became necessary.

For the first time, the home secretary indicated the possibility of extraditing some of the Nazis to West Germany. He said that there had been some discussion of a change in the treaty with Israel to enable extradition of war criminals to that country, but he considered such a move a long shot. Perhaps most importantly, the home secretary indicated that the government was willing to consider changes in the criminal law of the United Kingdom that might enable prosecution for crimes not committed there during World War II. He stated that this would depend upon the significance and gravity of the evidence from the Wiesenthal Center, the Soviets, and others.

Hurd's comments were appreciated by the Wiesenthal Center and the parliamentary group in London as a sign of progress.

In the months to come, there was an amazing shift in the international perception of the British prime minister. The problems facing Pres. Ronald Reagan, and the fact that he was completing his last term, helped Thatcher emerge as the forceful leader of the West. On March 31, 1987, when she visited the Soviet Union, it became clear to the world that this "Iron Lady" had emerged as far more than a strong prime minister. It also indicated a breakthrough in British relations with the Soviets. It was only natural, given Thatcher's growing profile of power, and the relaxation of relations between the United Kingdom and the Soviet Union, that the issue of cooperation in war crimes investigations would come up. During her visit to the Soviet Union that March, Thatcher was asked by journalists about war criminals living in the UK, and responded that "we do not have strict evidence yet against those names."

On April 7, 1987, the home office contacted Merlin Rees and advised him that it had discovered three more individuals on the original list of seventeen alive and well in the UK. That brought the total to nine. (We had reached that count three weeks earlier and shared the information with colleagues in various British newspapers who were assisting us in the preparation of this section.) The Nazi war crime issue was pushed further to the fore when, on April 28, 1987, amidst the storm of international reaction to the revelations about Kurt Waldheim's Nazi past, the British foreign office issued a statement. The United States had already officially barred Waldheim from reentering its borders as a private citizen by placing him on the Watch List.

The United Kingdom has no formal procedure comparable to placement on the Watch List, but the foreign office announced: "There are no plans whatsoever to invite Dr. Kurt Waldheim to the United Kingdom."

Meanwhile, pressure was building in New York for full disclosure of the United Nations War Crimes Commission files. The Waldheim case had become a bonfire, heating up arguments at the United Nations, in Washington, and in capitals throughout the world.

As mentioned earlier, Britain was quiet at the first meeting of the seventeen nations involved when they discussed reopening the files. Then it appeared to join a growing consensus favoring limited access to the files, but through a procedure so highly guarded that the world would probably not learn much about the materials. The pressure was heavy, but the British government maintained that it did not "currently support full access to the files." On April 30, 1987, and again on May 7, 1987, Rees, Rhodes-James, Janner, and others spoke out again publicly, urging the British government to take formal diplomatic action on Kurt Waldheim and inquiring about the British position on the United Nations Nazi war crimes archive. The situation remained unchanged.

On July 1 an exasperated All-Party War Crimes Group went public. Sidestepping the normal exchange of letters with the foreign office or raising of questions in Parliament, it held a press conference outlining what was hidden in the UN files and demanding greater access for the world. The next day Greville Janner, in a heated speech in Parliament, insisted that the British govern-

ment support the move to open the files. A week later, Merlin Rees sent by
hand to the foreign secretary a letter with evidence that when Kurt Waldheim
had been categorized as a suspected war criminal in 1948 by the seventeen-
member-nations meeting in London, the chairman of that group was British.
Rees suggested there might be British records about Waldheim.

In the weeks to come, Rees, Janner, and their group sent the foreign secretary more documents concerning the seventeen on the original list. The material had come from the Soviet Union, British historians, the World Jewish Congress, and other sources. It was clear and very convincing that those among the
seventeen who were alive and living in the UK had been involved in horrendous crimes. They had not been ordinary soldiers, but rather had committed
crimes against humanity and merited international attention.

Meanwhile, as a result of all of the pressure in the media about the U.N.
files, including the fact that at least four British newspapers editorialized in favor of full access, the foreign secretary finally said that the British government
was ready to consider proposals for a change in the rules. It was a great victory
for Greville Janner and the others—or at least so they thought.

Back on the issue of Nazis living in Britain, on August 6, 1987, the home
secretary wrote Merlin Rees and confirmed that seven individuals from the
second list of thirty-four names had been identified as still alive and residing in
the United Kingdom. Now there was a combined total from both lists of sixteen identifiable and reachable former Nazis living peacefully in the United
Kingdom. The tension was building.

Throughout the fall of 1987, there were repeated hints in London that the
British government was getting ready for a major change in its position with respect to Nazi war criminals. Perhaps there would really be an aggressive investigation, possibly prosecution, and even a necessary change in the law. On February 8, 1988, the British home secretary announced in the House of
Commons that the British government had established an inquiry team to investigate the issue of Nazi war criminals.

The announcement was overdue. The British had dragged their feet during
World War II in accepting the reality of the Final Solution despite evidence.
They had dragged their feet after World War II as the U.N. commission set
about gathering information on Nazi criminals. They had, perhaps most seriously, dragged their feet in 1987, when they already had much of the information that in 1988 finally pushed the British government to move ahead.

It was the constant lobbying of Jewish and other members of Parliament and
the incredible press attention given to the Waldheim case that forced the
change from the official foot-dragging.

On February 14, 1988, *The Sunday Express* of London reported, and the
world took note, that the British investigation of former Nazi war criminals liv-

ing in Britain was going to become a major inquiry and evidence would be collected from all over the world. Each of the sixteen identifiable men were contacted and each denied the allegations. Most claimed that the Simon Wiesenthal Center, the British authorities, and the Americans had been fooled by a communist plot to discredit anti-communist leaders who had immigrated to the West. The injunctions secured, as we have seen in chapter 5, by several of the accused effectively prevented media identification of their names.

The investigation into the backgrounds of these former Nazi war criminals has turned into a worldwide inquiry. British authorities are now dealing with the Russians to examine evidence firsthand. As a result of the pressure from *The Sunday Express*, the World Jewish Congress, the Simon Wiesenthal Center, and, perhaps, to a degree, from our nagging phone calls, the Home Office has really put some muscle into their campaign to find out which former Nazis are living in London, while simultaneously dealing with changes in their rules to make prosecutions possible in the UK.

Home Secretary Douglas Hurd has promised members of Parliament that he would be prepared to seek suspects who can be brought to trial in the UK if there is sufficient evidence.

Most of the known Nazis living in Britain are Latvians, who have settled quietly into the British way of life. Some are still working. The evidence that exists has, admittedly, been drawn up by avid anti-Nazis, but there has been sufficient cross-collaboration to name names and to move forward with the British government's investigation. The inquiry is now headed by Sir Thomas Hetherington (see below) who is in touch with the U.S. Justice Department in reviewing evidence and is dealing with the Soviet Union and Israel in seeking further evidence and witnesses with respect to those accused Nazis.

Among the moves in Parliament to change British laws, the easiest and most-supported proposal seems to be a law that would enable the British government to try in Britain those alleged war criminals who committed crimes against humanity. Another has explored a widening of the extradition treaty agreements to which Britain is a party. There is no treaty covering crimes of this nature between Britain and the Soviet Union, but it is thought that with her emerging international leadership role, and Mrs. Thatcher's ability to deal with Gorbachev effectively, the time might be right for such a treaty.

Because many of the offenses committed by accused Nazis living in England would come under the jurisdiction of the Soviet Union, extradition to that country could then result in prosecution.

There is a minority feeling in the British Parliament that an international court could be set up to deal with those cases where any one nation does not have true jurisdiction. It's not a question of reopening the Nuremberg trials, but rather of seeing whether a forum could be established through the United

Nations, as once suggested by the Israeli, to deal with just such cases.

An advertisement detailing the British inquiry appeared in newspapers throughout the United Kingdom in March 1988. It asked from anyone with information about a suspected Nazi to send it to the board. The inquiry board expects to report to the British government during the first few months of 1989. First, they will confer with American, Canadian, Australian, and even Soviet officials on available evidence about accused Nazis living in Great Britain.

Some in Parliament are hopeful but dubious. Even members of Thatcher's Conservative Party fear that the inquiry will provide an academic exercise, but, in the end, will rubber-stamp the lack of need for action. In other words, it will conclude that there is just not enough hard evidence to do anything.

On March 10, 1988, the Right Honourable Peter Archer rose in Parliament to introduce a proposed change in the criminal law of England. Under the Archer proposal, set forth on behalf of the All-Party War Crimes Group, the Criminal Justice Bill would be amended to broaden the possibility of prosecutions. If the bill had succeeded, and it would have become possible for those living in Great Britain now, regardless of their original citizenship, to be tried for murder, manslaughter, genocide, or torture. But it was not enacted.

The bill was referred to the committee studying revisions to the criminal code, but without government support it had no chance. The Thatcher government did not want to oppose the bill publicly. Instead, the government sent word that it was premature in view of the inquiry and urged that it be left alone until 1989, when the inquiry board finished and it could be determined whether prosecutions were warranted. After a very emotional debate in late March, the government prevailed.

The government has decided to adopt international-treaty references to torture to prosecute those in the UK accused of that inhumane act. But the government elected to restrict application to torture carried out in recent times. Some who oppose a change in the British law argue that "extraterritoriality," or the prosecution of persons who committed serious crimes outside the United Kingdom, is offensive. They are ill informed. The position of extraterritorial jurisdiction in British criminal matters and in international law is clearly established. With respect to murder, it has long been an option within the law. Many lawmakers find it repugnant to make any law retroactive. But the very nature of the conduct to be punished is so unconscionable that the need should outweigh the hesitance, in the view of Archer and many other British lawmakers. They point out that since the crimes involved were violations of basic international law anyway, the proposed changes in British law are merely procedural. No one has suggested making unlawful what was lawful at that time.

British authorities are well aware that Canada has already acted in this area and that the idea is also getting support in Australia.

West Germany—A Mixed Record

The one nation that is key to the process of bringing former Nazi war criminals to justice is West Germany. As part of the proceedings that set up the Nuremberg Tribunal, German federal and state courts were given jurisdiction to try "lesser" war criminals. Until 1949 that jurisdiction was limited to crimes that had been committed against German nationals and "stateless" people—and not against citizens of the other Allied nations. But since 1949 the jurisdiction has been expanded to include all war crimes, and the German national and state courts are now theoretically the primary place to which one seeking justice for war criminals must turn.

However, West Germany has a very complex legal system, and, as a nation, adheres more strictly than most to the letter of its laws. And it is Germany's legal system that, for all intents and purposes, has held it back it from assuming a leadership role in the ongoing attempt to make war criminals face up to and pay for their deeds.

Remember again Bohdan Koziy, the Ukrainian policeman in whose denaturalization proceedings four American courts found that there was overwhelming evidence that he had murdered civilians, including the child Monica Zinger. When the U.S. State Department requested that Germany extradite Koziy to stand trial for murder, as the Nuremberg process had envisioned, Germany declined because it did not believe he could be charged under German law. The reasoning is mind-boggling.

After carefully reviewing the findings of the American courts, and the underlying evidence, the Germans agreed completely with the conclusions reached by Judge Paine in the trial and affirmed by the Court of Appeals.

As stated in the official German reply to the extradition request by the U.S.: "According to the testimony of several eyewitnesses whose statements are in agreement, in the autumn of 1943 Koziy, by his own hand, shot to death a four-year-old girl in the yard of the police station at Lisets. The eyewitnesses further have accused him, around the same time, of having participated, together with a German policeman, in the shooting to death of several members of a

Jewish family, again in the courtyard of the Lisets police station. . . . In view of the very precise testimony by the witnesses, which is in agreement in all major points, there is no doubt as to Koziy's participation in the two aforementioned shooting incidents." But, said the German foreign ministry, "the witnesses' statements do not make any reference . . . [as] to what motives may have formed the basis for his actions. They are limited to this extent to solely their optical and acoustical impressions gained during the process of the shootings as such." In effect, because the United States could not offer proof as to why Koziy did what he did, they could not prosecute him for his crimes, although they agreed he was completely guilty as charged.

The crux of the problem is exactly how Germany defines the crime of "murder." Under the strict statute-of-limitations provisions of German law, no crimes committed during the war years could be prosecuted after January 1, 1980. But under intense pressure from the United States, Britain, Israel, and world Jewish organizations, on July 3, 1979, the West German *Bundestag* (legislature) abolished the statute of limitations for the crimes of murder and genocide. Even so, "murder" under German law is not the same as murder under U.S. or British law.

Black's Law Dictionary, the standard work in the United States on legal definitions, defines murder as "the unlawful killing of a human being by another with malice aforethought either expressed or implied." But under German law, the same set of circumstances might give rise to a charge that translates into English as "manslaughter" (but is not exactly the same as the American crime of manslaughter, which is defined as "the unlawful killing of another without malice") or "accessory to murder."

Lest you jump to the conclusion that putting a gun to the head of a four-year-old girl, listening to her cries for mercy, and then pulling the trigger constitutes murder in West Germany, the foreign ministry quickly pointed out that under the definitions contained in German statutes "the killings with which Koziy is charged . . . can be ascribed the weight as crimes of manslaughter or accessory to murder" in the absence of conclusive evidence as to why he did what he did, or what he was thinking when he did it. Under German law, what distinguishes murder from manslaughter or accessory to murder is the presence of "cruelty, iniquity, lust for murder, and base motives."

Again, lest any reader assume that putting a gun to a four-year-old's head and pulling the trigger is a "cruel" act, the foreign ministry quickly pointed out that "Cruelty, according to Section 211 of the Legal Code, would exist only if the perpetrator, beyond the purpose of executing the killings, had imposed special pain or torture on the victims out of a mentality entirely devoid of feeling or mercy. The available evidence does not prove any basis for such an assumption."

In other words, since the United States did not present any irrefutable evidence as to what Koziy was thinking when he pulled the trigger on Monica Zinger, he might have been sorry for what he was doing. In the absence of eyewitness testimony that he laughed while he did it, or that he first shot her in the kneecaps to inflict pain before killing her, the United States had made no showing that "cruelty," as defined under German law, was involved.

Should you think the foreign ministry had to stand logic on its ear to reach the conclusion that cruelty was not proved in Koziy's acts, they had to make even a greater stretch to find that neither "iniquity" nor "base motives," as defined by German law, were present. Under German law "treacherous iniquity" can be said to be present if it can be assumed that the perpetrator "exploited the lack of suspicion or inability of his victims to put up a defense." The document states that "the fact that one of the victims was a four-year-old child in itself does not suffice to establish a determination of underhanded killing according to Section 211 of the Legal Code." Obviously, the Germans concluded that the evidence failed to establish that Koziy wasn't afraid that four-year-old Monica might reach up and yank the gun out of his hands and beat him over the head with it.

As for "base motives," that could be proved only if Koziy killed Jews because he didn't like Jews: simply killing them did not prove he had any hatred for them. Further, they pointed out, Koziy himself had said often at his trial that he had no dislike for Jews, and no specific evidence had been introduced to refute this. "Even though his statements appear to be refuted by the testimony of the eyewitnesses, the witnesses apparently could not offer any concrete evidence leading to any conclusion as to the motive for the crime," said the official German statement.

Finally, they fell back on the old standby that he might have been just following orders. "Above all, they [the witnesses] were unable to testify as to who made the decisions to carry out the shootings, i.e., whether Koziy carried them out with or without orders from a superior. Even if Koziy was aware that he was being ordered to commit these murders by a superior who did possess base motives, that base motive cannot be ascribed to him under Section 50 of the German Legal Code."

Taking all this into consideration, said the German foreign ministry, "it does not appear likely that a warrant of arrest will be issued against Koziy in the German Federal Republic ... [nor that] any district attorney's office will charge him with murder." Thus it would not request his extradition.

Notwithstanding Germany's problems in trying accused war criminals, U.S. prosecutors were frankly stunned by the German reply to their request for prosecution of Koziy. They had made the request in the belief that the Koziy case was about as strong a case as they would ever have, short of another Eichmann, a Mengele, or some other mass murderer. What the German decision in the Koziy case meant was that almost every war criminal they would ever strip of citizenship or deport would probably be able to find refuge in West Germany without fear of facing trial. Seven former Nazis who had either been stripped of their U.S. citizenship or who surrendered it rather than face accusations in open court, had already returned to Germany. None had been prosecuted, and none faced the possibility of prosecution. It was a truly disheartening moment for many in the Office of Special Investigations.

As one top prosecutor puts it, "They [the West Germans] are our friends, and the State Department frowns on anything negative we have to say about them. And we have to work closely with them quite often in developing information on cases and in running investigations, and they have been and continue to be very helpful in that area. But you simply have to believe they will go to almost any length to avoid directly prosecuting a new war criminal. They desperately want to put all this behind them, and every time they prosecute it opens old wounds. You have to believe they have all but designed their legal system to avoid the problem."

All this is not to say that substantial numbers of former Nazis have not faced trial in Germany since the end of the war. According to statistics—and the West German government does keep meticulous records—91,160 suspected war criminals have been investigated by German authorities since the end of World War II. Of these actually brought to trial, 6,482 were convicted. Of these, 12 were sentenced to death, 160 to life imprisonment, and the rest to lesser punishment. The average sentence has been eight years and the actual time served has averaged less than four years.

However, as mentioned earlier, 75 percent of these trials resulted from indictments brought while the German courts were actually under Allied occupation control (1945-1949). Even when you look at these 5,228 pre-1950 indictments, only 100 were for serious crimes involving manslaughter or murder, and only 15 involved murders in concentration camps. Most were trials held en mass in denazification courts; very few of those convicted in a German court remain imprisoned.*

Many more were not prosecuted at all, including tens of thousands of cases involving SS men. They could have been prosecuted by West Germany. For example, there is the annoying case of August Heissmeyer, an SS general and an intimate associate of Himmler. After a great deal of pressure, he was finally prosecuted, but charged only with "giving a false name." Rather than going to

---

* Looking at this record, Karl Erlebeck, head of the German-based Association of Victims of Nazi Persecutions, says, "We think it is scandalous. It just points up an extraordinarily indifferent attitude toward old Nazis."

jail, he spent the rest of his postwar years as the West German director of a Coca-Cola subsidiary.

It may well take a followup book to deal with the bizarre events surrounding efforts to prosecute top German business leaders for war crimes. If the Paperclip Conspiracy focused on scientists who could help in the Cold War, there was a counterpart "copy machine" conspiracy in which thousands of industrialists personally involved on many levels with crimes against humanity were left alone to enjoy wealth and power in West Germany.

For example, in March 1964, West Germany honored Heinrich Butefisch, head of a chemical conglomerate. President Heinrich Lubke gave him the country's highest civilian award, the *Grosses Bundesverdientkreuz.* Incontrovertible evidence shows that, during World War II, President Lubke had designed concentration camps and had been an organizer of slave labor for the Buchenwald camp, where facilities were established to produce the V-rockets that killed British civilians and others. And the honoree, Butefisch, had been a senior manager of I.G. Farben (the key company in the German military-industrial complex) and had been convicted at Nuremberg for his part in Farben's Auschwitz project.

West Germany also has a very complex national psyche. On the one hand, it carries to this day a deep sense of shame for what was done in the name of Adolf Hitler. But perhaps more than any other nation—for obvious reasons— it would just as soon forget the past. The whole subject of Nazi war trials in Germany is today caught up in a growing debate, or rather debates, over how Germany should view its Nazi past. A significant segment of German society, primarily those old enough to have lived through the period, believes that Nazism is something that must be faced every day until the last vestige of it disappears from the earth. This group favors an aggressive approach to trying accused war criminals. But another sizable segment of German society, primarily younger people, believes it is time for the nation to move on, to bury the past. This view is called *Schlusstrich,* or, literally, drawing a bottom line on the past and closing the books on the Third Reich. This view is growing in strength, and among its proponents are Chancellor Helmut Kohl, whose conservative Christian Democrats toppled the leftist Social Democrats in 1982.

The dispute over whether to close the books on Nazism for the good of the present generation must be distinguished from another debate taking place in German society—a debate that is far more vicious and has a much greater potential for radically realtering German society.

The bitter, open debate, marked by charges that some prominent historians are trying to tone down the horror of Nazi atrocities, is capturing the attention of West Germans. The controversy has been the topic of a best-selling book and numerous newspaper articles and TV broadcasts. Known as the "Historians' Dispute," it has split prominent professors into feuding camps.

A small but growing number of right-wing German revisionist historians such as Andreas Hillgruber, of the University of Cologne, and Ernst Nolte of Berlin, are calling for a new perspective on the Third Reich and German identity forty-three years after World War II. Nolte and his supporters tend to compare what happened under Hitler to atrocities carried out by other governments, such as the deaths of millions in the Soviet Union under Stalin, or of the millions of Germans who fell victim to the advancing Soviet troops. They believe the Soviets are at least as guilty of a "holocaust" as the Nazis. Nolte also compares Nazi atrocities with those of Cambodia's Pol Pot regime in the 1970s. Some of the revisionists go even further, equating the U.S. act of dropping the atom bomb on Japan with the Holocaust.

Nolte sparked the historians' dispute with an essay called "The Past That Won't Go Away," published in the conservative newspaper *Frankfurter Allgemeine Zeitung* in June 1986. He suggested that Stalin's infamous forced labor camps and the communists' murder of millions of peasants were in a sense forerunners of Auschwitz and Hitler's genocide program. "Wasn't the Bolsheviks' 'class murder' the logical and actual precursor of the National Socialists' 'racial murder'?" Nolte asked in the essay. Nolte and his supporters claim that their arguments raise valid questions in historical interpretation. "Those who want to make the Nazis' mass murder stand alone by forbidding every comparison with other events are guilty of having an incredibly unhistorical attitude," Nolte told a newspaper reporter recently.

But the opponents of this movement toward revisionist history, led by Frankfurt University philosophy professor Juergen Habermas, say that the conservative historians use such comparisons to try to lessen the magnitude of Nazi crimes. Habermas, one of West Germany's best-known intellectuals, also says that his opponents are paving the way for nationalistic impulses.

Nolte's opponents have frequently called his phrasing unclear and open to many interpretations. His critics accuse him of trying to justify Hitler's motives for attacking the Soviet Union by arguing that the dictator was responding primarily to the Soviets' goal of spreading communism. "To Nolte, Hitler is a European citizen who was historically in the right in that he unwillingly went to war for democracy," the Bayerischen Rundfunk television show "Lesezeichen" said in reviewing Nolte's new book.

Habermas, in a newspaper essay, charged several conservative historians with rewriting history to justify and minimize the Nazi regime's crimes. The article appeared in the Hamburg-based weekly *Die Zeit* in July 1986. The Nazi crimes "lose their singularity" in Nolte's arguments, Habermas wrote. Many historians hold that the Nazi genocide cannot be compared validly with other atrocities. "Never before had a state, with the authority of its responsible leader, decided and announced it would completely kill off a specific group of people" and put the plan into action, wrote historian Eberhard Jaeckel of Stuttgart University in a 1986 essay in response to conservative arguments.

However, the debate has moved far beyond academic circles. A book documenting the dispute made the best-seller list, and new arguments regularly make headlines in leading newspapers. It is also tending to lap over into the *Schlusstrich* debate on whether a curtain shouldn't simply be drawn on the past.

Some German intellectuals say that too much dwelling on the Nazi past could cause West Germans today, particularly younger ones, to resent what they may see as a steady stream of accusation. "Many Germans today are at least one generation removed from the Nazi period," Professor Christian Meier of the University of Munich recently told the Associated Press. "But the [West] Germans are constantly being reminded of past actions. If it goes too far, it could even provoke a counter-reaction."

Those Germans who want to draw the bottom line on their Nazi past saw Ronald Reagan's trip to the Bitburg cemetery, where forty-seven SS soldiers are buried, as an affirmation of support in Washington for their movement. That visit seemed to stir up memories of Christian indifference to the Holocaust and lend support to those who were arguing that the hunt for Nazis should not continue.

The Bitburg scenario began when West German Chancellor Helmut Kohl invited Reagan to add a visit to Germany to his itinerary for an economic summit meeting. The occasion would mark the fortieth anniversary of Nazi Germany's surrender to the Allies at the end of World War II. Kohl, for political reasons, was anxious to demonstrate U.S.-German reconciliation.

Originally, Kohl suggested that the ceremonies include visits to both a concentration camp and a military cemetery. For some reason, an aide to President Reagan—perhaps only to save time—arranged that he would not visit the concentration camp, but only the cemetery. On May 21 at a press conference, the president was asked about it, and he said that the German people have "a guilt feeling that is imposed upon them and I think it's unnecessary." He said that visiting a concentration camp site would only "reawaken" painful memories.

When it was announced on April 11 that President Reagan would, in fact, visit the Bitburg cemetery and the discovery was made that among the 2,000 German soldiers buried there were 47 members of the notorious Waffen SS, there was an uproar all over the United States and in Jewish communities around the world.

But it was not only Jewish leaders who were telephoning and wiring the president and, in some cases, calling congressmen to ask for their support in getting Reagan to cancel the proposed trip. It was not only those devoted to the ongoing Nazi hunt who were concerned that this gesture by the president would undermine the work of the Office of Special Investigations in ferreting out Nazis in the United States, and the international movement to find the remaining ringleaders as well.

The American Legion, the National Council of Churches, and the National Association for the Advancement of Colored People (NAACP) were among the groups who voiced protests, and individuals ranging from former president Jimmy Carter to Archbishop John J. O'Connor of New York joined in opposing the Reagan trip.

The President met with a delegation of Jewish leaders and announced that he would still go to the cemetery, but he was also going to visit a concentration campsite. The critics were not satisfied.

"A courtesy call at a conveniently located concentration camp cannot compensate for the callous and obscene scandal of honoring dead Nazis," Dr. Norman Lamm, President of Yeshiva University, told 5,000 delegates to a Holocaust memorial service the following day. The United States Senate sent a letter to the president "strongly urging" him not to visit the cemetery. Members of the U.S. Holocaust Memorial Council, who are presidential appointees, discussed a mass resignation.

Matters got worse when the President described those who were buried at Bitburg as "victims of Nazism also." Some said it was an oblique suggestion that Hitler's soldiers should be thought of in the same way as those innocent Jews they had executed in the gas chambers.

The following day, Elie Wiesel received the Congressional Gold Medal of Achievement and chose the occasion to urge the president to cancel the Bitburg visit. He said to the president and to the world, "Your place is with the victims of the SS." But acting on the advice of those around him, President Reagan—who had always been a staunch supporter of Israel and of Jewish causes, appeared unmoved. He told the press that the cemetery visit was "morally right." Reagan's press aides went to great lengths to assure all who asked that the visit in no way meant a change in policy for the United States with respect to the operation of the Office of Special Investigation in the hunt for Nazi war criminals.

Just before the president departed, having said that he was going to Germany to affirm the "miracle" of postwar reconciliation, not to pay tribute to Nazis, Congress passed resolutions asking him to change his timetable and cancel Bitburg. The Senate voted for the resolution by voice, and in the House of Representatives irrespective of party affiliations, the resolution was passed by a vote of 390-26. But Reagan's trip went ahead, and at both Bergen-Belsen and Bitburg, the president of the United States delivered, as only he can, the most sensitive of all remarks. He aimed his comments specifically at survivors of the Holocaust and the relatives of those who did not survive when he said, "Many of you are worried that reconciliation means forgetting. But I promise you we will never forget."

Even as we were completing the editing of this book in March 1988, there was a significant development in Geneva, Switzerland, where the Human Rights Commission of the United Nations was meeting. A debate and a confrontation took place that showed clearly a major shift in the policy of the Federal Republic of Germany in regard to the hunt for Nazi war criminals and the involvement of Chancellor Kohl. While opinions differ as to whether or not the Kohl government made a diplomatic error in urging President Reagan to go to Bitburg, there was still hope that the West German policy would encourage the prosecution of Nazis in their country. But the bizarre and discomfiting crisis in Geneva makes it very clear that West Germany, under Kohl, is no longer inclined to recognize the need for a hunt, let alone to assist in any way.

These perturbing developments occurred at the forty-fourth session of the United Nations Commission on Human Rights, where West Germany made clear the change in its attitude toward the Holocaust and public references to Nazi war crimes. The West Germans opposed a resolution which was, in fact, adopted on March 8, 1988, entitled "Prosecution and Punishment of All War Criminals and Persons Who Have Committed Crimes Against Humanity." That resolution was presented by the United States without a co-sponsor.

None of the Western European countries present wanted to put their names to it because of Kohl's strong opposition. The text had been shared by the United States with the other delegates two weeks earlier and Kohl, himself, had spoken against it. He became so incensed at the proposed resolution that he contacted the State Department to register his country's complaint. Essentially, the resolution was a proposed reendorsement of a previous statement entitled "Detention and Punishment of War Criminals and Persons Guilty of Crimes Against Humanity." West German opposition was based on the belief that "The time has come to stop talking about Nazi war crimes." They had no objection to general comments about war crimes, but they did not want any reference to "Nazi" war crimes.

In a confidential memorandum from Jewish representatives attending the commission meeting, the West German opposition to the American proposal was described as "acrimonious and virulent." No fewer than three protests were filed with the State Department by the West German government. German representatives of the Human Rights Commission suggested that the resolution could compromise their support for another resolution proposed by the United States, concerning Cuba, that was due to be discussed. What amazed the American delegates, World Jewish Congress representatives, and journalists who attended was the intensity of the West German reaction.

After using every procedural stumbling block imaginable, the West Germans took advantage of the fact that they were holding the chair at the commission to manipulate the Belgian, Italian, French, and Irish delegations. But they failed. The United States was adamant, and it had assistance from the World Jewish Congress observers who were in attendance. The U.S.S.R. and other socialist states supported the proposal, and the African delegations did not oppose it. Passage of the resolution was a victory for the United States and Israel and a notice to the West Germans that if they are changing their policy with respect to "remembering" Nazi atrocities and dealing with them when they can, such a change would attract worldwide attention and criticism.

The resolution, dated March 4, 1988, condemned any attempt to deny the acts of genocide committed as a result of Nazi and fascist ideology and practices. The resolution went on to commend those nations who are providing fair trials and just punishment for important war criminals and singled out France for the prosecution of Klaus Barbie. It also commended the interest in the Nazi problem shown by numerous member states and pointed out that all the evidence indicated that a large number of those accused were still living peacefully in U.N. member nations. Finally, it urged all nations to take the necessary measures, in accordance with their national constitutional systems, to ensure full international cooperation for "the purpose of securing, preferably in the place where they committed their deed, the prosecution and just punishment of all those who had committed war crimes and crimes against humanity."

It was a shove, not a push, at those countries whose procedural limitations prevented the prosecution of Nazis known to be living within their borders.

Given this combination of a complex legal system and a growing national desire to close the books on the past, what is the prospect for continued prosecutions of war criminals in West Germany?

West Germany's Office for Nazi War Crimes Investigations is headquartered in the southern German city of Ludwigsburg and headed by chief prosecutor Alfred Streim, an experienced and dedicated Nazi hunter. In the spring of 1988, Streim told us that his office has open files on 1,164 individuals suspected of Nazi war crimes. After the U.N. files were opened in 1987, West German investigators were able to compile a list of 18,000 names of potential war criminals who might still be alive and subject to German jurisdiction, many because they are German, are possibly living in Germany, or because their alleged crimes were committed there.

The original list of 18,000 was quickly whittled down to 4,500, after eliminating the considerable number who had either been convicted or acquitted in previous trials or who had died. That number has now been further reduced to 1,164 persons.

Streim is sure that some prosecutions will result from these open files, but he says it is difficult to obtain eyewitnesses and evidence. We heard this argument often from West German officials and prosecutors. They used an unfounded excuse that the documents necessary for aggressive searches and effective prosecutions have been beyond their reach—that for the past forty years, they have been unable to get access to the enormous quantity of evidence seized by the Eastern European countries. They also allege that the Berlin Document Center* is under American and not German control.

But many observers, especially in the world Jewish community, believe that the West German government has been reluctant to ask for documents because the lack of evidence provides a convenient excuse for failing to prosecute. In fact, staff members of the Berlin Document Center told us that they are eager to support the Bonn government when and if it prosecutes and that the Germans have not availed themselves of the evidence there.

It is true that during the Cold War, Eastern European archives were frozen,

---

* One of the most important resources in the ongoing hunt for Nazi war criminals is the State Department-run Berlin Document Center (BDC). It holds a unique and extensive collection of files and other materials relevant to the Holocaust and to the operations of the Nazis prior to and during World War II.

The BDC opened in April 1946 to handle worldwide requests for accurate information about the Nazi Party and is the principal depository for captured German documents. The material is divided into two basic libraries, biographic and nonbiographic. Most of the nonbiographic material has been turned over as of 1988 to the German government and placed in the *Bundesarchiv Koblenz*. But the comprehensive biographical material on war criminals, consisting of 28 separate collections, is still in the active archive of the BDC. The archive houses the official files of the Nazi Party and its spin-off organizations during the Third Reich. When Allied troops located these materials, as they conquered Germany, they recognized this importance to history—and as a guideline to prevent future tragedies. Today, the BDC furnishes information from its files to Western governments and assists individual researchers.

The master file consists of 10,704,000 index cards maintained at Nazi Party headquarters in Munich. They identify more than 10 million members of the Nazi Party and reflect their dates of involvement and their particular service. Some 600,000 applications for Nazi Party membership include backgrounds on the applicants. And there are hundreds of thousands of other files reflecting disciplinary action taken by the Party against violators of its rules and general information on Nazi activities. Perhaps one of the most fascinating rooms at the BDC is a library of books from the Nazi era on the philosophy behind the Holocaust and the scope of Hitler's lust for conquest. Records of the German government contain information about German nationals who left Germany and returned there during the Nazi regime.

There are two-and-a-half million files from the central immigration office *(Litzmannstadt)* with detailed information on individuals of ethnic German origin who came into Germany on a large-scale program during World War II. Finally, 185,000 files from the Reich Chamber of Culture detail organizations and their memberships under Nazi rule.

By its sheer size, the Berlin Document Center is an instant reminder that while there may have been a handful at the top, there was a broad base of support for the Holocaust, for Hitler and his grand design, and for the war itself.

and the West Germans were among those who could not gain access. However, documents seized by the United States have been available ever since World War II to German prosecutors proceeding on Nazi cases. Until 1958, on specific orders from senior government officials, German prosecutors did not ask for help. It's understandable when you consider that so many of the senior governmental, judiciary, civil service, and police officials in Germany during the 1950s were former Nazis.

Nuremberg prosecutor Robert Knepner confirmed that after those trials the prosecution turned over most of its evidence to representatives of the German government. "Thousands of files were handed over. Documents with the signatures of the criminals; complete proof in many cases showing very clearly the responsibility of those criminals, their orders for murder, giving green lights to other agencies to murder—for example, from the foreign office to an agency for deportation." Asked what the Germans had done with all that material, Knepner replied, "they put them in good order, in their filing cabinets."

If West Germany thought it was unable to prosecute Bodhan Koziy because it could not be sure of his motives in killing a four-year-old Jewish child, how, then, to evaluate prosecutor Streim's assurance that many former Nazis will still face prosecution in German courts? If not Koziy—who? In answer, Streim and others point to the January 1988 conviction of Gottfried Weise, sixty-six, a former SS guard at Auschwitz.

A district court in Wuppert found Weise guilty of five counts of murder with malice and sentenced him to life imprisonment. Witnesses testified that on two separate occasions Weise killed young inmates—an eight-year-old boy and a seventeen-year-old girl, after forcing them to place tin cans on their heads so he could practice target-shooting. Effectively, he killed them when he missed. He was also found guilty of killing two male prisoners who tried to escape from the camp by hiding on a supply truck and another prisoner who did not report quickly enough for an inmate head-count.

Presiding Judge Wilfried Klein, in summing up the case, said that Weise had used his victims "as toys to satisfy his own moods. Before Weise killed his victims, he subjected them to inhuman physical and mental torture." Observers of German Nazi war crimes trials said that Weise might have escaped prosecution had it not been shown that he had used the children for target practice. It is worth noting that the evidence against Weise was so overwhelming that most courts could have tried him in a matter of days. The actual Weise trial took fifteen months.*

German prosecutors and officials would have one believe that the Weise

---

* As this book is written, Weise remains free on a low bail while he appeals his case. More cynical observers in Germany believe he has a good chance of winning a reversal.

case represents the kind of results that will be forthcoming from the German courts. But many in Germany—those with a much more pessimistic outlook—say that the case of Friedrich Paulus may forecast the future more accurately. There is no dispute about the fact that Friedrich Paulus is about as evil a Nazi as ever donned an SS officer's uniform. A former Waffen SS captain, he is accused of personally participating in the mass execution of 161 civilians near the Polish village of Lublin in 1940. The massacre was meant to be a lesson for Polish partisans and was carried out in retaliation for their alleged murder of a German. Paulus led the company that rounded up the hostages, and he helped organize and carry out the executions.

Paulus first went on trial for the 161 murders in Hamburg in 1971 and was acquitted under the statute of limitations then in effect. But West Germany's Supreme Court reversed the ruling and ordered a new trial. Three more trials and appeals followed until Paulus was finally convicted in 1986. His sentence was a stern one: four years' imprisonment. The court decided to be "tough" despite the fact that in ruling on a previous appeal, the West German Supreme Court had decided that the suggested sentence was too harsh.

Paulus successfully appealed the 1986 conviction, and still another trial was ordered last year—his sixth. But now legal proceedings against Friedrich Paulus have ended. The Frankfurt state court, where he was ordered for retrial, dismissed all the charges, ruling that at age eighty-one Paulus is simply too old and sick to face any further proceedings. Court doctors testified that his health had deteriorated beyond the point where he could defend himself. Paulus, who was brought to court in a wheelchair, had lost a leg in the war. The court also ruled that the twenty-year duration of the proceeding violated the International Human Rights Convention.

The results of other recent West German war criminal trials is very mixed, at best. Many have resulted in acquittals—some, according to observers, because it is becoming more difficult to find eyewitnesses, and others because the jury could not find it in their hearts to jail very aged and frail defendants. The harshest sentence, life imprisonment, was meted out to former SS sergeant Karl Frenzel, seventy-four, for participating in the mass murder of Jews at the Sobibor extermination camp. It was his second trial; the first had resulted in a hung jury. But Frenzel's sentence was almost unique. More common was that given former Gestapo official Helmut George Krizons, sixty-eight, who was sentenced to three years in prison for complicity in the deportation and the ultimate murder of 15,000 Jews from various Polish ghettos. His trial and appeals had lasted six years.

In Dusseldorf, also after a retrial, former SS sergeant Heinz Wisener, sixty-eight, was sentenced to five years in prison as an accomplice in the murder of two prisoners at the Riga-Kaiserwald concentration camp. In the Waldshut-

Tiengen district court, former Nazi lieutenant Kurt Rahauser went to prison for three years for his personal participation in the murder of eight Lithuanian slave workers in April 1945. In Traunstein, Johann Honorner, sixty-eight, a former Russian auxiliary officer, was sentenced to three years for complicity in the murder of over 100 Jews in the Ukraine in 1942. In one extraordinary decision, former Nazi police officer Otto Siemers, seventy, was found guilty of involvement in the murders of about 1,000 Jews at the Lublin concentration camp in 1941. But the jury spared Siemers any punishment after witnesses for him testified that what was happening at the camp finally became too much for him and he left, saying that he was ashamed to be a German.

In a Hamburg courtroom in July 1987, despite eyewitness testimony to the contrary, former Gestapo official Harri Schulz, seventy, was acquitted after being charged with murdering seven Polish Jews. The same month, the trial of former SS Captain Modest Graf Korff, seventy-six, was adjourned indefinitely on procedural grounds while he was being charged with involvement in the murder of 70,000 French Jews. In Luneburg, also on procedural grounds, a new trial was ordered for former SS sergeant Horst Sir-Czerwinsky, sixty-two, charged with killing eight inmates at the Auschwitz subcamp of Lagischa.

In all of the above cases, evidence was obtained from the Berlin Center and in three of them, additional confirming evidence had been sent back to Germany from the United States by the Office of Special Investigations which had uncovered it.

West Germany is an important ally of the United States. Our interviews with politicians, journalists, and prosecutors convinced us that, for the most part, German officials are sincere in their desire to do what is right. In the opinion of most observers, the combination of paying reparations to Jews and others whose property was confiscated, paying monies to Israel, and prosecuting known Nazis comprises justice. How this program will be implemented and with what results is a matter of conjecture. As to whether West Germany is doing enough; that, in the final analysis, must be left to the court of last resort: public opinion.

The Private Hunters

International Nazi hunters, whether they are governmental bodies, sophisticated organizations, or simply dedicated individuals, disagree occasionally as to procedure and emphasis. Some have more tact and diplomacy than others. Some utilize the media, both as an effective vehicle for gathering information and, unfortunately, sometimes for boastfulness that can interfere with the hunt. Others work very quietly and nothing is heard or read about their exploits until a Nazi is found and his identity is confirmed.

The war-criminal-hunting agencies of the world's governments have the money, manpower, and muscle. But, with one glaring exception, they are accomplishing relatively little. Were it not for Neal Sher and previously Allan Ryan (of the U.S. Department of Justice's Office of Special Investigations), whose determination has produced so many successes, the record of official Nazi hunting in recent years would be dismal.

The private hunters, on the other hand, have the savvy, the spirit, and the single-mindedness that has resulted in unprecedented achievements. The private hunters have global volunteer networks of firsthand witnesses who trust them. In many cases the names of the hunters once appeared on the rolls of the death camps.

Some are well known and others you will meet here for the first time. Many are old enough to remember being forced to watch their families tortured and killed. Others learned about the Nazis sitting in a history class in the 1960s. Most are affiliated with large, dedicated organizations that must deal with the issues of anti-Semitism, the survival of Israel, and international prejudice before, during, and after the hunt. To their credit, nary a one limits his or her hunting or passion for justice to those instances wherein Jews were killed. They personify dedication and are also wily, clever detectives.

THE WORLD JEWISH CONGRESS

In 1936 Adolf Hitler, a former housepainter, arranged for 2,000 other painters to cover up the swastikas and anti-Jewish hate slogans that appeared on buildings and walls throughout Berlin. He had to. It wouldn't have been appropriate for the athletes of the world who were arriving in Berlin for the Olympics, and the scores of journalists who would accompany them, to see the real face of Nazism in Germany—at least, not yet.

As the Olympics were getting underway, in neighboring Switzerland 280 delegates, representing the Jews of 32 countries, were creating the World Jewish Congress. Preparatory steps had been taken as early as 1927, when a conference of 65 leading Jewish personalities from 13 nations, representing more than 40 Jewish organizations, had met in Zurich to set a framework within which to defend Jewish rights when and if the need should arise.

In 1931 the Seventeenth Zionist Congress, under the chairmanship of Dr. Stephen Wise, was asked to mobilize Jewish solidarity throughout the world against what was already perceived as the Nazi menace. In 1932 ninety-four delegates from seventeen countries, representing major Jewish organizations, convened in Geneva, and established the groundwork for doing what could be done to warn the world about the Nazis. By the time the second preparatory conference in Geneva in September 1933 ended, the Nazis were already in charge of Germany.

At the time, Dr. Wise said, "As a people we are not yet risen to a sense of collective responsibility and obligation in an hour of overwhelming peril." Wise was warning Jews around the world to be wary about deceiving themselves about the danger Hitler represented. Of course, history shows that he was right, and the danger was even worse than he or anyone else imagined.

In 1936, as the Congress was founded, the swastika had already cast an ominous shadow over much of Europe. It was this group of Jews who warned Jews and the world at large of the impending dangers of the Nazi Party in Europe.

The record of the World Jewish Congress during the war years in defending the rights of the Jewish people was impressive. It called for a boycott of the Berlin Olympics, which, while unsuccessful, did result in focusing media attention on what was behind the paint that Hitler had used to cover his hate messages. It was the year of Jesse Owens' victory, and Hitler could not bear to watch an American black athlete beat his German supermen. He insulted the Olympians and disgraced his nation by walking out.

Unquestionably, the most visible Jew-hater, next to Hitler himself, was Goga, the prime minister of Romania. In an early example of international political muscle, the World Jewish Congress went to the League of Nations and its appeal led to Goga's resignation.

It was up to the World Jewish Congress, five years before the United States entered World War II, to fight for the admission of Jewish refugees into still-neutral America. In London, at the same time, it was pressing the British government and the governments in exile resident there, to organize assistance for Jews in Germany.

France has been criticized, with justification in many cases, for its soft line on Nazism and for the level of cooperation that French fascists gave Hitler's troops when they occupied the country. But in 1940 the World Jewish Congress won a battle, in the form of a public promise from General Charles de Gaulle, that once France had been liberated, he would repudiate all of the Vichy measures that had been directed against the Jews.

In August 1942, the organization's Geneva representatives attempted to alert the world to Hitler's secret plan for the Final Solution. The World Jewish Congress would break the wall of silence about the Holocaust. Leaders of the British and American governments and their counterparts worldwide were dubious of the extent of the plan that the congress said Hitler was about to implement. It took mass demonstrations by the World Jewish Congress and repeated statements to the press to impel the Allies into the proclamation simultaneously issued in Washington, D.C., London, and Moscow that after the war was over retribution would be exacted from the Nazi killers (December 1942).

The World Jewish Congress continued its fight on behalf of the Jews of the world. It interceded with the Vatican in an effort to protect Jews in Roman Catholic Croatia and Slovakia. It assembled tens of thousands of food parcels to go to concentration camp inmates and sent tons of food and medicine to the Jewish communities in occupied Europe.

The congress initiated a concerted effort in 1943 to save 50,000 Bulgarian Jews, and partially succeeded. From France, Jewish children were brought to neutral Spain, Portugal, and Switzerland for safety. And congress efforts to focus media attention on Hitler's plans for the deportation of Turkish Jews from France helped prevent the plan's implementation.

In 1943 the World Jewish Congress obtained a license from the United States government to transmit funds to Europe to rescue and assist persecuted Jews. It was that program that led ultimately to the creation of the United States War Refugee Board.

In 1945, when World War II finally ended, the world rejoiced—the Nazis had been conquered, freedom was alive and well, and there would be a good life. World Jewry celebrated for a moment, but could not rejoice with the memory of six million of its people dead. The World Jewish Congress compiled the monstrous statistics on innocent victims and put together the most accurate facts about the devastating losses of lives and property. Then it devoted itself to assisting those who had survived.

As the war ended, tens of thousands of Jews who had been liberated by the Allies roamed through a bombed-out Europe in search of their families. In most cases, their homes were gone. Thousands of orphaned children aimlessly wandered the streets of a hundred cities.

Survivors who were released from concentration camps by Allied soldiers clamored for admission to Israel and it was willing to welcome them.

The United Nations established a relief agency that herded the Jews into displaced persons camps throughout the war zone. In the Soviet zone and throughout Eastern Europe, where Stalin ruled, Jewish survivors could not even be counted because of the restrictions he placed on access.

The world had not listened quickly enough to the warnings by the World Jewish Congress that the Nazis were implementing a Final Solution. Perhaps the world would now follow if it led the way with the work that had to be done. The congress' Committee for Overseas Aid collected a vast quantity of food, medical supplies, and clothing, for dispatch to Europe. The European Tracing Office established by the congress in London assisted no fewer than 125,000 persons in locating their missing relatives. To do the job more effectively, the congress set up branch offices in Czechoslovakia, Hungary, and Romania.

The Department of Culture and Education of the World Jewish Congress took charge of trying to recover the cultural treasures and archives of world Jewry that had been taken over by the Nazis as they conquered Europe. It printed new prayer books for distribution among survivors. And it pressured the Vatican constantly to assist in the recovery of Jewish children through Catholic agencies worldwide. Representatives participated in the first Landsberg War Crimes Trial and helped formulate the principles that would govern the Nuremberg trials.

To recover Jewish property which had been confiscated by the Nazis, the World Jewish Congress established the Jewish Restitution Successor Organization (JRSO) and a Jewish Trust Corporation. Finally, the Congress was instrumental in working with other key organizations throughout the world in establishing the International Refugee Organization.

When the leaders of Nazi Germany were placed in the dock at the Nuremberg trials, Dr. Jacob Robinson, director of the World Jewish Congress' Institute of Jewish Affairs, was a key advisor on Jewish affairs to the U.S. chief counsel. The congress had also assisted by providing the prosecution team with documentation and witnesses.

To ensure that the horrors of the Holocaust would not be or forgotten or forgiven, the World Jewish Congress set itself the difficult task of compelling the new Federal German Republic to make some kind of restitution for the horrible wrongs inflicted on the Jewish people by the Third Reich. This required the establishment of relationships that would permit the most sensitive negotiations.

Dr. Nathum Goldmann of the World Jewish Congress developed a working rapport with the then German chancellor, Dr. Konrad Adenauer. It was Goldmann who was the chief architect of the historic Luxembourg agreements of 1952 by which West Germany agreed to pay Jewish survivors for property losses and so gave millions in reparations to Israel. And the congress has tried to maintain a dialogue between Germans and Jews even while doing all in its power to bring war criminals to justice.

After Jacob Robinson had served as an advisor at Nuremberg, the World Jewish Congress lobbied for German legislation to declare the wearing of Nazi uniforms and the publication of Nazi material illegal in that country. As a result of that lobbying, the German government set up a central office to prosecute war criminals and formally invited the World Jewish Congress to help trace them.

The congress led the lobbying effort to persuade the German government to change statutory limitations within its criminal code that would have made it impossible to prosecute any of the crimes against humanity. In 1979 the German *Bundestag* abolished that statute of limitations.

The congress has been in the forefront of the hunt for Nazi war criminals. It was the painstakingly compiled list of fifty-nine suspected Nazis living in the United States, turned over to the Immigration and Naturalization Service in 1973 by the congress's Dr. Otto Karbach, that revitalized the American Nazi hunt. Throughout the 1980s, the congress has processed material that comes from volunteer sources throughout the world. Some of it has gone directly to the Office of Special Investigations in Washington, because it concerns the location of Nazis believed to be hiding in the United States. Other material has gone to the British, Canadian, and other governments.

Some alleged former Nazis were investigated directly by the World Jewish Congress, because of its concern that no accusations be made without proper documentation.

Staff members of the World Jewish Congress form a group, including both those who work quietly behind the scenes and those with international recognition. At a desk at the World Jewish Congress headquarters on Madison Avenue in New York is a woman who is now in her eighties—Bessy Pupko. She has received none of the tributes that have been heaped upon Edgar M. Bronfman, who has earned stature as a world leader through his leadership of the congress since 1980. Bessy has not held meetings with visiting heads of state anxious to receive the blessing of the World Jewish Congress for their activities in tracing down Nazis and in avoiding anti-Semitism. She did not accompany Israel Singer, the group's secretary-general, or Elan Steinberg, its executive director, to meetings at the United Nations or in Washington, D.C., to debate the latest crises facing world Jewry. Instead, Bessy works alone, sifting through her seemingly endless file boxes, filled with little cards that she has put together over forty years: the names and last known addresses of survivors of the Holocaust. As a result of her meticulous work, witnesses have been traced and found to appear at the trials of Nazis throughout the world.

Bessy has taken out small ads in Yiddish newspapers asking people to come forward to identify Nazis. She has spent hours on overseas calls, in many languages, trying to find someone who was somewhere at some precise time to be a witness in a pending case. If ever there was a dedicated Nazi hunter, it is Bessy Pupko, who will be at that desk with those cards as long as she is able.

At the beginning of this book, we pay tribute to Elan Steinberg, the "fists" of the World Jewish Congress. While that organization is blessed with incredibly talented leaders and workers, Steinberg must be singled out for his extraordinary role in the exposé of Kurt Waldheim and the ongoing fight to keep the world from forgetting who the Nazi war criminals are and what can be done about them.

Steinberg, a former college instructor and World Jewish Congress delegate at the United Nations, is one of those rare individuals who can get to anyone. Government officials, top journalists, controversial figures in the middle of important matters do not duck his calls. When there is a development in Israel or Vienna or Berlin or London or Washington, his is the phone that rings off the hook. It is a reporter from *The New York Times* or Reuters or the leading newspapers of a dozen countries wanting an explanation as to the impact. Periodically, you meet people of whom you think, "I'm glad he's on our side." Elan Steinberg is one of those people.

SIMON WIESENTHAL

Wiesenthal was invited to share a Sabbath dinner one Friday night at the home of a former concentration camp inmate, a man who had survived and come to the United States, and prospered over the years. He was now an extremely successful jewelry manufacturer and occupied a fancy home that was equipped with all the adult toys that reflect wealth. They gathered for dinner in the formal dining room, shared prayers and bread, and then, after dinner, the host asked, "Simon, if you had gone back to building houses, you'd be a millionaire. Why didn't you?"

Simon Wiesenthal smiled and thought for a moment, then answered quietly, "You're a religious man, and you believe in God and life after death. I believe, too. When we get to the other world and meet the millions of Jews who died in the camps and they ask us, 'What have you done?' everyone will have to answer. You will say, 'I became a jeweler.' Another will say, 'I built houses.' But I will say, 'I didn't forget you.' "

We first interviewed Simon Wiesenthal in Vienna in 1985. An Austrian policeman had to point out his Jewish Documentation Center, and show us the main-floor bell—there is no name plate because it has repeatedly been vandalized.

It is a three-room office packed with newspapers, books, and files. It's modst, cluttered, but you know instinctively that the man who works there knows where each single piece of paper is.

Wiesenthal has used the same armchair for more years than anyone can remember. On each side are huge stacks of books. A giant map on one wall pinpoints the location of each of the major Nazi death camps with the number of people who died in each scrawled by it. And there are awards—many awards—in the form of plaques and framed letters from nations and organizations around the world.

Wiesenthal showed us a document that originated with the World Union of National Socialists, a hate organization with headquarters just outside Washington, D.C., which has put a $40,000 price on Wiesenthal's life. Threats on his life by telephone and by mail are quite frequent. The Vienna Bomb Squad knows him well. In 1983, a bomb destroyed the front door of the little red-brick house in the middle-class Viennese suburb where he lives. The following year another bomb failed to go off in his office. This place, which is both his home and office, is protected by several security devices, and a policeman patrols regularly.

At the office, you can see the peephole to the corridor, and the video surveillance he has had to put in. But the policeman who is stationed just outside the office door takes frequent breaks, and even when on duty can usually be found deep in a newspaper or book. When Wiesenthal leaves, he drives himself in an old Peugeot, and he travels without any bodyguard. He is an unpretentious man and he appears to be gentle. But he does carry a gun. "If I worried about being shot, I would not be able to live. When my time comes, it comes. But I will protect myself," he told us, and has repeated it many times to journalists since.

Wiesenthal has indeed become a legend through his commitment. This small, balding man will not let go. He is the ultimate Nazi hunter. He wrote once that "forgiveness is a personal matter. You have the right to forgive what has been done to you personally. You do not have the right to forgive what has been done to others."

Simon Wiesenthal survived Nazi death camps. After he was released, he dedicated his life to documenting the crimes of the Holocaust and to hunting down the Nazi war criminals still at large. His explanation for his determination has not changed in the past twenty years. He said in 1968, and he told us in 1985 and 1987 that "when history looks back, I want people to know the Nazis were not able to kill eleven million people and get away with it."

If there is one man in the world today who is a symbol, a reminder of the past, and a warning for the future, it is Simon Wiesenthal. He founded the Jewish Documentation Center in Vienna immediately after World War II, and has operated independently, but, most often, with the cooperation of the governments of the United States, West Germany, Israel, and, occasionally, Austria. He has been personally responsible for ferreting out thousands of Nazi war criminals, including Adolf Eichmann, the man who ran Adolf Hitler's extermination plan; Franz Murer, "the Butcher of Wilno"; and Erich Rajakowitsch, who was responsible for the "death transports" in Holland.

He has written his memoirs, memorializing horror stories that are inspired by his hope that it will never happen again.

This extraordinary hunter was born on New Year's Eve in 1908 in what is today the Lvov Oblast in the Ukraine. Wiesenthal had applied to be educated in the Polytechnic Institute, and was turned down because there were rigid quotas on the number of Jewish students who could enter the better schools. He left for Prague and earned a degree in architectural engineering from the Technical University there in 1932.

At the beginning of World War II, when the Soviets occupied Lvov Oblast, there was a purge of the so-called bourgeois elements. Wiesenthal's stepfather was arrested and died in prison. His stepbrother was shot. Wiesenthal himself started a small business in Lvov but was forced to close it and take a menial job in a bedspring factory. At one point, threatened with deportation to Siberia, he bribed a local commissar and he, his wife, and his mother were able to survive.

In 1941 the Germans displaced the Russians in controlling the area. He narrowly escaped execution by the Nazis through the help of some Ukrainian former employees, but was arrested again because he was a Jew. Initially, he was sent to the Janowska concentration camp just outside Lvov. Then he and his wife were sent with a huge forced-labor unit to the Ostbahn works, a large railroad repair shop.

In 1942 the Nazis began to send orders to many command posts to implement the Final Solution. The plan to exterminate a whole people was the most terrifying news that could possibly reach any city. Throughout occupied Europe, Hitler's genocide program began. Even as British authorities dragged their feet in accepting the evidence coming to them from escapees, prisoners of war, and even government officials, Simon Wiesenthal's mother was sent to the Belzec death camp.

In September 1942, the key members of the U.S. State Department office who advised the president on Hitler's program of genocide were still skeptical of reports of the Holocaust. By that time, however, almost all of Wiesenthal's family and his wife's family were dead. A total of eighty-nine relatives of the Wiesenthals were killed in the Holocaust.

Wiesenthal met members of the Polish underground and gave them detailed charts of railroad junctions for use by saboteurs in disrupting Nazi transportation. In exchange, Wiesenthal obtained false papers for his blonde wife identifying her as a Pole named Irene Kowalska. She escaped from Poland in the autumn of 1942, lived in Warsaw for two years, and then worked as a forced laborer in the Rhineland. Her true identity was never discovered.

Wiesenthal escaped from the Ostbahn camp in October 1943, just a few weeks before the Nazis began "liquidating" all the inmates there. A combination of friendship, bribery, and luck enabled him to escape, but he was recaptured in June 1944 and sent back to the Janowska camp, where he faced certain death.

Simon Wiesenthal would have died in Janowska if his return there had not luckily coincided with the sudden collapse of the Nazi eastern front and the rapid advance of the Red Army. Ironically, Wiesenthal and some other survivors may have been kept alive by a Nazi unit afraid of being sent to another front. The SS guards at Janowska knew that if they had no prisoners, they would no longer be kept in the rear but would go into combat, probably against the advancing Red Army. To save themselves, they kept the last few inmates alive. There were 200 guards and so few prisoners that the Nazis increased their "responsibilities" by arresting the entire nearby village of Chelmiec. Janowska had been the home of 149,000 prisoners. When the guards finally fled west with their prisoners, thirty-four, including Wiesenthal, remained alive.

Most of the prisoners were half starved and exhausted from forced labor, and they died in the trek that ended at Mauthausen, in Upper Austria. There Wiesenthal met another inmate—the jeweler who later held the Sabbath dinner where Wiesenthal, now a free man and a Nazi hunter, would express his feelings so eloquently.

Wiesenthal barely survived Mauthausen.

On May 5, 1945, a U.S. Army armored unit liberated Mauthausen, and Wiesenthal, weighing less than 100 pounds, was found in a barracks filled with dead and dying prisoners. He survived more by force of will than medical attention. He had a mission. "I began gathering evidence on Nazi atrocities for the U.S. Army. I worked with the War Crimes section," Wiesenthal says.

When the war finally ended later that year, he did more work for the U.S. Army Counterintelligence Corps (CIC). He expressed himself well and had been through hell. He ended up heading the Jewish Central Committee of the United States Zone of Austria, a relief and welfare organization.

World War II was over but, for years to come, there would be many who never knew whether their families had lived or died. A few, though, were lucky or blessed. They found their loved ones. Simon Wiesenthal was reunited with his wife late in 1945.

Colonel James Carter, an officer of the unit that Wiesenthal worked with, says that "the evidence supplied by him was extremely important in the preparation for wartime trials." In 1947 the United Nations Wartime Commission turned over the files on Nazi war criminals to the United Nations for safekeeping. At that time, a policy decision was made by the Allies to allow the Nuremberg Trials to be the international tribunal that would try the most heinous of the captured Nazis. Simon Wiesenthal, with thirty other volunteers, opened the Jewish Historical Documentation Center in Linz, Austria, to assemble evidence for the trials that he hoped would take place. But after the riveting testimony on Nazi atrocities by Holocaust survivors and other victims, interest in the subject gave way to Cold War concerns. Also, the harsh truth was that many Nazis could be valuable to the West, so they were readily accepted, despite their Nazi past, in the United States, England, Canada, and elsewhere.

Wiesenthal's volunteers, lacking money and frustrated by the Allies' loss of interest in hunting down Nazi killers, drifted away. Wiesenthal continued alone. In 1954 he had to close the office in Linz and turn the files over to Israel for placement in the Yad Vashem archives.

Wiesenthal gave Israel everything but the dossier he had compiled on Adolf Eichmann. He continued his low-salaried welfare and relief program work; then he was asked to administer an occupational training school for Hungarian and other Iron Curtain-country refugees. At night and on weekends, Wiesenthal continued his hunt for the invisible Adolf Eichmann, who had disappeared instantly when the war ended. He admits readily that he was obsessed with finding Eichmann. He wore that obsession as a badge of honor.

Information came to him from a network of friends and well-wishers all over Europe. Friends had friends who knew relatives who had ideas and information. Wiesenthal became a living clearance center for facts that might help find Eichmann and the other hunted Nazi killers. He also worked closely with Israeli agents. Through their combined efforts, Adolf Eichmann was located in 1959 in Buenos Aires, Argentina.

Wiesenthal's success in locating Eichmann and the publicity of his trial brought new promises of support for the ongoing search for other Nazis still living in freedom. Encouraged by well-wishers in Israel and the United States, Wiesenthal reopened his Jewish Documentation Center, this time in Vienna, and he devoted himself exclusively to Nazi-hunting. High on his list of targets was a man named Karl Silberbauer. Silberbauer was the Gestapo officer who arrested Anne Frank, the fourteen-year-old Jewish girl who was murdered after hiding in a now-famous attic in Amsterdam with her family for two years.

The Anne Frank diary had been discredited by Nazi propagandists in Holland until Simon Wiesenthal actually located Silberbauer, who was serving as a police inspector in Austria. When finally confronted, Silberbauer confessed, "I arrested Anne Frank."

In October 1966, more than a dozen SS officers went on trial in Stuttgart, West Germany, for the killing of Jews in Lvov. Most of them had been located by Wiesenthal himself.

Then there was the case of Fritz Stangl, commandant of the Treblinka concentration camp in Poland. A network of Wiesenthal informants heard rumors that Stangl was in Argentina or Cuba. They were close, but wrong. Wiesenthal finally located Stangl in Brazil, and the pressure he exerted, plus worldwide publicity, resulted in Stangl's being remanded to West Germany for imprisonment in 1967.

Later that year, Wiesenthal came to the United States to be interviewed by the media and to address various groups about the Nazis he was hunting. The visit was also designed to shore up support for his center and to reinforce American members of his network. When he arrived in the United States, he boldly announced that Mrs. Hermine Ryan, a New York housewife, was actually a woman named Braunsteiner. According to Wiesenthal, she had supervised the murder of several hundred children during the war. As we have seen in Chapter 5, Wiesenthal made his case to the authorities and she was extradited to West Germany for trial in 1973.

Despite the glamorization in such films as *The Boys from Brazil* starring Gregory Peck and others, Simon Wiesenthal does not himself track down each fugitive. His task is to gather and analyze evidence. His vast informal network consists of Jews and non-Jews, many of whom are friends and colleagues; others are simply sympathizers whom he has never met. Many German Army World War II veterans are also voluntary sources of information for Wiesenthal. They, too, were appalled at the horrors they witnessed during the liberation. Wiesenthal says that on occasion he also gets tips from former Nazis who may have been involved in crimes against humanity themselves, but who suffer feelings of guilt or hold a grudge against other former Nazis.

Wiesenthal's methods are simple. He combs every available document in detail and then cross-references repeatedly. He reads the personal accounts of survivors and compares them, painstakingly, until a pattern emerges and he can put together sufficient information for action against a Nazi war criminal.

Wiesenthal has been described as having the thoroughness of a great scholar with the investigative mind of a good cop. He admits that he is happiest when he finds some obscure or apparently irrelevant piece of information and puts it together with other incomplete facts to build a case. Authorities know that when Simon Wiesenthal brings them a case, it is generally solid. OSI's director, Neal Sher, says that "Wiesenthal has an incredible track record and he has been able to accomplish alone more than most governments have been able to do with all of their resources." Simon Wiesenthal has a secret weapon: it is his complete dedication to the cause of hunting Nazis.

Journalists throughout the world are always anxious to hear what he has to say. And that, too, becomes a weapon against those governments who, for whatever reason, hesitate to take action when a Nazi is located in their midst.

When Wiesenthal goes to the press and generates public outrage, it becomes a powerful tool. He is most aggravated when a Nazi is discovered to be in a position of importance and influence in industry or, even worse, government. Often prosecution follows. "We have just scratched the surface," Wiesenthal says. "The majority of former Nazis who committed serious crimes are still free."

Detective and investigator, Wiesenthal must also be the persuader. The authorities and the public must continue to be convinced that the trial of a given individual is in society's best interest, regardless of how old the evidence is, or how difficult it is to accumulate.

The world has recognized Simon Wiesenthal's dedication as a Nazi hunter. He has been honored by the French and Austrian resistance movements and has received the Dutch Freedom Medal and the Luxembourg Freedom Medal. The United Nations League has given him its highest award, and he received a special gold medal from President Jimmy Carter in 1980. In 1986 he was awarded the French Legion of Honor. But while he accepts the plaques and platitudes, he is most honored by the successful prosecutions that rely upon the evidence he and his international volunteer network have unearthed.

As we shall see, the case of Kurt Waldheim presented unique and very difficult problems for Simon Wiesenthal. First, there was the obvious: Wiesenthal is living in Austria and functioning there as a high-profile Jew. Waldheim is the head of his government. Wiesenthal has often been at odds with the 5,000-strong Jewish community of Vienna, whose members are largely supporters of the Socialist Party of former Austrian chancellor Bruno Kreisky, despite that political party's pro-Palestinian policies. It was still a more comfortable political home for Austrian Jews because of the party's domestic policies. Wiesenthal could never agree.

He prefers to take refuge with his family and counts on the visits with his three grandchildren in Israel. When members of his family or friends say, "You have done enough, it is time to stop," he has a simple answer: "I cannot stop because I would feel like a traitor." Wiesenthal's wife, Cyla, says she feels as if she is "not married to a husband, but married to millions of dead people."

Obviously, the exposé of Kurt Waldheim's Nazi past by the World Jewish Congress and others created a furor in Austria. Nevertheless, Austrians elected Kurt Waldheim their president despite at least some knowledge of his Nazi involvement. The attendant media coverage refocused the division of opinions as to Austria's role in World War II. Proportionately, there were more senior officers from Austria in the death camps than from Nazi Germany itself. While it is unfair to condemn a country because of the madness of a few of its citizens, it is not inappropriate to note the long list of senior Gestapo officials who were, in fact, Austrian.

In the beginning, Simon Wiesenthal took a soft line on Waldheim. After all, he was not, even if the new accusations were proved, one of the major Nazis responsible for the atrocities. At worst, he could be accused of knowing more than he admitted—or so it seemed in the beginning. There were heated arguments between Wiesenthal and leaders of various Jewish groups, including the Simon Wiesenthal Center in the United States. Most Jewish leaders actively supported the U.S. decision to bar Waldheim. The Austrian president went to great lengths to capitalize on the fact that Wiesenthal, in the beginning, did not share the views of other Jews with respect to him and the demands for his resignation. But, as the international commission of historians appointed by Austria to study the Waldheim case was completing its deliberations, Simon Wiesenthal spoke out. On September 29, 1987, he said that when the commission had finished its investigation, Kurt Waldheim should resign if, in fact, it was proven that the military unit to which he was attached was involved in war crimes. "It is obvious that we must draw some conclusions. If the commission cannot conclusively resolve these matters, then Waldheim must make the decision himself, but should act in Austria's interest."

Wiesenthal became embroiled in the work of the commission when Silvana Konieciny-Origlia, a sociologist who had worked for him for several years, admitted to the media that she had secretly copied confidential documents incriminating Kurt Waldheim and taken them to Italy for publication. The documents had come from a British historian, Gerald Fleming, destined for safekeeping in Wiesenthal's "private archive." At that point it was suggested that Fleming should leave the international commission to which he had been appointed for "suppressing the evidence." He did not! Instead, Fleming's became one of the loudest anti-Waldheim voices as the commission drew to a close and concluded that the president of Austria had lied repeatedly and was directly involved in many of the incidents at issue.

By 1987, when he reached seventy-eight, the deep lines in Wiesenthal's face showed the wear and tear of a lifetime of hunting. Those in his network of contacts are concerned because he has trained no successor to run the document center after his death. There is also concern that in the past few years, Wiesenthal's personal system of tracking down war criminals has not been organized in any way that even a designated successor could possibly take over. He has been very much a one-man show.

Wiesenthal brags that only four of the more than 1,100 persons he has named have sued him for libel; he says that none has succeeded.

Recently, Wiesenthal talked with us again briefly and said that he was still dependent upon his lifelong system of thorough review followed by comparison with reports of sightings of Nazis supplied by informants throughout the world. When he compares those bits of information with the library of tracings that he has accumulated, he often hits pay dirt.

For Wiesenthal the only proper punishment for a war criminal is one given out by the courts. He opposes assassinations or any other extreme measures, even in those cases where the known Nazis cannot be brought to Israel or some other country for trial. (Nazi hunters like Beate and Serge Klarsfeld have publicly condoned assassinations, but only if that is the only way to exact punishment for severe wartime crimes. In fact, that unusual Paris-based couple, who were instrumental in locating Klaus Barbie in Bolivia, readily admit that they once considered a plan to hire killers to assassinate him in La Paz.)

To a large degree, Beate Karsfeld has replaced Wiesenthal as a high-profile Nazi hunter. She has become a central figure in most publicity-generating demonstrations, if she is convinced that it will either help apprehend Nazis or at least keep the public focus on the hunt. Perhaps her most animated demonstration was her appearance in chains in the Bolivian capital sixteen years ago to draw the world's attention to the fact that Barbie was living there and to link that country to Nazism. Klarsfeld has also marched in the demonstrations against Kurt Waldheim the United States and Europe. More recently, she flew to Argentina to present testimony in the federal appeals court from Holocaust survivors against Joseph Schwammberger, in support of West Germany's extradition request. In recent years she has largely assumed the role of professional conscience on war criminals—the role played so well for so many years by a younger Simon Wiesenthal. But then Wiesenthal has never marched in such demonstrations, and indeed his initial hesitancy to join others in demanding Waldheim's resignation has separated him to some degree from other Jewish leaders. Wiesenthal, at one point, criticized the World Jewish Congress for acting too hastily and accusing Waldheim before getting all the evidence. Now that the Austrian commission's report is a reality and all of the evidence has been sifted through, even the most critical examiner will admit that, in this case, the World Jewish Congress was on point and accurate and Wiesenthal was wrong.

Throughout his career, the motto of Simon Wiesenthal has been: "I am fighting for the truth, the historic truth—without emotions." In the pursuit of that goal, he has been unyielding in his public criticism of countries that refuse to move aggressively against known Nazis. For example, he has protested for twelve years the Canadian government's failures to prosecute several hundred known Nazis, many of whom Wiesenthal located. He has said that despite the recent announcement of prosecutions there, he will not visit that country until the twenty alleged key Nazis are brought to trial.

Wiesenthal is supported by hundreds of thousands of dollars donated annually by supporters, mostly unsolicited, around the world. Today, he and his wife Cyla are the only two survivors of their combined family of ninety-one who were sent to Nazi concentration camps during the war. They spend most of their time together, have little social life, read a great deal, review their files, and answer letters from around the world. They have been married for fifty-two years.

He refers to his wife often and says that she constantly asks him "Haven't you done enough?" The answer, Wiesenthal says, was obvious: "I survived to represent and speak for those who did not—and the job is never done."

THE SIMON WIESENTHAL CENTER

"It has taken a generation for the people who experienced the horrors of the Holocaust to be able to talk about it openly. Many held their feelings in until quite recently, then some wrote books to make their experiences clear; now, through films and books, Holocaust themes are before the entire public," says Rabbi Marvin Hier, dean and founder of the Simon Wiesenthal Center in Los Angeles. The institute that was created in 1977 has become highly respected for its ongoing study of the Holocaust.

It is much more than a library and goes beyond recording specific historical events and keeping tabs on which Nazi killer killed how many Jews. The center has become a leader in worldwide concern for studying and publicizing the implications of the Holocaust and related human-rights issues. Rabbi Hier, as its leader, has become respected not only as a Nazi hunter, but as an articulate spokesperson for world Jewry.

The center also maintains offices in New York, Chicago, Washington, D.C., and Toronto. More recently, it has opened offices in Jerusalem to continue its research with respect to Nazi war criminals and international anti-Semitism.

Rabbi Hier has said that the Western Allies feel a certain level of guilt because they ignored for so long the truth about Hitler's Final Solution and were slow to be concerned about the victims of Auschwitz and the other death camps. Now, he suggests, these nations are alleviating some of that guilt by helping round up Nazi war criminals.

The Wiesenthal Center has been largely responsible for preserving the memory of the Holocaust through education and awareness. The goal is simply that education represents the best chance of avoiding atrocities of such magnitude in the future. The center reaches out through the media and into schools and conducts broad-based activities that have affected members of the business community, students around the world, and even governments. But the Wiesenthal Center is also a Nazi-hunting organization. It, too, receives large numbers of unsolicited letters and phone calls with information about former Nazis in hiding. It has become very effective in communicating such information to heads of governments with appropriate media attention to create a demand for prosecution.

Wiesenthal Center officials, and the man for whom the center is named, met with U.N. Secretary-General Javier Perez de Cuellar, when accusations of a Nazi past were first leveled against Kurt Waldheim. The center lobbied heavily for the release of all U.N. files. When Congress and the Reagan administration dealt with the issue of whether or not to bar Waldheim from the United States, center officials were in the forefront urging them to do so. Over one million postcards that said "No to Waldheim" were circulated to U.S. and Canadian officials. But long before the Waldheim case, the center joined the World Jewish Congress in mobilizing global opinion against West Germany's attempts to preclude the prosecution of Nazi war criminals by enacting a statute of limitations in 1979.

Rabbi Hier and his team of dedicated researchers, historians, and supporters monitor and speak out against the Institute of Historical Review and a handful of other revisionist groups who claim that the Holocaust is a hoax. They also challenge white supremacists, neo-Nazi organizations, and other disseminators of anti-Semitism.

In Canada, the Simon Wiesenthal Center has taken a high profile through the establishment of the Toronto office as part of its commitment to pursuing Nazi war criminals living in the country.

There is another very special function carried out by the Simon Wiesenthal Center in the ongoing hunt for Nazi war criminals. You can see it at work when you visit the facilities in Los Angeles and see students—some Jewish, many not—touring the building and learning about the Holocaust. To many, World War II is a set of statistics that they may or may not have heard about in a history class. But the effective presentation by the Wiesenthal Center staff, and a glance at the material and memorabilia there, makes it obvious that visitors become impressed with the need to know more. The Simon Wiesenthal Center knows that as the clock ticks and people get older, younger generations will have to understand the "why" of Nazi-hunting if there is to be a continued search for the monsters of the Third Reich.

THE ANTI-DEFAMATION LEAGUE

Elliot Welles is the director, heart and soul, army, and chief investigator for the Task Force on Nazi War Criminals of the Anti-Defamation League of B'nai B'rith—in short, he is that task force. While the Anti-Defamation League has earned worldwide acclaim for its achievements in fighting anti-Semitism and bigotry in every form, it has not had a substantial organization to chase down Nazi war criminals and to join other private and public hunters in distributing information that would help bring about prosecutions. But the league does not really need a sizable organization while it has Elliot Welles.

When Welles speaks about Nazi war criminals, or explains to skeptics why the hunt must go on, he talks from personal experience. Both he and his wife Ceil are survivors of concentration camps. They were married in 1946, after losing their families to the Nazis. Elliot's relatives had died in various Nazi death camps and Ceil's were killed either in Estonia or in Kovno, Lithuania.

The spirit of the Anti-Defamation League's efforts is perhaps best understood through Welles's words. On December 29, 1986, newspapers throughout the United States published a letter to the editor signed by Elliot as Director of the Nazi Task Force of the ADL. He took issue with a widely circulated column by the articulate conservative William F. Buckley. Welles wrote:

> As a victim of Nazi concentration camp torture during World War II, I was distressed to read William F. Buckley's column on the deportation of Karl Linnas.*
>
> Buckley admits that Linnas was "a guard at a Nazi camp in Estonia," that he participated "in arrangements to slaughter Estonians," that he "lied" about his past in seeking entry to the United States and that therefore "his citizenship was invalidated."
>
> But let us not deport Linnas, Buckley says. Why? Because he has "lived as an exemplary citizen." Because "the appropriate penalty in 1986" for a Nazi concentration camp guard is open to question.
>
> There are no open questions about Linnas. I attended Linnas' denaturalization hearings. It was one of the fairest trials a man could ever hope for. Indeed, Linnas has received extensive due process from the American judicial system. For murder and torture there is a price one should pay, sooner or later.
>
> No time should be spared in facilitating Linnas' deportation.

Welles is often called upon to testify before Senate committees and other groups who are studying the ongoing hunt for Nazis. He stated his philosophy clearly when he told senators, in speaking about the Mengele case and the remaining Nazi criminals, "What is the difference if they killed 400,000 people like Mengele or 15,000? Who can weigh one human life against others?"

As we have seen, Alois Brunner has been and remains a particular target for Welles. Brunner sent Welles's mother and other relatives of his to their deaths when he was Eichmann's top henchman in the concentration camp system. It's not surprising that Welles is assisting the District Attorney's office in Frankfurt, West Germany, by trying to line up witnesses in support of West Germany's efforts to find a way to get Brunner back from Syria to face trial.

---

* Linnas was the Greenlawn, New York, resident who was accused of murdering Jews at a concentration camp in Tartu, in his native Estonia. He was ordered deported to the Soviet Union in April 1987 based on Soviet-supplied evidence. He died of heart failure in July 1987 in a Leningrad hospital while awaiting trial. His case has become a cause célèbre in the anti-Soviet community that Buckley represents.

In December 1987, at the request of the German authorities, a short note sent by Elliot Welles appeared in Jewish newspapers throughout the world. It read:

> *I would appreciate your assistance in connection with a request that we received from Fritz Weinschenk, New York [based] Commissioner for the District Attorney's Office in Frankfurt, West Germany.**
>
> *Weinschenk advises that the Frankfurt prosecutor is actively pursuing the case of Alois Brunner, who heads the list of major Nazi war criminals still at large. In this connection, witnesses are needed to Brunner's wartime activities in Berlin, Czechoslovakia and Greece.*
>
> *Would you please share this information with your readers?*
>
> *All replies should be directed to Weinschenk. His address is Hamburger, Weinschenk, Molanar, and Busch, 36 West 44th Street, Suite 810, New York, New York 10036. Weinschenk's telephone number is 212-719-5930. Collect calls will be accepted.*
>
> *Thank you for your help.*

It is not uncommon for notices from Welles to appear in newspapers that reach survivors of the concentration camps and relatives of those who were less fortunate. As a result, he has become a one-man clearinghouse for essential firsthand information that often assists prosecutors.

He does not have the luxury of a big office or a computerized filing system, and his weapons are worn-out files with handwritten notes, a huge far-reaching list of telephone numbers, and what is in his head and heart. He is obviously obsessed, but the occasional victories appear to make it all worthwhile. It was an old, handwritten notation in his Brunner file that enabled us to update the story of the most wanted remaining Nazi criminal. He spent a few minutes enjoying that accomplishment, but then he moved on to another piece of evidence for his lifetime hunt.

---

* The West German government has long retained the services of Fritz Weinschenk as its official representative for its prosecution arm, especially for the investigation of Nazi criminals.

The Future Hunt

The principal Nazi hunters disagree on what will happen in the next few years with respect to their efforts to seek, capture, and prosecute many of the major Nazi war criminals who are still living throughout the world. Unquestionably, the trial of Barbie and a series of lesser judicial victories, coupled with the monumental shift in public opinion following the revelations concerning Kurt Waldheim, are encouraging to those who want prosecutions to increase in aggressiveness and frequency.

On the other hand, who would have believed that after all the researchers, lawyers, investigators, and journalists had finished piecing together Kurt Waldheim's role in World War II, he would not have vanished from the public scene? But Waldheim is still president of Austria, and it seems likely that he will remain in office until removed by illness or retirement. It's not that those who are dedicated to seeing Waldheim fall are giving up. Not only are they angered by his deeds, but they see him as a symbol of "forgiving the Holocaust." Talks are taking place in a dozen countries about plans for economic pressures on Austria to force Waldheim from office. Within Austria, intellectuals, college students, members of both major political parties, and even some former Waldheim loyalists are scheming on how to get him removed. Public demonstrations in Vienna become a regular event.

Some months ago, senior Austrian officials "floated" a plan to Jewish leaders which would, in effect, offer huge sums of money to Israel and to Nazi victims who suffered in Austria, in exchange for help in salvaging that country's devastated tourism business.

The West German government has paid out $47 billion in monies, goods, and services primarily to victims of the Nazis and, in part, to Israel itself. In 1987 East Germany, for the first time, accepted the principle of such reparations payments and serious talks continue in an effort to have them join West Germany.

Austria has steadfastly insisted that it was a Nazi victim, not a Nazi ally, and thus it would be inappropriate for reparations of any kind to be made to "fellow victims." But during the weeks following the announcement of the International Commission's report, which condemned Waldheim as a liar and linked him to war crimes, interesting conversations were taking place by transatlantic phone and in New York.

Jewish leaders were approached by friends of the Austrian government to see whether or not there was interest in resuming talks about Austrian reparations and linking those talks to assistance by the World Jewish Congress in resurrecting Austria's tourism. The government of Austria has been hesitant to talk about the exact dollar figure of their losses due to the Nazi hunt that led to their presidential doorstep. But even Waldheim's staunchest supporters admit that the results have been catastrophic.

The hint in those conversations about reparations was that, if a deal could beworked out, the last of those in the Austrian government supporting Waldheim would desert him "for the good of Austria," and he would be gone. Those secret talks are still underway as this book goes to press. The resignation of Kurt Waldheim would be a giant step toward maintaining the high energy of the hunt for remaining Nazis all over world.

It will take years to digest all the new information that has been uncovered with the opening of the United Nations Nazi archives. During that period, if the trend continues, more and more documents will emerge from the Soviet Union, Yugoslavia, Greece, and other sources.

Recent news from Europe has been mixed, but it seems that the steam is going out of the pursuit in many countries, including the Netherlands, which may serve as an example.

In the Netherlands, the recent death of one of the country's most notorious Nazi war criminals may have signaled the end of any serious attempt to bring Dutch war criminals to justice. Pieter Nicolaas Menten, who had become a millionaire art collector, died at age eighty-eight in a nursing home. Menten was convicted in 1980 for the killings of dozens of Jews in Podhorece, a village in Poland, while he was serving with a Nazi SS unit in 1941. Originally sentenced to ten years in prison, he was released in 1985 after serving only half his sentence.

For more than twenty-five years, Menten and his wife, Meta, lived in obscurity in a forty-room mansion twenty miles outside Amsterdam. In 1949 he had served an eight-month prison term after being convicted of collaborating with the Nazis, and in the early 1950s Poland had tried unsuccessfully to have him extradited for war crimes on two occasions. In 1976 Nazi hunters focused on Menten, and under intense public pressure, the Dutch government started an investigation. Menten fled to Switzerland but was ordered deported back to Holland to face trial.

What followed was said to be the most expensive court battle in Dutch legal history, costing the government in excess of $5 million. After a long and complex trial, Menten was acquitted of participating in one massacre, but was found guilty of murdering more than twenty Polish Jews in Podhorece on July 7, 1941.

Then the Dutch Supreme Court reversed the conviction on the basis that Menten had been promised immunity in 1952 by a former Dutch justice minister in recognition of his "contributions" to postwar Holland. The government successfully appealed this ruling, and the conviction was reinstated. Then Menten tried, unsuccessfully, to avoid prison by pleading insanity. Finally, in 1980, he started his sentence.

Since the trial it is widely believed that Menten would be the last Nazi to face trial in the Netherlands. The process has simply become too costly and complex.

At one time there was a list of 314 suspected war criminals believed to be living in Holland, most of whom have probably died or moved to countries that will not extradite them. In some cases, the Dutch statute of limitations has run out on the crimes they are accused of. Yet two German war criminals in Dutch prisons, Ferdinand H. Aus der Fuenten and Franz Fischer, were denied freedom by the authorities, who said that to release them, even now, would cause needless suffering to the "victims of Nazism."

East Germany has not been among the most vigorous pursuers of former Nazis. But in 1987 it caught a big one, and it moved quickly. Henry Schmidt, the former Gestapo chief in Dresden, disappeared from sight in 1945. But using information supplied by Western Nazi hunters, East German authorities located and arrested him in late 1986. In September 1987, Schmidt, now seventy-four, was convicted by a court in Dresden of responsibility for the deaths of 720 Jews. He was given a life sentence, and that sentence has been affirmed by East Germany's highest court.

The Soviets also showed that they continue to pursue Nazi war criminals. Last year Dmitri Maslo, a Soviet citizen, was convicted of war crimes and sentenced to fifteen years in prison. Tass, the official Soviet news agency, said that Maslo was found guilty of "high treason" and other charges because he joined the Nazi police force in the Ukrainian city of Krasnoarmeisk and tortured Ukrainians and Jews, and "on many occasions he took part in the shooting of peaceful civilians." He was also accused of helping kill prisoners in the Krasnoarmeisk jail in 1943, as Soviet forces retook the area. But the sentence also showed that the Soviets are less rigorous then they were. In the past, such a conviction would probably have resulted in a quick execution.

Nazi hunters have new leads. We are told that there are at least six former war criminals high in the diplomatic service of West Germany and that they can be named soon. At the same time, in the United States, the Office of Special Investigations has been able to move ahead relatively quickly with the investigation of several hundred accused Nazis. Again, their hands are tied when it comes to criminal prosecutions. But the combination of kicking a former Nazi out of the United States for lying on an application for citizenship and the attendant media coverage is a victory for the Nazi hunters and could well provide the impetus for other governments to prosecute.

In West Germany, the ultimate dilemma still exists. There is no question that prosecutors there would like to have their hands untied so that they may bring to trial not only former Nazis deported from the United States, but many others who have lived there for years and have been identified but remain free. An effort to change the criminal procedural laws to do away with existing restrictions is expected in Bonn in the near future.

In Great Britain, the Thatcher government has taken the first step ever toward the prosecution of Nazis living in the United Kingdom. The British government has agreed to study proposals for changes in criminal law that would allow trials. Despite all the British losses during World War II, nothing has had the impact of the new documentation on the abuse and murder of British POWs as the war drew to an end. The enthusiasm for prosecution of these cases and others—subject to the findings of the new Nazi Inquiry Board—is best reflected by the surprising unanimity of editorial support in the British press. Unlike the United States, each of the major British newspapers has an announced political philosophy and either supports or opposes the Conservative Party of Margaret Thatcher. While they are not absolute and parochial in judging every act of government, no Briton is in doubt about the political preference of his newspaper.

And all but one of the national newspapers has given some support to a more aggressive stance on the prosecution of Nazis and a reopening of the Waldheim case.

A half-dozen Nazis living in the United Kingdom have been identified in this book, but their names and photographs are yet to appear in any British newspaper or on television. The judicial system, from which we in America inherited so much, bends over backward to protect their rights. The injunctions that have been issued, even though they are challenged, will result in long delays of public information on Nazis now living in the UK.

More telephone calls and letters, with new accusations, are coming in to the headquarters of the World Jewish Congress then ever before. That organization has earned worldwide respect, not only for its handling of the Waldheim matter, but for its relentless efforts to separate fact from fiction on accused war criminals.

In fact, it was the World Jewish Congress that prevented media attention from being focused on an official of the United Nations whose name was the same as one that appeared in the U.N. archive. Eager journalists from New York to Tel Aviv were about to seize on the fact that an ambassador to the United Nations was listed as having been responsible for horrendous crimes. Elan Steinberg used his indefatigable network of Jewish community leaders to confirm that while the name was the same, the date of birth was not. And additional evidence proved irrefutably that the ambassador was guilty only of having the same name as a Nazi, not of war crimes. That kind of responsible action has resulted in the World Jewish Congress becoming an international repository for information about Nazis that originates with both former victims and government officials in a dozen nations of the world.

Similarly, in Los Angeles, the Simon Wiesenthal Center for Holocaust Studies has rejoiced in the attention given to the material it has presented to governments in the United Kingdom, Australia, Canada, and South America, as well as the United States. The center has been disturbed by hesitancy on the part of many governments to evaluate evidence that originated in the Soviet Union. But there seems to be a break even in that resistance, due partially to improved relations between the United States and the Soviet Union.

In his tiny cluttered office at the Anti-Defamation League in downtown Manhattan, Elliot Welles peers over the huge stack of files on his desk and talks about active investigations for next year. "We are close to finding many more monsters and in the next several months, we will do so," he told us.

Unfortunately, Israel is plagued with an incredible shift in world public opinion as a result of the tragedies arising from unrest in the Palestinian territories this year. The nation that has most often been glamorized as the "oasis of democratic progress" in that part of the world is now host to a huge number of journalists who have reported intensely on those incidents of brutality and reverse discrimination that have so embarrassed the government of Israel and so alienated many Jewish leaders. It would be very difficult for Israel to expect world support as it moves ahead against Nazis while it is being called upon to defend what some critics call "Israeli terrorism."

In Europe, there are many havens for Nazi criminals. Simon Wiesenthal Center representatives have repeatedly visited Carta Blanca, one of the most beautiful resort areas not only in Spain, but in all of Europe. That area has been a comfortable hideaway for several former Nazis.

Originally, Generalisimo Francisco Franco granted shelter to Nazis after World War II. The Socialist government in Spain has for the past few years been embarrassed by the large number of former Nazis residing there, and would like to have a means for dealing with the situation. Occasionally, there is a showcase. The Spanish extradited one Nazi war criminal to stand trial in the Netherlands—the first instance of such an extradition in almost forty years.

When we talked in Vienna, Simon Wiesenthal mentioned Spain. "The country is amazing," he said. "It gave refuge to 25,000 Jews during the war and absolutely refused to extradite them. Then, after the war, it gave refuge to thousands of Nazis and refused to extradite them. The difference is that the Jews haven't done anything and the Nazis have."

Spain is a target for Nazi-hunting organizations throughout the world. Plans are underway to focus media attention on former Nazi war criminals living there, capitalizing on the momentum from the Waldheim publicity.

Latin America has been the most comfortable haven for former Nazis. First, in many nations, the political sentiment embraces the idea of *caudillismo,* which describes their traditional acceptance of dictatorships, of strong-willed Perón-type leaders. Second, many of the war criminals who remain hidden from the hunters are able to buy their peace in their declining years. They stole enough from their victims and from the citizens of the territories they conquered to live like kings. They prefer to live quietly, but payoffs to local police officials and, in some cases, senior government leaders are a way of life for former Nazis, as well as others trying to escape the laws of the United States and other countries in Latin America. Nazi hunters from the Anti-Defamation League and the World Jewish Congress have estimated that as many as 40,000 to 50,000 Nazis found refuge in Latin America after the war. They have traced their movements in Argentina, Bolivia, Brazil, Paraguay, and to a lesser extent, in Chile and Uruguay.

Many of those Nazis, now aged, have been living in the same South American haven for nearly forty years without giving a hint of the sordid past that they left behind in Europe. Some were German military experts, others civilian technocrats invited to help build the economy and the military in their Latin American host country, much as rocket scientists were invited to help strengthen the United States against Soviet competition. Thousands of Nazis still live in Latin America relatively openly without much fear that they will be next to stand trial.

The Barbie case in Bolivia, which took such a dramatic turn when President Siles Zuazo took office in October 1982 and agreed to play a crucial role in bringing Barbie to justice in France, has sparked renewed interest in other Nazi war criminals in South America. Nazi organizations there try to offset search efforts by stirring up anti-Semitism wherever they can. A decade ago, one anti-Semitic group in Argentina circulated throughout that country and neighboring nations "captured proof" of an alleged plan known as "The Nadinia Program." It was described as a Jewish plot to establish a second Israel in South America and designed to appeal to nationalistic feelings and turn them into anti-Jewish action.

Germany always had great ambitions in Uruguay and other parts of Latin America. There was major German immigration to countries there, and substantial investment in real estate and businesses as early as the 1920s. A vast network of agents ready for espionage and propaganda existed by the time Germany and the United States went to war. At one time, early in World War II, there were reports that Uruguay would become a colony under the protection of the Third Reich. Today, Nazi hunters continue to infiltrate Uruguay and to ferret out the war criminals hiding there, with little or no cooperation from the government—a condition that prevails throughout the region.

The biggest enemy of the Nazi hunters is time. The older the remaining Nazis get, and the more feeble they appear when a camera focuses upon them, the more difficult it is to convince people who were not alive at the time of Hitler's horrors that these men should still be prosecuted.

The United Nations is often the scene of discussions about setting up some kind of international tribunal again to deal with those cases which should result in public judicial proceedings, but which are hampered by the laws of a given nation. When Alois Brunner told German reporters a few years ago that he would "stand trial before an international tribunal but not go to Israel," he was safe, since no such tribunal exists. But if cases that are known to have sufficient evidence to begin trials in Great Britain are blocked by the lack of an extradition treaty between that country and the Soviet Union, an international tribunal might well be the answer.

Finally, there is the moral issue raised by the argument that it is time to stop the hunt.

In the United States, if Charles Manson or any other mass killer had escaped arrest for forty or fifty years, it is doubtful that anyone would suggest patting him on the back, giving him his pension, and forgiving him. Thus, it must be asked that if someone has killed one thousand or perhaps one hundred thousand times more people than a Charles Manson, by what logic do we forgive and forget?

The story of the Nazi hunters is not over. In a sense, with the opening of the UN Archive, it's just beginning. In Germany, chief Nazi prosecutor Alfred Streim has his thousand-plus active files. In the United States, OSI director Neal Sher has his more than 500 open files. This is clearly not a story even near its end.

The hunt goes on.

Appendix

*Cases brought against accused Nazi war criminals in
the United States through June 15, 1988*

CASES BROUGHT BY THE IMMIGRATION AND
NATURALIZATION SERVICE (INS)

Cases Still Open

KAMINSKAS, BRONIUS — Hartford, Connecticut — 1976
Accused of participating in the murder of several hundred Jews in Lithuania. Was found incompetent to stand trial. (See page 42)

MAIKOVSKIS, BOLESLAVS — Mineola, New York — 1978
Accused of persecuting Jews and others while the police chief of Rezekna in Latvia. In 1984 the BIA ordered him deported to the Soviet Union. An appeal to the Supreme Court was denied in 1986. A further appeal is pending. (See page 202-03.)

Closed Cases

AGH, LASZLO — Newark, New Jersey — 1959
Accused of leading persecutions against Jews while a Hungarian army officer. Ordered deported, the BIA reversed the decision. The government did not appeal. (See page 189.)

ARTUKOVIC, ANDRIJA — Los Angeles — 1951
Accused of the responsibility for the deaths of tens of thousands of Jews and Serbs. Originally ordered deported in 1952, was finally extradited to Yugoslavia in 1986 where he was tried and sentenced to death. He is still appealing that ruling in Yugoslavia. (See pages 186-88.)

BRAUNSTEINER (RYAN), HERMINE — New York City — 1964
Accused of torture and murder while a guard at Majdanek. In 1974 West Germany asked for her extradition to stand trial. She was ordered deported and is now serving a life sentence in Germany. (See pages 190-91.)

FEDORENKO, FEODOR — Waterbury, Connecticut — 1977
Accused of the persecution of Jews while a guard at Treblinka. Ordered deported to the Soviet Union in 1984. Tried there and found guilty, he was executed in July 1987. (See pages 203-05.)

FRIEDMANN, HEINRICH — New York City — 1953
Accused of abusing fellow Jews while a labor camp kapo near Mielec, Poland. An INS hearing examiner found no conclusive proof he committed persecution based on religion and dismissed the charges. (See page 186.)

HAZNERS, VILIS — Albany, New York — 1977
Accused of taking part in reprisals against Jews and partisans while a member of the Latvian *Schutzmannschaft*. Deportation proceedings were begun in 1977. In 1980 the charges were dismissed for lack of evidence. The OSI appealed, but the BIA upheld the dismissal.

KOWALCHUK, MYKOLA — Philadelphia, Pennsylvania — 1977
Accused of Jewish persecutions while a member of the Ukraine police in Lubomyl. He is the brother of Serge Kowalchuk, another accused war criminal. Charges were dismissed when a key witness died before giving depositions. (See footnote on pages 200-01.)

KRASNAUSKAS, FELIX — Worchester, Massachusetts — 1956
Accused of being the chief of a Lithuanian police unit. An INS judge ordered him deported, but the BIA overturned the ruling and dismissed the charges. (See page 188-89.)

LANG, KORNEL (aka JANOS TOKAJI) — New York City — 1968
Accused of participating in persecutions while a member of a Hungarian para-military unit. Evidence ruled insufficient to force deportation given he had married an American and had children who were citizens by birth.

LEWY, JONAS — New York City — 1954
Accused in the persecution of fellow Jews while a kapo in the Piotrkow ghetto in Poland. An immigration judge ordered him deported to Poland, but they refused to accept him. In 1964 a new trial was ordered, but it was never held. Lewy died in 1980. (See page 186.)

SPOKEVICIUS, ANTANAS — Chicago, Illinois — 1953
Accused of being a member of the Lithuanian police auxiliary in Kaunas. Ordered deported, but the BIA reversed and ordered charges dismissed. (See page 188.)

TENCER, JAKOB — New York City — 1953
Accused of abusing fellow Jews while a kapo at a forced labor camp in Pionkii, Poland. An immigration judge ordered him deported, but the BIA dismissed the charges. (See page 186.)

VAJTA, FERENC — New York City — 1948
Accused of fostering persecutions while pro-Nazi Hungarian consul-general in Vienna. Eventually ordered deported and left voluntarily for Colombia. (See pages 189-90.)

WALUS, FRANK — Chicago, Illinois — 1976
Accused of the murder of Polish Jews while member of elite SS unit. Citizenship ordered revoked after 1978 trial. Order reversed by Court of Appeals based on new evidence. (See pages 192-97.)

CASES BROUGHT BY OFFICE OF SPECIAL INVESTIGATIONS

Cases Still Open

BERNOTAS, ANTANAS — Hartford, Connecticut — 1983
Accused of acts of persecution while a member of the Lithuanian 2nd Battalion. His trial has not yet begun. (See page 42)

BLACH, BRUNO KARL — La Habra, California — 1985
Accused of being a SS guard and dog handler at the Dachau and Wierner Neudorf death camps. Appealing a 1987 deportation order. (See page 44.)

DIDRICHSOS, VALDIS — Mercer Island, Washington — 1988
Accused of killing civilians while serving in the *Arajs Kommando*, a Latvian Security Auxiliary Police unit. (See page 46.)

ECKERT, JOSEF — La Puente, California — 1987
Accused of being a Waffen-SS Death's Head Battalion (SS-Totenkopf Sturmbann) guard at three Polish death camps. (See pages 43-44.)

ENSIN, ALBERT — Stoughton, Massachusetts — 1987
Accused of persecuting Jews while a Death's Head Battalion guard at Auschwitz. (See page 43.)

GUDAUSKAS, VYTAUTAS — Worchester, Massachusetts — 1984
Accused of being a member of the Lithuanian 2nd Battalion. Pretrial motions are still pending. (See page 41.)

HABICH, JAKOB — Chicago, Illinois — 1987
Accused of being a Death's Head guard at three camps. (See page 43.)

KALEJS, KONRADS — Chicago, Illinois — 1985
Accused of being a member of the *Arajs Kommandos.* (See page 46.)

KATIN, MATTHEW, (MOTIEJUS KATINAUSKAS) — Norwood, Mass. — 1984
Accused of serving in the Lithuanian 2nd Battalion. (See page 41, 236.)

KAIRYS, LIUSDAS — Chicago, Illinois — 1985
Accused of serving with SS guard units at various concentration camps. Stripped of his citizenship in 1986, he was ordered deported to the Soviet Union in 1987. Order on appeal. (See page 44.)

KAULS, JURIS — Sun City (Phoenix), Arizona — 1988
Accused of being the second-in-command of a series of fourteen Nazi slave-labor camps in and around Riga, Latvia. (See Page 47.)

KIRSTEINS, MIKELIS — Utica, New York — 1987
Accused of membership in the *Arajs Kommandos.* (See page 46.)

KUNGYS, JUOZAS — Clifton, New Jersey — 1983
Accused of participating in the massacre of Jews while a member of the Lithuanian 2nd Battalion. Trial court ruled in his favor. Court of Appeals reversed. Supreme Court remanded the case to the appeals court for a re-review. (See page 42, 235-36.)

LAIPENIEKS, EDGARS — San Diego, California — 1980
Accused of the murder and beating of civilians, including Jews, at the Riga Central Prison while a member of the Latvian Security Police. In 1982, immigration judge ruled government had failed to prove its case. BIA overruled judge. In 1985 Ninth Circuit Court of Appeals overturned BIA ruling. Government is appealing. (See pages 234-35.)

LEHMANN, ALEXANDER — Cleveland, Ohio — 1981
Accused of ordering persecutions while serving as deputy police chief of Zaporozhe in the Ukraine. Ordered deported to West Germany, the order was stayed pending an appeal and then stayed again for health reasons. (See pages 46-47.)

PALCIAUSKAS, KAZYS — St. Petersburg, Florida — 1982
Accused of the persecution of Jews while the mayor of Kaunas, Lithuania. Ordered denaturalized in 1983. Deportation proceedings still pending. (See page 47.)

PASKEVICIUS, MECIS (MIKE PASKER) — St. Petersburg, Fla. — 1977
Accused of the murder and beating of Jews while a Lithuanian 2nd Battalion member. In 1979, he consented to the revocation of his citizenship. He was then found mentally unfit for deportation trial. (See page 43.)

PETKIEWYTSCH, LEONID — Cincinnati, Ohio — 1985
Accused of being an SS guard at Kiel-Hassee concentration camp. (See page 44.)

QUINTUS, PETER — Shelby Township (Detroit), Michigan — 1987
Accused of being a Death's Head guard at several camps in Poland. (See page 44.)

REGER, STEFAN — Yardville, New Jersey — 1987
Accused of being a Death's Head guard at Birkenau, a section of Auschwitz. (See page 44.)

SCHELLONG, CONRAD — Chicago, Illinois — 1980
Accused of being an SS officer in charge of the training of new SS guard recruits at several death camps. Ordered denaturalized in 1983. Deportation proceedings proceeding. (See Page 44.)

SOKOLOV, VLADIMIR — New Haven, Connecticut — 1984
Accused of being a Nazi propagandist. Ordered denaturalized in 1986. Deportation proceedings begun after Supreme Court refused to review decision in 1988. (See page 47.)

THEODOROVICH, GEORGE — Albany, New York — 1984
Accused of the persecution of Jews while a member of the police force in Lvov in the Ukraine. Ordered denaturalized in 1984 and is currently appealing deportation order. (See page 47.)

VIRKUTIS, ANTANAS — Chicago, Illinois — 1983
Accused of the murder and torture of Jews, other civilians, and Allied prisoners while the warden of the Nazi prison in Lithuania. (See page 47.)

Closed Cases

ARTISHENKO, BASIL — East Brunswick, New Jersey — 1982
Accused of taking part in the execution of gypsies, including women and children, while a member of a local police unit in Byelorussia. He agreed to give up his citizenship in exchange for a government agreement not to seek his deportation to the Soviet Union.

AVDZEJ, JOHN — Roselle Park, New Jersey — 1984
Accused of taking part in atrocities while a member of a local police unit in Byelorussia. He voluntarily renounced his citizenship and departed for West Germany on March 2, 1986.

BARTESCH, MARTIN — Chicago, Illinois — 1986
Accused of being a Death's Head guard at Mauthausen. As part of a pre-trial settlement he departed for Austria on May 27, 1987. (See pages 45-46.)

BENKUNSKAS, HENRIKAS — Chicago, Illinois — 1984
Accused of being a Lithuanian 2nd Battalion member. He died in 1986 before case could be heard.

DEMJANJUK, JOHN — Cleveland, Ohio — 1977
Accused of operating the gas ovens at Treblinka where he was an SS guard. His citizenship was revoked in 1981 and eventually he was ordered deported to Israel in 1986. Tried there he was found guilty and ordered executed. Is appealing that decision. (See pages 225-31.)

DERCACZ, MICHAEL — Brooklyn, New York — 1980
Accused of participating in Jewish executions while a collaborator with the Ukrainian police in Lvov. Ordered denaturalized in 1982, he died one week before his deportation hearing was scheduled to begin in August 1983.

DETLAVS, KARLIS — Baltimore, Maryland — 1978
Accused of taking part in the persecution of Jews while a member of the Latvian Auxiliary Security Police. In February 1980 an immigration judge ruled that the government had failed to prove its case and the BIA upheld the ruling. He died in July 1983.

DEUTSCHER, ALBERT — Chicago, Illinois — 1981
Accused of taking part in the murder and persecution of Jews as a member of a fascist paramilitary unit in the Ukraine. The next day Deutscher stepped in front of a train and was killed. His death was ruled a suicide.

HRUSITZKY, ANATOLY — Orlando, Florida — 1983
Accused of the murder and persecution of Jews while a member of a police unit in the Ukraine. Voluntarily left for Venezuela, from which he had emigrated to the U.S., and formally renounced his U.S. citizenship in Caracas.

JUODIS, JURGIS — St. Petersburg, Florida — 1981
Accused of being a Lithuanian 2nd Battalion officer. Died before case completed. (See page 43.)

KARKLINS, JALIVALDIS — Los Angeles, California — 1981
Accused of persecuting Jews as a member of the Latvian police and later as the commandant of the Madona concentration camp. A month before his trial was set to begin in March 1983, he died of natural causes.

KISIELAITIS, JUOZAS (JOSEPH) — Boston, Massachusetts — 1984
Accused of being a member of the Lithuanian 2nd Battalion. He fled to Canada before his deportation trial could begin in 1984. (See page 41-42.)

KLIMAVICIUS, JONAS — Kennebunkport, Maine — 1984
Accused of being a member of the Lithuanian 2nd Battalion and also as a member of the Gestapo-led Iron Wolf terrorist squads. He was ordered denaturalized in September 1987. That order is on appeal. (See page 42-43.)

KOZIY, BOHDAN — Ft. Lauderdale, Florida — 1979
Accused of the murder of Jews and other civilians as a member of the Ukrainian police. Fled to Costa Rica after citizenship was ordered revoked and before his deportation hearing could begin. (See Chapter 6)

KOWALCHUK, SERGE (SERHIJ) — Philadelphia, Pennsylvania — 1977
Accused, like his brother Mykola, of being a member of the Ukrainian police in Lubomyl. Ordered stripped of his citizenship in 1983 and left voluntarily for Paraguay after deportation proceedings started. (See footnote pages 200-01.)

KULLE, REINHOLD — Chicago, Illinois — 1982
Accused of serving as a Death's Head guard and group leader of prisoners at Gross-Rosen. Eventually stripped of his U.S. citizenship and ordered deported to West Germany. (See page 45.)

LEILI, STEFAN — Clifton, New Jersey — 1986
Accused of serving as a Death's Head guard at the Mauthausen. After he was stripped of his citizenship in 1986, he left voluntarily for West Germany. (See page 45.)

LEPRICH, JOSEPH — Clinton Township, Michigan — 1986
Accused of being a Death's Head guard at Mauthausen. He was ordered denaturalized in July 1987, and voluntarily departed for West Germany. (See page 45.)

LINNAS, KARL — Greenlawn, New York — 1979
Accused of being the chief of the Tartu death camp in Estonia. Denaturalized and ordered deported to the Soviet Union in 1983, the order was carried out in 1987 after appeal expired. He died on July 2, 1987, of heart failure, in a Leningrad hospital.

LIPSCHIS, HANS — Chicago, Illinois — 1982
Accused of being a Death's Head guard at Auschwitz. Voluntarily agreed to deportation to West Germany rather than stand trial. (See page 45.)

OSIDACH, WOLODYMER — Philadelphia, Pennsylvania — 1979
Accused of leading the extermination of Jews in the town of Rava-Ruska in the Ukraine where he was police chief. His citizenship revoked in 1981. He died while waiting appeal.)

POPCZUK, MICHAEL — Lynn, Massachusetts — 1983
Accused of personally torturing and helping to execute dozens of Jews while a member of a local police unit. Eight days after the charges were filed, committed suicide by shooting himself in the head.

SCHUK, MYKOLA — Allentown, Pennsylvania — 1983
Accused of the persecution, beating, and murder of Jews while member of a Ukrainian police unit. He voluntarily agreed to give up his citizenship and to cooperate with the Justice Department in the prosecution of other accused war criminals in exchange for being allowed to remain in the United States.

SOOBZOKOV, TSCHERIM — Trenton, New Jersey — 1979
Accused of having been a member of the Waffen SS, the German Army North-Caucasian Legion and the Tachtamukai Town Police. The charges were dropped after it was determined that State Department knew this when he was admitted to U.S. (See page 220.)

SPROGIS, ELMARS — New York City — 1982
Accused of assisting Nazi persecution of Jews and of killing Soviet POWs while deputy police chief of Latvia. Trial court ruled in his favor citing lack of evidence. Government appeal was denied.

TANNENBAUM, JAKOB — New York City — 1987
Accused of collaboration with the Nazis and taking part in persecutions while serving as a kapo at the Goerlitz concentration camp. In a plea-bargaining arrangement, voluntarily relinquished his citizenship in exchange for a guarantee that he would be allowed to remain in the U.S. with no fear of deportation. (See page 208.)

TRIFIA, VALERIAN — Detroit, Michigan — 1975
Accused of being the leader of the fascist Iron Guard in Romania. After coming to the U.S. became the Archbishop of the Rumanian Orthodox Episcopacy. After fighting denaturalization, consented to the revocation of his citizenship in 1980. He then appealed his own consent decree. In August 1984, Portugal agreed to accept him and he lived there until his death in 1987.

TRUCIS, ARNOLDS — Philadelphia, Pennsylvania — 1980
Accused of the murder and abuse of Jews and while a member of a Latvian Auxiliary Security Police unit. He died in 1981 before his denaturalization trial could begin.

VON BOLSCHWING, OTTO — Sacramento, California — 1981
Accused of being an agent for the Reich Central Security Office for Jewish Affairs and later the head of the SD office in Bucharest. He voluntarily surrendered his citizenship in December 1981. Died of natural causes before deportation proceedings could begin.

WIELAND, JOSEPH — Burlingame, California — 1986
Accused of being a Death's Head guard at Mauthausen. He relinquished his U.S. citizenship and voluntarily departed for West Germany. (See page 45.)

WOJCIECHOWSKI, CHESTER — Chicago, Illinois — 1985
Accused of serving in two Nazi police units in Poland and as a Waffen-SS guard at the Majdanek camp. In 1987, voluntarily agreed to be denaturalized and departed for Paraguay. (See page 46.)

Index

Rickhey, Georg, 215
Riegner, Gerhard, 255
Riga-Kaiserwald concentration camp, 278
Robinson, Dr. Jacob, 283, 284
Rockler, Walter, 198, 200, 206, 233
Rodal, Dr. Alti, 241, 242, 243, 249
Rodal Report, 241
Roder, Anni, 20
Roncaglia, General, 96
Roosevelt, Elliott, 66
Roosevelt, Franklin Delano, 50, 52, 52n,
  55, 56, 57, 58, 59, 64, 65, 66, 67, 68, 69, 70,
  71, 72, 158, 256, 257
Rosenberg, Alfred, 78n, 79
Rosenman, Judge Samuel, 69, 71, 72, 73
Ross, Michael, 97
Royal Canadian Mounted Police (RCMP),
  40, 238n, 239, 240, 241, 242, 243, 246n,
  247n
Roziner, Liusia, 156
Rudenko, Roman, 199, 200, 200n,
Rudolph, Arthur, 215, 216, 220-221
Rumba, Leopolds Fricis, 36
Rust, Bernard, 65
Ryan, Allan, Jr., 119, 144, 197, 198, 200,
  200n, 201n, 204n, 205, 206, 209, 221n, 228,
  229, 233, 280
Ryan, Hermine Braunsteiner, 190, 191,
  221, 222, 226n, 290, 305
Ryan Report, 144, 145, 149
Ryan, Russell, 190

Sachsenburg concentration camp, 44
Sachsenhausen, 26
Salinger, Pierre, 110n
Sauckel, General Fritz, 78n, 79, 117n
Schacht, Hjalmar, 78n, 79
Schaefer, Konrad, 219
Scheide, Ralph, 88, 102
Schellong, Conrad, 44, 307
Schirach, Baldur von, 78n
Schmaldienest, Alois, 26
Schmidt, Henry, 300
Schmidt-Richberg, General Erich, 98, 99,
  100
Schreiber, Dr. Walter, 218, 219
Schuk, Mykola, 309
Schulz, Harri, 279
Schumann, Horst, 34
Schutzmannschaft (Latvian Aux. Police),
  38, 41, 42, 43, 207, 259, 305
Schwammberger, Josef, 30, 31, 32, 33, 293
Sedlmeier, Hans, 134, 138
Seidman, Hillel, 83, 84, 85
Seyss-Inquart, Arthur, 78n, 79

Sher, Neal, 13, 16, 40, 50, 114, 115, 116,
  166, 206, 208, 209, 231, 234, 237, 280, 290,
  304
Shimoni, Yehudah, 131
Shultz, George, 63n
Siemers, Otto, 279
Silberbauer, Karl, 289
Silverman, Sidney, 55, 255, 256
Simon, John A. (Lord), 51, 52, 53, 55, 60,
  64, 65, 66, 67, 70, 72, 74, 75, 76
  war criminal proposal, 65
Singer, Israel, 14, 63, 86, 284
Singur, Anna, 155
Sir-Czerwinsky, Horst, 279
Sivchev, Dorothy, 113
Snow, Dr. Clyde, 121
Sobibor, 226, 228, 278
Sokolov, Vladimir, 47, 208, 307
Solarz, Steven (Congressman), 83, 84, 85,
  88, 102, 104
Soobzokov, Tscherim, 220, 200n, 309
Soviet Foreign Ministry, 200
Soviet participation in UNWCC, 54
Special Investigations Unit, 254
Speer, Albert, 78n
Spilarewicz, Yadwiga, 169
Spokevicius, Antanas, 42, 188, 306
Sprogis, Elmars, 309
St. Laurent, Louis, 242
Stalin government, 53
Stalin, Joseph, 54, 56, 66, 67, 71, 75, 155,
  158, 271, 283
Stammer, Geza, 133, 135, 138
Stammer, Gitta, 133, 138
Stangl, Fritz, 290
State Department, 191, 192, 222, 224, 274,
  309
State-War-Navy Coordinating Committee
  (SWNCC), 213
Stebelsky, Ivan, 229
Steinberg, Elan, 14, 15, 63, 85, 86, 87, 88,
  284, 285, 302
Stettinius, Edward R., Jr., 58, 71
Stimson, Henry, 58, 70, 71
Stojic, Arsov, 101
Streicher, Julius, 78n, 79
Streim, Alfred, 28, 275, 277, 304
Stroessner, Alfredo, 133, 134, 136
Strughold, Hubertus, 215, 217-218
Supreme Court, West German, 278

Tannenbaum, Jakob, 208, 310
Tartu death camp, 309
Task Force on Nazi War Criminals (Anti-
  Defamation League), 295, 296

317

Waffen SS, 122, 272, 278, 306, 309, 310
Waldheim, Kurt, 7, 9, 11, 13, 14, 29, 30,
  50, 63, 82-119, 262, 263, 285, 291, 292, 293,
  295, 298, 299, 301
Wallach, Dr. Yehuda, 103, 107,
Walus, Frank, 192, 193, 194, 195, 196, 197,
  197n, 200n, 208, 306
Walus, Franz, 194
Wannsee Conference, 69n
War crime convictions, 17
War criminal definition, international
  debate over, 64-78
War Refugee Board, 59, 60
Warnstorff, Lt. Col., 91
Warsaw ghetto, 55, 83
Warzok, Friedrich, 33
"Watch List," 8, 45, 46, 116, 125, 262
Watkins, Judge Henry, 178
Waxman, Henry, 31
Wehrmacht, 89
Weinschenk, Fritz, 297, 297n
Weise, Gottfried, 277, 277n
Welles, Elliot, 14, 18, 26, 27, 28, 295-297,
  302
Welles, Sumner, 256
West Bosnian Combat Group, 93, 94
West German, criteria for prosecution of
  criminals, 10
West German Federal Archives, 99
West German post-war statistics, 269
West Germany, Central Office for the
  Investigation of Nazi Crimes, 28
Wev, Bosquet, 213
Wheeler, John, 259
White Book, 88, 102, 103, 105
White, Justice Byron, 205
Wieland, Joseph, 45n, 310
Wiener Neudorf death camps, 44, 306
Wiesel, Elie, 16, 273
Wiesenthal Center for Holocaust Studies,
  8, 12, 14, 30, 31, 32, 38, 39, 40, 139, 238,
  240, 251, 253, 258, 259, 260, 261, 264,
  292, 294-295, 302
Wiesenthal, Simon, 8, 14, 16, 31, 33, 39,
  131, 134, 136, 137, 146, 190, 193, 196, 207,
  228, 244n, 249, 285-294, 302
  awards and honors, 291
Williams, Judge John, 234, 235, 236

Willis, Thomas A., 175
Winant, John, 51
Winchell, Walter, 189
Winter, General August, 98
Wise, Rabbi Stephen, 55, 256, 281
Wisener, Heinz, 278
Wislenceny, Dieter, 19, 19n, 21, 25, 26
Wojciechowski, Chester, 46, 310
Wolf, Michael, 166, 167, 168, 172, 173,
  174, 178, 179
World Jewish Congress, 8, 9, 10, 13, 27, 55,
  63, 83, 85, 86, 87, 96, 99, 102, 103, 108, 110,
  111, 114, 117n, 118, 119, 127, 191, 226,
  255, 256, 258, 261, 263, 264, 274, 275, 280-
  285, 291, 293, 295, 299, 301, 302, 303,
  Department of Culture and Education,
  283
  European Tracing Office, 283
  Institute of Jewish Affairs, 283
  Jewish Restitution Successor
  Organization, 283
  Jewish Trust Corporation, 283
  Control Office, 192
World tribunal concept, 12
World Union of National Socialists, 286
World War II
  East European Jewish statistics,
  39
  East European policy during, 39
Wulecki, Fritz, 193
Wyman, David, 61

Yad Vashem Center, 15, 289
Yalta Conference, 71, 158
Yetter, Wayne, 239
Yugoslav State Commission, 90, 90n
Yugoslav War Crimes Commission, 94, 96,
  101
Yugoslavian anti-Nazi resistance, 7

Zaoui, Michel, 153
Zinger, Dr., 157
Zinger, Monica, 155, 156, 157, 165, 169,
  175, 178, 266, 267, 268
Zionist Congress, 17th, 281
Zuazo, Hernon Siles, 150, 303
Zumbakis, Paul, 226
Zutty, Sam, 185, 191, 192

319